D1285396

INTEREST RATE SWAPS

INTEREST RATE SWAPS

edited by
Carl R. Beidleman
DuBois Professor of Finance
Lehigh University
Bethlehem, Pennsylvania

IRWIN
Professional Publishing
Burr Ridge, Illinois
New York, New York

This publication is designed to provide accurate and
authoritative information in regard to the subject matter
covered. It is sold with the understanding that neither the
author nor the publisher is engaged in rendering legal, accounting,
or other professional service. If legal advice or other expert
assistance is required, the services of a competent
professional person should be sought.

*From a Declaration of Principles jointly adopted by a Committee
of the American Bar Association and a Committee of Publishers.*

Project editor: Lynne Basler
Production manager: Diane Palmer
Jacket designer: Renee Klyczak-Nordstrom
Compositor: Bi-Comp, Incorporated
Typeface: 11/13 Times Roman
Printer: R. R. Donnelley & Sons Company

Library of Congress Cataloging-in-Publication Data

Interest rate swaps/edited by Carl R. Beidleman.
    p.   cm.
    Rev. ed. of: Financial swaps/Carl R. Beidleman. c1985.
    ISBN 1-55623-207-1
    1. Forward exchange. I. Beidleman, Carl R. II. Beidleman, Carl
R. Financial swaps.
HG3853.B45 1990   90–33697
332.4′5—dc20   CIP

Printed in the United States of America
5 6 7 8 9 0 DOC 7 6 5 4

To Inge

PREFACE

The first edition of *Financial Swaps* was published in 1985. It was a solo effort based extensively on discussions with financial intermediaries and users of financial swaps. The book was an attempt to document the evolution of swaps, the rationale for their development, and the applications for which they were useful financial instruments. At that time financial swaps were in their infancy. Markets were not yet fully developed, documentation not standardized, pricing was fee-based rather than spread-based, liquidity was limited, and most players were quite far down on the learning curve.

When it came time to consider revision in 1988, I toyed with the idea of reworking the book myself and producing a second edition that built on and updated the first, a practice employed successfully by many authors. Review of the developments in financial swaps that had transpired since the first edition quickly made me realize that the markets had moved too far and applications had become too comprehensive for that approach. Modifications to basic instruments had transformed their uses in many ways; pricing and portfolio risk management had become more sophisticated and efficient; and credit risk, regulatory concerns, and accounting and taxation issues had all reached such new levels of complexity that I did not believe it possible for any single writer to do justice to the advanced state of the art that had been reached by financial swaps by the beginning of 1989. Hence, I decided to rely on my understanding of the subject and my association with scholars and practitioners in the field of swaps to assemble a body of material that could adequately treat this burgeoning subject. The result will consist of two volumes, each concerned with a major subset of financial swaps. This book, *Interest Rate Swaps,* will treat those issues concerned with altering interest flows in a common currency. *Interest Rate Swaps* will be followed by a companion volume, *Cross-Currency Swaps,* that deals with swapping cash flows in multiple currencies. The second volume will follow the first in less than a year's time.

Interest rate swaps have flourished in the recent overall surge of financial activity. Despite the fact that the full range of material integral to this subject is unusually far-reaching, I have attempted to gather together the basic knowledge intrinsic to the successful deployment of interest rate swaps. The book examines most of the factors responsible for the rapidly growing interest in this area. Part 1 begins with the basics of cash-flow management, moves quickly into the role of swaps in the menu of modern financial instruments, and describes basic terminology, applications, and instruments. It then covers variations to basic instruments that give them unique features for arbitrage and hedging applications.

Part 2 follows, with extensive material on widely diverse applications of interest rate swaps. Parts 3 and 4 cover valuation and conceptual issues and should be of special interest to students of the rapidly growing field of financial engineering. Much of the material in these parts represents advanced thinking on the subjects of valuation of streams of cash flows and the conceptual relationships between interest rate swaps and related financial instruments. This is the area where the realm of swapsdom is currently making its greatest strides and which should appeal most to advanced thinkers seeking a better understanding of modern financial products. Part 5 covers the essential issues of regulation, accounting, and taxation. The last chapter looks forward to the next generation of swappers and rounds out the book.

I have been very pleased with both the capabilities of the chapter contributors and the quality of their manuscripts. They are all prestigious experts in their respective sectors of financial swaps. The book is intended to provide a foundation and framework upon which serious swappers and financial engineers can build. It will also provide a useful guide for the uninitiated, as well as a handy reference for experienced swappers. It should prove useful to financial managers and portfolio managers, whose function is to source or manage funds. CEOs and corporate directors should also find it useful in developing an understanding of the effective management of interest rate risk. Analysts and executives of financial intermediaries should use it frequently as they seek to manage their own balance sheets or offer advice and service in assisting clients in matters of asset and liability management.

The book should also be useful in advanced undergraduate and MBA courses in financial management, in banking and executive seminars concerned with fixed income instruments, and as a resource volume for financial intermediaries and general business practitioners. Finally, commercial and investment banks, institutional investors, and international organizations will find *Interest-Rate Swaps* a very valuable aid in training sessions for employees and clients.

Acknowledgment of assistance in extensive undertakings such as this can never be complete. I am, of course, especially grateful to the individual chapter contributors who have all done a remarkable job in covering the material that was assigned to them. I wish to express my appreciation to Richard W. Barsness, Dean of the College of Business and Economics at Lehigh University, for establishing the environment in which efforts such as this can reach fruition. I am grateful to many members of the community of investment and merchants bankers and to users of interest rate swaps for generously sharing their perceptions of the development of the swapping process. While it is not possible to name them all, a few have been especially helpful from an early stage until the present and merit special thanks: John W. Townsend of UBS Securities, New York; Jeffery D. Hanna of Salomon Brothers, Tokyo; David P. Pritchard of RBC, London; Victoria D. Blake of Bear Stearns, London; and William L. James of Hill Samuel, London. I am also grateful to Janice Schaeffer who assisted greatly with the administrative burden that underlies any enterprise of this sort.

The editorial and production staffs at IRWIN *Professional Publishing* were thoughtful and helpful throughout the process leading to the publication of this book and made it a more enjoyable undertaking.

Finally, I thank my wife, Inge, for her confidence and encouragement during the continuing process that led to the completion of this endeavor. She alone remembers when it all began.

Any errors of omission or commission that remain are mine.

Carl R. Beidleman

THE CONTRIBUTORS

Raj Aggarwal is the current appointee to the Edward J. and Louise E. Mellen Chair in Finance, John Carroll University. His research interests cover finance, accounting, and business strategy and their global dimensions. In addition to John Carroll, he has taught at other universities including Toledo, Michigan, South Carolina, Hawaii, Indiana, and Kent State. Professor Aggarwal's education includes a degree in mechanical engineering, an M.B.A., a D.B.A. (in corporate finance and international business), and postdoctoral work in international trade and economics. He attended the Indiana Institute of Technology, Kent State University, and the University of Chicago. He has published eight books and over 50 scholarly papers. He has held a number of elected and appointed positions in professional organizations, including program chairman of the Academy of International Business and vice president of the Eastern Finance Association.

Marcelle Arak is a professor at the University of Colorado in Denver. She previously directed the Capital Markets Analysis Unit and interest rate options desk at Citicorp Investment Bank, New York. Prior to that she was vice president and director of domestic research at The Federal Reserve Bank of New York. She holds a Ph.D. in economics from M.I.T.

Gioia Parente Bales was an analyst in the International Bond Market Research Group at Salomon Brothers Inc. She focused on both dollar and nondollar international floating-rate markets and has written numerous publications describing the market and assessing relative value. Mrs. Bales holds a bachelor of science degree in journalism and a masters of business administration in finance. In 1989 she joined Hofstra University School of Business as a professor of finance.

Carl A. Batlin is managing director in charge of risk management research at Manufacturers Hanover Trust Company. He has also worked at Chase Manhattan and Chemical Banks and as professor of finance at the University of Michigan. He holds a Ph.D. in financial economics from Columbia University and has published articles on various financial topics in a number of academic and trade journals.

Carl R. Beidleman joined the Lehigh University faculty in 1967 and was awarded the Allen C. DuBois Distinguished Professorship in Finance in 1975. In 1983 he was appointed the first chairman of the newly organized Department of Finance. A graduate of Lafayette College, Dr. Beidleman earned the M.B.A. degree at Drexel University and the Ph.D. at the Wharton School, University of Pennsylvania. He is a member of the boards of directors of the Martin Guitar Corp., Independence Bancorp Inc., and Bucks County Bank and Trust Co., and he has served as a consultant to commercial banks, legal counsel, and industrial firms.

Jeffry P. Brown, vice president of Morgan Stanley & Co. Incorporated, is product manager for swap and derivative products. Mr. Brown received his B.A. from the University of Wisconsin in 1975, his J.D. from the University of Wisconsin Law School in 1978, and his M.B.A. from UCLA in 1981. His experience includes project finance, mergers and acquisitions, corporate finance, corporate bond trading, and special situations trading and selling.

Keith C. Brown is the Allied Bancshares Centennial Fellow and an assistant professor of finance at the Graduate School of Business, University of Texas at Austin. He received his M.S. and Ph.D. degrees in financial economics from the Krannert Graduate School of Management at Purdue University. He specializes in teaching investments and capital markets courses at the M.B.A. and Ph.D. levels. From June 1987 to July 1988 he was a senior consultant to the Corporate Professional Development Department of Manufacturers Hanover Trust Company. He has also lectured extensively in executive development programs and spent 13 months as a senior planner with a financial planning firm based in San Diego, California. In August 1988 he received his charter from the Institute of Chartered Financial Analysts.

Frederick D. S. Choi is Research Professor of International Business at New York University's Stern School of Business. He served as chairman of NYU's Area of Accounting, Taxation and Business Law from 1983–86 and is former director of the Vincent C. Ross Institute of Accounting Research. Professor Choi has contributed more than 50 articles to scholarly and professional journals and is the author or coauthor of 10 books on the subject of international accounting and financial control. He is the recipient of five literature awards from the National Association of Accountants, and his textbook, *International Accounting,* with G. Mueller, was recently awarded the Wildman Gold Medal by the American Accounting Association. He is currently serving as editor-in-chief of a new specialist journal, *The Journal of International Financial Management and Accounting,* published in the spring of 1989. He has served as a consultant to multinational companies, international accounting firms, financial organizations, and academic institutions and is a frequent lecturer in executive development programs in the United States and abroad.

Paul G. Cucchissi is a vice president in the Capital Markets and Risk Management Group at UBS Securities Inc. He is responsible for U.S. domestic and Euromarket financings, as well as interest rate and currency risk management for both corporate and financial institution clients. Prior to joining UBS Securities in 1987, Mr. Cucchissi spent three years with Citicorp in the Rate Risk Management Group responsible for West Coast marketing to financial institution clients. Mr. Cucchissi holds a B.S. in economics from the Wharton School, an M.B.A. from the University of California, Berkeley, and he is a certified public accountant.

Arturo Estrella is vice president of The Federal Reserve Bank of New York in charge of banking studies. He has held a number of other positions in that institution, including managing the domestic financial markets division. He holds a Ph.D. in economics from Harvard University.

Ellen L. Evans has been an analyst in the International Bond Market Research Department at Salomon Brothers Inc. Prior to joining Salomon Brothers, Ms. Evans was an economist at the Federal Reserve Bank of New York. Ms. Evans holds masters degrees in economics and in international affairs from Columbia University.

Laurie S. Goodman is vice president responsible for capital markets analysis at Eastbridge Capital Inc.—a position that encompasses both market research and consulting for financial institutions. Prior to joining Eastbridge, Ms. Goodman spent two years at Goldman Sachs & Co., where she was a vice president in the Financial Strategies Group. Her responsibilities included developing and applying financial models for the capital markets trading desks. She also managed 12 quantitative analysts in Goldman's New York and regional offices. Ms. Goodman was previously a vice president in the Capital Markets Analysis Group at Citicorp Investment Bank for four years, and, prior to that, she spent four years as a senior economist at the Federal Reserve Bank of New York. Ms. Goodman received a B.A. in mathematics and a B.S. in economics from the University of Pennsylvania in 1975. She graduated *magna cum laude* and is a member of Phi Beta Kappa. Ms. Goodman received an M.A. and a Ph.D. from Stanford University in 1978.

George Handjinicolaou is an executive director of Security Pacific Hoare Govett Limited, with responsibility for derivative products in Europe. He joined Security Pacific's swap group in New York in 1986, and since the spring of 1987 he has been the head of European market-making activities in derivative products in London. Before joining Security Pacific he was with the World Bank, where he was instrumental in building the World Bank's swap program and implementing several innovative borrowings. Prior to that, Dr. Handjinicolaou taught finance at New York University and Baruch College of the City University of New York and has also worked at Salomon Brothers and Josephthal & Co. Inc. in New York. He holds a B.A. in economics from the University of Athens and an

M.B.A. and a Ph.D in economics and finance from New York University.

Benjamin Iben is vice president for General Re Financial Products Corporation. He was vice president for Swaps and Foreign Exchange Research, Manufacturers Hanover Trust Co. He graduated with honors in economics from the University of California, Berkeley, and did graduate work at the Graduate School of Business of the University of Chicago, where he completed the M.B.A. with a specialization in finance. During this time he was an exchange student at ESC, Paris, France. His early career included work at the Federal Reserve Bank of San Francisco, where, as a research associate, he focused on the relationships among market concentration, profitability, and new entry. In his recent work at Manufacturers Hanover, he designed and implemented zero coupon–based pricing and hedging systems for all swap products and is responsible for monitoring exposure of all interest rate options positions.

Ira G. Kawaller is vice president–director of the New York office for the Chicago Mercantile Exchange. In this capacity, he is charged with educating potential users of the exchange—including brokers and professional financial managers—about the various futures and option contracts traded on the exchange. After receiving a Ph.D. in economics from Purdue University in 1976, Mr. Kawaller served as an economist at the Federal Reserve Board in Washington and at AT&T, and as a financial strategist for J. Aron Company Inc., a major precious metals dealer and commodity trading firm. In addition, he has been an adjunct associate professor at the Graduate School of Business of Columbia University. He also serves on the board of directors of the National Option and Futures Society, and he has published articles in numerous trade and professional journals.

Suresh E. Krishnan is currently vice president for international fixed-income research at Merrill Lynch. His responsibilities cover global asset-liability management, international fixed-income trading strategies, global bond indices, and currency risk management. Prior to joining Merrill Lynch, he was a senior consultant to Manufacturers Hanover Trust, Bank of America, and Chase Manhattan Bank. He has also served as a faculty member at Pennsylvania State University and the University of Michigan. He received his doctorate in international finance from the University of Michigan.

Victoria Lasseter is a vice president in the Exposure Management Division of Citibank and is a senior originator for the Currency and Foreign Security Risk Management Unit. Ms. Lasseter is responsible for advising customers on transactions related to non-U.S. dollar exposures, as well as for the structuring of pricing and closing of such transactions. She has responsibility for domestic and European customers. Her previous positions at Citicorp include financial controller for the Exposure Management Division and four years in Corporate Accounting Policy, specializing in treasury and investment bank products. Prior to Citibank, she was a senior auditor at Peat, Marwick, Mitchell and Co. Ms. Lasseter holds a B.A. from the University of Virginia and an M.B.A. from New York University.

Keat Lee is a group senior accounting manager at the Australia and New Zealand (ANZ) Banking Group. Prior to joining ANZ, he was a director of audit in the Office of Auditor General, Victoria. He started his career in the Melbourne office of Arthur Andersen & Co., qualifying as a chartered accountant while there. He is a commerce graduate (B.Com.) from the University of Melbourne and holds a M.B.A. from Monash University. Mr. Lee has been extensively involved in developing and formulating accounting policies on financial instruments, particularly off-balance sheet instruments, at the ANZ Banking Group.

John G. Macfarlane is treasurer of Salomon Inc and managing director of Salomon Brothers Inc and manager of the firm's Finance Department. He is also a member of the firm's Credit and Asset/Liability Committees. Mr. Macfarlane served as head trader of the Interest Rate Swap Group and manager of the mortgage finance trading desk prior to assuming his current responsibilities. He was appointed managing director in January 1988. Mr. Macfarlane earned a B.A. degree in classical studies from Hampden-Sydney College of Virginia in 1976 and an M.B.A. from the University of Virginia in 1979.

James E. McNulty teaches in the finance department at Florida Atlantic University in Boca Raton. In addition, he has worked at the Federal Home Loan Bank of Atlanta for 18 years, and was vice president–economist from 1983 to 1989. He served on the bank's Asset-Liability Management Committee and provided financial management research services to both the banking and regulatory functions within the bank. He has been doing research on interest rate swaps since 1984. His other research interests include interest rate risk management and financial institution performance. He received his bachelor's degree from the College of William and Mary, his master's degree from Northwestern University, and his doctorate from the University of North Carolina. He served as an adjunct professor in both finance and economics at Emory University from 1981 to 1989.

Ian Mordue is assistant general manager of financial engineering at the Investment Bank subsidiary of the Australia and New Zealand (ANZ) Banking Group. A science graduate from the University of Newcastle majoring in pure mathematics and applied mathematics, Mr. Mordue has worked for transnationals and governments in operations research and management science. He has spent the past 11 years in the finance sector, where he has been involved in the swaps market since its inception in Australia.

John J. Pringle is visiting professor of business administration, International Institute for Management Development (IMD), Lausanne, Switzerland. He is currently on leave from the Graduate School of Business, University of North Carolina, Chapel Hill, where he is professor of finance. Pringle specializes in financial management and is author of four books and numerous articles. He has acted as financial management consultant to numerous firms and financial institutions and has held the directorships in two corporations. Professor Pringle holds a B.E.E. degree from the Georgia Institute of Technology, an M.B.A. from Harvard, and a Ph.D. from Stanford.

Daniel R. Ross is a vice president in the Real Estate Finance Department of Salomon Brothers International Limited. He has previously worked in Salomon's capital markets and swaps efforts in London, Tokyo, and New York. Before joining Salomon Brothers in 1983, he practiced law with Cravath, Swaine & Moore in New York City. Mr. Ross is a member of the bar associations of New York and Virginia. He is a graduate of Harvard University and the School of Law at the University of Virginia, where he was an editor of the Virginia Law Review.

Janet L. Showers is a director of research of Salomon Brothers and the manager of the Hedge Group in the Bond Portfolio Analysis Department. Her major responsibilities include the quantitative analysis of fixed-income and foreign exchange hedging products, the development of hedging strategies for asset and liability problems, and new product development. The group is also responsible for the development of valuation models of government bonds, corporate bonds, and high-yield debt, including the analysis of bonds with embedded options and option pricing models. She joined Salomon in 1983 after holding various positions at Bell Telephone Laboratories and at the Chase Manhattan Bank. Ms. Showers holds a Ph.D. in operations research from Columbia University, an M.S. in operations research from Stanford University, and an Sc.B. in applied mathematics from Brown University.

Andrew Silver is a senior analyst for asset-backed securities at Moody's Investor Services. He previously served as vice president in the Capital Markets Analysis Unit at Citicorp Investment Bank, New York. Previously, he was chief of the Domestic Financial Markets Division of the Federal Reserve Bank of New York. He holds a Ph.D. in economics from the University of Michigan.

Donald J. Smith is an associate professor of finance and economics at the School of Management, Boston University. He received his M.B.A. and Ph.D. degrees in economic analysis and policy at the School of Business Administration, University of California at Berkeley. He specializes in teaching money and capital markets and futures and options courses at the undergraduate and M.B.A. levels. He has published widely in academic and practitioner-oriented journals. From August 1986 to August 1987 he was a senior consultant to the Corporate Professional Development Department of Manufacturers Hanover Trust Company. He has also developed executive education curriculum on capital markets and financial risk management using futures, options, and swaps for a number of major financial institutions. He was a Peace Corps volunteer in Peru and has traveled extensively.

Sharon L. Stieber has been a vice president of Barrentine, Lott and Associates since 1985; she advises depository and mortgage lending institutions in asset/liability management and the use of financing tools such as CMOs and interest rate swaps. She is a former member of the Asset/Liability Committee of the Student Loan Marketing Association (SLMA) and Union Commerce Bank and former chief economist of two federal credit agencies. As SLMA's chief economist and vice president of economic research, she developed the interest rate swap concept for use in domestic credit markets. She counseled the FHLBB on the development of regulations permitting savings and loans to participate in interest rate swaps and advised financial institutions, such as S&Ls, on the effective use of such swaps. Ms. Stieber has taught economics at the University of Saskatchewan. She holds a B.A. in economics from the College of Wooster in Wooster, Ohio, and has completed doctoral studies and exams in economics at the University of Edinburgh in Scotland.

Reto M. Tuffli is a vice president and head of Risk Management Products Group at UBS Securities Inc. The risk management group is a market maker in interest rate and currency swaps, caps, floors, and swap options. Mr. Tuffli joined UBS Securities in October 1985, following two years in the Rate Risk Management Group at Citicorp. Before that he worked as an international economic analyst at Crocker National Bank in San Francisco, assessing the credit worthiness of less-developed countries. Mr. Tuffli holds a B.A. degree in economics and an M.B.A from the University of California, Berkeley.

Lee Macdonald Wakeman is a managing director in Global Trading and Distribution at Continental Bank. Previously, he started the interest rate options trading desk for Chemical Bank and was head of the bond research and risk evaluation groups at Citicorp, London. Before that, he was an associate professor of finance at the

University of Rochester, specializing in corporate finance and international finance.

Larry D. Wall is the research officer in charge of the financial team at the Federal Reserve Bank of Atlanta and an adjunct assistant professor of finance at Emory University. He is also a C.P.A. He received his B.S. from the University of North Dakota and his Ph.D. from the University of North Carolina at Chapel Hill. Mr. Wall's research interests are in the areas of financial intermediation and corporate finance, and he has published articles in a variety of academic and trade journals.

Samuel C. Weaver earned a Ph.D. in finance and economics from Lehigh University in 1985. Prior to joining Hershey Foods as manager of Corporate Financial Analysis (1984), he was an assistant professor of finance at Elizabethtown College and was a consultant to Hershey Foods. In 1988, he became a member of the board of directors of the Financial Management Association and was recently listed in *Who's Who in Finance* (1989). Additionally, he is a certified management accountant and an adjunct professor in the M.B.A. program at Lehigh University.

CONTENTS

PART 1
GENERIC INTEREST RATE SWAPS

1   The Role of Interest Rate Swaps in Managing Cash Flows   3
    Carl R. Beidleman, Lehigh University, Bethlehem, Pennsylvania

2   The Place of Interest Rate Swaps in Financial Markets   25
    George Handjinicolaou, Security Pacific Hoare Govett, London,
    England

3   Plain Vanilla Swaps: Market Structures, Applications, and
    Credit Risk   61
    Keith C. Brown, University of Texas-Austin
    Donald J. Smith, Boston University

4   The Development and Standardization of the Swap Market   97
    James E. McNulty, Florida Atlantic University, Boca Raton,
    Florida
    Sharon L. Stieber, Barrentine Lott and Associates,
    Washington, D.C.

5   Variations to Basic Swaps   114
    Jeffry P. Brown, Morgan Stanley & Co., New York

6   Interest Rate Swaps: An Alternative Explanation   130
    Marcelle Arak, University of Colorado, Denver
    Arturo Estrella, Federal Reserve Bank of New York
    Laurie S. Goodman, Eastbridge Capital, New York
    Andrew Silver, Moody's Investor Services, New York

PART 2
APPLICATIONS OF SWAPS

7   Capital Market Applications of Interest Rate Swaps   147
    Laurie S. Goodman, Eastbridge Capital, New York

8   Asset Based Interest Rate Swaps   175
    Suresh E. Krishnan, Merrill Lynch Capital Markets, New York

9   Swaptions Applications   188
     Paul G. Cucchissi and Reto M. Tuffli
     UBS Securities, Inc., New York

10   Non-U.S. Dollar Interest Rate Swaps   214
     Victoria Lasseter, Citicorp, New York

PART 3
VALUATION OF SWAPS

11   The Interest Rate Swap Market: Yield Mathematics,
     Terminology and Conventions   233
     John Macfarlane, Daniel R. Ross and Janet Showers
     Salomon Brothers, New York

12   Interest Rate Swap Valuation   266
     Benjamin Iben, General Re Financial Products Corp.,
     Stamford, Connecticut

13   What Drives Interest Rate Swap Spreads?   280
     Ellen Evans and Gioia Parente Bales, Salomon Brothers,
     New York

14   The Duration of a Swap   304
     Laurie S. Goodman, Eastbridge Capital, New York

PART 4
CONCEPTUAL RELATIONSHIPS

15   The Portfolio Approach to Swaps Management   317
     Lee M. Wakeman, Continental Bank, Chicago

16   Integrating Interest Rate Derivative Products   346
     Lee M. Wakeman, Continental Bank, Chicago
     Reto M. Tuffli, UBS Securities, Inc., New York

17   Linkages between Interest Rate Swaps and Cross-Currency
     Swaps   359
     Carl A. Batlin, Manufacturers Hanover Trust Co., New York

18   Swap Rationalization: Equivalence of Short-Date and
     Long-Date Interest Rate Swap Strategies   374
     Samuel C. Weaver, Hershey Foods Corp., Hershey,
     Pennsylvania

19   A Swap Alternative: Eurodollar Strips   390
     Ira B. Kawaller, Chicago Mercantile Exchange, New York

PART 5
PERIPHERAL ISSUES

20   Interest Rate Swap Credit Exposure and Capital Requirements   407
     Larry D. Wall, Federal Reserve Bank of Atlanta
     John J. Pringle, Univ. of North Carolina at Chapel Hill
     James E. McNulty, Florida Atlantic University, Boca Raton

21   Assessing Default Risk in Interest Rate Swaps   430
     Raj Aggarwal, John Carroll University, Cleveland

22   Accounting and Taxation for Interest Rate Swaps   449
     Frederick Choi, New York University

23   Mark-to-Market vs. Accrual Accounting for Interest Rate Swaps   479
     Keat Lee, ANZ, Melbourne, Australia
     Ian Mordue, ANZ McCaughan, Melbourne, Australia

24   Innovations, New Dimensions, and Outlook for Interest Rate
     Swaps   492
     Carl R. Beidleman, Lehigh University, Bethlehem, Pennsylvania

Index   505

PART 1

GENERIC INTEREST RATE SWAPS

CHAPTER 1

THE ROLE OF INTEREST RATE SWAPS IN MANAGING CASH FLOWS

Carl R. Beidleman
Lehigh University
Bethlehem, Pennsylvania

THE CHARACTERISTICS OF CASH FLOWS

In its broadest and, perhaps, simplest context, finance may be thought of as study of cash flows. Each of the myriad applications of finance deals with the movement of funds toward or away from an entity. As we examine interest rate risk management, we should place it properly in context as part of a broader set of financial issues. This can be accomplished by briefly focusing on the characteristics of cash flows and evaluating the alternative means available to modify or manage an entity's (or firm's) cash flows.

In a purely domestic context, the fundamental characteristics of cash flows are limited to just four. They are (*a*) the size of the flow, (*b*) its direction (in or out), (*c*) its timing, and (*d*) its quality or degree of uncertainty. These characteristics may seem extremely simplistic considering the multibillion-dollar magnitude of the financial services industry; nonetheless, domestic cash flows can be defined by *size, direction, timing,* and *quality*. Whether we consider credit analysis, project finance, security valuation, capital markets, insurance, portfolio management, risk assessment, or even the current exotics (i.e., financial futures, options on securities, options on indices, and options on futures), these four attributes of cash flows form the foundation for financial analysis and decision making.

In nondomestic applications, a fifth characteristic often enters the picture—the *currency* of the cash flow. The currency of cash flows warrants attention only when it differs from the currency in which the financial results are to be measured. Although questions of foreign exchange surface frequently when transactions cross national borders, many international transactions can be conducted exclusively in terms of home currency. You can, for example, denominate an international transaction in your home currency or conduct international financing or investing in the Euromarket with your home currency.

It is not possible, however, to have an international commercial transaction denominated in the home currency of both parties. Moreover, Euromarkets are not always available or appropriate for all international financial or investment transactions. Hence, many large and small transactions have been arranged in foreign currencies from the point of view of one of the parties to the transaction. This additional currency characteristic rounds out the fundamental components of the nature of cash flows. Since financial management is concerned with the efficient management of cash flows, examining the available ways to modify the characteristics of cash flows so as to make them more amenable to the needs or preferences of financial managers is desirable.

MODIFYING THE CHARACTERISTICS OF CASH FLOWS

Expectations for cash flows constitute the fundamental components of analytical input for all financial decisions. In developing expected cash flows for a course of action, each analyst must specify the four or five characteristics outlined above. Cash flow formulation may be extremely difficult for many financial ventures, especially those where the quality or uncertainty of the flows is so large that it seriously reduces the accuracy of the size and timing of the flows. In extreme cases even the direction of the expected flow may be unclear. Such high risk may be associated with state-of-the-art investment projects involving new products, processes, or markets.

Despite the uncertainty of many financial decisions, a very large set of financial actions exists for which the quality of the underlying cash flows is remarkably high and the uncertainty connected with the flows is quite low (in some cases approaching zero). Cash flows of this sort are, of course, associated with fixed income or debt securities, where highest-quality flows (near-zero risk) are related to the obligations of the central government. In situations that involve high-quality cash flows, the underlying size, direction, and timing may be readily altered in the bond, bank loan, or money markets by implementing appropriate borrowing or investment strategies. Provided that active capital markets exist, straightforward portfolio changes can be made that shift the size, direction, and timing of expected cash flows to a revised but equivalent configuration as prescribed by the financial managers.

When evaluating the quality characteristic of expected cash flows, little can be done to alter the underlying risk profile of project, equity, or even low-grade, debt-related cash flows. However, as a result of recent innovations in financial instruments, modifications can be made, if desired, in the quality of interest payments on certain classes of debt instruments. These innovations involve the use of the recently developed financial instruments known as *interest rate swaps* and *cross-currency swaps*.

INTEREST RATE SWAPS

An *interest rate swap* provides a convenient means of altering certain aspects of the quality characteristic of expected cash flows. Its primary objective is to exchange floating-rate interest payments for fixed-rate payments, or vice versa. In the past most contractual interest payments were fixed over the life of a debt instrument. However, as a result of innovations in financial instruments, many debt issues in recent years call for interest or coupon payments that float or are revised every three or six months. The rolling over, or continued renewal, of short-term borrowings would also fit into this category. The basis for these revisions is some well-understood market rate such as the London Interbank Offer Rate (LI-

BOR), some short-term treasury rate, commercial paper rate, prime, or other index of rates. Such instruments are often called *floating-rate notes* (FRNs). Because the interest rate floats with market rates, floating-rate interest flows are less certain (and of lower quality) than the certain nature (high quality) of the coupon flows of fixed-rate instruments. Using currently available documentation, this question of quality or risk of the coupon cash flows can be altered by swapping the floating-rate coupon with a borrower who may be more willing to face a floating interest cost in return for another party servicing his fixed-rate coupon. Hence, an interest rate or coupon swap may be defined as an exchange of a coupon or interest payment stream of one configuration for another coupon stream with a different configuration on essentially the same principal amount. Moreover, a type of interest rate swap called a *basis swap* provides for the exchange of coupons on one floating-rate instrument for coupons on another floating-rate instrument, where the interest rate on each side of the swap floats on a different basis. These swaps would be done to alter the quality of the coupon cash flows and to make them more compatible with the floating-rate preferences of specific debt security issuers or investors. Investors or issuers of fixed- or floating-rate securities are now able to swap their coupon receipts or payments as their preferences dictate.

Similar instruments, called *cross-currency swaps,* provide for the exchange of coupon flows from one currency and interest basis to another. These instruments and their characteristics and applications are covered in detail in a companion volume to this book called *Cross-Currency Swaps.*

LIABILITY MANAGEMENT

The development of the swapping of coupon or interest rate obligations has enabled financial managers to apply well-known portfolio management techniques to the liability side of the balance sheet in much the same way they were formerly applied to their asset positions. Through the use of interest rate swaps many of the concepts of modern liability management that have recently become available to financial managers of financial institutions can now also be extended to nonfinancial corporations. Just as the choices available among alternative types of short-term purchased funds currently used to finance banks and financial institutions have increased their flexibility, interest rate swaps provide a means of arranging and rearranging the long-date funding of financial and nonfinancial companies to better match their financial requirements.

We explore these intriguing possibilities in this chapter in order to become better acquainted with the role of interest rate swaps in managing cash flows. In doing so, we examine the nature of coupon risk, the financial characteristics of an interest rate swap, and the configuration of cash flows of various groups of potential users. This leads to a brief discussion of hedging, arbitrage, and speculative applications of interest rate swaps.

COUPON RISK

The concept of coupon risk is closely related to a broader phenomenon known as interest rate risk. In its most basic sense, *interest rate risk* is the risk or uncertainty associated with the course of interest rates. Although periods of exceptional stability of interest rates have not existed for decades, U.S. interest rates in recent years have become even more volatile. This has been due primarily to a major policy change announced by the Federal Reserve Board in October 1979. At that time the Fed announced that it planned to target its money management operations on the monetary aggregates rather than on the level of interest rates. As a result of that change in policy, movements in rates have become much more volatile than they were previously.

This change in Fed policy, coupled with the high inflation rates in the intervening period, has resulted in heightened volatility in interest rates and, hence, in unacceptably high levels of interest rate risk. In terms of its impact on financial management and its effect on a firm's profits and residual cash flows, this change ranks closely with the adoption of floating exchange rates over fixed exchange rates in 1973. The difficulties that each of these watershed events has imposed on financial managers regarding the increased uncertainty associated with changes in exchange rates and interest rates have been addressed by various means, including currency cover and coupon cover.

Whereas interest rate risk deals with the uncertainty in the course of interest rates, coupon risk is used to focus on the impact of changes in interest rates on the cash flows and market values of borrowers and lenders who employ contractually determined or fixed-income securities. These effects are also more commonly referred to as *reinvestment rate risk* and *price risk*. Additional dimensions of coupon risk are concerned with which side of an investment instrument a player is on (i.e., borrower or lender). This consideration is necessary because what would be a favorable outcome for one party due to a given change in rates could be an unfavorable result for the other.

The Borrower's View

Accepting the prospect that interest rates will continue to fluctuate, we direct our attention first to the impact of changes in interest rates on fixed-income securities of various maturities. Basically, the longer the maturity of a fixed-income security, the longer the period until the principal or some part of it must be repaid, and the longer the period over which the level of interest payments is held rigid and fixed. Thus, from the standpoint of a borrower, a long-date bond would lock in an interest cost over a long period and would delay repayment or defer amortization of principal. Borrowers who have stable, long-term cash flow or profit expectations, such as might be expected from investment of the borrowed funds in manufacturing or distribution facilities, may demonstrate a strong preference for such long-term, fixed-cost capital. A necessary proviso, of course, is that the after-tax expected return on the investment projects exceeds the overall after-tax cost of capital. Thus, by locking in a positive spread of their expected return in excess of their expected cost of funds across a long investment horizon, these players have properly matched both the yield versus the cost and the maturity of their assets and liabilities. For such firms a substantial fraction of their assets is long lived, and they can tolerate the rigidity of fixed-interest cost over the expected lives of their underlying fixed assets.

Others that borrow funds to finance shorter-term assets or

assets with yields subject to change may choose to avoid having their interest cost fixed over long periods of time. They prefer the flexibility of refinancing in the short term at the current rate of interest. Borrowers who view interest rates as being cyclically high and anticipate a subsequent decline in rates would also fall into this category. Such borrowers could obtain the flexibility they desire by financing with short-term debt and rolling the debt over each three or six months at the market rates that prevail at the time of refunding. Alternatively, if such a borrower wished to avoid the uncertainty and nuisance of this requirement to refinance its short-term debt continually, it could establish a line of credit at a bank and pay the appropriate administered market rate of interest (i.e., prime or LIBOR plus some risk premium). Or it might source its funds using floating-rate term notes where the interest rate is reset each three or six months based on some predetermined formula related to short-term market rates. In any of these cases, the borrower has obtained the flexibility of paying a floating-rate for its finance based on current market rates and has avoided the funding rigidity associated with long-term fixed rates of interest.

The market valuation of a fixed-income security like a bond or note also fluctuates in response to changes in market rates of interest. The direction of the change in value is inverse to the direction of the change in interest rates. Thus, an increase in the market rate of interest would cause the market value of a debt instrument to fall, and vice versa. The magnitude of the change in market value of a fixed-income security for a given change in market rate is directly, but not linearly, related to the maturity of the security. Thus, market values of long-date debt instruments tend to fluctuate a great deal more than market values of short-date instruments for a given change in the level of interest rates.

The financial mechanics requires that, if interest rates go up from the time of issue, the market value of fixed-rate debt falls, and vice versa. However, if borrowers elect to continue to service their debt until maturity, their principal may not be affected. The major economic effect on the borrowers will occur if the debt issue has a sinking fund. Under these conditions, if interest rates have risen since the time of issue, the borrowers may be able to profit from a periodic retirement of debt at market prices below the debt's par value or principal. Furthermore, if the issuers have sufficient liquidity to retire the issue or choose to execute an equity for debt swap or other type of defeasance of the debt, they may be able to augment income by effectively retiring the debt at the below-par market value associated with the rise in rates since the debt was issued. On the other hand, if rates go down, the borrowers may, within the limitations set forth in their debt agreement, consider refinancing at the lower current market rates. Certain duplicative costs are associated with refinancing debt issues that preclude this option in cases where interest rate changes have not been significant or when the current period to maturity becomes rather short.

In summary, the impact of coupon risk on financing costs can be managed effectively if borrowers properly match the maturity of their liabilities to the maturity of their assets. The impact of price risk on borrowers is not terribly significant and often operates in their favor. We turn now to the impact of coupon risk on investors, and focus on the uncertainty of interest flows and market values for various periods to maturity.

The Investor's View

From the point of view of an investor, the dual dimensions of coupon risk can, unless properly managed, have extremely serious implications as interest rates change. Foremost among these implications is the fact that the market value of a fixed-income security moves in the opposite direction to the change in interest rate, and the magnitude of the change increases with the maturity of the security. This is the risk of principal or price risk faced by investors. And price risk on long-term debt instruments can be much more significant to investors than to borrowers. We see this significance surface in the potential adverse impact on long-term securities if investors are forced to dispose of them following an increase in rates or if they are required to finance their investment with higher-cost, floating-rate funds.

As before, effective asset and liability management involves carefully matching the maturities of assets and liabilities. Thus, life insurance companies and many pension funds with distant liabilities can, in a more or less cavalier fashion, invest in long-term fixed-rate bonds with little concern for interest rate induced changes in market values. This carefree attitude is possible because these investors fully intend to hold their assets to maturity in order to match the maturity of their liabilities or claims.

On the other hand, investors with short-dated liabilities would view long-dated investments with great apprehension because of the possible loss in asset value if interest rates subsequently rose. The potential gain in portfolio value associated with a decline in rates receives little attention from prudent investors using the same investment strategies. This potential is overshadowed by the serious loss possibilities if rates were to rise. As a result, investors with short-dated liabilities prefer short-term or repriceable instruments for their portfolios. Contrariwise, investors with long-dated claims prefer higher-yielding, long-term instruments through which they can lock in known interest returns over a long period and set up principal receipts that approximate the maturity of their claims.

The second dimension of coupon risk to an investor deals with the uncertainty associated with the reinvestment rate that may be earned on the repaid principal. Here the impact of the risk runs counter to the risk of principal. A long-dated bond provides a known fixed rate of interest over the life of the bond, whereas the owner of a short-dated instrument faces the risk of reinvestment at more frequent intervals. Given that interest rates are expected to continue to fluctuate, investors in short-dated instruments cannot be assured of what their interest returns will be beyond the maturity of each of their holdings. If investors depend on their investment income for their support or to support some enterprise, this risk can be quite serious. For instance, if a college endowment fund is totally invested in short-term instruments and rates fall, the reduced level of income may be insufficient to provide such necessities as basic facility maintenance, faculty salaries, and student aid, all of which were expected to be maintained by investment income. Management of reinvestment-rate coupon risk for such investors may be accomplished by holding a strip or sequence of medium-term instruments so that only a few mature in each year, thereby reducing the impact of reinvestment at a different current rate on the total income provided by the portfolio.

While some investors are averse to the risk of changing reinvestment rates, others prefer it. In the latter category would be investors that have liabilities that are also being continually repriced. Notable examples of this type of investor are commercial banks that face variable-rate funding costs, where some of the rates may change on a daily basis as market rates change. These investors would prefer to hold matched variable-rate assets whose returns also fluctuate with market rates but at a sufficient spread above funding costs to provide the necessary net interest margin to the bank.

The Function of Interest Rate Swaps

As market participants seek to match the maturity of the asset and liability cash flows that redound from both interest and principal payments or receipts on fixed-income securities, players tend to favor either long-date or short-date instruments. As these characteristics of market participants become sorted out, players tend to seek the maturity of financing or investing that suits their needs. However, because of certain market anomalies, attaching funds with undesired maturities is often easier than obtaining funding with preferred maturity characteristics. Moreover, some anomalies have been large enough to provide a significant cost advantage to those who move to breach the market imperfection in order to obtain a more preferable form of finance. The instrument available for this maneuver is called the *interest rate swap*. We turn next to the financial characteristics of an interest rate swap and then focus on the nature of the cash flows of typical users.

FINANCIAL CHARACTERISTICS OF INTEREST RATE SWAPS

An interest rate swap is a straightforward arrangement wherein the parties agree to bear the obligation to service the interest cost on a common principal amount with the same maturity but at a different basis for interest determination. Interest rate swaps generally exchange a fixed-interest obligation for a floating-rate or variable-rate interest obligation. However, floating versus floating-rate interest rate swaps have also become popular in certain applications.

Note that in a straight interest rate swap, the principal is in the same currency and is not swapped. Only the debt service or coupon is swapped. Hence, the principal can be new or existing debt and is only notional to the transaction. As a result, principal is not at risk, and the resulting credit exposure is significantly lessened. Moreover, in straight interest rate swaps, only one counterparty is at risk at any point in time, depending upon the direction of the change in interest rates since the inception of the swap.

The risk that is incurred or removed in an interest rate swap is the risk associated with changes in interest rates (i.e., coupon risk). Floating-rate payers and receivers encounter a relatively short maturity until they face a possible revision of contract interest rates and incur the coupon risk associated with short-term instruments. On the other hand, fixed-rate payers and receivers are locked into a fixed coupon rate over the term of the swap and incur the coupon risk earlier identified with term instruments. Therefore, depending upon the characteristics of players' underlying operating cash flows, they may be natural floating-rate payers or natural fixed-rate payers, if borrowers, or natural floating-rate receivers or natural fixed-rate receivers, if investors.

CHARACTERISTICS OF INTEREST RATE SWAP PARTICIPANTS

Whether a potential participant to an interest rate swap is a natural floating-rate or fixed-rate payer or receiver depends upon its underlying operating cash flows. In classifying players in the interest rate swap market, we look first at natural fixed-rate payers followed by natural floating-rate payers. We then direct our attention to fixed-rate and floating-rate receivers.

Natural Fixed-Rate Payers

Natural fixed-rate payers are entities whose minimum cash flows are reasonably predictable regardless of the level of interest rates. A reliable minimum level of revenue and net income sufficient to provide a margin of safety necessary to service fixed-rate debt is essential to the successful placement of long-term fixed-rate obligations.

A large class of natural fixed-rate payers (borrowers) are manufacturing and distribution firms in the developed countries. The cash inflows to these firms arise from their manufacturing and/or distribution activities. Although the cash flows may be cyclical, they can be forecast with some degree of assurance. Moreover, if the borrowing firms had not previously engaged in excessive debt or financial leverage, they would normally be expected to generate sufficient cash inflows to service their fixed-rate debt annually.

In addition to their expected ability to service a moderate volume of fixed-rate debt, many managements of production and distribution firms prefer fixed-rate debt because of the assurance that it provides to their cost of capital and to the capital investment decision process. For instance, if a capital investment in production or distribution facilities is expected to produce an after-tax return of 15 percent, a firm may be quite willing to undertake the project if its overall cost of capital is 14 percent after taxes. Such an after-tax cost of capital may have been based on a fixed-rate debt component that has a pretax cost of, say, 12 percent and approximately 8 percent after taxes and an after-tax cost of equity of, say, 17 percent. This favorable deployment of financial leverage would be beneficial to the stockholders provided the capital cost was fixed. On the other hand, if the pretax debt cost floated up to, say, 22 percent, driving the overall cost of capital above the 15 percent earned by the fixed-asset investment, the elevated interest bill would erode earnings, and both management and shareholders would be disappointed. Thus, fixed-rate debt with predictable cost is desirable for many borrowers.

This preference for fixed-rate debt comes through with even stronger force for one group of borrowers that have done extensive financing in past years. The gas and electric utilities have a special interest in the predictable cost features of fixed-rate debt because of the impact of regulators on a utility's performance. When a utility submits a request to a regulatory agency for a rate increase, the regulators need to know the utility's costs, a difficult procedure regarding interest costs unless rates are fixed.

Another major class of natural fixed-rate payers is financial institutions with large portfolios of fixed-rate assets. During the period of rapid escalation of interest rates after the change in Federal Reserve Board policy in 1979, many thrifts and savings and loan associations (S&L) suffered serious earnings erosion. This phenomenon, frequently referred to as the *S&L syndrome,* was the result of extensive maturity mismatch of assets and liabilities. At the outset the asset portfolios of thrifts and S&Ls were largely filled with fixed-rate mortgages. When market interest rates rose and deregulation eliminated many of the ceilings on rates paid to depositors, thrifts faced a grave profit squeeze, which caused erosion of reserves, near failures, numerous financial restructurings, and the thrift bailout at enormous costs to taxpayers.

There are two potential solutions to this problem of maturity mismatch. One is to shift the current portfolio of fixed-rate assets (mortgages) to variable-rate instruments. The other is to swap the extant stock of variable-rate, or floating-rate, liabilities for fixed-rate debt with a low enough coupon to allow a reasonable net interest margin. Of course, some combination of the two would also be appropriate. Although much effort has been undertaken to write variable-rate mortgages and other floating-rate assets have been added to thrift asset portfolios, this strategy does not change the payment features of outstanding fixed-rate instruments. Hence, the process of shifting to variable-rate assets has been slow and unpredictable. On the other hand, during periods of lower market interest rates, the swapping of a floating-rate interest obligation for a fixed-rate commitment represents a rapid means of shifting the maturity of liabilities to match the maturity of assets more properly. Moreover, the existence of a major market anomaly (in the form of differential credit risk premiums in the floating- and fixed-rate markets) and its appropriate arbitrage have helped reduce the cost of fixed-rate money below that obtainable by a thrift directly in the fixed-rate market.

Many of the smaller U.S. banks have also suffered from the S&L syndrome and should be included in the group of natural fixed-rate payers. Because the size of their maturity mismatch is modest relative to many of the larger players, the interest rate swap requirements of individual small banks and thrifts may have to be packaged together in some way to accommodate a larger swap counterparty. Such assembling or syndication of interest rate swap demand has been performed by market intermediaries as the swap market has become more standardized or productized.

Another set of international natural fixed-rate payers is the national agencies of certain developed countries that have difficulty accessing fixed-rate funds because of local capital market or regulatory constraints. Examples here would include various national agencies of modestly high inflation-rate countries. These agencies prefer fixed-rate debt with predictable debt service for planning purposes, but they cannot readily access fixed-rate money in their currencies. The relatively protracted high inflation rates experienced in these countries have made term loans something of an endangered species in their currencies. These agencies, with sovereign guarantees, have been able to access floating-rate Eurocurrency debt, which because of their preference for fixed-rate debt, they have been inclined to swap with natural floating-rate payers.

The foregoing major types of players have been instrumental in launching the concept of interest rate swaps. Undoubtedly other classes of natural fixed-rate payers will come to the fore as the swap market continues to develop. Next, we examine their natural counterparties, those that have underlying operating cash flows that make them natural payers of floating or short-term market rates of interest.

Natural Floating-Rate Payers

Whereas natural fixed-rate payers are primarily concerned with locking in a cost of funds across some borrowing horizon and have relatively reliable cash inflows with which to service the fixed-rate debt, natural floating-rate payers tend to be more sensitive to changes in short-term market rates of interest. This sensitivity is found mainly in large money center or regional banks that have large portfolios of floating-rate assets. The interest rates on the assets held in their loan portfolios may be indexed to U.S. prime rates, LIBOR, or other short-term market rates. These assets produce an income stream that is tied to short-term market rates and should be matched with liabilities whose interest cost is similarly indexed. Hence, we find a preference among large money center banks for floating-rate liabilities.

The demand for floating-rate liabilities by money center banks had surfaced initially on the part of non-U.S. Eurobanks. The large European banks have participated actively in extending Eurodollar credits to borrowers where the interest rates are based on LIBOR.

Because of deposit structures abroad, sourcing sufficient variable-rate deposits to fund the Eurobank's assets tied to a LIBOR or some other market index has become difficult. Hence, the large European money market banks have sought variable-rate funds in large amounts and became the natural floating-rate payers to serve as counterparties to natural fixed-rate payers in an interest rate swap.

When interest rate swaps were first introduced in spring 1982, the floating-rate payers were primarily European money market banks. Soon afterward the large Japanese international banks entered the picture and have since become a major factor in the supply of fixed-rate funds to the coupon swap market. In fact, of the interest rate swap volume undertaken in later years, Japanese banks have been estimated to exceed the European banks in participation. The rationale in each case was the same (i.e., to procure floating-rate liabilities at attractive rates [sub-LIBOR] to be used to fund the bank's floating-rate assets).

U.S. money center banks have been slower to participate directly in interest rate swaps for their own accounts primarily because of the large availability of floating-rate deposit liabilities that accompanied deregulation of financial institutions since interest rate swaps were launched. More recently, however, some large U.S. money market banks have participated in interest rate swaps as floating-rate payers to augment their domestic sources of floating-rate funds. U.S. bank participants are also driven by the cost savings inherent in the swap transaction that enable them to create cheaper floating-rate debt than is otherwise available. In a contrary vein, U.S. international money center banks also find use of the interest rate swap market appropriate to procure fixed-rate funds at a cost below equivalent-term U.S. government bonds (treasuries) without putting demand pressure on fixed-rate markets.

The role of international money center banks as natural floating-rate payers has been paramount in the organization and early development of the interest rate swap market. In fact, for quite some time a bank had represented at least one side of nearly every interest rate swap. Moreover, because the international money center banks have placed so much demand on the private-placement, fixed-rate market in Eurocurrencies, rates have increased relative to fixed-rates paid by potential counterparties, reducing the advantage of the market anomaly that initially made interest rate swaps so attractive.

Although large international banks have recently somewhat diminished their participation in swap transactions, the market has continued to prosper. This has occurred, in part, because other floating-rate payers have become attracted to the cost advantages of a swap. High-quality corporations' swapping new or existing fixed-rate debt service for floating-rate payments indexed to LIBOR has not been uncommon.

A related class of natural floating-rate payers includes borrowers who have fixed-rate debt outstanding and prefer to convert it to floating-rate debt. This group would include those who have low-coupon fixed-rate debt and could obtain, by swapping, a very low floating-rate cost of funds. That is, if a 5 percent fixed-rate coupon were swapped when equivalent risk fixed-rate rates were, say, 10 percent, this issuer could expect to pay a floating-rate of nearly 5 percent under LIBOR. If LIBOR were to drop below 5 percent, a negative interest rate to the floating-rate payer could be produced.

Unfixing of fixed-rate debt could be desirable for other reasons as well. The operational nature of a player's cash flows might have changed such that they feel more comfortable with floating-rate debt. Or a player's asset or liability structure may have been reassessed suggesting a shift in the nature of its liabilities. The newly found application of liability management concepts on the right-hand side of the balance sheet may suggest the unwinding of a given long-date obligation. This flexibility is now available to finance managers and introduces a considerable volume of supply of floating-rate payers.

Natural Fixed-Rate Receivers

In most cases interest rate swaps have been put in place with natural fixed-rate payers servicing fixed-rate debt that is owed by borrowers who prefer floating-rate obligations but have been able more handily to access fixed-rate funds. On the other side, natural floating-rate payers serviced new or existing floating-rate borrowers that prefer the certainty of fixed-rate debt service but are unable to place fixed-rate debt at reasonable rates. In addition, one more class of market participants is natural fixed-rate receivers.

The natural fixed-rate receivers are well known in the capital markets and are the primary sources of fixed-rate funds. Institutions such as life insurance companies, pension funds, wealthy investors, and managed trust accounts are notable examples of natural fixed-rate receivers. Although most such funds find their way into original fixed-rate issues, natural fixed-rate receivers can become quite interested in taking down floating-rate instruments at market rates to be subsequently swapped for above-market fixed-rate coupons at no incremental risk to principal. This application of interest-rate swaps entails an asset hedge, which is discussed in detail in Chapter 8.

Natural Floating-Rate Receivers

Investors sometimes park funds in short-term instruments because they think interest rates will subsequently rise, at which time they will move the money to higher-interest fixed-rate instruments. Because many floating-rate instruments are of intermediate-term maturity, say 4 to 10 years, there is some credit risk if they are used for this purpose, and other reasons must be sought for their demand. The primary preference for floating-rate income is from investors who fund their assets with variable-cost funds (i.e., funds whose costs are indexed to some base rate such as LIBOR, prime, treasury bills, certificates of deposit, or commercial paper). If such investors can lock in a reasonable net interest margin or spread between their return on floating-rate instruments and their floating cost of funds, they can enjoy a positive return at the end of the day. Such investors are typically the funds managers of financial institutions, especially smaller commercial banks and thrifts.

The smaller banks and thrifts have displayed a strong preference for floating-rate income as an alternative to fixed-rate finance in their attempt to match the maturity structures of their assets and liabilities. Since the supply of floating-rate assets has been more institutionalized and accessible than the supply of fixed-rate liabilities to banks and thrifts, most astute banks and thrifts have sought out floating-rate assets in their attempt to manage the interest sensitivity of their institutions.

The other large class of floating-rate receivers is the large international money center and regional banks. These banks source their funds in the interbank market at short-term market rates and want to place floating-rate assets on their books, usually indexed to LIBOR. These banks represent the primary source of funds to the floating-rate borrowers that enter into interest-rate swaps to obtain fixed-rate financing.

Credit Risk on Interest-Rate Swaps

For the most part interest rate swaps have been arranged between natural fixed-rate payers or natural floating-rate payers and a financial intermediary such as a commercial or an investment bank. In some cases credit enhancement might be necessary because of the unknown or unacceptable credit risk of the parties. However, in most cases where a commercial bank was a party to the swap, the need for credit enhancement was removed. The reasons for this are that (1) most banks are sufficiently creditworthy to satisfy most nonbank players and (2) banks have adequate credit-rating capabilities to assess and assume the credit risk of their counterparties.

From a credit viewpoint, note that in no case is principal at risk. Each party maintains the obligation to repay the principal and interest on its own debt when due. Hence, the credit risk reduces mainly to the willingness and ability of each counterparty to honor its chosen variety of debt service. And even here the risk is not the total risk of full debt service but only the risk of the *difference* between the periodic floating-rate payment and the fixed-rate payment, or vice versa. A related risk in the event of default is the risk of refinancing or reinvesting the fixed-rate principal at the then-current rates. This component of risk is evaluated more fully in Chapter 21.

BASIC APPLICATIONS OF INTEREST RATE SWAPS

Our discussion of the characteristics of interest rate swap participants and the conceptual basis for interest rate swaps has led us through an examination of the primary types of applications. As we have observed, swaps can be used to improve the match between the parties to a debt contract based upon their underlying preferences in order to hedge their balance sheet exposure. In addition, they can also be utilized to arbitrage opportunities that arise due to differential credit-risk premiums in the fixed- and floating-rate markets. Other applications arise in the use of swaptions to arbitrage the differential pricing of option premiums in the bond and swap-option markets. These applications will be covered in detail in Chapters 7 and 9.

In addition to risk management, hedging and arbitrage, interest rate swaps can be used in trading or speculative applications. Little has been written about this last set of applications because they entail an excessive risk posture in that the view on interest rates that drives the swap strategy may turn out to be wrong. Basically, interest-rate swaps enable a speculator who believes that interest rates will fall to enter into a swap agreement to receive fixed and pay floating rates of interest on a given notional principal. If the speculator's view was for rising rates, he would want to receive floating rates and pay fixed rates throughout the swap period. Although the volume of speculative swaps is not known, it would be naive to believe that it was negligible. Given the risks involved, it would appear that the bulk of such applications would lie in the shorter range of the swap maturity spectrum.

ORGANIZATION OF THE BOOK

In the foregoing introductory section, I have attempted to identify the characteristics of financial flows and to illustrate how certain of them may be altered to suit the needs or preferences of financial managers. I have also briefly described how interest rate swaps may be used to accomplish these objectives. These tasks are elaborated on as the book progresses. In the balance of this chapter, I provide a succinct preview of the material that lies ahead and its order of presentation.

The book is divided into five parts. In the remaining chapters of Part 1, accomplished academics and practitioners who are presently involved in interest rate swap activity present their thoughts on the generic aspects of interest rate swaps. Chapter 2 was prepared by the director of swaps activity of the London office of Security Pacific, Hoare Govett, Ltd. In it he describes the place of swaps among financial market instruments by focusing on the environmental and comparative advantage factors that have led to the emergence of swaps. In Chapter 3 two academics with prior experience in the New York financial market cover the basics of plain vanilla swaps. This is followed by a chapter on the development and standardization of the swap market, jointly written by a former thrift regulator and a person who was on the scene with Sallie Mae when they first contemplated the use of interest rate swaps to obtain lower-cost floating-rate funding (Chapter 4). This strategy went on to become a significant stimulus to the development of the interest-rate swap market. In Chapter 5 a practitioner who is on the swap desk of the New York office of a major investment bank offers a thorough development of the variations to basic swaps, with applications provided throughout. The final chapter in Part 1 deals with the role of swaps in allowing a debt issuer to separate interest rate risk from credit risk and hedge the desired amount of each (Chapter 6). It was written by a team of professionals from a commercial bank, investment bank, and central bank and provides intense insight into the rationale for interest rate swaps.

Part 2 covers applications of swaps. Each chapter describes a set of applications in detail and is well dosed with case studies and examples that illustrate each specific application. Chapters 7 and 8 deal with capital market or liability oriented applications and asset-based applications. They were written by research and strategy professionals at prominent New York investment banks. The latter two chapters in Part 2 cover swaptions applications and the extension of interest rate swaps to non-U.S. dollar applications (Chapters 9 and 10). They were written by extremely capable personnel who are actively involved on the swap desks of the New York offices of a large Swiss merchant bank and U.S. commercial bank, respectively.

In Part 3 we examine the critical material that deals with the valuation of interest-rate swaps. Chapter 11 is a seminal piece in the evolution of swap valuation practices. It was prepared by a group of research associates at a prominent New York investment bank which was a leader in the evolution of swaps from the outset.

Chapter 12 adds a critical dimension to the swap valuation process, that of using zero-coupon pricing rather than traditional bond pricing to value the fixed-rate side of an interest rate swap. It was written by a financial strategy associate of a large New York commercial bank. It is followed by a chapter prepared by research analysts of a significant New York investment bank that looks into the determinants of interest-rate swap spreads over fixed-rate term treasuries. The final chapter in Part 3 considers the topic of the duration of swaps. This is approached by examining the duration of each side of the swap and identifying the timing of changes in duration and other factors that influence the ability of an interest rate swap to help manage interest rate risk. This chapter was developed by a research strategist of a large investment bank in New York.

Part 4 covers conceptual relationships among swaps and other interest rate–derivative products. Here we examine how a swap market maker can manage the risk of its swap portfolio, relying on much of the material on zero-coupon pricing and duration analysis (Chapter 15). This work was done by a very successful U.S. commercial bank and fostered by the director of its swap group. He then collaborated (Chapter 16) with a leader in the swap activity of the New York securities group of a major Swiss merchant bank in developing a chapter that deals with the integration of the variety of interest rate–derivative products that are available in today's financial markets. Chapter 17, written by another strategist at a prominent U.S. commercial bank, considers the linkages between the two most common types of swaps (interest rate and cross-currency) and identifies their common foundations and conceptual relationships. Chapter 18 deals with the relationships and assumptions that are necessary for a strip of short-date forward contracts to equate to the long-date cover that is obtainable from an interest rate swap. It was drafted by a practitioner who understands the role of swaps in his own set of treasury operations. The section on conceptual relationships is rounded out with a thorough discussion (Chapter 19) of the use of Eurodollar futures contract strips to substitute for a short-date interest rate swap. With the recent extension of the maturity of Eurodollar futures contracts to four years, this alternative can substitute for certain characteristics of a larger number of swaps. It was written by the director of the New York office of the Chicago Mercantile Exchange, which is the leading marketplace for Eurodollar futures contracts.

Certain peripheral issues are covered in Part 5, which begins with a chapter covering the very topical question of interest rate swap credit exposure and capital requirements (Chapter 20). This work was prepared by a former thrift regulator, the senior economist for a bank regulator, and an academic, all of whom are intensely familiar with the forces that impinge on the credit risk inherent in swaps and the need for requisite capital by swap intermediaries. This chapter is followed by a related chapter on default risk in swaps wherein an attempt is made to identify the potential exposure of swaps to default risk and to report on available data regarding default behavior (Chapter 21). It was prepared by an academic active in the evaluation of default experience. Accounting and taxation of swaps constitute a very comprehensive area with numerous ramifications that may differ from country to country. These concepts are covered in Chapter 22 by a very capable professor, long active in accounting for financial transactions. Here he has attempted to summarize the accounting and tax implications inherent in undertaking an interest-rate swap strategy. This work is followed by a chapter written by swap practitioners who carefully evaluate alternative ways of accounting for interest rate swaps (Chapter 23). Finally, in the last chapter I have tried to identify the ways in which the swap market has evolved and innovated during its brief life span. I attempt to catalog some of the new and pending dimensions of the market and provide some outlook for what may lie ahead. As it has turned out, the evolution of the market has far exceeded anything that any of us could have expected in its short existence, so any attempt to forecast its future prospects may be little more than frivolous or naive.

CHAPTER 2

THE PLACE OF INTEREST RATE SWAPS IN FINANCIAL MARKETS

George Handjinicolaou
Security Pacific Hoare Govett Ltd
London, England

INTRODUCTION

Among the most successful of the innovations in financial techniques that have taken place over the course of the 80s decade have been the currency and interest rate swaps. These transactions were first made famous by the World Bank–IBM swaps in 1981, and markets for currency and interest rate swaps have developed beyond the expectations of users and banks who put together the first swap transactions. Swaps are essentially agreements between two counterparties to exchange cash flows (which are usually exchanges of interest obligations but sometimes also of principal in the case of currency swaps) undertaken for the mutual benefit of the parties concerned. Depending on the type of cash flows exchanged, swaps are classified into *interest rate, currency,* and *cross-currency–interest rate* swaps. In an interest rate swap, the parties exchange fixed-rate for floating-rate cash flows in the same currency. In a currency swap, the parties exchange cash flows expressed in different currencies, while in a cross-currency–interest rate swap the parties transform both the currency and the type of cash flows exchanged.

From the few structured proprietary transactions that were first put together in the late 70s, an enormous market has developed over the past 10 years. According to surveys conducted by ISDA (the International Swap Dealers Association), an estimated $1.6 trillion in interest rate and currency swaps were outstanding as of the end of 1988, and both markets see no signs of abatement in the rate of growth. The development of swaps as a technique of finance has been particularly rapid over the past two years, despite the fact that the technique has been available for some time. Why this phenomenal growth?

The reasons for this development are complex, but, by and large, they rest on the volatility of interest rates and exchange rates and the dramatic changes that have taken place in the world financial markets over the past 10–15 years. The increased volatility, combined with deregulation steps in a number of capital markets, has led to an explosion of financial innovation. These developments have brought the various capital markets around the world much closer, opening up new investment and funding opportunities. Swaps have been one of the most successful of the innovations that have come out of this process. Most important, the growth of the swap market has been fed by the above developments. Today, many participants around the globe—financial institutions and corporate, supranational, or sovereign entities—utilize swaps for asset/liability management purposes. By combining the issuance of debt in accessible markets with an interest rate and or currency swap, borrowers can create synthetic liabilities that cost less than traditional financing, while investors can create synthetic assets that yield more than conventional investments of the same risk class. For example, borrowers of Swiss francs who want U.S. dollars can swap their liability with a borrower of U.S. dollars who wants Swiss francs, and in the process both parties can reduce their borrowing costs. Fixed-rate borrowers can exchange their funds for floating-rate liabilities, and vice versa.

An important feature of the cash flow exchanges involved in swaps is that they offer a way to hedge risk, whether foreign exchange risk, interest rate risk, or both. In the interest rate area, swaps offer the means of matching the maturity and price characteristics of liabilities (e.g., floating and short-term) with the characteristics of assets to reduce interest rate risk. Savings and loans, for example, can swap their variable-rate deposit liabilities into fixed-rate, long-term capital market liabilities to match their long-term assets such as mortgages through a swap of interest streams with a counterparty whose funding requirements demand variable-rate borrowings. Both parties can obtain the type of financing they need through the other party. Such opportunities have led to an explosion in the use of interest rate swaps over the past eight years. It is estimated that at the end of 1988 the outstanding notional amount of interest rate swaps contracts exceeded $1.0 trillion. This compares with an estimated volume of $680 billion in 1987, $100 billion in 1984, and zero in 1981. Although the swap market first emerged in, and was primarily limited to, the U.S. dollar markets and a couple of other currencies (pound sterling, Swiss franc), over the last two to three years, new interest rate swap markets have emerged in all the other major international reserve currencies (i.e., Japanese yen, deutsche marks) as well as in the currencies of emerging capital markets such as French francs; European Currency Units (ECUs); Australian, New Zealand, and Hong Kong dollars; Belgian francs; Danish and Swedish kroner; Spanish pesetas, and Italian lire.

In the currency area, swaps are important in reducing the risks associated with trade finance and asset/liability management in international business more effectively than more traditional hedging alternatives. For the importer or exporter with foreign currency payables or receivables, swaps offer advantages in increased certainty and lower cost over such alternatives as offshore funding, leads or lags in payments, or short-term hedges in the forward foreign exchange markets. Swaps, moreover, accomplish these purposes without the destabilizing effects on the foreign exchange market or the added capital market access requirements associated with the comparatively awkward techniques previously available. It is estimated that an additional $0.7 trillion in currency swaps was outstanding at the end of 1988, compared with the few transactions (perhaps a few hundred million dollars) that first took place in the 1979–1980 period. In addition, the growth of this market segment has been further boosted by the emergence of interest rate swap markets in many capital markets around the world.

Table 1 presents information about the relative size of the various swap markets around the world.

TABLE 1
Estimated Volume of Outstanding Swaps (End of 1988—$ Billions)

	Interest Rate	Currency	Total	Percent
U.S. dollars	728,166	269,477	997,643	60.69%
Japanese yen	78,488	131,033	209,521	12.75
Deutsche marks	56,466	33,979	90,445	5.50
Swiss francs	14,610	73,983	88,593	5.39
Pound sterling	52,265	17,704	69,969	4.26
Australian dollars	29,341	32,637	61,978	3.77
Canadian dollars	15,771	29,259	45,030	2.74
ECUs	9,197	24,497	33,694	2.05
French francs	18,871	5,178	24,049	1.46
New Zealand dollars	2,042	7,473	9,515	0.58
Dutch guilders	2,086	6,164	8,250	0.50
Hong Kong dollars	2,348	390	2,738	0.17
Belgian francs	554	1,867	2,421	0.15
Total	1,010,205	633,641	1,643,846	100.00%

Source: International Swap Dealers Association (ISDA).

The demand for hedging was a necessary condition for the emergence and further growth of swaps. But by itself it would not be sufficient to support the rapid growth that has taken place in this market. The sufficient conditions came in the form of two major factors: First, an environment that was conducive to the development of the swap market, that is, an environment characterized by financial deregulation, innovation, and a trend towards increased globalization; second, by attracting more market participants who were willing to stand on the other side of such hedging transactions. Such participants came in either as parties with complementary hedging interests or as players attracted by the arbitrage opportunities that the hedgers, in search of liquidity, were creating. Arbitrage has been the other prime motivation for using swaps. And, although the initial economic need satisfied through swaps was hedging, arbitrage is what has glorified the swap markets.

The themes of this chapter are volatility, hedging, innovation, arbitrage, and comparative advantage and how they were combined to lead to the creation and growth of a market, as enormous as the swap market. The objectives in writing this chapter are twofold. First, it aims at providing a description and an analysis of the factors that led to the emergence, growth, and development of the swap market. Second, it hopes to provide a framework within which the concepts of hedging and arbitrage of swaps can be visualized and analyzed in the context of the overall financial markets. In this respect it serves as a "big picture" chapter for swaps by focusing on the economics that drive a swap.

The chapter is organized into five sections. Section 2 focuses on the factors that have led to the emergence of swaps. It argues that the increased volatility in interest rates and foreign exchange rates has been the major reason for the emergence of swaps. The collapse of the Bretton Woods agreement and the shift in the implementation of monetary policy in the United States in controlling money supply were the two events that led to the increased volatility. The hedging needs and the demands of asset/liability management (which, in conjunction with the volatile interest rate environment, where the necessary conditions for the emergence of swaps) are touched upon.

Section 3 turns to the factors that have contributed significantly to the growth and development of the swap market: deregulation, innovation, and the trend towards increased globalization on the swap markets. These concepts serve as the platform for introducing the sufficient conditions for the development of the swap markets.

The focus of Section 4 is on the use of swaps as a tool to take advantage of the arbitrage opportunities that became available as a result of all the changes in the world financial markets over the past two decades. The concept of the *comparative advantage,* borrowed from the theory of international trade, is the analytical tool used to facilitate the presentation. A few examples are used to illustrate the deployment of swaps as a tool for capturing gains emanating from firms acting upon their financial comparative advantage. The nature of arbitrage and its utilization for lowering the cost of borrowing or enhancing asset returns are also illustrated through these examples. The implications of such arbitrage activity are also explored.

Finally, Section 5 summarizes the chapter and draws its conclusions.

FACTORS THAT HAVE CONTRIBUTED TO THE EMERGENCE OF SWAPS

Although the exact date of the appearance of the first swap is still debated, it is generally acknowledged that swaps first appeared in the late 1970s. Looking back with the benefit of history, one can see that the emergence of swaps in that period was not accidental. The 1970s (and in this respect the 1980s) will be remembered as a time when the financial landscape was reshaped. The changes in the world financial markets have been enormous and have been caused by a number of factors, from fundamental changes in the underlying economic environment to changes due to advances in regulation, technology, and communications. The objective of this section is to focus on the changes that have led to the emergence of the swap market, namely, the unprecedented increase in the volatility of interest rate and exchange rate levels. It starts by providing the reader with an overview of the prevailing economic and financial environment of the early 1970s and the developments that led to the increases in volatility we have experienced in recent years.

The World Economic Environment in the 1970s

If one were to have taken a snapshot of the world financial markets as we were entering the 1970s, the following observations would have been made.

First, developed financial markets, in the sense of the word used today, existed only in the United States and to some extent in Europe, centered around the so-called Euromarkets. In the United States the size of the economy, the prosperity of the postwar period, a well established legal and regulatory framework, and a "promarket" philosophy in combination with a stable political system had allowed the development of a wide spectrum of large liquid markets that served as efficient vehicles for transferring funds from investors to borrowers. Even in the United States, however, the various market segments were not integrated in one single market in which pressures in one segment were relieved by offsetting movements of funds from the other segments. The emergence of the Euromarkets, on the other hand, had its origins in a series of events (large U.S. balance of payments deficits, reluctance of several countries to deposit money in the United States, and tax considerations) which led over a period of time to the creation of large pools of U.S. dollars abroad, outside the U.S. system, that were deposited primarily with London-based financial institutions. Over time a network of markets emerged, ranging from deposits to securities, through which funds changed hands but that were not subject to the supervisory, regulatory, and tax-imposing arms of any monetary authority. Domestic financial markets in other countries were in an embryonic stage, isolated from each other and closely regulated by national authorities. Nonresident access to these capital markets was limited and tightly controlled while the scope of instruments available to borrowers and investors was very limited.

Second, the primary vehicle for transferring financial flows from investors to borrowers was by means of traditional commercial banking instruments, primarily syndicated loans, and securities played a comparatively modest role. Lending in the form of medium-term (5–7 years of maturity), U.S. dollar–denominated floating-rate syndicated loans was the main form of channeling such resources.

Finally, most international financial transactions were conducted in U.S. dollars. This was due to the critical role of the U.S. dollar as the linchpin of the international financial system. Under the Bretton Woods agreement, the values of all the currencies of the western world were pegged to the U.S. dollar which, in turn, had a fixed price vis-a-vis gold. Thus, the U.S. dollar in effect was the international medium of exchange as well as the main reserve currency.

Two major events took place that unravelled the environment and led to the sequence of events that changed the economic landscape. The first was the collapse of the Bretton Woods agreement in 1971, and the second was the change in the conduct of the U.S. monetary policy in 1979 from targeting interest rates to controlling money supply. These two events account for most of the unprecedented levels of volatility in interest rates and foreign exchange rates over the past 15 years.

The Collapse of the Bretton Woods Agreement

The year 1971 marked the end of the international monetary system as it had functioned since the Bretton Woods agreement in 1944. Under this system, the U.S. dollar had been the linchpin in the system through its fixed price vis-a-vis gold, and the values of all western currencies had been pegged to the dollar. As a result, exchange rates had been fixed, and the countries had agreed to manipulate their economic policies in order to maintain these rates. These policies ended when the convertibility of the U.S. dollar into gold was suspended in August 1971. Foreigners were no longer able to turn their dollars to the U.S. Treasury and exchange them for gold. Exchange rates were no longer fixed; instead they floated—that is, they were determined by free market forces. The major casualty of these developments was the U.S. dollar, which, given the overhang of U.S. dollars worldwide, started a long period of sustained depreciation that lasted until the end of the 1970s. During the same period, the demand for other hard currencies to substitute for the role of the U.S. dollar as an international reserve currency led to significant appreciation in the values of currencies such as deutsche marks, Swiss francs, and Japanese yen.

The significant changes in the values of these currencies had a significant impact on both internal and external sectors of the various economies around the world. For example, the devaluation of the dollar meant that the purchasing power of the U.S. dollar changed dramatically. Imported goods into the U.S. cost more, affecting the domestic price level, while at the same time higher-valued imports and lower-valued exports widened the external trade deficit. Most important, since the U.S. dollar was de facto the international reserve currency, most international trade was denominated in U.S. dollars; thus, the effect of the weaker U.S. dollar on inflation and trade accounts was expanded worldwide. Revenues of firms associated with exports and/or imports fluctuated dramatically; the valuation of official reserves was affected while commodity prices started following the price of gold.

In 1972 the signs of worldwide inflation began to emerge, with a 50 percent increase in commodity prices due to poor harvests and, in November 1973, the oil price shock, which was largely due to the reaction of the oil-producing countries to reduced oil export revenues (since oil prices were denominated in U.S. dollars). What followed was tremendous variance in inflation rates between countries as different countries adopted different economic policies in tackling the wealth effects caused by the major transfer of economic power from the oil-consuming to the oil-producing countries. The resulting differences in interest rates and price levels among countries and the varying balance of payments accounts added another source of currency fluctuation on top of an already volatile environment.

Since then, volatility has become a feature with which participants in the international economic system have had to cope. An appreciation for the magnitude of the economic changes induced by the collapse of the Bretton Woods agreement and the resulting divergence of exchange rates can be gained by looking at Figure 1, which shows how widely the value of the main trading currencies

FIGURE 1

Exchange Rate Fluctuations, 1971–1989 (Monthly Data, January 1970 to August 1989)

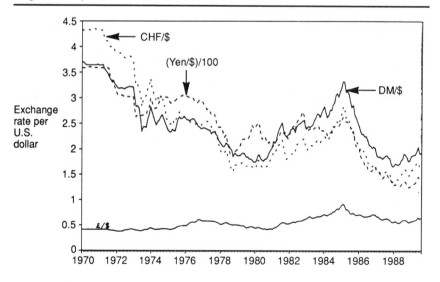

Source: Security Pacific Hoare Govett Limited.

fluctuated against the U.S. dollar between January 1970 and August 1989.

Almost all parties have felt the volatility of exchange rates and interest rates. Not only have exporters and importers suffered from the exchange rate volatility, but also foreign investors and those who borrowed overseas. As a result, the need for protection was keen for almost all participants active in international financial markets. Exporters, international corporations, and importers all require hedging vehicles to be able to compete. Exporters want assurance of the value of the currency they will be paid in, importers want to safeguard the amount they will be required to pay, and multinational corporations want to protect their activities in different parts of the globe. Currency swaps, which provide protection against currency fluctuation, were one of the answers the marketplace came up with as a means of protecting participants from increased foreign exchange uncertainty.

Controlling Money Supply as a Means of Conducting Monetary Policy

As discussed in the previous section, the first signs of prolonged interest rate uncertainty are traceable to the breakdown of the Bretton Woods agreement. However, interest rate volatility became a permanent feature of the financial landscape in 1979, when the U.S. Federal Reserve Board, responding to the lack of confidence to the U.S. dollar internationally and mounting inflationary pressures domestically, changed its monetary policy by focusing on controlling the money supply instead of targeting interest rates in the hope of bringing monetary growth under control. The results were dramatic. Interest rates in the United States reached unprecedented levels by historical standards. Most important, under the policy of controlling money supply, interest rates became a residual policy-making tool, resulting in greater movements in interest rates than at any time in the postwar period.

Repercussions of the change in the conduct of U.S. monetary policy went beyond the U.S. dollar markets and resulted in wider fluctuations in the levels of interest rates in other countries. The pursuit of independent monetary policies in various European countries and Japan was made more difficult because of the effects of floating exchange rates, which meant that the monetary authorities had to make a choice between domestic (domestic interest rates and inflation) or international (exchange rate) objectives. In most cases, monetary authorities allowed their domestic rates to be influenced by interest rate levels in the United States in order to protect their currencies, leading to worldwide interest rate increases.

The extent of interest rate volatility in the major economies around the world is illustrated in Figure 2, which portrays the movement of short-term interest rates (six-month LIBOR) in selected currencies from January 1980 to August 1989.

As inflationary expectations were sweeping the economy, raising funds became exceedingly difficult for corporations, finan-

FIGURE 2

Fluctuations in the Six-Month LIBOR Rates, 1980–1989 (Monthly Data January 1980 to August 1989)

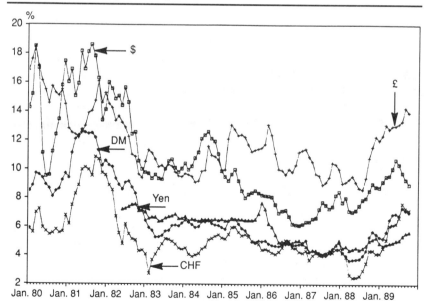

Source: Security Pacific Hoare Govett Limited.

cial institutions, and even the U.S. Treasury (particularly fixed-rate funds). Savers were reluctant to invest their savings in long-term financial assets that were losing value rapidly; they expressed a preference for short-term, floating-rate investments, which offered protection against such losses. Such developments led to the emergence of variable-rate funding. However, borrowing entities such as industrial corporations, which traditionally need long-term fixed-rate funding to finance the acquisition and/or construction of long-lived assets such as plant and equipment, were exposed by variable-rate funding to significant interest rate risks arising from mismatches in their assets (long-term, fixed-rate producing) and their liabilities (short-term, variable rate). Similarly, for deposit-accepting financial institutions, where credit risk has been traditionally the most important risk and, as such, the most important determinant of earnings, the new environment led to the emergence of a new class of risk, spread income risk, that is, the risk of being squeezed between the rate they were earning on their assets (which were either fixed or floating) and their liabilities (which, again, were either fixed or floating).

The consequence of this volatility has been that the management of interest rate risk has taken on much more importance. The need for hedging interest rate risk grew acute, and interest rate swaps came about in response to that need. For example, industrial corporations, by utilizing their access to funding (i.e., bank funding and/or short-term markets such as commercial paper), were in a position to convert it into fixed-rate funding by hedging it through interest rate swaps. Financial institutions were able to reduce the sensitivity of their liabilities to interest rate fluctuations, and thus protect themselves from rising interest rates, by transforming floating-rate liabilities into fixed-rate liabilities. Most important, interest rate swaps have provided institutions with the tools to manage more effectively the choice between fixed and floating rates and to protect themselves from interest rate fluctuations, or for the more daring participants, to take advantage of such fluctuations in locking in profits.

Investors were another group that benefited from the emergence of interest rate swaps. The versatility and flexibility of interest rate swaps make them ideal for combination with other assets in order to create packages that offer higher return for the same level of risk and, more generally, create assets that have the desirable risk/return profile. As explained in Section 4, one of the first uses of interest rate swaps was the packaging of fixed-rate bonds with an interest rate swap to create floating-rate assets (by swapping out the fixed stream of coupon payments for floating) that yielded significantly more than other floating-rate assets of the same risk class.

Of course, interest rate swaps were not the only measures used to manage risk. Other asset/liability management tools were developed, such as financial futures contracts, options, and other over-the-counter products. Yet among all of these, the interest rate swap is perhaps the most flexible and versatile instrument available for hedging interest rate risk.

FACTORS THAT HAVE CONTRIBUTED TO THE GROWTH AND DEVELOPMENT OF SWAPS

The extreme volatility in interest and foreign exchange rates that prevailed in the late 1970s provided a fertile environment for the emergence of swaps. However, the swaps market would not have grown to its current size unless a number of other developments had taken place. The objective of this section is to focus on these factors. In particular, this section contains a discussion of the three critical trends in financial markets, namely, deregulation, innovation, and globalization through advances in technology, communications, and transportation, that have been shaping the new environment and as such have contributed to the development of swaps and other derivative products. Although these trends emerged separately, in their evolution they fed each other and have now become closely intertwined, affecting and reinforcing each other.

Financial Deregulation

Financial deregulation has been the principal factor in the emergence and acceleration of financial innovation and the trend towards closely linked capital markets around the globe. It has been responsible for opening new markets and increasing the availability of choices to borrowers and investors by bringing into the market new instruments and structures that have enabled participants to compose or decompose risk and thus create assets and liabilities with the desired risk profiles.

The U.S. financial market has long been a leader in financial innovation. Because of its depth, liquidity, and the wide variety of financial instruments being traded in a well-organized environment, it has been responsive to the needs of the borrowers and investors. Yet the scope of innovation has been limited because of the relative stability that had prevailed in the postwar economic period. The international markets, on the other hand, have been far more active over the past few years in bringing forth new instruments and methods of financing and investing. Apart from the increased volatility caused for reasons reviewed earlier, the creation of new financial instruments in overseas markets has been to a large extent due to the steps that have been taken in deregulating financial markets in several key countries.

The focal point of all these activities has been the Euromarkets, where the Pandora's box of financial deregulation was opened. Operating in a regulatory vacuum beyond the reach of any tax and monetary authority, these markets attracted large amounts of funds which in turn were offered to investors that preferred anonymity and no tax burden. The emergence and the dynamic growth of these markets and the gravity they exerted on international money flows in the 1970s and early 1980s induced several monetary authorities to revisit the regulations they have been building to control capital flows. It became increasingly obvious to the respective monetary authorities that delaying the process of deregulating their domestic markets was not a choice available to them. It was a matter of assuring the survival of their local markets, which were in danger of being overshadowed by the activity in the Euromarkets. What we observed over the past 10 years was an effort by several key countries with developed capital markets, especially Japan, West Germany, Switzerland, and Britain, to prevent such overshadowing by liberalizing their financial markets. In the remainder of this section we briefly review the major steps that have taken place in various countries.

In the United States a critical step in this direction was the decision to abolish the 30 percent withholding tax on coupon payments of U.S. dollar–denominated bonds issued by U.S. corporations and held by foreign investors. Eurobond instruments traditionally have been havens for investors wishing to avoid taxation on investment income. This had been accomplished primarily by the issuance of bearer bonds (as opposed to registered bonds), which conceal the identity of the bondholder and thus the tax liability incurred from holding such bonds. By abolishing the withholding tax, U.S. authorities provided an additional level of comfort to investors wishing to avoid such taxes. The new provision afforded foreign investors an incentive to hold U.S. dollar–denominated securities as opposed to securities denominated in other currencies.

Similar steps were taken in Germany. The threat that German banks would shift their international bond operations away from Frankfurt to London was the catalyst for the reforms that took place in Germany. Among the OECD countries, Germany had been in the forefront of fiscal conservatism, prohibiting the use of money market instruments. The first step was to remove the 25 percent withholding tax imposed on domestic DM investments held by foreigners, offsetting the advantage offerred to investors holding Euro-DM denominated investments. Following that, authorities opened up the Euro-DM bond market by eliminating the mandatory queue for Euro-DM bond issues and by allowing foreign institutions with a banking presence in West Germany to lead-manage such issues. Finally, they permitted the issuance of nontraditional bonds issues, including FRNs, zero coupon bonds, and dual currency issues, thus enhancing the appeal of the deutsche mark to the international investors.

Similar considerations led the Swiss and Dutch authorities to proceed with reforms to partially deregulate the Swiss franc and Dutch guilder bond markets. For example, restrictions regarding the issuing queue and the size of bond issues in the Swiss franc market were eliminated. And the Dutch authorities lifted the restrictions regarding the use of new instruments such as FRNs and money market instruments. Additional moves, such as the creation of a Euro-Swiss franc (offshore) bond market are also under active consideration.

In the British capital markets radical changes in the structure of the stock and bond markets took place in October 17, 1986. The new measures transformed the existing market structures in accordance with the U.S. prototype in which securities firms act as both principals and agents. The functions of the jobbers (market makers who traded gilts—U.K. government securities—but were not allowed to distribute to clients) and brokers (who intermediated between jobbers and clients) had been separated. Similarly, in the stock market, the system of minimum commissions was eliminated. The consolidation of the two functions has led to increased competition among the many market participants (including several non-British entities) for the benefit of the final investor.

The country in which the most extensive reforms have occurred is perhaps Japan. As in most major currency countries, three segments constitute the so-called Japanese capital market: the domestic capital market, where domestic issuers finance themselves in Japanese yen; the Samurai market, which is located in Japan and where nonresident borrowers finance themselves in Japanese yen; and the Euroyen market, in which primarily nonresidents obtain financing by funds provided by non-Japanese investors. The reforms cut across all three markets. First, market forces have been allowed to set interest rates in the domestic markets replacing a vast array of administered rates. Second, access to Samurai and Euroyen markets, which was formerly restricted to supranational and sovereign credits, has become available to most market participants. Finally, restrictions on currency swaps and forward foreign exchange transactions have been lifted. The objectives of these reforms have been to open the Japanese capital markets, enhance the use of the yen as an international currency, and facilitate the flow of the large surpluses of savings this country currently enjoys to corporations or sovereign entities in need of funds.

What followed has been more or less predictable. Many innovations that had been initiated and tried in the Euromarkets started appearing in several domestic markets. For example, the past few years have seen the issuance of first Japanese yen and deutsche mark floating-rate notes (FRNs), the emergence of the first zero coupon bonds in three of these countries (Switzerland, Germany, and the United Kingdom), the issuance of dual-currency bonds, and the first foreign currency–denominated bonds in the domestic Japanese market (Shogun bonds). In turn, the appearance of new instruments accelerated the arbitrage process through swaps (as explained below) by making it possible to capture arbitrage profits which otherwise would only be observable.

In conclusion, financial deregulation has had positive effects. By eliminating tax considerations, it has induced economic units to make decisions based on fundamental economics, thereby improving the allocation of funds. Elimination of restrictions regarding the type of instruments available has enhanced the menus available to both investors and borrowers. Finally, deregulation has induced swap activity, which in turn has increased market efficiency by facilitating the process of transferring funds in the most efficient way from the savings surplus to the deficit surplus economic units.

Financial Innovation

In the previous section financial innovation was identified as the major by-product of the deregulation process. An equally important factor accounting for the emergence of financial innovation has been the continued high price and interest rate volatility and the general economic uncertainty caused by the divergence in the fiscal and monetary policies of the major industrialized countries. More generally, however, innovation is spurred when market participants respond to changes in the surrounding economic environment by introducing new techniques, new instruments, and new ways of transferring funds from investors to borrowers. The innovation process, by its very nature, creates funding and investment opportunities for the various financial market participants that otherwise would not have been possible. It allows borrowers to obtain financing at reduced financing costs, compared with traditional techniques. At the same time, the process of composing and decomposing risk that is embedded in the innovative techniques also creates more alternatives for investors by offering yield improvements, compared with similar risk assets. Examples of such major innovations, apart from swaps, that have taken place over the past 15 years are discussed in the following paragraphs.

Floating-Rate Financing
Perhaps the most far-reaching of the many changes introduced in the past two decades has been floating-rate financing. This technique combines the characteristics of a money market instrument,

providing stability of market value to the investor with long tenure, which is a feature of traditional fixed-rate bond financing. As such, it enables investors to insulate themselves from the interest rate risk by quickly passing on increases in the cost of their sources of funds to borrowers. At the same time it provides borrowers with funding when the traditional sources of funding (i.e., fixed-rate bond financing) are closed. The first FRN appeared in 1970 in the Euromarkets, but it was the inflationary environment since then that induced the growth of floating-rate instruments and their rapid expansion in both domestic and international markets. Over the past few years two more developments extended the scope of variable-rate financing. First, the markets witnessed a proliferation of note issuance facilities (known with acronyms such as NIFs and RUFs) which are essentially syndicated financing arrangements that guarantee an issuer access to a volume of floating-rate funding for a prescribed period. Second, FRNs and note issuance facilities emerged in currencies other than the U.S. dollar.

The significance of the emergence of FRNs as another source of floating-rate financing was that it gave a further impetus in the growth of the swap market. It has enabled borrowers to further decompose the funding decision from the decision as to the form and type of their liabilities (i.e., fixed or floating). At the same time, it has equally enabled investors to expand the universe of instruments that would typically be considered as investment choices. For example, a bank wishing to expand its floating-rate asset portfolio now routinely considers asset swaps (i.e., packages of fixed-rate bonds which, together with interest rate swaps, emulate the risk profile of a floating-rate asset) among its choices.

Futures and Options
The emergence of options and futures, whether foreign exchange or interest rate, was another response by market participants to the increased volatility of the last decade. As with swaps, these new instruments provide borrowers and investors with more choices and flexibility in managing their assets and liabilities. The recent explosive growth in these markets is an indication of how the management of risk has evolved. These instruments and their markets are briefly reviewed below.

Options contracts are agreements that give the holder the right (but not the obligation) to buy (call option) or sell (put option) an underlying asset at an agreed-upon price (the exercise price) within a specified period of time (expiration time). Depending on what the underlying asset is, we distinguish between interest rate options (the underlying asset is a fixed-income security) and currency options (the underlying asset is a foreign currency). Option holders benefit from price changes while, at any point of time, the maximum loss is known with certainty and is equal to the premium paid to acquire the option. The asymmetric characteristics of options (either unlimited gain with known maximum loss or unlimited loss with known maximum gain) make them particularly attractive among market participants in connection with borrowing, investing, and commercial activities. Currency options have been used extensively over the past years to hedge a growing volume of non-dollar borrowings and/or investment securities, in large part, because of the record volatility in the currency markets. Recently, the use of interest rate options has also expanded rapidly as their role as interest rate "insurance policies" (such as interest rate caps and floors) has become more widely recognized.

Futures contracts are agreements that give the holder the right *and* the obligation to buy or sell an underlying asset at an agreed-upon price at a specified time. Depending on what the underlying asset is, we distinguish between interest rate futures, currency futures, as well as a whole series of commodities futures. Futures holders benefit from price changes, but unlike option holders, their profits and losses are unlimited since they are binding contracts. The symmetric properties of futures contracts make them ideal for hedging activities arising in connection with borrowing, investing, and commercial activities. The unprecedented volatility in the exchange and interest rate markets has led to a proliferation of a variety of futures contracts be they currency futures or GNMA, Eurodollar and Treasury bond contracts.

Securitization

The term *securitization,* in its strict sense, is used to describe the process by which nontradeable, private assets such as bank loans are packaged together to create homogeneous asset units that are offered to investors through public offerings in a tradeable security format. The beginnings of securitization go back to the early 1970s, when pools of mortgages were created and homogeneous participations in them were sold as securities (GNMAs, FNMAs). However, in its most general context the term securitization is used to describe the process by which funds, which before were channelled from investors to borrowers through some sort of intermediation, are now channelled directly through the issuance of publicly offered, tradeable securities. In this broader context, over the past 10 years securitization has been greatly expanded in several directions and has played a catalytic role in the whole process of financial innovation. The broadening of securitization has taken place in several directions.

First, an increasing variety of good-quality assets have been used to collateralize this class of instruments (including assets such as credit card receivables and automobile loans). In addition, by cleverly packaging these assets, new types of securities, such as the Collateralized Mortgage Obligations (CMOs), have emerged, with cash flows resembling those of traditional bonds (semiannual payments as opposed to the monthly payments on GNMAs and floating-rate structures).

Second, over the past 10 years an increasing number of high-quality borrowers, such as highly rated corporations and sovereign entities, have been securitizing their borrowings. These entities, which traditionally have used bank credit as their main source of borrowed funds, have been bypassing intermediating institutions, raising funds directly through the issuance of securities in the markets. The emergence and rapid growth of the FRN and Eurocommercial paper markets are prime examples. Corporations and sovereign entities that once obtained financing through syndicated loans are now satisfying their needs, to a large extent, by utilizing the floating-rate security and Eurocommercial paper markets. Again, this process has enabled borrowers to further decompose the funding decision from the decision about the form and type of their liabilities (i.e., fixed or floating) and enhance their ability to lower borrowing costs by employing swap-related debt management techniques. At a broader level, it has intensified the competition between commercial banks (the traditional suppliers of loans) and the securities houses (the beneficiaries from securitization), inducing the former to work off their comparative advantage (their strong balance sheets) in order to reclaim the lost business.

Third, securitization has extended to the lesser credit quality assets. In particular, lower-rated entities such as start-up companies, which traditionally have relied upon bank credit and/or other more expensive forms of fund raising (i.e., issuance of equity or debt convertible to equity), have increased access to securities markets thanks to the innovative steps of a handful of U.S. investment banks. Another variation in this theme has been the increased tradeability of traditional bank loans. Increasingly, traditional banking loans have been syndicated and subsequently sold out to other smaller banks and investors.

The securitization process offers advantages to both borrowers and investors. Borrowers benefit in two ways: First, they can mobilize otherwise unutilized assets to create borrowing capacity, and, second, they can lower their funding costs. Lower costs occur because the expenses associated with issuing securitized debt are typically lower than those associated with loans. Similarly, investors benefit as well. The new securities enhance the choices available to investors, offer improved yields compared with other high-quality assets because they cost less to issue, and, finally, offer liquidity since they are tradeable. However, securitization, which transforms obligations from nonmarketable to marketable, encourages debt growth.

Globalization of Financial Markets

The third important trend characterizing financial markets over the past 10 years has been the growing trend towards increased internationalization, or *globalization,* of financial markets. This term is used to describe the trend towards financial integration of the various capital markets around the globe. The trend towards globalization of financial markets is the product of the other two developments, namely, deregulation and innovation, coupled with rapid technological advances in computing and communications.

Deregulation has brought down many of the barriers that previously existed (whether in the form of taxes or restrictions and controls) and prevented the free flow of capital. Innovation has provided the tools with which the "bridging" of the various capital markets can be accomplished. In this respect swaps are the perfect example of an innovation that has contributed significantly towards an integrated international capital market. The interest rate swap markets are integrally linked to the local money and capital markets. At the same time, the interest rate swap markets are intimately linked with their currency swap sectors, which, in turn, comprise an international webb of satellite markets forming an efficient mechanism for transmitting changes from one market to the others. The whole process has received a tremendous boost from the rapid advances in communications and the computer technology. These advances have led to a collapse of the constraints imposed by time and distance, permitting the immediate exchange of information and intensifying competition among the various financial centers.

The result has been that the major borrowers and investors no longer perceive their borrowing and investment opportunities within the framework given by their local markets. Now they seek the best terms by borrowing and investing around the globe in all the major (and minor) financial centers of the world, whether they are in Europe, the United States, or Japan. Issuers and investors have a wider range of currencies, instruments, and markets from which to choose, and their ability to arbitrage across markets has been enhanced. As a result, the role of financial institutions and the capital markets is being redefined. The distinction between investment banks and commercial banks in the United States and Japan is becoming more and more blurred, and both kinds of banks are reorienting themselves internationally. In this environment, financial institutions from every major country in the world compete with each other to attract the business of entities that need to raise funds (whether corporate or sovereign credits) or invest excess cash. In the process, they continuously invent new ways of transferring funds that give an edge to the borrowers, or the investors, or the financial institutions themselves—and sometimes (if the new ways are true innovations) to all of the above.

The outcomes of globalization have been good news for the international economy because they have caused markets to become more efficient. As such, they better fulfill their role as the mechanism for distributing investments and savings among the various economic units. The result has been greater efficiency in the real economy and the creation of more and more demand for products such as swaps.

THE USE OF SWAPS AS AN ARBITRAGE TOOL

The discussion in the previous sections focused on the conditions that made the appearance of the currency and interest rate swaps necessary as a tool for commercial and financial hedging. The need for hedging vehicles was a necessary condition for the development of swaps, but it was not a sufficient one.) However, another important factor behind swaps has been the motivation to take advantage of arbitrage opportunities that exist because of capital market inefficiencies. Such arbitrage has attracted a great deal of attention in the financial press, which has glorified this use of swaps, and has been a main selling point used by banks in convincing many corporations and financial institutions to enter the swap market. The objective of this section is to address the issue of how swaps help in capturing arbitrage gains. This is explained in the context of the theory of comparative advantage, which is well established in economics. Finally, the section addresses the issues of where these arbitrage opportunities come from and what their implications are for financial markets.

The Liability Interest Rate Swap Arbitrage

Swaps can be used to capture arbitrage gains in many different ways. However, the use of swaps as an arbitrage tool in connection with funding has done the most to popularize the technique. To illustrate just how this advantage comes about and how it can be exploited through a swap, we start by taking a look at an example of interest rate swap arbitrage in connection with creating a new liability. Using illustrative typical cost spreads that one might find in the same capital market for two different borrowers, we identify the economics that underlie these transactions and demonstrate how the arbitrage gain arises and how it can be captured with the help of swaps.

Let's consider a Fortune 500 industrial firm with a BBB credit rating that wishes to raise $250 million in 10-year, fixed-rate funds in order to finance the acquisition of another company. Given its BBB credit rating, the firm can borrow 10-year funds in the U.S. dollar market at a fixed rate of 11.00 percent, or at a spread of 200 basis points over the 10-year U.S. Treasury bond. The company, for a variety of reasons, does not have immediate access to the U.S. fixed-rate bond market because of its weak credit rating and the fact that it has tapped the fixed-rate bond market frequently over the past few years. Unable to proceed unless willing to pay the required spread over Treasuries, the treasurer of the firm contacts his investment banker and asks for suggestions to lower the cost of borrowing.

At the same time, the investment banker is aware that a financial institution with a better credit rating (its obligations have been rated AAA by Standard & Poors and Moody's) wants to take advantage of the favorable market conditions to raise medium-term variable-rate funding in order to finance its expansion program. If the financial institution were to decide to access the floating-rate market directly, it could raise the funds at an all-in cost of LIBOR + ¼ percent. The firm, however, is exploring alternatives for reducing the cost of such borrowings. Given its AAA credit rating, the firm could access the U.S. dollar bond market and raise the amounts at an all-in cost of 9.50 percent, or a spread of 50 basis points over the 10-year U.S. Treasury bond. Firm AAA is well regarded in the U.S. dollar market, has not tapped the fixed rate market recently, and as such can obtain favorable borrowing terms.

Before the appearance of swaps and other hedging instruments, industrial firms with access to the capital markets would typically tap them for fixed-rate funds. Similarly, financial institutions would rarely issue fixed-rate funds and would concentrate primarily on raising floating-rate funding. Given these propensities, one would expect that commercial banks should have a relative comparative advantage in raising fixed-rate funds while industrial firms should have a relative comparative advantage in raising floating-rate funds. The investment banker realizes that there is a potential for a swap between these two firms. Upon further inquiry with his trading and sales force, he comes up with the following cost assessment for the two firms in the two different markets. Table 2 summarizes the funding costs of the two firms in the two markets.

TABLE 2
Relative Borrowing Costs in the Two Markets

	Fixed-Rate Market	Floating-Rate Market
Firm AAA	9.50%	LIBOR + 25 bp
Firm BBB	11.00%	LIBOR + 75 bp
Credit spread	150 bp	50 bp
Arbitrage opportunity	100 bp	

Careful examination of the relative funding costs of the two firms reveals some interesting points.

First, as one would expect, Firm AAA, being a better credit risk, has an absolute advantage in both markets since it can raise funds at a lower cost than Firm BBB.

Second, while Firm AAA has an absolute advantage in both markets, its relative advantage is in the fixed-rate market since it can borrow at a cost 150 basis points lower than that of Firm BBB. By comparison, Firm AAA's borrowing advantage over Firm BBB in the floating-rate market is only 50 basis points. That is, Firm AAA's comparative financial advantage, which can arise from any one of the market inefficiencies discussed later, is thus in the fixed-rate market. Similarly, Firm BBB, disadvantaged in both markets, has less of a disadvantage in the floating-rate market, where its borrowing disadvantage vis-a-vis Firm AAA is only 50 basis points (as opposed to 150 basis points in the fixed-rate market).

Third, the difference in funding costs between the two companies in the two markets is not identical. In the fixed rate market the difference in costs is 150 basis points while in the floating rate market is 50 basis points. That is, the credit premium between the two firms, which is defined as the difference (spread) in their funding costs in the two markets, is different. Investors in the fixed-rate market assess the difference between the two credits to be worth 150 basis points while investors in the floating-rate market assess it to be 50 basis points. This difference gives rise to a classic arbitrage situation since an otherwise identical item (the credit difference between the firms) has different prices in two different markets.

If the arbitrage difference were to be captured, it would be possible for one or both firms to lower their funding costs. As in any other arbitrage opportunity this can be accomplished by selling the item (the credit spread) in the more expensive market and buying it back in the cheaper market. We mentioned above that Firm AAA has a comparative advantage in the fixed-rate market while Firm BBB has the comparative advantage in the floating-rate market. If each firm issues in the market where it can borrow at the lowest absolute cost and then exchanges payments through an interest rate swap, both borrowers can lower their borrowing costs. The specific steps involved are presented in Table 3.

It is clear that the level of payments made between the two firms is critical to the success of this structure. If the two firms were to simply pass their respective costs of borrowing, the structure would never work. Firm AAA would never enter the agreement because the fixed-rate funds would cost the firm 11.00 percent, while it could obtain the same funds at 9.50 percent on its own, that is, 150 basis points cheaper. And Firm BBB would have U.S. funds at 9.50 percent, 150 basis points less than it would have had to pay in a direct borrowing. Clearly, such an arrangement would not be sustainable. The typical outcome is that the parties divide their differences in borrowing costs in the two markets. This can be accomplished according to the relative bargaining strength of the borrowers or on the basis of other factors. Typically, Firm AAA, the stronger credit, and the one that can borrow at the lowest cost in both markets, will take most of the savings, but it will, in most circumstances, share some of the savings with the Firm BBB in order to induce it to enter into the transactions.

In this case, there is a net cost savings of 100 basis points to be divided (an easy way to calculate the net savings is by observing that Firm BBB benefits by 150 basis points while Firm AAA loses 50 basis points if interest payments are simply exchanged). In order to complete the example, let's assume that Firm AAA obtains

TABLE 3
Steps Necessary to Lock in Arbitrage Gain

Firm AAA	Firm BBB
• Raise $250 million fixed-rate at 9.50%	• Issues $250 million floating at LIBOR + 75bp
• Receive fixed-rate payments from BBB	• Receive floating-rate payments from AAA
• Make floating-rate payments to BBB	• Make fixed-rate payments to AAA

FIGURE 3
Swap Payment Structure

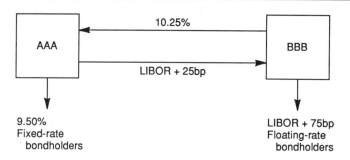

9.50%
Fixed-rate
bondholders

LIBOR + 75bp
Floating-rate
bondholders

75 basis points of savings and Firm BBB gets the remaining 25 basis points. A final minor technical point is how these savings will be delivered to each party. For simplicity, we assume that Firm AAA gets the 75 basis point savings in the form of lower fixed interest rate payments it receives from Firm BBB. Figure 3 shows how these arrangements are finalized.

This transaction benefits both parties. Firm AAA has been able to raise floating rate funds at 75 basis points below cost (LIBOR − 50 basis points compared with its direct cost of LIBOR + 25 basis points). Firm BBB has been able to obtain fixed-rate funds at 25 basis points below cost (at 10.75 percent compared with its direct cost of 11.00 percent). The cost savings that these swap payments translate to for each party is demonstrated in Table 4.

TABLE 4
Cost after the Interest Rate Swap

Firm AAA		Firm BBB	
Receives from Firm BBB	10.25%	Pays to Firm AAA	10.25%
Pays to bondholders	9.50	Pays to bondholders	LIBOR + 75 bp
Pays to Firm BBB	LIBOR + 25 bp	Receives from Firm AAA	LIBOR + 25 bp
Net cost of floating-rate debt	LIBOR − 50 bp	Net cost of fixed-rate debt	10.75%
Direct cost of floating-rate debt	LIBOR + 25 bp	Direct cost of fixed-rate debt	11.00%
Net savings	0.75%	Net savings	0.25%

By exploiting its financial comparative advantage, Firm AAA has been able to transform its advantage in accessing the fixed-rate bond market into a cost-effective way of creating a floating-rate liability of similar maturity. Firm BBB has done the reverse.

Finally, the above example has been instrumental in demonstrating a few common elements that form the basic principles of swap activity in connection with borrowing arbitrage:

- In order for an interest rate swap to lead to arbitrage gains for one or both parties, at least one party must have an advantage in at least one market. Arbitrage gains occur only if each party borrows in the market where it has the comparative advantage.
- The total arbitrage gain available to both parties reflects the comparative advantage of the two issuers in the two markets. If one party has an absolute advantage in both markets, the total arbitrage gain is the difference between the differential borrowing costs. If each party has an advantage in only one market, the total arbitrage gain available is equal to the sum of the comparative advantages.
- The allocation of arbitrage gains depends on the relative bargaining strengths of the two parties involved.

The Asset Interest Rate Swap Arbitrage

The above example is an accurate representation of the prevailing conditions in the early 1980s and demonstrates to a large extent the first use of interest rate swaps as an arbitrage instrument. Swaps were popularized through the liability side of the business—hence, the term, used initially, *liability* swaps. Furthermore, the arbitrage gains achievable through combinations of borrowings and swaps highlight the high public profile of swap activity. However, arbitrage opportunities also exist on the asset side of the balance sheet. In fact, shortly after the appearance of the liability swaps, the first asset packages involving interest rate swap arbitrage were put together.

In the typical asset swap, the investor (say a bank) would be interested in obtaining a variable-rate asset which yields a margin over LIBOR which roughly represents its cost of funds in the interbank market. The bank, by acquiring an asset yielding a spread over LIBOR, say 25 basis points, and financing it at LIBOR, locks in the spread. The typical source of such assets are the FRNs and/or syndicated loans markets. An alternative way of creating a floating-rate asset is by buying fixed-rate assets (i.e., fixed-rate bonds) and swapping out the fixed-income receipts for floating receipts based on LIBOR through an interest rate swap. To the extent that the interest rate at which fixed payments made under the swap is less than the interest rate at which fixed payments are received from the fixed-rate asset, a spread over the LIBOR is created. If this spread over the LIBOR is higher than what is achievable by directly buying an FRN or syndicated loan from the same issuer, the asset package (the fixed-rate bonds plus the interest rate swap) is preferable. The following example is typical of so-called asset-swap activity, which continues until today. Table 5 portrays the yields that we observe on the secondary market values of the obligations of Firm XXX in the fixed-rate and floating-rate markets, respectively. Alongside we state the yield on the fixed-rate leg of an interest rate swap of similar maturity.

The reader may observe that these three markets are not in equilibrium with each other because combinations of two of them result in a package of similar risk but with a different return from the third market. For example, if the holder of fixed-rate bonds enters an interest rate swap where it pays fixed and receives 6-month LIBOR, he or she can create a floating rate package with a 25 basis points spread over LIBOR which is higher than the spread of 15 basis points observed in the floating-rate paper of the same issuer. It is discrepancies of this nature that are exploitable through asset interest rate swap arbitrage. Table 6 and Figure 4 portray the arrangement of such a combination.

This is another example of how interest rate swaps are being used to capture arbitrage gains.

TABLE 5
Relative Yields in Various Markets

Fixed Rate	Floating Rate	Swaps
10.50%	LIBOR + 15 bp	10.25% versus LIBOR Flat

FIGURE 4
Asset Swap Structure

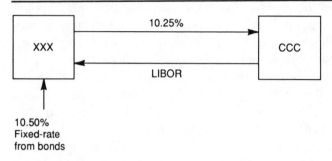

Where Does the Arbitrage Come From

The examples used in demonstrating how swaps can be used as a tool for capturing arbitrage profits are a good representation of how corporations are able to lower their borrowing costs and/or enhance the return on their investments. In the previous section, we argued that the benefit of lower costs derives from the utilization of a firm's comparative advantage in particular markets. In what follows, we explore the sources of this comparative advantage.

Capital markets exist for the purpose of efficiently channelling funds from the economic units with excess funds (savers) to economic units in need of funds (borrowers). Interest rates are the means by which an equilibrium is brought between the supply of funds by savers and the demand of funds by the borrowers in each capital market. The levels of interest rates determined in this way

TABLE 6
Yield Enhancement after the Interest Rate Swap

• Receives from fixed-rate bonds	10.50%
• Pays to swap counterparty CCC	10.25%
• Receives from swap counterparty CCC	LIBOR
• Net return from floating-rate asset	LIBOR + 25 bp
• Direct return from floating-rate asset	LIBOR + 15 bp
• Return enhancement	0.10%

in the various markets are related to each other. The forward exchange markets, for example, relate and reflect the interest rate levels between two currency markets. If markets were perfect, a firm should not have an advantage in raising funds in a particular capital market and/or in a particular currency. Interest rate parity would ensure that the cost would be identical regardless of the currency in which the borrowing were denominated. In practice, however, markets are neither perfect nor totally integrated. Finance theorists, when they talk about perfect markets, assume that these markets have the following characteristics:

- Markets are frictionless (no transaction costs, taxes, divisible assets, regulations).
- There is perfect competition so that everybody is a price taker (no individual can affect the price).
- Markets are informationally efficient; that is, information is costless and available to everybody.
- Economic units are rational and are allowed to maximize their wealth.

If any of the above conditions is violated, then inefficiencies exist in the system that create comparative advantage, which, in turn, can be exploited through arbitrage. Following the above classification, such inefficiencies can be classified in the following categories: regulatory constraints, imperfect information, imperfect competition, and portfolio saturation. These are analyzed below.

First, regulatory constraints or frictions create cost differentials which the market, to the extent it can, tries to exploit. One form in which these constraints take place is by the imposition by the appropriate monetary authorities of controls that limit access to the capital markets. The monetary authorities of most countries do not permit, or permit in a constrained manner, nonresidents to enter their capital markets. The control takes the form of refusing entry outright, restricting access to certain maturities, imposing formal or informal queuing systems, requiring approvals by capital markets committees, or, simply, enforcing gentlemen's agreements that reflect some of the above. Strictly speaking, not a single domestic market is free from all access controls. By contrast, the Eurodollar market (because of the lack of any formal regulations) and the market in European Currency Unit (ECU) bonds (because

ECUs are not the currency of any country) are free from access controls. But every other market, in one way or another, is subject to access controls. The result is that some issuers have access to certain currencies, and other issuers have no access at all even though they have a desire to be in those currencies. Firms that have access to the currency (whether they are domestic or nonresident), in effect, generate the comparative advantage for themselves because of their monopoly situation created by the regulation of the market.

Another way that access to the market is regulated is through the imposition of various taxes, mostly in the form of withholding taxes. In virtually every country in the world, investment income in one way or another is subject to taxes, and this gives investors the incentive to pay a premium for the opportunity to avoid being subject to taxes. Thus, for example, bearer bonds (in which the identity of the investor is not revealed) in the Eurobond market are placed at yields lower than those of their domestic markets. All of these factors cause yield discrepancies, and therefore are typical sources of comparative advantage. In light of the developments that have taken place in the world financial markets over the past 10 years (discussed in Section 2), it is not surprising that the availability of arbitrage has been diminishing over the same time period.

A second source of comparative advantage is informational inefficiencies. If markets were perfect and every participant in every market possessed the same information, then corporations would be evaluated identically and thus raise funds at the same credit risk premiums. However, in practice, market participants in, say, the Benelux countries, are not totally familiar with top-credit U.S. corporations in the U.S. capital market. Similarly, U.S. investors may not be familiar with top-credit European corporations. The result is that although you may have two issuers (say, one German and one U.S. corporation) of identical credit standing, they might face different risk premiums in raising funds in the United States and German capital markets. In particular, the German corporation may have an advantage vis-a-vis the U.S. corporation in the German market while the opposite might be true for the U.S. corporation in the U.S. market. Therefore, imperfect information is an additional source of comparative advantage. Again, with the advent of communications and information technology the source of such arbitrages has been diminishing.

A third source of comparative advantage may be the noncompetitive financial structures that exist in several countries. For example, in most European countries (especially Germany and Switzerland), the financial systems are dominated by the banking sector, which, in turn, is dominated by a handful of large banks (the three big banks in Switzerland, Deutsche Bank in Germany). These structures do not allow the market-clearing process to work efficiently, resulting in interest rate levels that may deviate substantially (lower or higher) from competitively driven market interest rates and that, in turn, leads to arbitrage opportunities and are thus another source of comparative advantage.

A recent, fourth source of comparative advantage, stemming again from lack of perfect competition, is the swap intermediation costs. As detailed elsewhere in this book, swaps expose the user to the risk that the counterparty to the swap transaction may become insolvent and thus stop serving its swap obligations. To avoid this risk, most players in the swap market will not deal with lesser-quality counterparties directly; instead, they put a bank in the middle, and the bank, for an intermediating fee, in effect substitutes for the lesser credit in the transaction. If the bank does not properly assess the risk involved and as a result charges a smaller fee, then, in effect, the bank creates comparative advantage. In a perfectly competitive environment, credit risk assessment should not be different depending on where this assessment takes place, whether by the public in the bond markets or by the credit analysts in the insurance companies or commercial banks.

Finally, another source of creating cost differentials among otherwise identical issuers from a credit standing point of view is the lack of diversification in individual portfolios. If flows of funds are controlled and investors choices are constrained, then saturation of the portfolios of investors in particular markets may occur. The primary reason for this is, again, the restricted access to the various markets which forces investors in these markets to hold suboptimally diversified portfolios, that is, portfolios in which "local" securities are held in proportions higher than efficient diversification would suggest. Investors in these currencies/markets have very strong desires to diversify their portfolios to include a broader range of international credits. The result is that investors would be willing to pay a premium to hold securities of names underrepresented in their portfolios while, at the same time, they would need a yield inducement to hold securities of names overrepresented in their portfolios. Thus, depending on the relative volume of their respective borrowings and the frequency with which they go to a particular market, borrowers of identical credit quality may pay markedly different rates of interest. A prime example of portfolio saturation has been the case of the World Bank in the Swiss capital market. The Swiss capital market has been a major source of funds for the World Bank over the past 20 years. As a result, World Bank bonds are overrepresented in the portfolios of the Swiss franc market investors, and the credit spread of the World Bank vis-a-vis other, less-creditworthy issuers has worsened substantially. Scarcity value and portfolio saturation are important determinants in pricing new issues and cause yield differentiation for identical credits. Therefore, they are a source of comparative advantage.

Implications of Swap Activity for Financial Markets

The discussion of the previous section highlighted the fact that there are several factors that lead to the creation of financial comparative advantage. The discussion also pointed out that the comparative advantage arises from inefficiencies that are created mostly by regulators and/or policy makers. These inefficiencies introduce temporary or long-term differences in the credit spreads which, through the vehicle of swaps, can be exploited to reduce borrowing costs and/or to increase asset returns.

The arbitraging activity, apart from being beneficial for the parties involved in these transactions, has beneficial effects on financial markets in general by improving the markets' ability to distribute funds from savings units to borrowing units more efficiently. The improvements in the market efficiency gained through the arbitrage activity come in a number of different ways. To begin with, swaps serve as linkage among the various markets. Before the appearance of swaps, fixed-rate and floating-rate markets were isolated from each other. Market participants would move from one market to the other on the basis of their expectations about the level and/or shape of the yield curve. Funds would flow from one market to the other only to the extent that expectations changed. However, with the advent of swaps, market participants do not have to restrict themselves to the market that they have chosen for borrowing or investment. Instead, having formed their opinion about future interest rates, they now have the ability to look at both markets simultaneously to search for the best deal. For example, a borrower wanting to raise fixed-rate funds considers not only the fixed-rate market but also the combination of floating-rate funding with an interest rate swap. This process ensures consistency of pricing between the fixed- and floating-rate markets and helps alleviate pressures that may build in the various market segments.

Another example of market integration that occurs as a result of swap-driven arbitrage can be seen in asset swaps. As discussed previously, floating-rate investors actively consider alternative packages of fixed-rate bonds and interest rate swaps. By doing so they ensure that the yields prevailing in the secondary markets are consistent with those of the primary market. For example, if the yields prevailing in the secondary fixed-rate market are higher than those in the primary market, market participants would buy the higher-yielding bonds, combine them with interest rate swaps, and create packages yielding a spread over 6-month LIBOR, in excess of that obtained by buying newly issued fixed-rate bonds (and combining them with interest rate swaps). Again, the process leads to more efficient market to the extent that new issues are priced in a manner that is consistent with the secondary markets.

Arbitrage of this nature continues even today, although the arbitrage gains achievable are much lower because of market integration. In fact, one of the reasons swap markets have emerged in various parts of the world is in pursuit of arbitrage opportunities in markets which, because of their size or lack of sophistication, such opportunities still exist. Moreover, it is processes like these, taking place in all the financial markets where interest rate swap markets have developed, that have led to efficiencies in a number of domestic financial markets around the world. In addition, these markets have been further integrated through the existence of the cross-currency swap market. Just as interest rate swaps ensure pricing consistency among market segments within a particular financial market, so also do cross-currency swaps ensure pricing consistency across financial markets in different currencies. Developments such as these have pushed globalization of financial markets even further, creating a global marketplace composed of a series of interlinked markets. Events affecting a particular market are transmitted through swaps throughout the global network of markets.

Clearly, the new global environment has implications for the conduct and efficiency of monetary policies of various countries around the world. Actions of the monetary authorities in one country, particularly from the reserve currency countries, are transmitted to the other financial markets around the world, thus affecting the monetary variables in other countries and offsetting or reinforcing actions taken by the local monetary authorities. As a result, there is an increasing need for cooperation among the key monetary authorities around the world in order to coordinate their policies more closely in an increasingly interlinked global marketplace.

SUMMARY AND CONCLUSIONS

The objective of this chapter was to describe the environment that led to the emergence of the swap market in the context of financial markets. In doing so, the changes that have taken place in the world financial markets over the past 10–15 years were described. We saw that this period was characterized by an unprecedented increase in the volatility in foreign exchange rates and in interest rates. In particular, the collapse of the Bretton Woods agreement, the oil crisis, and the subsequent divergence in the monetary policies of the leading western countries, and of the United States especially, were identified as major sources of the volatilities that provided the necessary conditions for the emergence of swaps as a prime hedging instrument.

In addition to an increasingly volatile environment, a number of other factors have significantly contributed to the growth and development of the swap market. Within this context, the trends towards less regulation, financial innovation, and global market integration were discussed.

Finally, the important role of swap-driven arbitrage was discussed, focusing on the benefits of this activity and its implications, concluding that market participants have benefited and, as a result, capital markets have become more efficient in their role of channelling funds from investors to borrowers.

CHAPTER 3

PLAIN VANILLA SWAPS: MARKET STRUCTURES, APPLICATIONS, AND CREDIT RISK

Keith C. Brown
University of Texas at Austin
Donald J. Smith
Boston University

INTRODUCTION

A plain vanilla interest rate swap is a very straightforward transaction. Two interest rates are compared on certain settlement dates, one rate that is constant throughout the life of the agreement and one that fluctuates with changing market conditions. The difference between these two rates, adjusted first for the fraction of the year that has elapsed since the last settlement and then multiplied by some dollar amount of notional principal, is paid by one counterparty to the other. As an example, consider a five-year, semiannual settlement, $10 million notional principal, fixed-versus-floating interest rate swap between a company and a bank. The company agrees to pay a fixed rate of 10 percent and to receive six-month LIBOR (the London Interbank Offered Rate). When LIBOR is above 10 percent, the bank makes net settlement payments to the company; when LIBOR is below 10 percent, the company makes net settlement payments to the bank. In essence, the swap is merely an exchange of coupon cash flows on bonds of equivalent value, where one bond has a fixed coupon rate and the other a floating rate. A swap is not a funding transaction, so the principal amount is only notional, a figure used to calculate settlement payments.

That some swaps are described as *plain vanilla* suggests that, in general, a great deal of variety exists in the way these transactions can be structured. Indeed, a swap is an extremely flexible instrument since the terms of the agreement need only be mutually acceptable to the two counterparties. Despite the myriad of extant possibilities, however, plain vanilla interest rate swaps are predominant in the market. These are fixed-versus-floating swaps for which three- or six-month LIBOR is the floating reference rate and both interest rates are denominated in the same currency. The notional principal is a constant amount throughout the life of the swap. There is no cash payment or exchange at origination, and the agreement is immediately in force. Departures from these standard terms define other swap formats: A *basis swap* is one where both rates are floating (e.g., LIBOR versus a commercial paper index rate); a *currency* swap is one where the rates are denominated in different currencies (e.g., a fixed rate in Japanese yen versus U.S. dollar LIBOR); an *amortizing* swap has a notional principal that declines over the lifetime of the agreement; an *off-market,* or *non-par-value,* swap is one for which one party makes an initial payment to the other; a *forward* swap defers the start date of the agreement into the future.

Our focus in this chapter is on plain vanilla interest rate swaps. There is little doubt that plain vanilla transactions comprise the largest sector of the entire swap market. The International Swap Dealers Association (ISDA) estimated that, by the end of 1987, the outstanding notional principal for all swaps approached $1.2 trillion, with interest rate swaps accounting for roughly 80 percent of the total amount. In fact, to indicate the pervasive influence the swap market has had in other financial markets, *The Wall Street Journal* (November 20, 1987) reported that during the latter part of 1987 as much as 40 percent of all new corporate debt offerings were linked to an interest rate swap in some manner.

Our objective is to explain the economic nature of an interest rate swap and its use in financial management. We start with an overview of the structure of swap transactions to illustrate the development of the market from brokered to intermediated deals. We then review swap market pricing conventions and use a numerical example to calculate settlement cash flows. Next, we offer two theoretic interpretations of a plain vanilla swap, one as a combination of capital market instruments and the other as a series of over-the-counter futures contracts. Following this, we provide detailed examples of the three classic applications of an interest rate swap—hedging, speculation, and arbitrage. Finally, we discuss the credit risk that is inherent in a swap transaction.

TRENDS IN SWAP MARKET STRUCTURE

Coincident with the phenomenal growth of the interest rate swap market over the 1980s has been a change in the structure of swap transactions. Of particular interest is the evolution of the role played by the financial institution that serves as the third-party agent in a typical transaction. Exhibit 1 presents a stylized "box-and-arrow" view of the three different forms of market interaction that have characterized the market since 1981. The first interest rate swaps were highly customized deals that the two ultimate end-users negotiated and transacted directly between themselves. The financial institution acting as the middleman—usually a commercial or investment bank—had no continuing role in the swap; its compensation came solely from the services it provided to the counterparties as an information *broker* helping to structure the terms of the agreement. Accordingly, such compensation was called the swap arrangement fee. This situation is illustrated in Panel A of Exhibit 1. Beyond the initial identification of the eventual counterparties, the terms that the financial institution helped to establish included the designation of the notional principal amount, the dates and logistics of the net settlement payments, and the specification of the floating and fixed rates. Notice that from the financial institution's standpoint the brokered swap transaction entails no credit risk since it is not a principal party in the deal. Instead, the two companies are forced to make independent assessments of the default potential of the other and then attempt to quantify this possibility as a relevant potential cost of the swap.

EXHIBIT 1
Swap Market Structures

Panel A. Broker market

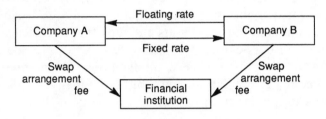

Panel B. Dealer market

Panel C. Intermediate market

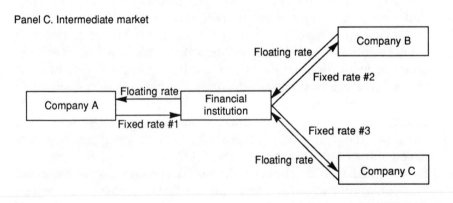

One of the main problems with the brokered swap transaction is that it requires the third party to have simultaneous knbwledge of two firms with exactly offsetting interest rate risk profiles, in terms of both timing and dollar amount. As the swap market expanded in the early 1980s, financial institutions found that it was increasingly difficult to adequately service their clientele in the passive manner just described. This factor, along with the pressure to develop nontraditional sources of revenue, led financial institutions to become principals in the same swap transactions they had previously brokered. This often required the bank itself to make a commitment to enter the swap with one company before the other half of the transaction had been located. In this fashion, financial institutions began "warehousing" swap commitments for short periods of time, which eventually led them to assume the role of market makers. Panel B of Exhibit 1 diagrams the same swap transaction in a *dealer-oriented* market structure.

Several important distinctions develop in the swap market when the role of third party changes from that of broker to that of dealer. Most important, notice that although the two ultimate end users (Company A and Company B) remain the same, they are no longer transacting the swap agreement directly with one another. Rather, both of the corporations contract separately with the financial institution, which then becomes the counterparty to each. A potential advantage of this arrangement to Company A and Company B is that they are now assuming the credit risk of the financial institution. Also, notice that there is no direct payment of a swap arrangement fee in a dealer-oriented market. Since the third party now stands directly in the middle of the swap transaction, its compensation comes from the markup, or spread, that it can extract from the two end users. From Panel B it is apparent that this bid-ask spread takes the form of a differential on the fixed-rate side of the swap transaction. More precisely, while the dealer makes no adjustment to the floating rate involved in the swap, the fixed rate that it receives from Company A is set at a *higher* level than that paid to Company B. On each settlement date the financial institution merely acts as a conduit passing the net cash flows through to the appropriate counterparty after taking the spread as its compensation. However, it should also be noted that because the financial institution is now exposed to the default potential of two different companies, the bid-ask spread must be set so as to allow adequate remuneration for this risk.

The dealer-oriented market for plain vanilla swaps as just described has one serious shortcoming. Since the swap dealer must often make a firm commitment to one company before it locates another company with offsetting needs, it can be exposed to sudden movements in interest rates. To see this, assume that for the deal illustrated in Panel B the financial institution first agrees to terms with Company A and that the notional principal on this swap is $20 million. Since the bank will be receiving cash flows based on a fixed rate, it is exposed to sudden increases in the level of interest rates. If rates indeed rise, the fixed rate the dealer receives from Company A may be lower than what it will eventually have to pay to Company B once that counterparty is finally found. Clearly, then, the swap dealer is more affected by the degree of liquidity in the market than is the swap broker.

The swap dealer's interest rate exposure has another dimension as well. Suppose that while separate deals with Company A and Company B are consummated before market conditions change appreciably, Company B is only willing to commit to a $12.5 million plain vanilla swap. The financial institution is still exposed to rising interest rates since on every settlement date the net payment it must make to Company A will be based on a far larger notional principal than that received from Company B. One way for the bank to immunize itself against this exposure is to find another counterparty (Company C) willing to receive the fixed rate side of swap for the remaining $7.5 million in notional principal. This situation is illustrated in Panel C of Exhibit 1. In practice, financial institutions that transact in the swap market use the Treasury cash and futures markets to hedge the mismatch between their pay-fixed and receive-fixed positions. For example, the bank that enters the swaps with Companies A and B could sell futures contracts to gain if market rates unexpectedly rise. That gain then offsets the loss from eventually closing out the swap with Company C at the higher fixed rate.

Although it is a more subtle change than the difference between the broker-oriented and dealer-oriented regimes, the series of swap transactions displayed in Panel C nonetheless represents a third, distinct market structure. This distinction is best seen by recognizing that while the first two cases represented different methods of linking the same two counterparties, the final form requires the financial institution to effectively repackage the swap agreement from Company A across multiple counterparties. In this sense, the financial institution is serving a truly *intermediary* function. Implicit in this repackaging is the notion that a swap agreement is nothing more than a series of cash flows (both receipts and payments) that can be unbundled and re-created in other ways. The importance of this market structure, which typifies the way the swap market exists today, is that the intermediary can think of doing "half deals" with a single counterparty and not worry about finding a second end user with exactly offsetting needs. Instead, any particular swap commitment can be effectively hedged through an appropriately formed portfolio of alternative positions. This approach to swap market making is sometimes referred to as running a *dynamic book* and has allowed financial institutions to develop many of the more creative swap varieties, such as forward swaps and amortizing swaps.

SWAP MARKET PRICING CONVENTIONS

Swap market terminology is a confusing blend of banking, capital market, and futures market trading vocabulary. Exhibit 2 provides a box-and-arrow illustration of a plain vanilla swap agreement, assuming that the floating reference rate is six-month LIBOR and that settlement payments are made on a semiannual basis. By convention the floating-rate side of the exchange is quoted without adjustment, or *flat*. The two parties to the agreement are designated the *pay-fixed* (Counterparty A) and the *receive-fixed* (Counterparty B) sides of the swap. It is also common, although not as widely used, to refer to the fixed-rate payer as having *bought* the

EXHIBIT 2
Swap Market Pricing Mechanics

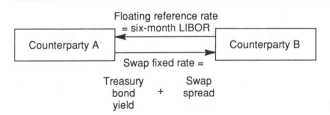

swap, or, equivalently, taken the long position in the swap. Conversely, the fixed-rate receiver is sometimes said to have *sold*, or to be *short*, the swap.

At first glance, it may seem strange to characterize an arrangement in which either counterparty might be responsible for making a net settlement cash flow payment with terms such as *buying* and *selling*. Perhaps the best way to understand this terminology is to recognize that Counterparty A in Exhibit 2 has agreed that on each settlement date in the future it will receive a LIBOR-based cash flow in exchange for a set amount that depends only on the predetermined fixed rate and the notional principal. Thus, Counterparty A can be thought of as having a contract to buy LIBOR at each settlement date for the single fixed rate agreed upon at the outset. Similarly, Counterparty B—the fixed-rate receiver—can be viewed as having contracted to sell LIBOR on each settlement date for a prespecified price. In this sense, LIBOR is the traded commodity and the fixed rate is its price.

Another swap market convention evident in Exhibit 2 is that the fixed-rate side of a plain vanilla swap is quoted in the form of two separate components: (*a*) the Treasury bond yield and (*b*) the swap spread. The particular Treasury bond yield selected as the base depends on the maturity, or *tenor*, of the swap agreement. For instance, the fixed rate on a five-year swap agreement would be the yield to maturity of the *on-the-run* (i.e., most recently issued) five-year Treasury, plus the swap spread for a tenor of five years.

One of the most convenient facets of the market conventions just described is that it reduces the quotation of the entire swap transaction to the specification of the swap spread. That is, since it is commonly accepted that the floating-rate side of a plain vanilla swap will trade LIBOR flat and that the fixed-rate side will trade as an increment over the appropriate Treasury bond yield, the only remaining piece to the pricing puzzle is the swap spread. In fact, so pervasive is this convention that market makers usually quote two different swap spreads—one for deals in which they will pay the fixed rate and one where they will receive the fixed rate. For example, a dealer might quote five-year swaps at "70-76," meaning that it will buy a swap at 70 basis points over Treasuries and sell a swap at 76 basis points over Treasuries. (Recall that a market maker entering a swap in which it will be the fixed-payer is said to be buying the swap. Thus, the *bid* quote would be applicable since the bid-ask spread is always interpreted from the point of view of the market maker. Conversely, the *ask* swap spread would be quoted in situations where the market maker receives the fixed rate.)

Panel A of Exhibit 3 lists a representative set of swap quotes for June 10, 1988. Two aspects of this display merit special mention. First, notice that as the maturity of the swap lengthens, the absolute level of the swap spread tends to rise. Thus, it is apparent that at any point in time there exists a term structure of swap spreads in addition to the term structure of Treasury yields. Second, across all maturities the bid-ask differential never exceeds seven basis points. Since this spread serves as the market maker's profit margin, it is also clear that this swap market has become quite competitive as it has grown in size and importance. To see this last point more graphically, Panel B of Exhibit 3 illustrates the five-year swap assuming that Counterparty B serves the role of the

EXHIBIT 3
Swap Market Rate Quotation Conventions

Panel A. Representative Market Quotes for June 10, 1988, for Interest Rate Swaps Based on Six-Month LIBOR

Swap Maturity	Treasury Yield (Percent)	Bid Swap Spread (Basis Points)	Asked Swap Spread (Basis Points)	Effective Fixed Swap Rate (Percent)
2 yr.	7.98%	67	74	8.65–8.72%
3 yr.	8.17	72	76	8.89–8.93
4 yr.	8.38	69	74	9.07–9.12
5 yr.	8.50	70	76	9.20–9.26
7 yr.	8.75	71	77	9.46–9.52
10 yr.	8.94	73	79	9.67–9.73

Panel B. The Five-Year Swap Illustrated

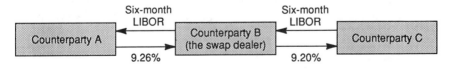

Source: Globecon.

swap dealer. Once again, barring default by either Counterparty A or Counterparty C, the middleman in this transaction is unaffected by fluctuations in six-month LIBOR since these cash flows will simply be passed through. The annual compensation for the dealer amounts to the difference between the fixed rate it receives and the fixed rate it pays (i.e., 9.26 percent − 9.20 percent, or six basis points) times the notional principal common to the two transactions.

To now see how these quotation conventions translate into an exact set of cash flows throughout the life of the swap, let us focus on the transaction between Counterparty A and Counterparty B. Suppose that after the initial agreement had been reached, the terms of the transaction were confirmed as follows:[1]

Initiation date: June 10, 1988.

Maturity date: June 10, 1993.

Notional principal: U.S. $20 million.

Fixed-rate payer: Counterparty A.

Fixed rate: 9.26 percent (semiannual bond basis).

Fixed-rate receiver: Counterparty B.

Floating rate: 6-month LIBOR (money market basis).

Settlement dates: June 10th and December 10th of each year.

LIBOR determination: determined in advance, paid in arrears.

It is very important to recognize that the fixed and floating rates in this deal are not directly comparable. Specifically, the fixed rate of 9.26 percent assumes a 365-day (bond basis) year, like U.S. Treasury notes and bonds. On the other hand, U.S. dollar LIBOR is a money market yield based on a 360-day year. Further, since these rates are annualized, they both need to be prorated to the actual number of days that have elapsed between settlement dates to calculate the payments. The precise formulas for determining

---

[1] For a more detailed discussion of the swap agreement confirmation procedure, see J. Walmsley, *The New Financial Instruments* (New York: J. Wiley & Sons, 1988).

the fixed-rate and floating-rate settlement cash flows are as follows:

Fixed-rate settlement payment

$$= (.0926) \left(\frac{\text{no. of days}}{365} \right) (\$20 \text{ million})$$

Floating-rate settlement payment

$$= (\text{LIBOR}) \left(\frac{\text{no. of days}}{360} \right) (\$20 \text{ million})$$

Once the number of days between settlement dates (no. of days) is determined, the complete fixed-rate payment schedule can be calculated. The floating-rate schedule, though, depends on future levels of LIBOR and therefore cannot be established at the time of the initial agreement. As noted above, the usual convention in the swap market is to fix LIBOR one settlement date ahead of the payment date. That is, the floating rate corresponding to the first settlement date on December 10, 1988, would have been the six-month LIBOR that prevailed on June 10, 1988. This implies that the next net settlement payment, both the amount and the owing counterparty, will always be known six months in advance. Exhibit 4 illustrates this settlement process from Counterparty A's perspective for a hypothetical LIBOR series. The final column of the display indicates the net swap payment or receipt. As the fixed-rate payer, Counterparty A makes (receives) the net settlement

EXHIBIT 4
Swap Cash Flows from Counterparty A's Perspective

Settlement Date	Number of Days	Current LIBOR	Fixed-Rate Payment	Floating-Rate Receipt	Counterparty A's Net Payment
6/10/88	—	8.25%	—	—	—
12/10/88	183	8.50	$928,527	$838,750	$ 89,787
6/10/89	182	8.75	923,463	859,444	64,019
12/10/89	183	9.00	928,527	889,583	38,954
6/10/90	182	9.25	923,463	910,000	13,463
12/10/90	183	9.50	928,527	940,417	−11,880
6/10/91	182	9.75	923,463	960,556	−37,093
12/10/91	183	9.50	928,527	991,250	−62,713
6/10/92	183	9.25	928,527	965,833	−37,296
12/10/92	183	9.00	928,527	940,417	−11,880
6/10/93	182	—	923,463	910,000	13,463

payment whenever the bond basis–adjusted level of LIBOR is less than (exceeds) 9.26 percent. Finally, notice once again that no exchange of the $20 million principal amount takes place at either inception or maturity, indicating that this is a par-value, or *at-market,* swap.

ALTERNATIVE APPROACHES TO A PLAIN VANILLA SWAP

Consider now a five-year, semiannual settlement, $10 million notional principal, 10.00 percent-versus-LIBOR interest rate swap between Company A and Bank B, structured similarly to the swap between Counterparties A and B in Panel B of Exhibit 3 (i.e., Company A is the fixed-payer and Bank B the fixed-receiver). Generally speaking, such an archetypical plain vanilla swap agreement is the most efficient way for these two counterparties to exchange fixed and floating interest rate payments. Nevertheless, the same pattern of settlement cash flows could have been obtained from the proper structuring of other financial transactions, such as (*a*) a combination of buying and selling capital market instruments or (*b*) a series of over-the-counter futures contracts. A closer examination of these two alternative approaches to obtaining equivalent payoffs is useful to see the swap's economic function and to identify what is innovative about its structure.

Alternative Interpretation 1: A Capital Market Approach

Suppose that Company A can issue a five-year, $10 million, 10.00 percent coupon rate bond in the public capital market. It would be obligated to make a series of ten coupon payments of $500,000, based on semiannual interest, and then to redeem the principal at the end of the fifth year. Assuming that the bond is issued at par value and neglecting any underwriting fees, the promised cash flows can be pictured as in Panel A of Exhibit 5. The boxes above the time line refer to cash inflows, below the time line to outflows. The coupon interest boxes are shown to be the same size to indicate that the bond is a fixed-income security.

EXHIBIT 5
Pay-Fixed Swap as a Combination of Capital Market Instruments

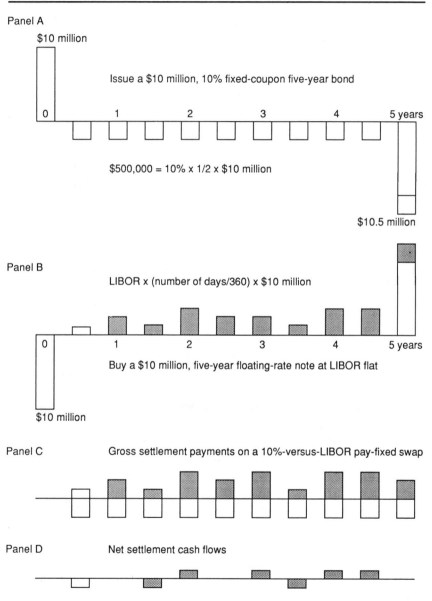

Panel A

$10 million

Issue a $10 million, 10% fixed-coupon five-year bond

$500,000 = 10% x 1/2 x $10 million

$10.5 million

Panel B

LIBOR x (number of days/360) x $10 million

Buy a $10 million, five-year floating-rate note at LIBOR flat

$10 million

Panel C   Gross settlement payments on a 10%-versus-LIBOR pay-fixed swap

Panel D   Net settlement cash flows

In addition, suppose that Company A can purchase a five-year, $10 million floating-rate note (FRN) issued by Bank B. This FRN resets the coupon at LIBOR flat every six months and is also priced at par value. The promised cash flows on this security appear in Panel B of Exhibit 5. The shaded boxes represent the uncertain future coupon receipts; they are drawn in various sizes to illustrate the idea of a floating rate security. Notice that the initial coupon payment is unshaded since that amount is known in advance. That is, FRNs (like swaps) usually settle in arrears—the rate is determined at the beginning of the period, the settlement payment is made at the end of the period.

The cash flows on these two capital market transactions are merged in Panel C. The principal flows at issuance and redemption are dropped since they cancel out. The resulting picture fully describes the gross settlement payments on a pay-fixed/receive-floating plain vanilla interest rate swap at 10.00 percent versus LIBOR. The net settlement payments, given that arbitrary path for future LIBOR, are shown in Panel D. Notice that while the first settlement payment is known, the remainder are uncertain and depend on the specific path LIBOR takes. However, it is reasonable to conclude that the present value of the (expected) future coupon cash flows is the same for each counterparty, since both bonds currently trade at par value. Therefore, the present value of the expected net settlement payments and receipts in Panel D is zero, as of date zero.

To restate this last point in a slightly different manner, at origination a plain vanilla interest rate swap has an economic value of zero. Of course, that does not mean it is of no worth—surely it must have value to both companies entering into the transaction. However, the swap's *use value*, which depends on the specific application of the swap to the end user, should not be confused with its *intrinsic value*. An economic value of zero simply means that neither counterparty needs to pay anything initially to induce the other to enter into the agreement. The swap cannot be sold or assigned to a third party for a profit. Also, if either counterparty were to walk away from the deal immediately after signing, there would be no financial loss to the other, assuming that the same terms are available from other market participants.

The idea of zero economic value at origination is linked to the assumption that each hypothetical capital market instrument trades at par value. To see this more fully, suppose that Company A can also issue a five-year $10 million bond at a coupon rate of 11.00 percent. Clearly, since the earlier 10.00 percent bond over the same maturity is priced at par, this new instrument could be sold at a premium to its face value, or for $10.386 million. Therefore, if the par-value swap has terms of 10.00 percent versus LIBOR, an 11.00 percent-versus-LIBOR swap must be nonpar-value (i.e., off-market), meaning that the economic value at origination is not zero. Specifically, a firm would agree to pay an above-market fixed rate of 11 percent against receipt of LIBOR flat only if it received some initial compensation; in fact, an amount on the order of $0.386 million. This capital market approach to a swap is useful in practice to value such off-market swaps and, as we shall see in a later section, to value an existing swap when market conditions have changed or when one counterparty defaults.

Viewing a plain vanilla swap as a combination of par-value capital market instruments leads to two summary statements:

1. A pay-fixed (receive-floating) interest rate swap is equal to buying an FRN at LIBOR and issuing a fixed-rate bond at the swap fixed rate.
2. A receive-fixed (pay-floating) interest rate swap is equal to issuing an FRN at LIBOR and buying a fixed-rate bond at the swap fixed rate.

Since the cash flows on a swap can be duplicated by existing securities, one might wonder what is new or innovative about its structure. The answer is that a swap agreement provides the given set of cash flows more efficiently and at less expense and risk than would the combination of capital market instruments. Some of the advantages to a swap are fairly obvious. First, the coupon payment dates on the fixed-rate bond and the FRN in the above discussion would have to exactly coincide to be equivalent to a swap. In most cases buying one bond and selling the other would involve some timing risk since the coupon payments and receipts would not likely occur on the same day. Second, issuing a capital market instrument always involves an underwriting expense that can be avoided with the swap structure. Third, the swap is an off-balance sheet transaction, so an otherwise desirable debt/equity ratio is not increased as it would be by simultaneously buying and issuing new capital market securities.

While each of these factors suggests a basic efficiency gain of an interest rate swap over balance sheet restructuring to obtain the same net cash flows, the original impetus for swaps arose from a different consideration—credit risk. Interest rate swaps developed in the early 1980s from currency swaps, which in turn developed from parallel and back-to-back loans. Those original transactions were designed to circumvent restrictions on international capital flows and involved one firm lending to a second firm in one currency while borrowing in another. The loan agreements were legally separate documents, so default on one did not necessarily allow an offsetting default on the other.

Currency swaps, and subsequently interest rate swaps, lessen the credit risk problem since they are *executory* contracts. This means that execution of the terms of agreement depends on the other party's executing its obligation. Therefore, a swap falls under contract, not security, law and legal jurisdiction. Consider again the company that could buy the FRN from the bank and issue a fixed-rate bond in lieu of entering a pay-fixed swap. If the bank defaults on its FRN, the company could not just cancel its own debt issue. It still would be required to pay the series of coupon and principal payments even though its receipts from the FRN had disappeared. However, if the bank counterparty to the swap defaults on its floating-rate payment, the firm does not have to meet its fixed-rate obligation. Consequently, swaps have significantly less credit risk than the combination of capital market instruments. However, the remaining credit risk is not necessarily trivial, a point that we will return to in a later section.

Alternative Interpretation 2: A Futures Market Approach

An interest rate swap also can be viewed as a series of futures contracts. A number of exchange-traded futures contracts on debt securities have been developed over the last 15 years to address risks associated with the unprecedented rise in interest rate volatility. In a typical transaction, the buyer of the futures contract (the *long*) agrees to take delivery of a specified security on a certain future date and to pay a predetermined price. The seller of the contract (the *short*) agrees to make delivery of the same security under the same conditions. Actually, both the buyer and the seller strike their deals with the futures exchange itself—that transfers the credit risk from the counterparty to the exchange. In turn, the exchange manages the credit risk of the two parties by requiring a margin account from each, valuing (i.e., *marking-to-market*) the contract daily, and then debiting and crediting the appropriate margin accounts. Futures contracts are rarely held until the delivery date. Usually they are closed out by offsetting transactions; that is, a long position takes on an equivalent short position, and vice versa. The presence of an organized exchange fosters the liquidity of the futures contract.

Exchange-traded futures contracts require standardization with respect to the terms of the specified contract and the delivery date. For instance, the contract might be based on a 90-day, $1 million Treasury bill (T-bill) deliverable on the third Friday in either March, June, September, or December. Standardization and the subsequent limitation on the number and types of traded contracts are necessary to maintain liquidity. However, the essential features of an exchange-traded futures contract—margin accounts, daily valuation and settlement, and standardization—also limit its applicability to the corporate end user. Risk management with futures entails *basis* risk when the characteristics of the hedge instrument do not correlate closely to the nature of the risk exposure. As an example, a firm that is exposed to unexpected movements in the 30-day commercial paper (CP) rate in July and hedges that risk with the September 90-day T-bill futures contract bears three types of basis risk: the credit spread between CP and T-bills, the yield curve spread between 30-day and 90-day maturities, and the timing spread between expected rates for July and for September.

Interest rate swaps are like a series of over-the-counter, cash settlement futures contracts that have been stripped of their margin accounts, daily valuation and settlement, and standardization. That is, the settlement payoffs on a swap—the consequence of future interest rate movements—are fundamentally the same as on a series of futures contracts. Note that while the seller of the futures contract often can make actual delivery of the underlying security, settlement on a swap always is in cash since the underlying principal is only notional. Also note that a futures contact has a single delivery date while a swap has a series of settlement dates. Swaps are not traded on an exchange and, despite the presence of a dealer market, cannot be as liquid as a futures contract. However, swaps are much more flexible in design since the terms to the swap agreement—the choice of settlement dates, the floating reference rate, and tenor—can be negotiated directly between the counterparties. That reduces the basis risk to the corporate end user. However, the absence of margin accounts and daily valuation and settlement means that a swap entails more credit risk than an exchange-traded futures contract.

As an illustration of these points, consider again the five-year, semiannual settlement, $10 million notional principal, 10 percent-versus-LIBOR swap between Company A and Bank B. The company, as the fixed-payer on the swap, has in effect sold a series of hypothetical futures contracts to the bank, one contract for each settlement period. Each futures contract calls for the delivery of a $10 million, six-month, Euro-time deposit that pays an interest rate of 10 percent. Therefore, the company is committed, in principle, to deliver this security to the bank and the bank is committed to pay $10 million to receive it. Said differently, the company goes short and the bank goes long on the Euro-time deposit futures contracts.

The flows on this transaction are illustrated in Panel A of Exhibit 6 for the delivery date on one of the futures contracts. It is assumed that the bank obtains the $10 million to meet its obligation by issuing a par-value, six-month Euro-time deposit at LIBOR flat on the spot market and that the company uses its $10 million receipt to buy a similar security. Panel B shows the payments on the time deposits six months later at maturity. The company has a net gain if LIBOR is greater than 10 percent, and the bank has a net gain if LIBOR is less than 10 percent. These net cash flows are exactly the same as those on a 10 percent-versus-LIBOR swap that determines the reference rate at the beginning of the period and settles in arrears at the end of the period. Note that if there were margin accounts and if the futures contracts were valued and settled daily, the ultimate payoff would only approximately equal that of the swap agreement. In technical terms, the swap payoffs would depend only on the level of LIBOR on the specific determination

EXHIBIT 6
Swap as Series of Futures Contracts

Panel A. Settlement at the delivery date on the futures contract
(At the beginning of the semiannual settlement period)

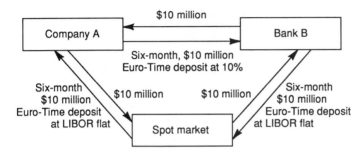

Panel B. Cash payment flows at the maturity date of the Euro-Time deposits
(At the end of the semiannual settlement period)

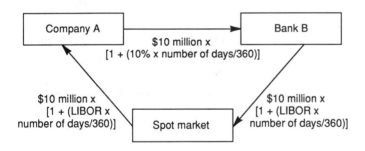

dates, whereas the payoffs on the series of futures would depend also on the particular path of LIBOR between determination dates.

This example has illustrated that Company A can obtain the same net cash flows by paying the fixed rate on an interest rate swap or by selling a series of over-the-counter futures contracts. But, as we mentioned previously, market terminology is that the fixed-payer buys, or goes long on, the swap. So, selling futures is the same as buying a swap! This apparent contradiction can be clarified by noting that futures refer to *prices* and swaps to *rates*. Since prices and rates are inversely related, selling futures contracts is fundamentally equivalent to buying a swap. The seller of a debt futures contract gains when futures prices fall (and rates rise); the fixed-payer on a swap gains if rates rise.

The main difference between an interest rate swap and a series of futures contracts is the time horizon of the transaction. The swap market is active for maturities out to 10 years, but delivery dates on exchange-traded futures contracts extend only to 3 years. Moreover, most of the trading activity and liquidity in the futures market is in the nearest-term contracts. Notice that it is the time to delivery, not the time to maturity of the underlying security, that constrains the applicability of exchange-traded futures. That is, a futures contract on a 10-year Treasury note deliverable in two months provides interest rate risk management for the next two months, not the next 10 years. For practical purposes, then, the swap market extends, and is not duplicated by, the exchange-traded futures market.

Even if futures exchanges were to provide a more expansive set of contracts, extending actual delivery dates out to 10 years, an over-the-counter product like a plain vanilla swap might still be preferable to many corporate end users. Swaps clearly have greater design flexibility than standardized futures but also more operational ease. Margin accounts and daily settlement, procedures that mitigate credit risk, demand daily oversight. However, the need for additional accounting and information systems can be a costly nuisance to some firms. Swaps, with periodic net settlement within an ongoing banking relationship, place less burden on cash management. Futures exchanges, reflecting their roots in physical commodities, are structured to maintain a key role for the individual participant. Therefore, the institutional design of the exchange and its procedures place a premium on controlling credit risk. On the other hand, the swaps market is institutional; the main participants are money center investment and commercial banks, major corporations, and governments. Credit risk is always a concern, but unlike a market that includes relatively small individual participants, it does not need daily settlement procedures. Also, commercial banks act as intermediaries on many swap structures, and managing credit risk is the heart of their traditional line of business.

BASIC SWAP APPLICATIONS

All applications for plain vanilla swaps, or any other risk management instrument for that matter, fall into one of the following three categories: (*a*) hedging, (*b*) speculation, and (*c*) arbitrage. Each attempts to alter the basic trade-off between risk and return in some way. In general, hedging applications aim to reduce risk (or, more precisely, the variability of some financial holding), while speculative applications aim to increase the return on assets (or to reduce the cost of funds). Arbitrage strategies are opportunistic and attempt to exploit some pricing inefficiency across markets to either increase return or reduce risk. The phenomenal growth of the swap market during the 1980s ultimately can be traced to the ease and efficiency with which swaps address all three types of applications. At first, interest rate swaps were used primarily in arbitrage strategies, but as more corporations and financial institutions moved up the swap learning curve, the opportunities for profitable exploitation of mispricing across markets became fewer. Of course, this was to be expected in a largely efficient financial market.[2] In recent years the search for arbitrage opportunities continues, but often involving more complex swap structures and financial strategies. Meanwhile, hedging and speculative swap transactions have become increasingly important.

Swap Application 1: Hedging

Suppose that two years ago Company X issued a five-year floating-rate note that pays semiannually a coupon rate equal to LIBOR + 1 percent. Assume further that when the firm issued this debt instrument its net revenues were closely tied to short-term interest rates.

---

[2] On this point, see C. Smith, C. Smithson, and L. Wakeman, "The Market for Interest Rate Swaps," *Financial Management*, Winter 1988, pp. 72–81.

Therefore, the FRN provided a natural internal hedge since the interest rate characteristics of its liabilities matched its assets. Using the concept of *duration*—a technical, statistical measure of a financial instrument's price elasticity relative to changes in yield— one would say that the company was *immunized* from interest rate risk since the short-duration FRN balanced the short-duration assets. Since both revenue and coupon interest cash flows would respond quickly to shifts in the level of interest rates, the market values of the assets and liabilities, and hence the value of the firm, were not very interest sensitive. Now suppose that there has been a fundamental change in the nature of the firm's assets such that net revenues are expected to be roughly constant in nominal terms over the next few years. Clearly, the company is exposed to the risk that interest rates will increase, thereby raising the interest expense of the FRN without any compensating rise in revenues. In terms of market value, the longer-duration assets would decline in price by more than the shorter-duration liabilities.[3]

Two ways Company X can protect itself from rising rates are (*a*) issuing a new three-year fixed-coupon bond in an amount sufficient to buy back the remaining portion of the existing FRN or (*b*) combining the FRN with a three-year pay-fixed interest rate swap having semiannual settlement dates timed to match the bond's coupon payment dates. There are several reasons why the second solution is preferable from the firm's perspective. First, refinancing the existing debt issue requires a new capital market transaction and paying additional underwriting and registration fees. The interest rate swap, on the other hand, can be done with virtually no transaction costs. Second, in the absence of a call provision, an open market debt repurchase program is risky in terms of the total price to be paid and the total quantity of the notes that can be

---

[3] Durations of fixed-income securities are easily calculated since future cash flows are certain; see G. Bierwag, *Duration Analysis* (Cambridge, Mass.: Ballinger, 1987), for a thorough treatment of this topic. FRNs pose a problem since future coupons depend on unknown future interest rates. However, assuming no change in the credit quality of the Issuer, the implied duration of an FRN can be stated as the time until the next reset period. For example, an FRN with semiannual resets would have an implied duration of 0.50 years just after the coupon rate has been set. See J. Yawitz, H. Kaufold, Macirowski, and M. Smirlock, "The Pricing and Duration of Floating Rate Bonds," *Journal of Portfolio Management*, Summer 1987, pp. 49–56, for further discussion.

redeemed.[4] Finally, interest rate swaps can be reversed almost as easily as they can be implemented and, consequently, they can be thought of as a more flexible solution to a risk management problem that might be temporary.

The combination of the existing FRN and the pay-fixed interest rate swap is equivalent to a synthetic three-year fixed-rate bond with semiannual coupon payments. To see this, assume that the market maker's asking quote on a three-year swap against six-month LIBOR is 75 basis points over the Treasury yield, which currently stands at 8.50 percent. Once Company X agrees to these terms, two things will happen on each of its remaining coupon payment dates. First, since the original debt is still in place, the firm is responsible for making a coupon payment based on the prevailing LIBOR plus 100 basis points. Thus, observe that the swap agreement *supplements,* rather than replaces, the obligation that Company X has to its existing investors. Second, by the design of the swap, the firm receives from its counterparty payments based on the same six-month LIBOR that it must pay out on the FRN, while its swap obligations are payments based on the fixed rate of 9.25 percent.

These two steps are illustrated in Exhibit 7. This display also shows that, after adjusting for differences in rate quotation methods, the effective cost of the fixed-rate financing for Company X is 10.264 percent. An important caveat in interpreting this synthetic fixed rate is that it is not directly comparable with the fixed rate Company X would have obtained via the bond repurchase scheme since it involves credit exposure to the swap counterparty. Barring default on the part of the counterparty, however, the combination of the FRN and the pay-fixed swap has allowed the firm to hedge its exposure to rising rates.

Notice also that the plain vanilla swap has resolved the duration mismatch that arose between the assets and liabilities. Recall that it was a change in the nature of the asset base (and, in particular, that net revenues had become less sensitive to interest rates,

---

[4] J. Finnerty, A. Kalotay, and F. Farrell, *Evaluating Bond Refunding Opportunities* (Hagerstown, Md.: Ballinger Publishing, 1988), have noted that tender offers are only about 75 percent successful in obtaining the desired number of outstanding bonds.

EXHIBIT 7
Hedging Application

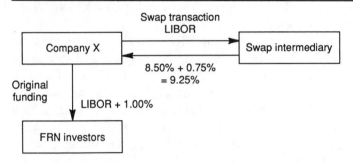

Effective Annual Financing Cost (on a 365-Day Bond Basis)

FRN coupon payment: LIBOR + 1.00%(365/360) = (LIBOR)(365/360) + 1.014%
Swap transaction: *(a)* Fixed-rate payment   = 9.25%
                  (b) Floating-rate receipt   = (LIBOR)(365/360)
Net cost of funds (9.25% + 1.014%)   = 10.264%

thereby lengthening the duration of assets) that created this mismatch. The pay-fixed swap effectively has lengthened the duration
of the company's liabilities, so that once again it is in an immunized
position. In the same vein, it is a simple matter to show that a
receive-fixed swap has the effect of shortening the duration of
fixed-coupon debt. These conclusions hold for swaps that are attached to liabilities, and the opposite holds for asset swaps: a pay-
fixed swap shortens, and a receive-fixed swap lengthens, the duration of the asset. In general, *sensitizing* the cash flows of a security
to interest rate changes in equivalent to shortening the duration;
desensitizing the cash flows lengthens the duration.

Swap Application 2: Speculation

Duration is an important concept in interest rate risk management
using swap agreements. In the present example, we will expand
and formalize this idea. Consider the stylized balance sheet in
Exhibit 8 for Company Y, a hypothetical financial institution.
Along with the current market values of the various assets and
liabilities, the durations of these instruments are reported. An

EXHIBIT 8
Hypothetical Balance Sheet and Asset/Liability Durations

Asset	Market Value ($)	Duration (Years)
Cash and cash equivalents	$ 100	0.10
5-year term loan, valued at par with an interest rate of 10%	300	4.17
10-year amortizing mortgage, valued at par with an interest rate of 10%	800	4.68
Total market value	$1,200	
Liabilities		
3-year zero-coupon bond, with a yield to maturity of 8%	$ 500	3.00
7-year zero-coupon bond with a yield to maturity of 8%	500	7.00
Total market value	$1,000	

$$\text{Duration of assets} = (0.10)\left(\frac{100}{1,200}\right) + (4.17)\left(\frac{300}{1,200}\right) + (4.68)\left(\frac{800}{1,200}\right) = 4.17 \text{ years}$$

$$\text{Duration of liabilities} = (3.00)\left(\frac{500}{1,000}\right) + (7.00)\left(\frac{500}{1,000}\right) = 5.00 \text{ years}$$

Source: Adapted from Kaufman (1984).

overall measure of the interest rate exposure for Company Y is the *duration gap* statistic, which takes the following form:[5]

$$\text{Duration gap} = \text{duration of assets}$$
$$- \left[\left(\frac{\text{market value of liabilities}}{\text{market value of assets}}\right) \times \text{duration of liabilities}\right]$$

Here the durations for the asset and liability sides of the balance sheet are simply weighted averages (using relative market values) of the component instruments in the two portfolios. For this particular firm these are calculated at the bottom of Exhibit 8, and so the duration gap measure can be computed as follows:

$$\text{Duration gap} = (4.17) - [(0.833) \times (5.00)] = 0.00 \text{ yr}$$

---

[5] See G. Kaufman, "Measuring and Managing Interest Rate Risk: A Primer," *Economic Perspectives*, January-February 1984, pp. 16–29, for a general discussion of the uses of duration in the measurement and management of interest rate risk.

The duration gap of zero indicates that Company Y has no net exposure to interest rate movements—a fully immunized status. That is, the firm is in an internally hedged position to the extent that as interest rates increase (decrease), the market value of its assets and liabilities will tend to fall (rise) by offsetting amounts. Suppose, however, that the treasurer for Company Y is willing to speculate on the possibility that interest rates are going to fall in the near future. To take advantage of this forecast, he or she will have to adjust the balance sheet so that the assets are more sensitive than the liabilities to rate changes (and, thus, appreciate more with declining rate levels). Said differently, the balance sheet will have to be restructured so that the duration gap statistic is positive.

There are two ways that this view on future interest rates can be made operational. As noted in the previous example, the treasurer can always change the composition of the existing asset-liability mix. In the present case, this would necessitate transferring funds from the shorter-duration assets to the longer-duration ones or, conversely, using shorter-term funding sources to replace the longer-term bonds currently in place. The disadvantage of this method is that it is likely to be quite expensive to implement because of the required capital market transactions. On the other hand, in the prior example it was shown that a plain vanilla swap can be employed to alter the interest rate sensitivity of a specific financial instrument. This concept is now extended such that the swap alters the character of an entire portfolio of assets and liabilities.

To understand this, recognize that since the duration of a portfolio of financial instruments is merely a weighted average of the component parts, the sensitivity of the entire portfolio will be affected by a swap attached to any of the underlying securities. Company Y can create a positive duration gap by either increasing the duration of the assets or decreasing the duration of the liabilities. This is analogous to either (a) turning a floating-rate asset into a synthetic fixed-rate asset or (b) turning a fixed-rate liability into a synthetic floating-rate liability. The key point is that the same plain vanilla swap can be used for either purpose. Whether treated as an *asset swap* or a *liability swap,* an agreement to pay the floating rate and to receive the fixed rate lengthens the duration of assets or shortens the duration of liabilities. It should also be mentioned that the notional principal level selected for the swap can be varied directly with the degree to which the treasurer chooses to gamble on future rate movements. This method of speculating, which does not alter the original composition of assets and liabilities, is sometimes referred to as *off-balance sheet* restructuring.

Swap Application 3: Arbitrage

The last two applications, while differing in their objectives for interest rate risk management, were similar in that each was motivated by the transactional efficiency with which the swap obtains the desired cash flows. But it is also possible that sufficient pricing discrepancies exist across markets to allow arbitrage profits as well. For instance, it is possible that the synthetic fixed-rate of 10.264 percent from the first example, obtained by combining the pay-fixed swap with the FRN, was considerably lower than Company X's best direct alternative in the fixed-rate bond market. However, as mentioned above, most arbitrage transactions at present are rather complex and require some unique features on either the capital market security or the swap. Here we shall show an example of an arbitrage strategy using an innovative security and a plain vanilla swap.

Suppose that Company Z is attempting to raise fixed-rate funds for the next five years and that its best capital market alternative would be a par-value Eurobond with an annually paid coupon rate of 10 percent. The Eurobond therefore would have a yield of 10 percent on an annually compounded basis or 9.76 percent for semiannual compounding. Suppose further that the choice of issuing an FRN and entering a pay-fixed swap does not dominate the Eurobond. However, the firm can issue a par-value *inverse* floating rate note, or "bull floater," paying a semi-annual coupon based on a formula of 19.50 percent *minus* six-month LIBOR. Notice that the inverse FRN differs from a traditional FRN in that coupon payments actually decrease as interest rates rise. Also, assume that the current quoted bid-ask spread for a five-year swap agreement involving six-month LIBOR is 70 and 76 basis points, respectively, and the on-the-run five-year Treasury yield is 9.50 percent.

If the firm issues the inverse FRN, it would then want to transform the coupon obligations into synthetic fixed-rate funding by means of a plain vanilla swap. Perhaps the best way to determine the requisite type of swap is to think of the inverse FRN as a

EXHIBIT 9
Arbitrage Application

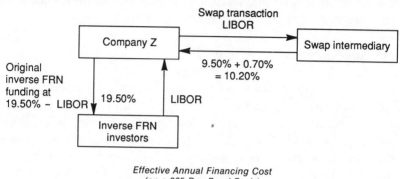

Effective Annual Financing Cost
(on a 365-Day Bond Basis)

Inverse FRN coupon payment: (19.50% − LIBOR)(365/360) = 19.77% − (LIBOR)(365/360)
Swap Transaction: (A) Fixed-rate receipt   = 10.20%
                  (B) Floating-rate payment   = (LIBOR)(365/360)
Net cost of funds (19.77% − 10.20%)   = 9.57%

combination of (*a*) two fixed-rate notes *issued* at 9.75 percent for a total of 19.50 percent and (*b*) one traditional FRN with a coupon of LIBOR held as an *asset*. Thus, to remove the presence of the floating rate altogether, the firm must pay LIBOR and receive the fixed rate in a supplementary swap agreement.[6] Exhibit 9 illustrates this process using the bid side of the fixed swap rate specified above and shows that the net cost of funds is 9.57 percent, assuming semiannually compounded rates, and that the swap fixed rate is on a 365-day basis, while LIBOR and the inverse FRN are on 360-day bases.

Exhibit 9 also indicates that the effective fixed-rate funding cost created by combining the inverse FRN with the receive-fixed plain vanilla swap is 19 basis points lower than the direct fixed rate issue (i.e., 9.76 percent − 9.57 percent). Thus, there is an apparent

---

[6] The implied duration of an inverse FRN is very long, in fact, typically about double that of a fixed-rate note of comparable maturity (see D. Smith, "The Pricing of Bull and Bear Floating Rate Notes: An Application of Financial Engineering," *Financial Management,* Winter 1988, pp. 72–81). This means that the inverse FRN is very sensitive to interest rate changes. Thus, from the issuer's perspective, a receive-fixed swap shortens the duration of the inverse FRN back to that of a fixed-rate note.

arbitrage opportunity due to a relative mispricing between the capital and swap markets. However, two important considerations mitigate against this conclusion. First, as mentioned in the previous examples and elaborated in the following section, any time a swap agreement is involved, there will be additional credit risk that must be considered. The synthetic fixed-rate financing scheme forces Company Z to accept the possibility that the swap intermediary will default. Of course, there is no such default exposure (from Company Z's viewpoint) with the direct issue of a fixed-rate Eurobond.

Second, and perhaps more important in this case, the effective yield of 9.57 percent does not represent a funding cost that is fixed with certainty. Since the coupon rate on the inverse FRN can never fall below zero, this instrument contains an implicit cap at LIBOR equal to 19.50 percent. Thus, Company Z is left unprotected against any movement in LIBOR above 19.50 percent since it would have to continue to make the higher net settlement payments on the swap without any offsetting reduction in its funding cost. To fully protect itself, Company Z would have to purchase an interest rate option (specifically, an interest rate *cap*) which would compensate it when LIBOR exceeds 19.50 percent.[7] Naturally, the cost of this option would have to be factored into the analysis of the synthetic strategy before a precise comparison can be made with the 9.76 percent yield available on the fixed-rate Eurobond. In any event, this additional expense makes the presence of any significant funding arbitrage more remote.

CREDIT RISK ON A PLAIN VANILLA SWAP[8]

The credit risk on a swap agreement is not at all comparable to that of a capital market instrument of similar amount and maturity. A swap is not a funding transaction; there is no principal payment at

---

[7] See K. Brown and D. Smith, "Recent Innovations in Interest Rate Risk Management and the Reintermediation of Commercial Banking," *Financial Management,* Winter 1988, pp. 45–58, for a more comprehensive treatment of the market for over-the-counter interest rate options such as caps, floors, and collars.

[8] This section is based in part on D. Smith, "Interest Rate Movements and the Credit Risk of Interest Rate Swaps," *Commercial Lending Review,* Winter 1988–89, pp. 39–52.

origination and no amount borrowed or lent. As noted earlier, the initial economic value of a plain vanilla swap is zero and so the initial credit risk must also be zero. Obviously, the credit exposure on a traditional debt security is the amount of principal, and that exposure can only decline in the future as principal payments are made. Further, the risk of a possible default is borne only by the bondholder. On the other hand, *potential* credit risk on a swap is *bilateral* in that risk exposure starts out at zero but can become a positive amount for either party. At any point in time, however, only one counterparty bears the credit risk of the other; that is, *actual* credit risk is *unilateral*.

An example will help to clarify the difference between potential and actual credit risk on a swap. Consider again a five-year, semiannual settlement, $10 million notional principal, 10.00 percent-versus-LIBOR interest rate swap between Company A (the fixed-payer) and Bank B (the fixed-receiver). Suppose that two years and four settlement payments pass without event. Then, just after the fourth payment is made, Company A falls into serious financial distress. The relevant question in the present context is how much would the bank lose if the company defaults on the remainder of the swap agreement? The answer depends on the terms that the bank could obtain on a *replacement* swap—namely, a *three*-year, semiannual settlement, $10 million, fixed-versus-LIBOR swap. The underlying notion here is that current swap market rates can be used to value an existing swap in a process similar to marking-to-market a traded security or futures contract.

Suppose that the replacement swap would call for exchanging a fixed rate of 9.50 percent against LIBOR flat. Note that the replacement fixed rate can be less than the original rate for any number of reasons: a downward shift in the Treasury yield curve; a downward shift in the swap spread curve; or, simply, movement along the same Treasury yield and swap spread curves (that is, lower rates for three-year maturities than for five-year). Under these circumstances, default on the part of Company A means that the bank suffers a loss of $25,000 per period for the remaining six periods (three years). The old swap specified fixed receipts of approximately (depending on the actual number of days in each semiannual settlement period) $500,000 and the new swap only $475,000. Using 9.50 percent as the discount factor, the present value of this annuity is $127,913. So, given a replacement fixed swap rate of 9.50 percent, the actual credit risk exposure to the bank is $127,913. This amount also represents the economic value of the original swap—a positive value to the bank since it has an agreement to receive what is presently an above-market fixed rate. It is important to notice, though, that a swap is a "zero-sum game" in that the positive value (and, therefore, risk) to the bank is fully offset by the negative value to the company, since it is paying the above-market fixed rate.

Now suppose that the replacement swap fixed rate is 10.50 percent instead of 9.50 percent. Under these market conditions the swap has positive economic value to the distressed company since it has under contract an agreement to pay the bank what amounts to a below-market fixed rate in exchange for LIBOR flat. The value of the swap is $125,884, slightly less than above since the same $25,000 annuity now is discounted by 10.50 percent. The increase in market rates has made the swap an asset to the company rather than a liability. Presumably, the swap could be assigned to a third party or closed out by negotiation with the bank to capture some or all of the economic value. In any case, the company (or the bank-ruptcy trustee) would not want to default on the swap despite the financial distress, regardless of the current level of LIBOR. For instance, LIBOR (adjusted to a bond basis) could be less than 10 percent on the fourth settlement date, meaning that the subsequent payment is due to the bank, and still the company would not ration-ally default. The value of the swap would be preserved by continu-ing to perform under the terms of the agreement. Note that there is nothing inconsistent with the current six-month LIBOR being be-low 10 percent when the three-year fixed swap rate is 10.50 per-cent; that might merely reflect higher expected future rates.

These examples illustrate that the key datum in valuing a plain vanilla swap is the current fixed rate on a replacement swap for the remaining maturity vis-a-vis the contractual fixed rate on the origi-nal agreement. Notice further that while current LIBOR is impor-tant from a cash management perspective since it determines the amount and direction of the settlement cash flow, it is not directly involved in the measurement of credit risk exposure. Naturally, though, there is a connection—in fact, one might say that the current fixed swap rate is some average of current and expected future path for LIBOR. For any given replacement fixed rate, however, the swap can have positive economic value to only one counterparty. Therefore, actual credit risk exposure at any time is unilateral.

The examples also demonstrate that two events are necessary for default loss on a swap: the actual event of default on the agreement and an adverse change in the fixed swap rate. More exactly, credit risk on a swap is a function of the joint likelihood of financial distress and interest rate movements. But those two factors are not mutually exclusive; some firms, like utilities and thrift institutions, are notoriously interest sensitive. As a consequence, the role that swaps play in the firm's financial structure can matter greatly. A swap used as a hedge can reduce credit risk; a speculative swap can increase it. In any case, both counterparties at origination must assess the possibility of a default by the other. It is in this sense that potential credit risk is bilateral.

The negotiated fixed rate on a plain vanilla swap typically includes an adjustment for the difference in credit risk between the two counterparties. But it is the differential credit risk, not the presence of risk itself, that matters for swap pricing. For example, two virtually risk-free entities could agree to the same swap terms as two very risky parties. But a less risky firm would only be willing to pay a lower fixed rate, or to receive a higher fixed rate, on a swap with a riskier counterparty. Alternative ways to manage credit risk differences, in addition to rate adjustments, include posting collateral and periodic marking-to-market and settlement. The latter arrangement is similar to topping-up clauses used in the foreign exchange market.

While potential credit risk is bilateral, it is not necessarily symmetric between the two counterparties. An obvious reason for this is that interest rates have a lower bound at zero. That puts a maximum on the potential economic value of the swap to the fixed-receiver. In practice, some argue that for institutional reasons there is an effective lower bound on market rates some percentage points higher than zero. Then one might say that, other things being equal, fixed-payers pose less credit risk than fixed-receivers to prospective swap counterparties.

A more subtle reason for the credit risk asymmetry is the inherent design of a plain vanilla swap. Suppose, for instance, that

LIBOR is currently 8 percent and is generally expected to rise smoothly and gradually to about 12 percent over the next five years and that the current five-year, fixed-versus-LIBOR swap rate is 10 percent. Assume further that the present values of the fixed and floating payment streams are equal, in other words that the swap is at par value. The expected settlement flows for the fixed-payer on the swap are displayed in Panel A of Exhibit 10. The shaded boxes

EXHIBIT 10
Asymmetric Credit Risk on a Plain Vanilla Swap

Panel A. Expected settlement cash flows on a pay-fixed, plain vanilla swap

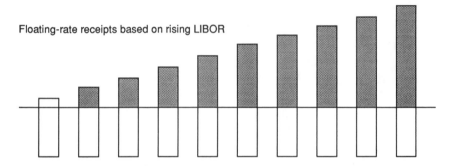

Floating-rate receipts based on rising LIBOR

Fixed payments based on 10% for each settlement date

Panel B. Expected settlement cash flows on a series of futures contracts

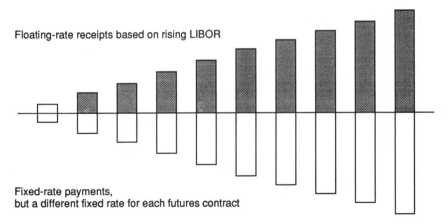

Floating-rate receipts based on rising LIBOR

Fixed-rate payments,
but a different fixed rate for each futures contract

represent the uncertain LIBOR-based receipts, and the unshaded boxes the certain fixed payments. On a net basis, the fixed-payer expects to be making settlement payments in the early years and receiving payments in the later years. Most important, the replacement swap fixed rate is expected to be rising in the future, increasing the credit risk exposure from the fixed-payer's perspective. The key point is that the asymmetry would arise even if the future path for LIBOR were known with certainty. That is, credit risk on a swap is ultimately due to the static design of the plain vanilla swap as well as the uncertainty of future interest rates.

The design characteristic that is the source of the asymmetry is that the same fixed rate is applied to all settlement periods. Recall that an interest rate swap can be viewed as a series of over-the-counter futures contracts. Suppose that the predetermined rate (and therefore the price) of each futures contract reflects expected LIBOR for that particular delivery date. Since LIBOR is expected to rise, the prevailing rate on the futures contracts also rises. The expected settlement flows are drawn in Panel B of Exhibit 10. Notice that on a net basis, the expected settlement is zero for each date. The credit risk exposure is zero at date zero and remains at zero as long as LIBOR follows its expected path.[9] At origination, each of the individual futures contracts has a zero economic value, as does the series in aggregate. On a plain vanilla swap, however, the individual settlement dates have negative and then positive economic values even though in aggregate they net out to zero.

CONCLUSIONS

The simplicity of a plain vanilla swap should not belie its importance as an innovative tool for interest rate risk management, per-

---

[9] This suggests that another way of dealing with swap credit risk, although deviating from the plain vanilla structure, would be to have a different fixed rate for each period to reflect market expectations. It is possible, for instance, to use the prevailing sequence of implied forward rates for this purpose. While this sort of structure would not provide the constant fixed rate that is useful in many arbitrage applications, it would provide a known fixed rate on the swap for each period. Basically, the latter is what is needed in most hedging and speculative strategies.

haps as *the* innovation of the 1980s, at least in terms of market impact. The extraordinary growth and depth of the swap market can be attributed to the range of its applications—from defensive hedging strategies, to aggressive speculative views on future rates, to arbitrage transactions that foster links between the various financial markets. Interest rate swaps over the last few years have passed through the classic stages of market development, from occasional customized brokered deals to standardized plain vanilla intermediated ones. Investment and commercial banks have become active market makers to meet their clients' risk management needs and have developed the analytic techniques to offer a wide range of swap products and variations.

A swap can be described as either a combination of long and short positions in capital market securities or as a series of over-the-counter futures contracts. The former interpretation is useful in establishing the swap's economic value and measuring credit risk exposure. The latter is useful to position swaps within the realm of derivative risk management products and, in particular, to see the unique aspects of swap credit risk. In spite of these alternative theoretical interpretations, however, it should be kept in mind that the swap agreement is a sufficiently unique form of contracting to prevent it from being easily duplicated in practice. Consequently, since plain vanilla swaps are likely to be at the forefront of financial innovation for years to come, a thorough understanding of both the instrument and its attendant market conventions would seem to be essential knowledge.

BIBLIOGRAPHY

Bierwag, G. *Duration Analysis*. Cambridge, Mass.: Ballinger Publishing, 1987.

Brown, K., and D. Smith. "Recent Innovations in Interest Rate Risk Management and the Reintermediation of Commercial Banking." *Financial Management,* Winter 1988, pp. 45–58.

Finnerty, J., A. Kalotay, and F. Farrell. *Evaluating Bond Refunding Opportunities*. Hagerstown, Md.: Ballinger Publishing, 1988.

Kaufman, G. "Measuring and Managing Interest Rate Risk: A Primer." *Economic Perspectives,* January-February 1984, pp. 16–29.

Monroe, A. "Firms Return in Force to Credit Markets with Debt Linked to Interest-Rate Swaps." *The Wall Street Journal,* November 20, 1987.

Smith, C., C. Smithson, and L. Wakeman. "The Market for Interest Rate Swaps." *Financial Management,* Winter 1988, pp. 34–44.

Smith, D. "The Pricing of Bull and Bear Floating Rate Notes: An Application of Financial Engineering." *Financial Management,* Winter 1988, pp. 72–81.

Smith, D. "Interest Rate Movements and the Credit Risk of Interest Rate Swaps." *Commercial Lending Review,* Winter 1988–89, pp. 39–52.

Walmsley, J. *The New Financial Instruments.* New York: J. Wiley & Sons, 1988.

Yawitz, J.; H. Kaufold; T. Macirowski; and M. Smirlock. "The Pricing and Duration of Floating Rate Bonds." *Journal of Portfolio Management,* Summer 1987, pp. 49–56.

CHAPTER 4

THE DEVELOPMENT AND STANDARDIZATION OF THE SWAP MARKET

James E. McNulty
Florida Atlantic University
Boca Raton, Florida

Sharon L. Stieber
Barrentine, Lott and Associates
Washington, D.C.

Interest rate swaps, which have become a very homogeneous and generic financial instrument, began life in the U.S. capital markets in a different form. Interest rate swaps were created to allow firms to transform short-term or floating-rate financing into long-term fixed-rate financing, or vice versa. In the early stages of the development of the interest rate swap market, the instrument was customized to best meet the needs of the two counterparties. Each swap was unique. While this served the customer, it also made swaps relatively illiquid. The market has gradually concluded that liquidity is more important than the advantages of tailoring a swap.

THE EARLY SWAPS

Origins of the Market

Interest rate swaps were spawned by the needs of less-than-premier quality credits in Europe for intermediate- or long-term fixed-rate financing. The Eurobond market, especially in the early 1980s when credit was tight and interest rates were high, was very selective in its acceptance of only the highest-quality issuers for fixed-rate securities. Firms that needed fixed-rate financing, but were excluded from acquiring it directly through their own issuance, could access it indirectly with an interest rate swap. Not only could the lower-quality institution acquire the much-needed, fixed-rate funds, but it could do it at an attractive rate.

The concept of swapping cash flows was not new. Currency swaps had existed since at least the mid-1970s.[1] Currency swaps are essentially long-term forward contracts that provide for the transfer of currencies between counterparties at the initiation of the swap and the reversal of these flows at the termination. This was normally done at the same rate of exchange but with a fee paid by the provider of the stronger currency to compensate for the expected changes in the exchange rate over the life of the swap.

The Student Loan Marketing Association, better known as Sallie Mae, imported the European currency swap concept to the American capital markets in mid-1982 and sparked a revolution in corporate finance. Like the fixed-rate issuers in the Eurobond market, Sallie Mae, as a quasi-government agency, was perceived as an extremely high-grade credit issuer and thus had the ability to access attractive fixed-rate intermediate-term debt at narrow spreads to the Treasury yield curve.

Sallie Mae was created by Congress in the early 1970s to develop a secondary market in guaranteed student loans. These student loans bought by Sallie Mae, or advances given to student loan originators collateralized by student loans, are intermediate-term floating-rate assets that are tied to the 91-day Treasury bill rate, on a bond equivalent basis. Despite the attractive pricing, Sallie Mae did not want to finance its floating-rate assets with these fixed-rate funds and incur a significant level of interest rate risk. Developing interest rate swaps allowed Sallie Mae to take advantage of its ability to access intermediate-term funds well below the cost of most corporations but avoid the interest rate risk (and the higher

---

[1] See Carl R. Beidleman, *Financial Swaps* (Dow Jones-Irwin, 1985), chapters 2–3, and 12–14. According to Beidleman, the commercial currency swap was introduced in 1976 (see p. 21).

cost when the yield curve is upward sloping) of borrowing long and lending short.

In the summer of 1982, Sallie Mae issued its first fixed-rate intermediate-term debt through a private placement and swapped it for floating-rate funds tied to the 91-day Treasury bill. It was said that ITT, the counterparty, saved 17 basis points by using this mechanism. This provided fixed-rate funds to the corporation at a cost below what it would have paid to acquire them directly and provided Sallie Mae with cheaper intermediate-term floating-rate funds than it could have obtained in the floating-rate note market. Thus both parties benefited from the transaction.

Tailoring a Swap

Although Sallie Mae's first swap was with a Fortune 500 company and was arranged through an investment banker, Sallie arranged many of the swaps that followed on its own. These were done directly with savings and loan associations (a natural counterparty) and, to a lesser extent, with commercial banks.

Sallie Mae's preferred index was Treasury bills since this index was closely correlated with the yield on their short-term assets. This index was ideal for thrifts as well because it was closely correlated with the cost of their short-term deposits. The swap thus resulted in minimal basis risk for both parties. (This high correlation with thrift CDs is not surprising since the six-month money market certificate had previously been directly tied to the Treasury-bill rate through regulation.) For the thrift, the swap converted their short-term certificates into intermediate-term fixed-rate funds that were a much better, but not perfect, match for funding mortgages.

Any fixed-maturity CD, bond, advance, or interest rate swap may not turn out to be a perfect hedge for a pool of mortgages because a mortgage does not have a fixed, known maturity. This significantly complicates the execution of a matched funding strategy. Despite this challenge, the swap market tried to oblige. Some large thrifts staggered the maturities through a series of smaller swaps that mirrored the expected prepayments. Later, amortizing swaps were developed that allowed for a declining balance on the swap, to reflect anticipated payoffs on the mortgage pools.

Associations could still face extension risk or refinancing risk if prepayments were significantly different than expected. For example, a thrift that negotiated a swap in 1983 would have faced four years of generally declining interest rates and very high prepayments, especially in 1986 and early 1987. This would have resulted in significant reinvestment risk. Most of the high-yielding mortgages of 1983 would have been refinanced and replaced by lower-yielding loans, probably at a negative spread relative to the swap.

The most common technique of calculating the monthly or quarterly index was a mean of the Treasury bill auction rate in that period, but true to the market's boutique character, anything was possible. One swap was tied to the secondary market quotes on Tuesday. Other swaps used the index at the beginning or end of the month or quarter. The first swap Sallie Mae executed involved payments by both parties. The inefficiency of this was almost immediately recognized and subsequent swaps involved a net payment by one counterparty.

Other Indexes

As the market developed, counterparties began seeking interest rate swaps that met their particular needs. Certificate-of-deposit rates were popular as an index, particularly among commercial banks. The basis risk between CDs and Treasury bills was moderate, allowing participants that might choose one to tolerate the other. Commercial paper was another common index requested of Sallie Mae, especially by large Fortune 500 companies, since commercial paper was their most common source of short-term financing. In both of these cases one-, three-, or six-month financing instruments could be used as the index. In addition, one could use a particular date near the end of the period or the average for the period as the index.

The Federal Home Loan Bank System's 11th District cost of funds was also occasionally used as an index, primarily by California thrifts. This index is less volatile than any of the previously mentioned possibilities. It reflects the cost of both long- and short-term liabilities of thrifts in Arizona, California, and Nevada. The inclusion of long-term liabilities that were acquired in previous interest rate environments tends to cause the index to remain higher than the short-term money market instruments in low interest rate environments, and lower than these instruments in high interest rate periods. Since it is calculated from individual thrift income statement and balance sheet data, there is a lag between the period of the index and the publication date. Nonetheless, this index was particularly attractive to 11th District associations because it reflects their cost of funds and is a common index for their adjustable-rate mortgages. Despite its attractiveness to these savings and loan associations, it was less attractive to most swap counterparties because of its low correlation with other market rates.

A slight variation on the 11th District cost of funds was a request for a swap priced off the Federal Home Loan Bank of Atlanta's variable advance rate. The FHLB advance rate is the rate at which these banks will lend to their members. Although it is an administered rate, it is generally priced in relation to the federal funds rate and the prime rate. Pricing was developed by Sallie Mae and offered to the counterparty, but the deal was never closed. Despite the fact that the swap was never consummated, this illustrates the boutique flavor of the market in this early period. Almost any index was considered if historical data were available so that the index could be modeled, and the potential swap market was large enough to warrant the time and effort to develop pricing.

RECOGNITION OF ADVANTAGES AND OPPORTUNITIES

As the swap market developed, many types of institutions began to recognize the advantages of swaps. Thrifts, as has already been mentioned, used swaps as vehicles to reduce interest rate risk. U.S. corporations discovered they could borrow at a lower rate by issuing a bond or borrowing from a bank and then doing a swap. U.S. and European commercial banks also discovered the arbitrage opportunities in swaps and, most important, became dealers in swaps. These firms turned to swaps because swaps had several advantages over other methods of changing the maturity of a financial instrument, such as financial futures. Each of these parties saw the advantages of swaps almost simultaneously, and the market expanded rapidly.

Advantages of Swaps[2]

A swap can be viewed as a series of privately negotiated forward contracts. The contract price of a swap remains constant for the life of the swap, whereas futures contracts are repriced daily. The private nature of the contract allows for customization of all aspects of the swap. Nonetheless, forward contracts have disadvantages which futures contracts do not have. These include the credit risk of the counterparty and the lack of public information about prices.

Every aspect of the swap contract can be subject to negotiation. This includes the size of the notional principal, the maturity of the agreement, and the timing of the periodic cash flows. The cost of executing a swap is higher than for futures, while the cost of maintenance would generally be expected to be lower.

The cost of establishing a futures position is low because an exchange exists and price information is readily available. The markets are liquid because of the presence of speculators. Commission costs are minimal, and the credit risk of establishing a position is reduced by the initial margins and the fact that the transaction is guaranteed by the clearing organization. Nonetheless, the cost of establishing a futures position also includes such items as collecting and analyzing past price data to evaluate the basis risk in the hedge. The costs of establishing a swap position include the expenses of collecting price information, locating a swap partner, researching the creditworthiness of potential counterparties, and paying arrangement fees.

Although the costs of execution may be higher for swaps than for futures, there are costs to futures positions during the life of the hedge which exceed the costs of interest rate swaps. These costs are related to the daily repricing feature of futures, the desired term of the hedge, and the customized nature of swaps.

---

[2] This section is adapted from Dennis E. Bennett, Deborah L. Cohen, and James E. McNulty, "Interest Rate Swaps and the Management of Interest Rate Risk for Mortgage Lenders," *Housing Finance Review*, Summer 1988, pp. 249–53.

As is well known, futures contracts are repriced daily through variation margins. Although this eliminates the credit risk of the counterparty as a factor in the transaction, it also creates unknown and potentially adverse cash flows during the life of the hedge. As interest rates change, the hedger must finance or invest the uncertain cash flows. Swaps have no variation margin requirements, which contributes to their attractiveness as hedging vehicles. With swaps, the fixed-rate cash flows are known in advance, and the timing of the variable-rate cash flows is also known, although the amount is unknown. As a result, there is no liquidity or reinvestment risk in the swap hedge from unanticipated variation margins.

Another difference between swaps and futures hedge maintenance results from the direct credit risk present in swaps. This occurs because the swap contractual obligation is with the counterparty rather than with a clearing organization. The risk of default raises the cost of doing business in the swap market. However, interest rate swaps, unlike most forward contracts, exchange only the interest payments. The notional principal is not at risk.

The notional principal of a swap may be $100 million, but the maximum amount at risk is much less than this. The amount of risk would be the expected future value of the interest differential between the fixed and floating rates. While it is difficult to generalize because rates have been volatile, in most cases the exposure probably amounts to no more than 3 percent or 4 percent of the notional principal for every year remaining on the swap contract. Default risk is further reduced because most swaps net the periodic cash flows of the two counterparties. The risk of default may be further reduced through the use of letters of credit, collateral, or other forms of performance guarantees.

The term of the desired hedge has a significant influence on the desirability of swaps relative to futures contracts. The term of interest rate swaps may extend beyond 10 years. However, a hedge using financial futures must be rolled over if the desired length of the hedge is beyond the three-year maximum expiration date of the posted futures contracts. This increases the basis risk of long-term futures hedges because of rollover risk. The need to roll futures positions forward also increases the transactions costs of futures hedges because of increased commissions and monitoring expense.

The ability to customize swaps allows the hedger to minimize basis risk relative to the basis risk present in a futures hedge. Basis risk in futures hedging arises from (*a*) the relationship of the interest rate on the instrument being hedged and that on the deliverable instrument of the futures contract, (*b*) the duration of the underlying instrument, (*c*) the contract expiration dates and their frequency, and (*d*) the liquidity of the futures contracts. The attractiveness of swaps is that a hedger may select a variable index, frequency of reset, and cash flows that have a high correlation with the repricing characteristics and cash flows of the instruments being hedged.

U.S. Corporations and the Swap Market

Chart 1 shows how a corporation can benefit from swaps. Assume the company can borrow using three-month commercial paper at

CHART 1
Differential Credit Risk Premiums

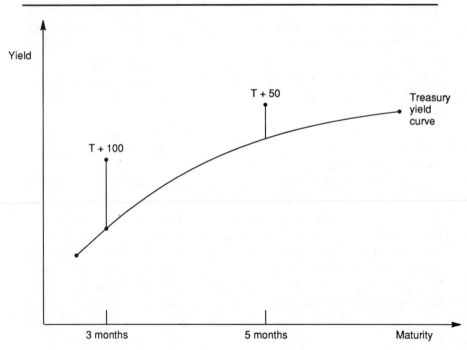

100 basis points over the three-month U.S. Treasury bill rate (T + 100). But it can also borrow five-year funds at 50 basis points over comparable maturity Treasury rates. If the company wants to borrow short-term funds, it can obtain these cheaper by borrowing five-year funds at T + 50 and then entering into an interest rate swap as the variable-rate payer. The fixed rate it receives on the swap will offset the interest on the bonds, and it will be left with a floating-rate obligation. The company thus has, in effect, borrowed funds at 50 basis points under the commercial paper rate.

One of the first published examples of corporate use of the swap market was by Detroit Edison.[3] As a BBB rated company, it faced long-term rates of 17.25 percent in the spring of 1982 to refund $60 million of mortgage bonds. By doing a swap through Continental Illinois, it was able to raise seven-year funds at 16.25 percent.

This was accomplished as follows: Continental formed a syndicate of banks to lend Detroit Edison $60 million through a seven-year floating-rate loan. The rate on this loan was at LIBOR plus 68 basis points. Continental then did an interest rate swap with Detroit Edison. The utility paid a fixed rate of 15.57 percent. (This included a swap rate of 15.39 percent plus 18 basis points in fees.) On the other side of the swap it received LIBOR. Since the company paid LIBOR plus 68 basis points on the loan, the 68 basis points can be added to the fixed rate to give the total cost of the long-term funds. This works out to 16.25 percent (15.57 percent + 0.68 percent). The LIBOR payments simply offset one another.

Continental offset the interest rate risk in the Detroit Edison swap by simply doing another swap, this one with a French bank, Banque Indosuez. This bank raised funds in Europe at 15.39 percent using Continental as underwriter. It then swapped payments with Continental, agreeing to receive the same 15.39 percent and pay LIBOR. The difference between the 15.57 percent paid to Continental by Detroit Edison and the 15.39 percent Continental paid to the French bank represents the above mentioned 18 basis points, which was Continental's profit on the swap transaction.

The number of such deals exploded in the early 1980s. They

---

[3] *Business Week*, December 13, 1982, pp. 85–86.

were especially popular for lower-rated companies whose cost of raising long-term debt (relative to some benchmark yield curve such as Treasury) would be greater than its cost of raising short-term debt.[4]

Thrifts

Thrift institutions were also active participants in the interest rate swap market. Having just been through the crisis of the early 1980s, when high interest rates caused 40 percent of the industry to fail, many thrifts were anxious to find longer-term sources of funds to match against their mortgage loans. As noted earlier, a large portion of the initial Sallie Mae swaps were done with thrifts for this reason. Swap brokers eagerly courted thrifts because these institutions are natural users of swaps. A sample of 114 swaps done by three major swap dealers between December 1982 and May 1984 included 65 that were done with thrift institutions.[5]

Thrifts were specifically encouraged by their regulators in 1983 and 1984 to practice gap management—the matching of maturities.[6] Each FSLIC-insured thrift was required by the Federal Home Loan Bank Board beginning in March 1984 to file data quarterly on the maturity distribution of its assets and liabilities. These raw data were adjusted for amortization and expected prepayments to produce an asset-liability gap report. These reports were to be discussed quarterly with the institution's board of directors as an indicator of the institution's overall exposure to changes in rates. Institutions with high gap ratios could be subject to regulatory criticism.[7] This further encouraged the use of swaps by thrifts.

The customized nature of swaps appealed to both corporations and thrifts. A corporation such as Detroit Edison could choose a swap maturity that corresponded precisely with that of its

---

[4] The reader should notice that this example is precisely the opposite of that depicted in Chart 1. This is deliberate because both types of transactions were undertaken.

[5] Dennis Bennett, Deborah Cohen, and James McNulty, "Interest Rate Swaps and the Management of Interest Rate Risk for Mortgage Lenders," *Housing Finance Review*, Summer 1988, pp. 249–64.

[6] The effect of thrift regulation on the growth of the swap market is discussed in more detail in Chapter 20, "Interest Rate Swap, Credit Exposure and Capital Requirements."

[7] Usually the focus was on the cumulative one-year and three-year gaps relative to assets.

fixed-term obligation. Thrifts could choose a swap maturity that provided a reasonable match with mortgages and still produced a reasonable profit. The swap yield curve is generally upward sloping when other capital market yield curves are upward sloping. This means that a thrift doing a 10-year swap to match the expected maturity of its mortgages may be unable to make a sufficient profit. However, if it were to do the swap for, say, five years, it could lock in an acceptable spread.[8]

The advantages of swaps relative to futures were also of importance to thrifts. A few thrifts had used futures in the early 1980s to extend the maturity of their liabilities. When rates came down, these short positions produced large losses at some thrifts. Many thrift financial managers turned to swaps because, as noted, it is possible to use them to hedge without incurring some of the adverse features of futures.

Commercial Banks and Investment Bankers

Domestic and European commercial banks also saw advantages to swaps. First, they saw the same arbitrage possibilities as other corporations and used swaps as a means to obtain a lower cost of funds. Since more of a bank's funds come from debt (of various forms, including, of course, deposits) than that of the typical corporation, credit-risk arbitrage is a particularly important advantage for banks. Banks went well beyond this application, however, and became swap dealers. In this endeavor they were also joined by the major investment bankers.

As noted previously, the early swaps were customized and involved putting together two or more counterparties interested in the same index, maturity, and amount of notional principal. With their extensive network of business relationships, large money center commercial banks in the United States and Europe were ideally suited for this role. In addition, commercial banks have developed extensive procedures for analyzing credit risk because

---

[8] While most fixed-rate mortgages have a term of 30 years, the estimated duration of many mortgages is somewhere in the neighborhood of 5 years because of amortization and prepayments.

of their commercial lending function. Since the swap dealer acts as principal (i.e., the two parties each swap with the dealer rather than with each other), the dealer is exposed to credit risk on both sides of the transaction. As a result, an established credit evaluation procedure is essential for a successful swap operation.

Commercial banks in particular have extensive and detailed procedures for analyzing the credit risk of their business customers in connection with the commercial and industrial loans that are the heart of their business. Banks were thus in a unique position to act as swap dealers. Many of the large commercial banks in New York, Chicago, San Francisco, Toronto, London, Paris, and Tokyo have set up swap departments and have become active participants in the market. Most large investment banking organizations were also very active in the early stages of this market.

With their knowledge of the swap market and their expertise in instruments like futures and options, commercial and investment banks were able to develop a wide variety of customized hedge programs for their corporate customers. Combining swaps and options, for example, could enable a bank to offer a corporation a hedge contract that would allow it to profit if interest rates moved in their favor without taking losses if rates moved against them. (Of course, this kind of protection costs money. As a result, if rates did not change, profits would be lower than if the institution had remained unhedged. The difference would be the cost of the hedge.) This is what's now known as an interest rate cap. A similar transaction can be set up to hedge against exchange rate movements.

As *The Wall Street Journal* put it in 1986, "With one phone call a company treasurer can get his interest or exchange rate capped, floored or collared, either now or in the future, at whatever level he's willing to pay for."[9] Customers often prefer this to doing the hedging themselves. One investment banker remarked, "Everyone reacts very negatively to complexity. We provide a mechanism where we take the burden of understanding the design of the instrument."[10] This enabled banks to take the expertise they

---

[9] "Tailor Made 'Hedges' Appeal to Big Corporate Customers," *The Wall Street Journal*, December 18, 1986, p. 6.
[10] Ibid.

had developed using swaps, options, and futures to hedge their own interest rate and currency risk, and use it to develop sophisticated risk management products for their corporate customers.

GROWTH AND STANDARDIZATION

Because swaps provide the opportunities described above for a broad range of both financial and nonfinancial firms, the growth of the market has been described by many analysts as explosive. Table 1 shows the notional principal of swaps outstanding from the inception of the market in 1982 through 1987, the latest data available at the time of this writing. While growth was substantial between 1982 and 1986, it is especially noteworthy that the outstanding principal more than doubled between 1986 and 1987 alone and then increased further in 1988. Data since 1985 are based on an annual survey done by the International Swap Dealers Association. The figures have been adjusted to avoid most double counting, which is possible since two parties could report opposite sides of the same swap.[11] It is clear from the table that the swap market is now an integral part of the overall capital market.

Table 2 shows swap maturities at the end of 1987. It is clear from this table that these run the entire gamut, although swaps out to five years are the most common.

Standardization

This growth could not have been achieved without standardization of the swap instrument. As the market grew, it became clear that it is not possible to do business efficiently when each dealer needs to find an exact match for each swap. Locating a counterparty willing to take precisely the opposite position and who agrees on the maturity, index, and size of the swap is cumbersome at best; in some

---

[11] Double counting is eliminated by eliminating one half of the notional principal of swaps between ISDA dealers. ISDA suggests that this may cause the total to be understated. In addition to the figures in Table 1, there were $180 billion in currency swaps outstanding at the end of 1987.

TABLE 1
Interest Rate Swaps Outstanding
(Amount of Notional Principal)

Year	$ Billions
1982	$3
1983	20
1984	90
1985	170
1986	310
1987	680

Source: International Swap Dealers Association and Cravath, Swaine and Moore.

TABLE 2
Swap Maturities (December 31, 1987)

Years to Maturity	Notional Principal ($ Billions)
1	$67
2	85
3	76
4	69
5	77
6	43
7	40
8	18
9	18
10	32
11	13
Over 12	2

Source: International Swap Dealers Association and Cravath, Swaine and Moore.

cases it may be impossible and the deal would not get done. In addition, given the volatility of rates, customers want to be assured of locking in their fixed cost at the time they place their first phone call. This could happen only if swaps were standardized.

In addition, firms frequently find it convenient or useful to liquidate a swap. In the early days of the market, they could do this only by entering into another swap with equal but opposite terms. This would require paying a new set of fees. It occurred to market participants that exit from swap positions would also be much easier if swaps were standardized.

By 1984–85 the market had become more generic. Several factors drove this increased homogeneity: (*a*) the number of indexes became too large to efficiently price and track, (*b*) a unique index was difficult to sell in the secondary market, and (*c*) some of the indexes were difficult to hedge, either by one of the counterparties or the investment bank or commercial bank that was temporarily taking a position in a swap. A plain vanilla LIBOR swap was easier and quicker to price, arrange, hedge, or sell if it later became necessary to unwind the position.

The administrative burden of customized swaps was also considerable. As noted, counterparties like Sallie Mae and investment bankers found that as the market grew, the number of indexes that were being utilized grew as well. More back-office time was needed to collect, calculate, and price swaps based on nonstandard indexes. Firms began to limit the indexes that they would deal in, or price nonstandard swaps less attractively in order to compensate for the added burden.

A secondary market in swaps began to develop. For example, Sallie Mae found that many of the early Treasury bill swaps with thrifts were sold to other counterparties, with Sallie Mae's approval, when interest rates went up. These sales produced an immediate accounting gain for the thrift institution since if an institution had locked in a fixed rate with a swap, the swap would be more valuable in a higher interest rate environment.[12] Nonetheless, a swap that was negotiated to a particular firm's needs was often less valuable to other potential counterparties, and was thus more difficult to sell.

As the market matured, a smaller percentage of swaps were done directly between counterparties. Instead, investment banks and commercial banks made a market in swaps. It was much easier to take a position in one index, such as LIBOR, that could be easily hedged, during the time that it took to locate counterparties for the other side of the swap. Although some of the larger swap dealers

---

[12] Naturally, the value of the firm would be unaffected by this type of activity. The motivation, for the most part, was purely in the accounting treatment of the gains.

will still negotiate special interest rate swaps, this portion of the market is now small.

The first formal move toward standardization came in 1984 when representatives of 18 swap dealers met to develop standard terms for interest rate swaps.[13] Further attempts at standardization took place with the formation of the International Swap Dealers Association (ISDA) in 1985. The group of participants grew from 18 to over 100, and ISDA now includes dealers from all over the world.

Standard wording was developed in 1985 with the publication of the first edition of the *Code of Standard Wording, Assumptions and Provisions for Swaps*. By 1987 a master agreement had been developed that covered both interest rate and currency swaps. The code standardized many aspects of swaps, including (*a*) wording of the contract, (*b*) rate setting, (*c*) the calculation of fixed and floating amounts, and (*d*) the calculation of the liquidation value of the swap. Master agreements are really complete swap contracts, so that swaps have become a homogeneous commodity.

SUMMARY

Hedging became easier for swap dealers as swaps became standardized. Under the old approach, the only way to hedge was to find a counterparty with the opposite risk profile. If the firm didn't do this precisely, some exposure to interest rate changes would remain. With nonstandard swaps it would be difficult to know accurately what this exposure would be.

If all swaps were based on the same index with the same repricing characteristics, it would be possible to calculate net exposure fairly easily using duration analysis. The firm could hedge its exposure by either doing an offsetting swap with another dealer or using the financial futures markets.

With standardization, swaps indexed to the Treasury bill rate have become a smaller and smaller part of the market. Capital

---

[13] William P. Rogers, "Interest Rate and Currency Swaps," unpublished manuscript, Cravath, Swaine and Moore, New York, April 1989.

markets have become global, and the international standard float-ing-rate index is LIBOR. Thus, increasingly, more and more swap contracts use LIBOR as the index for variable-rate payments. Ne-gotiated contracts using other rates continue to be done, but the user pays a premium for this type of contract and it is not as liquid. As a result, the customized contracts that dominated the swap market in its very early days, such as those arranged by Sallie Mae, have become a smaller and smaller part of the total.

CHAPTER 5

VARIATIONS TO BASIC SWAPS

Jeffry P. Brown
Morgan Stanley & Co. Incorporated
New York, New York

INTRODUCTION

The underlying structure of the generic interest rate swap has been modified in a variety of ways in order to accommodate alternative applications. As a result, the interest rate swap has become a very versatile instrument that lends itself to myriad applications. The basic idea of the swap, that of exchanging interest payments between parties, quickly became a basic financial engineering tool for the financial manager to apply to a variety of problems. In this chapter, we examine some of the more established variations to basic swaps. While our examples will be dominated by one currency, it should be remembered that these variations can be utilized in other major currencies or in more than one currency on a particular structure.

VARIATIONS TO BASIC SWAPS

Off-Market Swaps

The great majority of interest rate swaps are structured and priced at the market—that is, the floating leg is quoted flat (i.e., no spread to the floating-rate index), and the fixed-pay leg is at the currently quoted market for swaps of a given maturity. However, swaps can also be priced *off-market* in order to obtain a set of cash flows desired by the financial engineer structuring the swap. The swap is so structured that the value of the fixed-rate side, including a possible up-front payment, just equals the value of the floating-rate side under current market conditions, and the net value of the swap is zero. Off-market structures may involve oddly-dated or -sized cash payments between the parties, the setting of a lower or higher than market coupon on the fixed pay leg, a spread added to or subtracted from the floating leg, or some combination thereof.

The most common off-market swap is the swap assignment situation where a new counterparty pays (or receives) an up-front payment to (or from) an existing counterparty in exchange for assuming the original counterparty position in the swap. This results in a transfer of an existing swap position for an up-front price that represents the difference between the notional par value of the swap and its current market value (which is the present value of the remaining cash flows).

The price behavior of an outstanding swap is similar to the price behavior of a bond with a fixed coupon financed with a short-term loan. For example, if a counterparty receives a fixed rate on the swap and pays a floating rate, this is equivalent to the counterparty buying a bond with a fixed coupon and financing it with a loan pegged to a floating-rate index. If interest rates fall, the value of the swap increases (the counterparty can unwind at a gain); conversely, if interest rates rise, the value of the swap decreases (the counterparty can unwind at a loss). The gain or loss is somewhat mitigated by the change in the value of the floating-rate leg, which is analogous to a floating-rate loan.

In order to illustrate movements in swap value, consider a five-year swap with a notional principal of $100 million. The structure of the swap is that the counterparty pays fixed 8.90 percent annually, each July 15, for five years and receives six-month LIBOR semiannually.

Suppose that one year later the floating rate is unchanged but swap dealers value a swap paying 8.9 percent annually for four years hence at 9 percent annually. This higher fixed rate reflects an increase in interest rates or a widening in swap spreads. To produce an internal rate of return of 9 percent that is necessary to induce the existing floating-rate counterparty to assign its position to a dealer, the dealer must pay the counterparty an up-front payment of about $324,000.

Off-market swaps have a somewhat storied reputation due to their potential use to effect corporate tax planning. Examples include an off-market swap with a large up-front payment to a taxpayer wishing to offset net operating losses, or an off-market swap with a large up-front payment from a taxpayer wishing to accelerate deductions from income.

In response to perceived abuses in the utilization of off-market swaps for corporate tax planning, the Internal Revenue Service released Notice 89-21 on February 7, 1989. This announcement gave notice that the Internal Revenue Service would be issuing regulations requiring up-front payments to be amortized and reported as income over the life of the swap. Generally, the treatment of the up-front payment as ordinary income in the year of receipt was a critical feature of the tax-advantaged structures. Moreover, Notice 89-21 indicated that the forthcoming regulations would be effective retroactively to the date of the announcement. The effect of this announcement has been to curtail the use of off-market swaps for tax-advantaged purposes, but their application for specifically engineered structures remains.

Synthetic Securities

The term *synthetic security* refers to the use of swaps and derivative swap products to alter the characteristics of a fixed-income asset. The most common structure is the alteration of a fixed-rate security to a floating-rate security (or vice versa), thereby making the security of use or value to a new fixed-income investor. Alterations could also be accomplished in the timing of the asset's payments or the currency denomination of its cash flows. Such swaps may be off-market as they often utilize fixed coupons or payment schedules to produce a different cash flow pattern. Since these revised coupons or payment schedules are not part of the generally quoted swap market convention of "pay or receive a fixed-rate coupon versus LIBOR flat," they fall into the off-market category.

The buyers of synthetic securities are numerous. Historical floating-rate buyers, such as non-U.S. banks and international trading companies, have been the major investors in fixed-rate bonds that are swapped to floating-rate instruments. U.S. banks and thrifts are showing greater interest in floating-rate packages. Similarly, historical fixed-rate buyers, such as U.S. life insurance companies, have been major customers for floating-rate bonds that they simultaneously swap to fixed-rate instruments in order to obtain the fixed-rate cash flows that they desire.

The basic mechanics of the creation of a synthetic security using an interest rate swap are relatively straightforward and are presented in Figure 1. In this example, consider the following steps:

1. An investor buys a five-year fixed-pay corporate bond at par to yield 100 basis points ("bp") over the semiannual yield on the five-year U.S. Treasury note.
2. The investor enters into an interest rate swap to pay a fixed-rate coupon at plus 100 basis points over the five-year U.S. Treasury note and to receive three-month LIBOR plus 35 basis points. The investor funds the fixed-rate payment on the swap with the interest payments received from the fixed-pay bond.
3. The investor accounts for the position as a synthetic security yielding three-month LIBOR plus 35 basis points.

Similarly, a floating-rate note can be swapped into a fixed-pay asset. Assume a perpetual floating-rate note is priced at LIBOR plus 50 basis points. An investor could purchase the note and enter into a swap to pay LIBOR (funded by the floating-rate note) and

FIGURE 1
Fixed-Pay Cash Flows Swapped to Floating-Pay Cash Flows

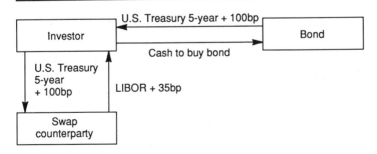

FIGURE 2
Floating-Pay Cash Flows Swapped to Fixed-Pay Cash Flows

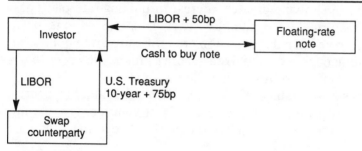

receive a fixed-rate coupon for 10 years at 75 basis points over the 10-year U.S. Treasury interest rate. As a result, the investor has fixed the note for 10 years at 125 basis points over the ten-year Treasury rate. The transaction is illustrated in Figure 2.

Derivative swap products such as caps, floors, and swap options can also be used to create or realize value in a fixed-income security. Typically, options embedded in outstanding securities (e.g., a 10-year bond that is callable after 5 years) are undervalued by the market because the investor buying such a bond is often not well compensated for the call risk. There is, normally, more value to be realized in selling an option in the swap market in order to create an optioned (callable) security than there is in buying an option to create a de-optioned security (e.g., converting a callable bond into a noncallable bond).

The mechanics of creating a synthetic security using derivative swap products is relatively less straightforward, owing to the more complex nature of derivative swap products. Although the number of buyers for such synthetic securities may be fewer, the opportunities these buyers encounter may be considerably greater. While the topic of derivative swap products (caps, floors, and swap options) is dealt with elsewhere in this book, a brief discussion of the subject's relation to synthetic securities is appropriate here.

Consider the creation of a synthetic callable bond. The underlying concept from the fixed-income trading viewpoint is as follows:

1. An investor sells a callable bond it currently owns.

2. The investor acquires a synthetic security consisting of the purchase of a noncallable bond and the sale of a swap option.
3. This combination produces a synthetic security that enables the investor to improve its yield in the process.

To illustrate this strategy, assume that a noncallable-for-life bond with a 9⅞ percent semiannual coupon maturing in five years is trading at plus 105 basis points to the five-year U.S. Treasury bond and is priced at par. To implement this strategy, the investor would sell a three-year callable bond maturing in five years that it currently owns at 115 basis points over the five-year U.S. Treasury and buy a synthetic security consisting of:

1. The purchase of 9⅞ percent semiannual coupon noncallable bond maturing in five years at 105 basis points over the five-year U.S. Treasury yield.
2. The sale of a call to a swap counterparty giving the swap counterparty the right to receive the 9⅞ percent semiannual coupon beginning in three years for an additional two years and to pay three-month LIBOR plus 30 basis points. Compensation for the call is 25 basis points.

The synthetic security is priced to yield 130 basis points over the five-year U.S. Treasury yield. The investor has been compensated 25 basis points for call risk, or 15 basis points more than the investor was being compensated for call risk in the original, callable bond. At the synthetic security call, if the counterparty exercises the option (i.e., if rates have declined), the investor pays the swap counterparty the 9⅞ percent coupon semiannually and receives three-month LIBOR plus 30 basis points. As a result, the fixed-pay asset is converted to a floating-pay asset. The investor's liability to pay 9⅞ percent fixed (semiannual) is funded by the coupon payment from the bond.

Note that we have assumed that the bonds are purchased at par and essentially yield their stated coupon. However, bonds actually used in creating synthetic securities may be trading at a discount or a premium, and this component of value may positively or negatively impact the economics of the resultant synthetic security. Overall, investors should remember that relatively cheap fixed-income securities (from a relative value perspective) are the most likely candidates for a synthetic securities treatment.

Other examples of synthetic securities using derivative swap products include:

1. An investor uncaps a capped floating-rate bond. The investor owns a collateralized mortgage obligation (CMO) capped at 12 percent. The investor buys a 12 percent cap with principal scheduled to match the expected redemption of the CMO.
2. An investor recaps a capped floating-rate bond. The investor owns a CMO floater capped at 12 percent. The investor buys a 12 percent cap and sells a 14 percent cap.
3. An investor monetizes the value of a putable bond. The investor sells the put to a swap counterparty (the right to pay the fixed coupon and receive LIBOR).

Non-Libor Swaps

Approximately 90 percent of all swaps use LIBOR as the floating-rate basis for the transaction; indeed, LIBOR is the dominant index for the floating leg of the interest rate swap market. However, a swap counterparty may wish to pay (or receive) some other floating index, such as commercial paper, the prime lending rate, Treasury bills, or a Federal Home Loan Bank 11th District Cost of Funds Index (so-called COFI swaps).

A non-LIBOR floating rate index often appears in swaps used to manage basis risk. In this context, basis risk refers to the possibility that the yield differential between two floating rate indices changes over time. For example, a bank may have floating rate assets (loans) whose interest receipts fluctuate based on prime. This same bank may have liabilities (funding) whose interest payments fluctuate based on LIBOR. Bank management has the choice of accepting the risk that the basis of its assets does not match the basis of its liabilities, or it can choose to manage the basis risk by using a basis swap.

The swap market uses a number of conventions for the floating leg of an interest rate swap. These conventions are summarized in Table 1. The effect of these conventions is that a non-LIBOR swap may not completely match the asset or liability risk that the non-

TABLE 1
Conventions Used in Floating Legs of Swaps

Type of Basis	Day Count	Source	Calculation
Commercial paper	Actual/360	Fed's H15 form*	As quoted by the source for one-, three-, or six-month commercial paper
Federal funds	Actual/360	H15	Simple average of the daily rate
LIBOR	Actual/360	Page LIBO on Reuters or 3750 on Telerate	As quoted by the source for one-, three-, or six-month LIBOR
Prime	Actual/360	H15	Simple average of the daily rate
T-bills	Actual/actual	H15	Simple average of the weekly average auction rate for three-month T-bills converted to a bond-equivalent basis

* The Federal Reserve Statistical Release, Form H.15 (519).

LIBOR swap is intended to manage. For example, a corporation that funds a capital project with commercial paper as its incremental cost of capital can enter into a swap to manage the risk of rising short-term rates that may impact negatively on the project's economics. Stated another way, the returns on the project are typically fixed on a long-term horizon, but the project is funded on a short-term basis with commercial paper issued by the corporation. To manage the risk that rising commercial paper costs may extinguish the economic benefit of the project, the corporation may enter into a swap to pay a fixed rate for 10 years and to receive a floating rate that is tied to the commercial paper rate of interest. The swap market pays commercial paper floating-rate payments based on a daily average of commercial paper rates, but the corporation probably issues paper using discrete maturity date settings. Unless the corporation issues frequently enough to generate an approximation of the same daily average commercial paper rate, it may be well served to enter into a swap based on its discrete setting. Furthermore, the corporation's commercial paper cost may differ from the published commercial paper rates used to construct the index, due to such differences as actual trade execution and offering costs.

Interesting trading arbitrages sometimes appear in basis swaps. In such cases, an investor may intentionally take a risk with the expectation of reversing the trade position. Rather than entering into the swap with the intent to make and receive payments for the term of the swap, the investor may expect to unwind (sell) the swap position as soon as the trading expectation is achieved.

The graph in Figure 3 shows an 11-year history of three-month LIBOR versus the 90-day bill rate. It can be inferred from the graph that the relationship is subject to great volatility in periods of yield curve inversions or flight to quality. During these periods, the investor may expect to reverse a basis swap position at a gain.

For example, suppose that on March 2, 1987, an investor entered into a swap for 24 months on notional principal of $50 million. The investor paid the weekly average of 90-day U.S. Treasury bill (paid quarterly) plus 110 basis points. The investor received three-month LIBOR. This swap can be illustrated as follows:

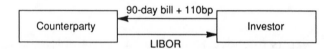

Three months later, the investor reversed the trade. On June 1, 1987, the investor reversed the position by unwinding the swap at the 90-day T-bill rate plus 200 basis points. The investor's profit was as follows:

Nominal: 200 − 110 = 90 basis points (semiannual) for the remaining one year and nine months of the swap on notional $50 million = $787,500.

Present Value: 7 quarterly period payments remaining of $112,500 each discounted at 10.0 percent quarterly (an assumed hurdle rate) = $714,306.

While the great majority of swaps will continue to be denominated as fixed versus LIBOR based, the swap counterparty who makes an effort to understand and use non-LIBOR swaps will have the ability to manage the relationships between various indices and profit from such management.

Zero Coupon Swaps

In general, payments are normally netted between the counterparties on the least frequent reset leg of the swap. Thus, on a five-year quarterly-paid fixed-rate versus three-month LIBOR swap, the

FIGURE 3
Three-Month LIBOR versus Three-Month Bill on a CD Basis
(1/1/78 to 1/30/89)

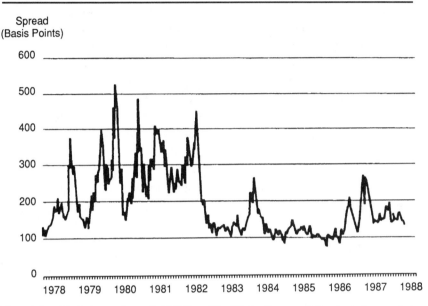

The relationship between 3-month LIBOR and the 90-day Treasury bill reflects key market events such as the October 1987 stock market crash.

Source: Morgan Stanley.

payments between the counterparties are netted each three months. However, the swap market can accommodate other financial engineering applications in which either one or both of the swap legs do not actually exchange a payment until the maturity of the swap. Called the *zero coupon swap,* this variation is an extreme example of an off-market swap. The applications of this type of swap are often related to a zero coupon bond. For example, a buyer or owner of a zero coupon bond could create a synthetic security that converts the zero coupon bond into a LIBOR-floating-rate bond or a semiannual fixed pay bond. In addition, the issuer of a zero coupon bond may use a zero coupon swap to manage the mismatch between this zero coupon–based liability and the non-zero coupon–based assets.

The term structure of interest rates tells us that in a positively sloped yield curve environment, the expectation is that interest rates will rise; conversely, in a negatively sloped yield curve environment, the expectation is that interest rates will fall. When interest rates change, the price of a fixed-income instrument will change in the opposite direction. The magnitude of the price changes of a fixed-income instrument depends on the coupon the instrument bears. This is called the *coupon effect*, and it requires an extension of our thinking about the implications of the term structure of interest rates to coupon and non-coupon-paying instruments.

We have seen that an at-the-market swap has fixed payments priced at a spread off the existing Treasury yield curve. This holds true whether that curve is positively or negatively sloped. However, the pricing of a zero coupon swap cannot use the stated current coupon yield curve as a pricing basis without ignoring the coupon effect. In order to take into account basic term structure theory and the coupon effect, a counterparty pricing a zero coupon swap must first create a zero coupon yield curve. A theoretical zero coupon yield curve, which may be derived from observations of the current coupon swap curve, is the product of the following question: Given the swap yield curve, does the investor need to be paid more for a zero coupon instrument of the same term or less for a zero coupon instrument of the same term?

In a positively sloping yield curve, there is an implied expectation of a rise in interest rates. As the investor receives coupons, the investor would expect to reinvest these cash flows at higher rates. Such an investor would require that a zero coupon instrument pay a higher rate than a current coupon instrument in order to compensate the investor for the loss of the expected ability to invest at higher-yielding rates in the future. Similarly, in a negatively sloped yield curve, the holder of a current coupon bond would expect interest rates to fall. Such an investor could be expected to accept a lower rate for a zero coupon bond since the investor would expect to be able to reinvest future cash flows at lower rates.

The swap counterparty thereby can create a zero coupon swap curve, which reflects interest rates at maturities at which the counterparty is indifferent to paying or receiving, for the same maturity on a zero coupon basis or a current coupon basis.

It should be noted that a receiver on a zero coupon swap (with periodic floating payments) can be expected to express a credit rate surcharge over the theoretical value in a quoted swap rate because the receiver's credit exposure grows on a compounded basis and is not relieved until maturity.

Obviously, given these subjective elements in the pricing of zero coupon swaps, pricing between dealers can show considerable variation. Such swaps are good illustrations of the "more an art than a science" nature of pricing swap products.

Prepaid Swaps

The prepaid swap is an interesting contrast to the zero coupon swap. In a zero coupon swap, one (or both) of the legs accumulate the payment stream and distribute the result at the maturity of the swap. In a prepaid swap, the future payments due under a leg (usually those under the fixed-pay leg) are discounted to a present value and paid at the start of the swap. The prepaid swap is analogous to an annuity. The premium paid for the annuity is the prepaid fixed leg, and the payments under the annuity contract are the variable payments under the floating leg of the swap.

Forward Swaps

Forward swaps are interest rate swaps whose cash flow clock commences at a later date, rather than at the current date. In other words, a forward swap offers the opportunity to lock in a fixed rate today, either as a fixed-rate payer or as fixed-rate receiver, but have payments under the swap begin at some future date.

By utilizing a forward swap, a counterparty can lock in a fixed rate today for an interest rate swap starting in the future and make no payments until the swap commences. In addition, because the swap market is fairly liquid, forward swaps are flexible and can be unwound at any time before or after the swap commencement date, should requirements change. Forward swaps are easy to execute and can typically be priced within a matter of minutes, depending on the complexity of the deal and credit position of the parties.

The difference between a forward swap and a swap option should be understood. A forward swap is a *commitment* to enter into a swap that starts at some future time at interest rates that are agreed upon today. The start date can be from four weeks to many years in the future. In contrast, a swap option is a right, but not the obligation, to enter into a swap, to terminate an existing swap, or to extend or shorten an existing swap at some future time at terms that have been agreed to at the outset of the option. Swap options are discussed in Chapter 9.

To illustrate a forward swap, assume that an investor wishes to enter into a forward swap to pay a fixed rate for three years and receive three-month LIBOR for three years beginning in two years. To the investor, the swap can be depicted as follows:

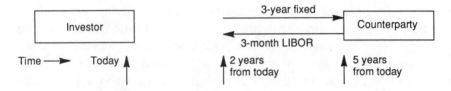

To the dealer pricing the swap, it appears as a combination of two swaps, which can be represented as follows:

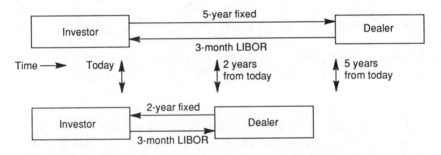

For the initial two years, the LIBOR legs cancel each other. The coupon difference on the fixed legs is amortized into the swap that is visible to the investor. As such, the shape of the swap yield curve (the government yield curve plus swap spread) influences the valuation of the swap from the investor's point of view. Because the forward swap starts at a forward period, forward rates, as indicated by the yield curve's shape and absolute levels, have specific valuation implications for the level at which the fixed coupon will be set in the forward swap. If the swap yield curve is positively sloped, the investor would pay a higher fixed coupon on the forward swap relative to a current swap. If the swap yield curve is negatively sloped, the investor would pay a lower fixed coupon on the forward swap relative to a current swap.

Forward swaps can be used to manage future interest rate risk in connection with an expected future financing. In this application, a corporation would enter into a forward swap today that would begin at the date of expected financing and have a final maturity equal to the maturity of the expected financing.

Extension Swaps

A forward swap can also be utilized to create an extension swap. The term *extension swap* refers to an interest rate swap product that effectively extends the maturity of an existing interest rate swap. An extension swap enables counterparties that have interest rate swaps already on their books to take advantage of current rates and lengthen the maturity of their swaps, hedging future exposure to adverse changes in future fixed swap rates when the swap would normally be renewed.

Under this transaction a counterparty has two alternatives:

- Enter into a forward swap today that would begin on the maturity date of the existing swap and have a fixed-rate coupon at today's forward rates. Under this alternative, no cash is exchanged up front.
- Enter into a forward swap as described above, except that the fixed-rate coupon is equal to that of the outstanding swap and an up-front cash payment is exchanged.

For example, if interest rates rise between now and the maturity date of the existing swap, a counterparty originally paying a fixed rate has the option of unwinding the extension swap at a substantial profit or of keeping the extension swap to maturity and benefiting from lower costs over time.

Amortizing Swaps and Step-Up Swaps

Until now, we have limited our financial engineering applications to situations in which the notional principal amount does not vary.

TABLE 2
Amortizing Swaps and Step-Up Swaps

Behavior of the Notional Principal	Type	Example
Notional principal increases on known schedule	Step-up	Real estate construction loan
Notional principal decreases on known schedule	Amortizing	Synthetic security using a private placement with a pro rata sinking-fund bond
Notional principal increases on schedule estimated to track anticipated behavior of asset or liability*	Step-up	Loan with capitalized interest and variable interest rate
Notional principal decreases on schedule estimated to track anticipated behavior of asset or liability*	Amortizing	Synthetic security using a CMO
Notional principal decreases and increases (or vice versa) on known schedule	Roller coaster	Project financing
Notional principal decreases and increases (or vice versa) on schedule estimated to track anticipated behavior of asset or liability*	Roller coaster	Revolving line of credit

* These financial engineering situations could involve a cancelable swap, which involves a swap option. Swap options are discussed in Chapter 9.

The amortizing swap and its reverse, the step-up swap (sometimes called the *accreting swap*), comprise the basis for accommodating a changing notional amount. The possibilities are listed in Table 2.

Assume that in the fall of 1988 the two-year interest rate swap market was quoted as customer pays a fixed rate at plus 62 basis points over the two-year U.S. treasury rate versus LIBOR flat. The swap yield curve was modestly positively sloped. A customer has entered into a contract to build a new plant and has set up a construction loan facility priced at one-month LIBOR plus 75 basis points. Drawdowns are made at the first of each month, and the facility will be rolled into a permanent financing on September 1, 1990. These cash flows are illustrated in Table 3.

The step-up swap can be done with the customer paying fixed at plus 82 basis points to the two-year U.S. Treasury rate and receiving LIBOR flat. Conceptually, this step-up swap is a series of small forward swaps. The costly nature of the swap in comparison to the straight swap rate of plus 62 basis points is driven by the combination of the rapid step-up and the positive slope of the swap yield curve. As discussed previously in the section on forward swaps, if the swap yield curve is positively sloped, the investor

TABLE 3
Step-Up Swap

First Of	Monthly Draw	Cumulative Draw/Notional
December 1988	$10,000,000	$10,000,000
January 1989	1,000,000	11,000,000
February 1989	2,000,000	13,000,000
March 1989	2,000,000	15,000,000
April 1989	3,000,000	18,000,000
May 1989	3,000,000	21,000,000
June 1989	3,000,000	24,000,000
July 1989	3,000,000	27,000,000
August 1989	2,000,000	29,000,000
September 1989	2,000,000	31,000,000
October 1989	2,000,000	33,000,000
November 1989	1,000,000	34,000,000
December 1989	1,000,000	35,000,000
January 1990	1,000,000	36,000,000
February 1990	1,000,000	37,000,000
March 1990	1,000,000	38,000,000
April 1990	2,000,000	39,000,000
May 1990	2,000,000	41,000,000
June 1990	1,000,000	42,000,000
July 1990	500,000	42,500,000
August 1990	500,000	43,000,000

must pay a higher fixed-rate coupon on a forward swap relative to a current swap.

SUMMARY AND CONCLUSION

In this chapter, we have examined many of the variations to basic swaps and provided examples of the applications of each variant. The application of basic techniques to satisfy the requirements of a given situation will continue to give rise to an ever-changing number of variations to basic swaps. It is hoped that these examples will serve to stimulate the imaginations of financial engineers and inspire them to design appropriate swap structures to accommodate any revision to cash flows that may be needed.

CHAPTER 6

INTEREST RATE SWAPS: AN ALTERNATIVE EXPLANATION*

Marcelle Arak
University of Colorado at Denver
Arturo Estrella
Federal Reserve Bank of New York
Laurie S. Goodman
Eastbridge Capital
New York, New York
Andrew Silver
Moody's Investor Services
New York, New York

The interest rate swap market, first developed in 1982, had an estimated annual volume of more than $360 billion in 1987.[1] Various reasons have been given for the existence and growth of the market, ranging from comparative advantage arguments to agency cost explanations to tax and regulatory reasons. However, each of the explanations is in some way inadequate in explaining the phenomenal growth of the market.

Prior to the introduction of swaps, the only instruments available to borrowers were long-term fixed rate, long-term floating rate, and short-term debt. The combinations that were possible with those instruments are shown in Exhibit 1. The introduction of swaps brought additional options to borrowers. When combined

---

* This chapter is reprinted from *Financial Management*, Summer 1988, pp. 12–18.

[1] This figure is based on first half of 1987 volume of $181 billion reported in The ISDA Report, First Quarter 1988, p. 5, International Swap Dealers Association, New York.

EXHIBIT 1
Combining Risk-Free Rates and Credit Spreads Prior to Swaps

Fixed Credit Spread Floating Credit Spread	Floating Risk-Free Interest Rate	Fixed Risk-Free Interest Rate
	Floating-rate note Short-term debt	Fixed-rate note Not available prior to swaps

with short-term borrowing in the credit markets, swaps enable borrowers to fix the risk-free component of their interest costs while allowing the credit risk components to fluctuate. This ability to provide borrowers with previously unattainable alternatives is the characteristic that makes swaps a true, and probably enduring, financial innovation.

I. PRIOR EXPLANATIONS OF SWAPS

The explanation for the existence and growth of the swap market appearing most frequently in the popular press and occasionally in the academic literature is analogous to the comparative advantage principle in trade theory.[2] Borrowers who are a strong credit with a cost advantage in both the fixed-rate and variable-rate markets, but have a comparative advantage in the fixed-rate market, may borrow in that market and swap ("trade") the fixed-interest stream for a floating-rate stream with other borrowers who raise funds at a variable rate. The gain from the swap (the "gain from trade"), so the story goes, is divided between the two borrowers involved in the swap, making them both unambiguously better off.

However, there is a problem with this reasoning. There are two ways in which a borrower can borrow at a variable rate. In the first case, the debt may be of a long-term nature with periodic repricing and, effectively, an automatic rollover. Examples of this include a bank loan priced at LIBOR plus some credit risk pre-

---

[2] See, for example, J. Bicksler and A. H. Chen, "An Economic Analysis of Interest Rate Swaps," *Journal of Finance,* July 1986, pp. 645–55.

mium, or a floating-rate note. But the comparative advantage argument then relies on the assumption that the relative credit risk premium on a term floating-rate instrument for a high-rated versus low-rated borrower is less than the relative premium on an equal-term fixed-rate instrument.[3] It is not clear why this should be so since the lender in either case has the same amount at risk for the same period of time.[4] Smith, Smithson, and Wakeman hypothesize that cases of apparent underpricing of floating-rate credit risk are actually the result of overlooking a call option that is embedded in some floating-rate agreements.[5] They claim that accounting for this call option would eliminate the supposed pricing differential, and hence the motivation for swaps. Furthermore, they argue that any additional apparent savings from borrowing at a long-term fixed rate via a swap can be attributed to the loss of the prepayment option that the firm would typically have if it borrowed directly in the long-term fixed-rate market. Thus, again, as Wall and Pringle point out, superficial interest rate savings from swaps are not necessarily motivation for swaps.[6]

Furthermore, as Smith, Smithson, and Wakeman note, if any interest rate differential simply represents market inefficiencies, it certainly should not persist for a long period of time since over time, the use of swaps to arbitrage would reduce the differential.[7] Thus, there would be less incentive for swap use, so the swap market should shrink rather than grow over time. Moreover, Turnbull points out that floating rate debt plus a swap is equivalent to fixed rate debt.[8] If the bond market is competitive and there are no externalities, then swaps must be a zero-sum game.

---

[3] See C. R. Beidleman, *Financial Swaps* (Homewood, Ill.: Dow Jones-Irwin, 1985), pp. 214–18, for a discussion of this anomaly.

[4] In fact, it could be argued that the lower-rated borrower should have a higher relative credit spread on term floating-rate debt since it presumably has less resources to deal with the potential for unexpectedly high interest rates.

[5] C. W. Smith, Jr., C. W. Smithson, and L. M. Wakeman, "The Market for Interest Rate Swaps," Working Paper Series No. MERC 86-04, University of Rochester, 1986.

[6] L. D. Wall and J. J. Pringle, "Alternative Explanations of Interest Rate Swaps," Working Paper No. 87-2, Federal Reserve Bank of Atlanta, April 1987.

[7] "The Market for Interest Rate Swaps," 1986.

[8] S. M. Turnbull, "Swaps: A Zero Sum Game," *Financial Management*, Spring 1987, pp. 15–22.

The second way in which a borrower can borrow at a variable rate is in the short-term market using, say, commercial paper or a short-term bank loan, or, for a thrift, short-term CDs, with the intention of rolling it over every three or six months. In this case, it is certainly conceivable that the relative credit premium on the short-term instrument for the high-rated versus low-rated borrower is less than the relative premium on a fixed-rate instrument. However, by borrowing in the short-term market and swapping into fixed, the low-rated borrower is accepting the risk that its credit premium may rise in the future. Thus, in this case, it cannot be said that the swap makes the low-rated borrower unambiguously better off. Wall and Pringle make a similar argument.[9]

Another explanation of the attractiveness of swaps relies on differences in agency costs between long- and short-term debt. Wall argues that after a low-rated borrower issues long-term debt, there is an incentive to make the firm riskier at the expense of the bondholders.[10] Although the bondholders share in the loss if bankruptcy occurs, they cannot receive more than the bond's promised rate of return. Bondholders understand this incentive and attempt to protect themselves by demanding a large premium required of higher-rated companies is not as large because these companies have already "paid their dues" and established a good reputation. Low-rated borrowers, however, can avoid the agency problem by issuing short-term debt and swapping into fixed payments; the firm is monitored each period as it enters the short-term debt market and consequently is not required to pay the long-term premium for agency costs. Wall and Pringle offer a similar agency cost argument related to the costs of monitoring insolvent firms.[11] These agency cost arguments appear to be quite reasonable and, in fact, can be viewed as special cases of our model, which looks at the general question of when a firm would find it desirable to allow the market to determine its credit premium on a short-term basis but to fix the risk-free component over the long-term.

---

[9] "Alternative Explanations of Interest Rate Swaps," April 1987.

[10] L. D. Wall, "Interest Rate Swaps in an Agency Theoretic Model with Uncertain Interest Rates," Working Paper No. 86-6, Federal Reserve Bank of Atlanta, July 1986.

[11] "Alternative Explanations of Interest Rate Swaps," April 1987.

Smith, Smithson, and Wakeman argue that, besides financial arbitrage (which cannot explain the continued growth of the market), there are three additional factors: management of rate exposure, tax and regulatory arbitrage, and market completion.[12] However, rate exposure can generally be better managed in other ways. Furthermore, as noted in these articles, tax and regulatory arbitrage do a better job of explaining the growth of the currency swap market than the growth of the interest rate swap market. In addition, the given explanation of tax arbitrage for interest rate swaps requires the firms make and receive swap payments on different days. In fact, most swaps involve only net payments, that is, a simultaneous exchange of payment, making the tax arbitrage scheme impossible. Finally, while swaps could be used to complete the interest rate forward markets, as the authors argue, most uses of the market do not involve establishing forward positions.[13] In the following sections a different market completion argument is advanced.

II. COMBINING RISK-FREE RATES AND CREDIT PREMIUMS PRIOR TO SWAPS

The borrower's cost of a long-term instrument can be thought of as consisting of four components: the risk-free rate, the risk premium associated with the future uncertainty of that rate, the credit premium attached to a specific borrower, and the risk premium associated with the future uncertainty of the credit premium. With a long-term instrument, both investors and borrowers have expectations of the future path of short-term risk-free rates. If the instrument is fixed-rate, the risk-free component (as well as all other components) is set over the life of the instrument. The cost of that compo-

---

[12] C. W. Smith, Jr., C. W. Smithson, and L. M. Wakeman, "The Evolving Market for Swaps," *Midland Corporate Finance Journal,* Winter 1986, pp. 20–32; "The Market for Interest Rate Swaps," 1986.

[13] L. D. Wall and J. J. Pringle, "Alternative Explanations of Interest Rate Swaps," Working Paper No. 87-2, Federal Reserve Bank of Atlanta (April 1987), present a comprehensive summary and critical evaluation of explanations for the existence of the interest rate swap market. They, too, find that the previous explanations are at best limited, with the possible exception of the agency cost argument.

nent in each period can be thought of as representing the lender's, or the market's, expectation of future one-period rates. Let us call this series of rates $r_{i,M}, i = 1, 2, \ldots n,$ where n is the term of the instrument. The borrower's expectations of interest rates, $r_{i,B,}$ may be different from the market's. With a fixed-rate instrument, even if the borrower's expectations are higher, it pays the lower market rate that is implicit in the fixed interest rate. However, with a floating-rate instrument, the series of risk-free rates that the borrower expects to pay is its own expectation, not the market's. This is true both with a term borrowing, such as a floating-rate note, or with a short-term loan that is continually rolled over.

Different participants value the uncertainty regarding the future course of short-term risk-free rates differently. These valuations are represented by a risk premium. On a fixed-rate instrument, the borrower pays the risk premium required by the market, $p_{i,M}^r,$ where the r superscript indicates that the premium is associated with the risk-free rate. However, again, on either a term floating-rate obligation or a series of short-term loans, the borrowers expect to pay their own valuation of the risk $p_{i,B}^r$ since they do not lock in the rate and instead subject themselves to the uncertainty.

With the third component of the borrowing cost, the credit premium specific to the borrower, there is a marked difference between floating-rate notes and series of short-term debt rollovers. On floating-rate notes, the credit risk premium is represented by a fixed markup over some risk-free rate, say the six-month Treasury bill rate.[14] Therefore, as in the case of fixed-rate borrowing, the credit spread is locked in at the market's level of expectations, $c_{i,M}.$ In contrast, on a series of short-term loans, the borrower does not lock in the credit spreads, and at the outset expects to pay its own set of credit premium expectations, $c_{i,B}.$

Similarly, the risk associated with the uncertainty of those future credit spreads is borne by the borrower on a series of short-term borrowings. The borrower, therefore, in this case expects to pay its own valuation of that risk, $p_{i,B}^c.$ However, on long-term fixed or floating-rate debt, the borrower shifts the risk to the

---

[14] The base rate on many floating rate notes is LIBOR, which is not a risk-free rate. This case is investigated in the final section.

lender, who requires a premium, $p_{i,M}^c$, that is incorporated in the interest rate.

The total cost of borrowing a dollar using fixed-rate, floating-rate, and short-term debt for a term of n periods can be represented as follows:

fixed-rate debt,

$$K_L = (1 + r_L)^n - 1$$
$$= \prod_{i=1}^{n} (1 + r_{i,M} + p_{i,M}^r + c_{i,M} + p_{i,M}^c) - 1; \tag{1}$$

floating-rate (variable-rate) debt,

$$K_v = \prod_{i=1}^{n} (1 + r_{i,B} + p_{i,B}^r + c_{i,M} + p_{i,M}^c) - 1; \tag{2}$$

and short-term debt,

$$K_S = \prod_{i=1}^{n} (1 + r_{i,B} + p_{i,B}^r + c_{i,B} + p_{i,B}^c) - 1; \tag{3}$$

where r_L represents the fixed interest rate and P denotes the multiplicative product operator.

Note that the essential differences among the three instruments are in the way that they combine fixed and floating risk-free rates and credit premiums. Fixed-rate debt fixes all the components, floating-rate debt fixes the credit spread while allowing the risk-free rate to float and short-term debt allows both the risk-free rate and the credit spread to float. The borrower would choose the instrument with the lowest total expected cost. If, for example, the borrower expected its future credit spreads to be lower than the market expected, then, *ceteris paribus,* it would choose short-term debt. On the other hand, if the borrower expected higher risk-free interest rates than did the market, then, *ceteris paribus,* it would choose fixed-rate debt.

The completion of possibilities accomplished with the introduction of swaps follows the same basic principles as the completion of securities markets in the seminal model of uncertainty developed by Arrow and Debreu.[15] The Arrow-Debreu result states

---

[15] K. J. Arrow, *"The Role of Securities in the Optimal Allocation of Risk-Bearing"* (Amsterdam: North Holland Press, 1970); G. Debreu, Theory of Value (New York: Wiley, 1959).

that if there are competitive markets in securities that have a positive monetary payoff in one and only one state of the world, and if there is one such security for each of the possible states, a pareto optimal distribution of risk-bearing may be achieved.[16]

The existence of the securities markets allows agents to divide their decision process into two parts. First, income is allocated to each state of the world. Second, once the true state is unveiled, the income is allocated to different commodities. In the absence of a complete set of markets, a nonoptimal distribution of risk-bearing will result.

While it is difficult to analyze the issue of swaps literally in this context, there is an immediate parallel in terms of the additional possibilities for the distribution of risk opened by the use of swaps. As argued in the following section, swaps enable borrowers to hedge fully their interest rate risk exposure, leaving the exposure to changes in their own credit premium fully unhedged. Using swaps in combination with other instruments, such as those discussed in this section, also makes it possible to hedge partially either the interest rate risk or the credit premium components of borrowing costs. Essentially, the existence of the swap market allows issuers to separate interest rate risk from credit risk and hedge the desired amount of each.

III. COMBINING RISK-FREE RATES AND CREDIT PREMIUMS USING SWAPS

To see how interest rate swaps, in combination with short-term debt, complete the possibilities, it is necessary to look at their cash flows. Suppose a borrower expects to borrow in the short-term debt market and swap floating for fixed payments with some part-

---

[16] It is assumed that there are also competitive commodities markets that operate normally once the state of the world is determined. The existence of the monetary securities, however, assures that an optimal solution is attainable without the need for markets in each commodity conditional upon each possible state of the world. That is, if there are m commodities and n states of the world, in the absence of securities there would be a need for $m \times n$ markets. With the securities, $m + n$ markets are needed.

ner. The expected cost in period i per dollar of the short-term debt would be

$$k_{i,s} = r_{i,B} + p^r_{i,B} + c_{i,B} + p^c_{i,B} \qquad (4)$$

The borrower would receive floating payments from its swap partner and make fixed payments. However, since no principal is exchanged, there is little cost of default, and both sides should be willing to execute at rates very close to risk free rates.[17] Therefore, the borrower would receive a floating rate with an expected cost of

$$k_{i,v} = r_{i,B} + p^r_{i,B}, \qquad (5)$$

and pay a fixed rate of

$$k_{i,f} = r_{i,M} + p^r_{i,M}. \qquad (6)$$

The net payment, $k_{i,swap}$, is then

$$
\begin{aligned}
k_{i,swap} &= k_{i,s} - k_{i,v} + k_{i,f} \\
&= r_{i,B} + p^r_{i,B} + c_{i,B} + p^c_{i,B} - (r_{i,B} + p^r_{i,B}) \\
&\quad + (r_{i,M} + p^r_{i,M}) \\
&= r_{i,M} + p^r_{i,M} + c_{i,B} + p^c_{i,B}. \qquad (7)
\end{aligned}
$$

By engaging in the swap, the borrower has thus replaced the floating risk-free rate components ($r_{i,B} + p^r_{i,B}$) in the short-term borrowing cost with fixed risk-free rate components ($r_{i,M} + p^r_{i,M}$). The borrower, then, is left with the fixed risk-free rate components, priced by the market, and variable credit spread components ($c_{i,B} + p^c_{i,B}$), to which the borrower attaches its own value.[18] The total borrowing cost of the combination swap and short-term debt is

$$K_{swap} = \overset{n}{\underset{i=1}{P}} (1 + r_{i,M} + p^r_{i,M} + c_{i,B} + p^c_{i,B}) - 1. \qquad (8)$$

---

[17] For an analysis of the risks involved in swaps, see M. Arak, L. Goodman, and F. Rones, "Defining Credit Exposure for Risk Management," *The Review of Research in Banking and Finance,* Winter 1987, pp. 60–72.

[18] Prior to swaps, a short-term borrower could have accomplished nearly the same thing by selling short a long-term Treasury security and buying a series of Treasury bills. However, this strategy has a number of disadvantages compared to swaps. First, it entails the additional transactions costs of periodic purchases of Treasury bills. Second, it requires the borrower to continually finance Treasury bills in the repurchase agreement (RP) market and

IV. CONDITIONS FOR SWAP PREFERENCE

Borrowers will prefer the combination of a swap and short-term debt to the alternatives if (and only if) its total cost, Equation 8, is less than the alternatives' costs, Equations 1–3. A sufficient condition for this is that the cost in each period is less than that of each of the alternatives, that is,

$$r_{i,M} + p^r_{i,M} + c_{i,B} + p^c_{i,B} < r_{i,M} + p^r_{i,M} + c_{i,M} + p^c_{i,M}, \tag{9}$$

$$r_{i,M} + p^r_{i,M} + c_{i,B} + p^c_{i,B} < r_{i,B} + p^r_{i,B} + c_{i,M} + p^c_{i,M}, \tag{10}$$

and

$$r_{i,M} + p^r_{i,M} + c_{i,B} + p^c_{i,B} < r_{i,B} + p^r_{i,B} + c_{i,B} + p^c_{i,B}. \tag{11}$$

This, in turn, will be true if, for $i = 1,2, \ldots ,n$, all of the following conditions hold:

1. The borrower's expectations of future risk-free rates are higher than the market's.
2. The borrower is more risk-averse than the market with respect to risk-free rates.
3. The borrower's expectations of its future credit spreads are lower than the market's.
4. The borrower is less risk averse than the market with respect to its credit spread.

Obviously, it is not necessary that all of the conditions hold simultaneously. For example, if Conditions 1 and 3 hold and the borrower's risk aversion is equal to that of the market, then the swap combination still dominates.[19]

---

borrow the long-term security in the RP market. However, the rate earned when one buys a security in the RP market is generally 20–40 basis points less than the rate one pays when selling a security, that is, there is an additional transaction cost of 20–40 basis points. Finally, the difference between the rates paid and received in the RP market is uncertain. At times, some securities go "on special," in which case the rate earned when buying the security in the RP market is far below other market rates. This adds considerable risk to this transaction.

[19] If interest rates were additive in the total cost function instead of multiplicative, then we could modify the requirement that Conditions hold for all i. Instead, it would be sufficient to require that they hold on average over the life of the instrument. For example, Condition 1 could be modified so that the borrower's average expected future risk-free rate was higher than the market's average expected rate.

As an illustration, consider the following two-period example. In the first period, the risk-free rate and the borrower's credit spread are known with certainty, so that

$$p_{1,M}^r = p_{1,B}^r = p_{1,M}^c = p_{1,B}^c = 0, \tag{12}$$
$$r_{1,M} = r_{1,B} = r_1, \tag{13}$$

and

$$c_{1,M} = c_{1,B} = c_1 \tag{14}$$

Let

$$r_1 = .06, \tag{15}$$
$$r_{2,M} = .06, \tag{16}$$
$$r_{2,B} = .07, \tag{17}$$
$$c_1 = .02, \tag{18}$$
$$c_{2,M} = .03, \tag{19}$$
$$c_{2,B} = .02, \tag{20}$$
$$p_{2,M}^r = p_{2,M}^c = 0, \tag{21}$$
$$p_{2,B}^r = p_{2,B}^c = 0; \tag{22}$$

then,

$$K_L = (1 + .06 + 0 + .02 + 0)(1 + .06 + 0 + .03 + 0) - 1$$
$$= .1772, \tag{23}$$
$$K_v = (1 + .06 + 0 + .02 + 0)(1 + .07 + 0 + .03 + 0) - 1$$
$$= .1880, \tag{24}$$
$$K_s = (1 + .06 + 0 + .02 + 0)(1 + .07 + 0 + .02 + 0) - 1$$
$$= .1772; \tag{25}$$

and

$$K_{swap} = (1 + .06 + 0 + .02 + 0)(1 + .06 + 0 + .02 + 0) - 1$$
$$= .1664. \tag{26}$$

Therefore, the swap, measured in future dollars, would cost 0.0108 less per dollar of principal than its nearest competitors (fixed-rate and short-term financing) over the life of the security, or about 50 basis points on an annually compounded basis.

To this point, it has been assumed that the borrower of short-term funds (who swaps into fixed) receives the entire benefit from the swap (i.e., the 50 basis points per year in our example). If it is assumed that the counterparty (the payer of floating) has "market" expectations and valuations of risk, then the counterparty is indifferent between the swap and some other instrument since the swap is being executed at "market" prices for each of the parameters. In general, though, the benefit from the swap could be divided any way between the counterparties—the short-term borrower would be willing to pay the counterparty up to 50 basis points per year in the example to enter into the swap.

In the swap market, this distribution of the benefit is seen in the terms of the swap. Generally, the swap is not executed at the risk-free rates, as we have assumed. Instead, the payer of fixed generally pays the risk-free fixed rate plus some spread, which varies from swap to swap over time depending on supply and demand conditions. The meaning of that swap spread, however, depends on whether the base rate on the floating-rate side of the swap is really a risk-free rate, such as the six-month Treasury bill rate or, as is often the case, a rate that is not risk-free, such as LIBOR.

If the floating rate was risk-free, then the variable rate received by the borrower in period i would be, as before,

$$k_{i,v} = r_{i,B} + p_{i,B}^r, \tag{27}$$

and the fixed payments would be

$$k_{i,f} = r_{i,M} + p_{i,M}^r + d_{i,M}, \tag{28}$$

where $d_{i,M}$ is the swap spread.

For the borrower who swaps into fixed payments, then, the net cost of the swap is

$$\begin{aligned} k_{i,swap} &= k_{i,s} - k_{i,v} + k_{i,f} \\ &= r_{i,M} + p_{i,M}^r + c_{i,B} + p_{i,B}^c + d_{i,M} \end{aligned} \tag{29}$$

The counterparty's net cost of borrowing in the long-term market and swapping into floating would be[20]

$$\begin{aligned} k_{i,swap}^t &= k_{i,L} + k_{i,v} - k_{i,f} \\ &= r_{i,M} + p_{i,M}^r + c_{i,M} + p_{i,M}^c + r_{i,M} + p_{i,M}^r \\ &\quad - (r_{i,M} + p_{i,M}^r + d_{i,M}) \\ &= r_{i,M} + p_{i,M}^r + c_{i,M} + p_{i,M}^c - d_{i,M}. \end{aligned} \tag{30}$$

---

[20] Note that the cost in the swap of the floating rate component $(k_{i,v})$ to the counterparty is valued using the market's valuations. This stems from the assumptions that the counterparty has market expectations and market valuations of risk. This was assumed for ease of exposition.

In the two-period example, if $d_{i,M} = .003$ for $i = 1, 2$, then the counterparty gains 30 basis points from the swap and the short-term borrower (the payer of fixed in the swap) gains 20 basis points.

In the case where the floating rate in the swap is LIBOR, the situation is a little more complicated. Let $1_{i,B}$ be the borrower's expectations of the credit premium implicit in LIBOR in period i. Then for the receiver of LIBOR in the swap,

$$k_{i,v} = r_{i,B} + p^r_{i,B} + 1_{i,B},\qquad(31)$$

$$k_{i,f} = r_{i,M} + p^r_{i,M} + d_{i,M},\qquad(32)$$

where, again, $d_{i,M}$ is the stated swap spread. Therefore, the net cost to this borrower is

$$k_{i,swap} = r_{i,M} + p^r_{i,M} + c_{i,B} + p^c_{i,B} + (d_{i,M} - 1_{i,B}),\qquad(33)$$

where $(d_{i,m} - 1_{i,B})$ is the true expected swap spread. For the counterparty,

$$k_{i,swap} = r_{i,M} + p^r_{i,M} + c_{i,M} + p^c_{i,M} - (d_{i,M} - 1_{i,M}),\qquad(34)$$

where $1_{i,M}$ is the market's (and by assumption, the counterparty's) expectation of the credit premium in LIBOR and $(d_{i,M} - 1_{i,M})$ measures the net gain from the swap to the counterparty.

V. SUMMARY

Swaps enable borrowers to fix the risk-free interest rate while allowing the credit spread to fluctuate from period to period. Some borrowers, especially those that are particularly pessimistic about future risk-free rates but optimistic about their own credit standing, would find that borrowing in the short-term market and swapping into fixed payments would be the preferred financing instrument. Finally, the expected cost saving from the swap would be split between the counterparties, depending on supply and demand conditions.

BIBLIOGRAPHY

Arak, M; L. Goodman; and A. Rones. "Defining Credit Exposure for Risk Management Products." *The Review of Research in Banking and Finance,* Winter 1987, pp. 60–72.

Arrow, K. J. "The Role of Securities in the Optimal Allocation of Risk-Bearing." In *Essays in the Theory of Risk-Bearing* (Originally published in France, 1953.)

Beidleman, C. R. *Financial Swaps.* Homewood, Ill.: Dow Jones-Irwin, 1985, pp. 214–18.

Bicksler, J. and A. H. Chen. "An Economic Analysis of Interest Rate Swaps." *Journal of Finance,* July 1986, pp. 645-55.

Debreu, G. *Theory of Value.* New York: Wiley, 1959.

Hakansson, N. "Welfare Aspects of Options and Supershares." *Journal of Finance,* June 1978, pp. 759–76.

Smith, C. W., Jr.; C. W. Smithson; and L. M. Wakeman. "The Evolving Market for Swaps." *Midland Corporate Finance Journal,* Winter 1986, pp. 20–32.

———. "The Market for Interest Rate Swaps." Working Paper Series No. MERC 86-04. University of Rochester, 1986.

Turnbull, S. M. "Swaps: A Zero Sum Game." *Financial Management,* Spring 1987, pp. 15–22.

Wall, L. D. "Interest Rate Swaps in an Agency Theoretic Model with Uncertain Interest Rates." Working Paper No. 87-2, Federal Reserve Bank of Atlanta, July 1986.

Wall, L. D. and J. J. Pringle. "Alternative Explanations of Interest Rate Swaps." Working Paper No. 87-2, Federal Reserve Bank of Atlanta, April 1987.

PART 2

APPLICATIONS OF SWAPS

CHAPTER 7

CAPITAL MARKET APPLICATIONS OF INTEREST RATE SWAPS

Laurie S. Goodman
Eastbridge Capital
New York, New York

As a result of the high and volatile interest rates of the early 1980s, firms began to emphasize active management of their liabilities as well as their assets. Issuers started to realize that the type of debt used and its maturity could make a considerable difference in their funding costs. At the same time, a number of new risk management products—futures, options, swaps, and caps—made it possible for firms to manage their liabilities more actively. Firms began to understand that debt could be transformed to take advantage of changing market conditions: Rates on floating debt could be fixed via futures or swaps, floating-rate debt could be capped, fixed rates could be transformed into floating rates, and issuers could hedge the cost of a new issuance by fixing or capping the rate. Moreover, corporate treasurers realized the cheapest way to issue a given variety of debt was not always the most straightforward. Issuers might find an opportunity to issue their initial debt offering more cheaply in one form than in other, perhaps ultimately more desirable, configurations. By using risk management products, they could transform the debt into the more desired form for an all-in cost lower than issuing directly in the desired form.

In this chapter, we consider some of the liability management or capital markets applications of one of the most important risk management products: interest rate swaps.

Swaps can have three purposes in liability management:

  a. Reducing the cost of current issuance.
  b. Locking in the cost or spread on a future issuance.
  c. Altering the cash flows on an existing liability.

Here we examine how interest rate swaps can be used for each of these purposes. To give a flavor of the versatility of interest rate swaps, we focus on new products and applications.

The interest rate swap market has contributed significantly to furthering the integration of the debt markets. While floating debt plus a swap may, at times, be cheaper than fixed debt, the disparities are not nearly as large as they were five years ago. Many of the applications looked at here are "window of opportunity" arbitrages that appear from time to time, but currently may not be generating transactions. Other applications may be used more frequently.[1]

I. REDUCING THE COST OF A NEW ISSUANCE

Issuers commonly use the swap market to reduce their borrowing costs. Via the swap market, a firm can obtain its desired financing at a lower cost than issuing the desired debt directly. For example, if a firm wants to issue fixed-rate noncallable debt, it has at least five alternatives:

  1. Issue the fixed-rate debt directly.
  2. Issue floating-rate debt and swap the floating-rate debt into fixed-rate debt.
  3. Issue callable fixed-rate debt and enter into a callable swap or write a swap option, or swaption.
  4. Issue putable fixed-rate debt and enter into a putable swap.

---

[1] The chapter considers the economics of various swap transactions. It does not consider tax and accounting issues. An issuer would want to take these into account before making a final decision as to the form the debt will take.

5. Issue a nonconventional instrument and enter into a swap to obtain the equivalent of a fixed-rate bond.

Exhibit 1 illustrates each of these funding strategies, and others. For instance, to obtain our fixed-rate noncallable debt (Row 2), any of the original debt issues (top row) can be transformed by adding the features of the call that intersects the applicable column and Row 2. Thus, callable fixed-rate debt (top row, Column 3) can be transformed into noncallable fixed-rate debt (Row 2) by writing a callable swap or entering into a swaption (Column 3, Row 2). The X indicates no transformation is necessary; the debt is in the desired form. Each of these alternatives will be discussed within this chapter. The reader may want to make repeated references to this exhibit.

The choice between the five alternatives outlined above will depend primarily on which is cheapest for the issuer. In all cases, the issuer will end up with fixed-rate noncallable debt. Astute issuers will generally check out all available alternatives to ensure that they achieve the cheapest funding for fixed-rate noncallable debt. In other words, the issuers should examine all of the alternatives across Row 2 to be sure of selecting the lowest-cost means to this method of funding.

In addition, many issuers will want to investigate other available funding opportunities, bearing in mind the consequences of the necessary trade-offs. For example, issuers would undoubtedly want to examine the cost of issuing fixed-rate noncallable debt versus the cost of issuing callable fixed-rate debt in order to evaluate the cost of the right to call the debt. They would want to see how much issuing a put bond might lower the required coupon on an issue. In terms of Exhibit 1, after finding the lowest-cost funding method in each row, issuers will also want to compare the various rows as alternative financing strategies. Thus, an issuer interested in ending up with fixed-rate debt should compare the least-cost entry in Row 2 with Rows 1, 3, 4, and 5.

As we proceed in this chapter, we first will investigate the various ways to create straight fixed-rate debt with no embedded options. Then we will investigate ways to create floating-rate debt, callable fixed-rate debt, and putable fixed-rate debt. The techniques discussed have all been used repeatedly in the market, al-

EXHIBIT 1
Using Swaps and Swaptions to Transform Debt

Transformed Debt	Original Debt				
	(1) Floating rate	*(2)* Fixed-rate Noncallable Nonputable	*(3)* Callable Fixed-Rate Debt	*(4)* Putable Fixed-Rate Debt	*(5)* Nonconventional
1. Floating-rate debt	X	Vanilla swap	Callable swap	Putable swap	FROG + yield curve swap
2. Fixed-rate noncallable nonputable debt	Vanilla swap	X	Callable swap + vanilla swap or swaption	Putable swap + vanilla swap	Inverse floater + vanilla swap **or** FROG + yield curve swap + vanilla swap
3. Callable fixed-rate debt	Swaption + vanilla swap	Swaption	X	Not economical	Not economical
4. Putable fixed-rate debt	Swaption + vanilla swap	Swaption	Two swaptions	X	Not economical
5. Nonconventional debt	Not economical	Not economical	Not economical	Not economical	X

This exhibit shows how swaps can transform one type of debt to another. The original form of the debt is given in the columns, the transformed debt in the rows. The entry in the cell shows the swap requirements that are necessary to accomplish the transformation. Thus, callable fixed-rate debt (Column 3) can be transformed into floating-rate debt (Row 1) via a callable swap (Column 3, Row 1). An X indicates no transformation is necessary. "Not economical" means the transformation has never made sense economically—the transformed debt has never been cheaper than the original.

though they may not always be appropriate for existing market conditions at a particular time.

Creating Synthetic Optionless Fixed-Rate Debt

The interest rate swap market provides a variety of ways to create noncallable fixed-rate debt using original debt of another form. We refer to debt for which the final form is different from its original form as *synthetic* debt. Synthetic fixed-rate debt is most often created in one of two ways: (*a*) When the original bond is a floater, a conventional, or "vanilla," swap is introduced; or (*b*) when the original bond is callable, a callable swaption is sold. Less frequent variations include putable bonds and nonconventional bonds as the original underlying instrument.

Transforming Floating-Rate Debt into Synthetic Fixed-Rate Debt

Firms with credit ratings lower than AA often find that they can achieve cheaper fixed-rate financing by using floating-rate debt plus a swap than by using a conventional fixed-rate issuance. This is because there is often a difference in the relative credit spread between the fixed-rate market and the floating-rate market. Firms with a lower credit rating often pay a smaller spread over a more highly rated borrower in the floating market than in the fixed market.

To illustrate how a swap can be used to take advantage of this circumstance, assume that an issuing firm would have to pay a fixed rate of 200 basis points (bp) over a 10-year Treasury (T_{10}). Alternatively, it could issue a floating rate note (FRN) at LIBOR + 50 bp. The swap rate that it faces is T_{10} + 70 bp. The firm could borrow via LIBOR-based financing and swap the proceeds for fixed at an interest rate equal to the 10-year Treasury + 70 bp. The firm would obtain synthetic fixed financing of T_{10} + 120 bp, calculated as follows:

Instrument	Action	Cash Flow
FRN	Firm pays	LIBOR + 50 bp
Swap	Firm receives	(LIBOR)
	Firm pays	T_{10} + 70 bp
Synthetic fixed	Net payment	T_{10} + 120 bp

This net payment should be compared with an original fixed-rate issuance of T_{10} + 200 bp. The net saving is 80 bp.

If the firm issues a floating-rate note as illustrated above, the payment on the synthetic fixed-rate instrument is locked in. Often, however, the firm chooses to issue floating-rate debt in which the credit spread is reset each period. Examples of this include short-term issuance in the Euromarket and commercial paper market. In these instances, the firm has not actually locked in a rate. However, for firms that do not expect credit spreads to widen significantly in the future, this is not a problem.

Transforming Callable Debt into Noncallable Debt Using Callable Swaps

Callable swaps are frequently used in conjunction with callable bonds in order to create synthetic noncallable debt. The reason: Bond investors demand less for the call option inherent in a callable bond than such an option will bring in the swap market. An issuer generally pays a slight premium to investors for the option to call the original bond after a stated period of time, say 10 years. In essence, the issuer has purchased a call option. He then is in a position to sell an equivalent call option but in the form of an option to call or terminate an interest rate swap. In this way, the issuer can obtain noncallable debt at a lower cost.

The mechanics of this transaction actually involve entering into two swaps, which can best be illustrated by means of a simple example. Say that a firm issues a 10-year note that can be called at par after 5 years. The note is sold to yield 10.20 percent. This option may add 20 bp to the cost of the debt. In other words, if the firm issued a noncallable bond, it would pay only 10.00 percent. But as we shall see, the issuer will ultimately be better off with the callable debt.

The firm next undertakes two transactions in the swap market. It enters into a callable swap—a swap with an option to call or terminate the swap after five years. The firm pays the floating rate and receives a fixed rate of 10.40 percent. The fixed rate on a vanilla swap is 10.00 percent. That is, the swap counterparty is willing to pay 40 bp per annum for the right to terminate the swap after five years. The swap counterparty will terminate the swap if rates decline—if it can enter into a new swap and pay less than

10.40 percent. Thus, the counterparty has purchased a call on the debt. The net effect is that the issuing firm pays a net floating rate of interest of LIBOR minus 20 bp. In order to transform the debt into fixed rate, the issuer can enter into a plain vanilla swap in which it agrees to receive floating and pay fixed. Assuming the fixed interest rate is 10.00 percent, the firm ends up with a net interest cost of 9.80 (10.20 percent on the bond less 10.40 percent on the swaption plus 10.00 percent on the vanilla swap), which is 20 bp less than it would have cost to issue the noncallable debt directly.

This series of transactions is illustrated in Exhibit 2. Let's also look at the transactions from the perspective of the issuer and the swap counterparty under different interest rate scenarios:

Scenario	Issuer	Swap Counterparty	Result
Interest rates are higher after five years.	No action on bond.	No action. Both swaps remain outstanding.	Issuer has ended up with 10-year fixed-rate money.
Interest rates are lower after five years.	Bond is called. Issuer funds floating.	Swap in which issuer pays floating and receives fixed is called. Swap in which issuer pays fixed and receives floating remains outstanding.	Issuer has ended up with 10-year fixed-rate money.

Thus, a callable swap is simply a swap in which the fixed payer (the counterparty) has the right of early termination without penalty. In either scenario, the issuer has achieved 10-year fixed-rate financing.

Other variants of this structure are, of course, possible. For example, rather than receiving 10.40 percent per annum on the callable swap, the bond issuer could receive 10 percent plus 2.00 percent to 2.25 percent as an up-front fee. In this case, the firm is

EXHIBIT 2
Using Callable Swaps to Create Synthetic Noncallable Debt

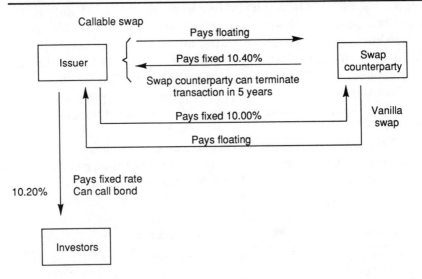

paying the same 10.20 percent to issue debt as initially, but has traded away its call option for a fee of 2.00 percent to 2.25 percent of the par value of the bond.

The major point about callable swaps is that they can be used to create synthetic noncallable debt that costs the issuer less than noncallable debt issued directly in the market.

Transforming Callable Debt into Noncallable Debt Using Swaptions

Thus far we have discussed how to achieve fixed-rate financing by transforming callable debt into noncallable debt using callable swaps. The same result can be achieved using swaptions. A swaption is an option providing a counterparty the right, but not the obligation, to enter into an interest rate swap at a future date. A callable bond and a swaption can be used to create fixed-rate funding to the call date and synthetic fixed-rate financing from the call date to the maturity date. The issuer is again able to take advantage of the fact that the call feature is priced more cheaply by the bond market than by the swap market.

In order to create five-year noncallable debt, this funding technique uses callable debt with a final maturity of five years and a *back-end fixed* swaption, or in other words, an option to enter into a swap to pay fixed and receive floating from the call date to the maturity date for five years on the notional amount of the debt. Alternatively, an issuer could facilitate the funding by issuing longer-maturity (10-year) debt with a call in 5 years and a *back-end floating* swaption to enter into a swap to pay floating and receive fixed for the balance of the 10-year maturity. Using a back-end fixed swaption simply means that the issuer pays fixed and receives floating if the swaption is exercised. With a back-end floating swaption, the issuer pays floating and receives fixed.

Let's look at an example of callable debt and a back-end fixed swaption. Assume an issuer wants five-year fixed-rate funding. It can be created by issuing a five-year bond, callable at par after three years, and selling a back-end fixed swaption. This swaption provides the buyer the option to enter into a two-year interest rate swap commencing in three years. The back-end fixed swaption would commit the issuer to pay fixed and receive floating if desired by the counterparty. We show the results below:

Scenario	Swap	Issuer	Result
Interest rates are higher after three years.	The swaption is not exercised.	The issuer does not call the bond.	Issuer has five-year fixed-rate money.
Interest rates are lower after three years.	The swaption is exercised. The issuer pays fixed and receives floating for years four and five.	The issuer calls the bond and funds floating for years four and five.	Issuer has five-year fixed-rate money.

Note that in both cases, the issuer has achieved five-year fixed-rate money.

An issuer can also obtain noncallable debt by issuing a 10-year note callable at par after five years and selling a back-end floating swaption. This swaption would allow the buyer the option to enter into a five-year swap, commencing in five years. The back-end floating swaption would commit the issuer to pay floating and receive fixed. Here are the results under the two interest rate scenarios:

Scenario	Swap	Issuer	Results
Interest rates are higher after five years.	The swaption is exercised. The issuer pays floating and receives fixed from Years 6–10.	The issuer does not call the bond.	Issuer has five-year fixed-rate money. Over Years 6–10, the issuer has floating money.
Interest rates are lower after five years.	The swaption is not exercised.	Issuer calls the bond.	Issuer has five-year fixed-rate money.

Again, the issuer has achieved fixed-rate funding for five years under either interest rate scenario.

One advantage of this structure is that if the swaption is exercised, and the issuer does not call the bond, he still has the call option. That is, the swaption does not extinguish the call on the bond. This option can be exercised if rates move down in the future.

The choice between these alternatives will depend on how cheap the embedded call option is vis-à-vis the back-end fixed swaption, the back-end floating swaption, and the callable swap. Again, in these examples, we are assuming that the issuer is interested in achieving the lowest possible funding cost on the synthetic noncallable debt.

Transforming Putable Debt into Optionless Debt

Putable swaps, like callable swaps, are used by issuers wanting to issue noncallable debt as cheaply as possible. With a put bond the investor purchases the right to put the bond back to the issuing firm. If interest rates rise, the investor may well want to exercise this option. For example, assume a firm issues a 10 percent 10-year bond with a put after 5 years. If after five years rates had risen to 12 percent, the investor would put the bond back to the issuer and reinvest at the 12 percent rate. Naturally, from an investor's perspective, a 12 percent reinvestment rate is preferable to the 10 percent rate implicit in the bond. If rates fall, the put bond remains outstanding. However, investors are often willing to pay more for the put feature than the theoretical price of the option.

A put bond can be used in conjunction with a putable swap to create inexpensive noncallable debt. With a put bond, the issuer writes an option. The issuer can then buy a putable swap to negate the exposure created by the put in the bond. This would be done only if the issuer can realize more by selling the put option on the bond than must be paid for the put on the swap purchased.

This funding strategy is achieved by using two swaps, as illustrated in Exhibit 3. In the putable swap the issuer receives a fixed rate and pays a floating rate. The fixed rate the issuer receives is lower than on a vanilla swap, reflecting the fact that the issuer can terminate the swap if rates rise. The issuer will terminate the swap if it can receive a higher rate than 9.60 percent at the expiration of the option—in other words, if interest rates have risen. The vanilla swap converts the then-floating rate payments of LIBOR less 10 bp into fixed payments. The issuer pays an effective interest rate on the noncallable, nonputable debt of 9.90 percent—9.50 percent on the bond less 9.60 percent on the swaption plus 10.00 percent on the vanilla swap. This is 10 bp cheaper than optionless debt with the same characteristics.

Under our alternative interest rate scenarios:

Scenario	Issuer	Swap Counterparty	Result
Interest rates are higher after five years.	Bond is put back to issuer.	Swap for issuer to pay floating and receive fixed is terminated. Swap for issuer to pay fixed and receive floating remains outstanding.	Issuer has 10-year fixed-rate money.
Interest rates are lower after five years.	No action.	Both swaps remain outstanding.	Issuer has 10-year fixed-rate money.

EXHIBIT 3
Using Putable Swaps to Create Synthetic Noncallable Debt

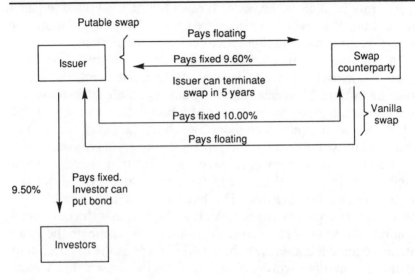

Note that a putable swap is a swap in which the fixed rate receiver (in this case, the issuer) has the option to walk away from the swap.

Creating optionless debt from put bonds is an arbitrage driven transaction—that is, it is done only if the optionless debt can be created synthetically more cheaply than it can be issued directly.

Transforming Nonconventional Debt: Inverse Floaters into Fixed-Rate Debt

Another, less frequently used method of obtaining fixed-rate financing is through the use of an inverse floating-rate security. An inverse floater is an instrument that pays a prespecified interest rate minus LIBOR. This is generally coupled with a swap in which the issuer receives fixed and pays floating.

We can illustrate this transaction with an example viewed from the issuer's perspective (see Exhibit 4). We assume the floater pays 19.50 percent minus LIBOR. The swap spread in this example would be T_{10} + 70 bp or 10.00 percent.

EXHIBIT 4
Synthetic Fixed Financing Using Inverse Floaters

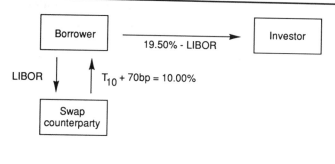

Borrower's net payments: 19.50% - LIBOR + LIBOR - 10.00% = 9.5%
bond   swap

The issuer's net payment is calculated as follows:

Instrument	Action	Cash Flow
Bond	Firm pays	19.50 percent − LIBOR
Swap	Firm receives	(10.00 percent)
	Firm pays	LIBOR
Synthetic fixed	Net payment	9.50 percent

Using an inverse floater plus a vanilla swap, the issuer has locked in a coupon payment of 9.5 percent. The coupon payments on a new fixed-rate issue would be 10.0 percent. Thus, the borrower has saved 50 bp over a traditional bond.

With this sort of funding strategy, a cap is necessary to protect against very high rates. Without a cap, if LIBOR happened to rise above 19.5 percent, the investor would owe the issuer money. Obviously, the issuer could not logistically collect from the investor. Thus, the issuer can buy a cap that will enable it to be paid if rates go above 19.50 percent. This cap is far out of the money, and the protection is very inexpensive.

This structure attracted a great deal of interest when introduced in 1986. Investors initially did not realize that it was equivalent to holding a long position in two fixed-rate bonds and a short position in a floating-rate instrument. Investors could easily re-create this position by purchasing a fixed-rate bond and entering into a swap in which the investor received fixed and paid floating. Investors showed interest in the security because they were con-vinced short rates would drop. When LIBOR rates fell, the coupon on an inverse floater increased. But once investors realized how easily this strategy could be replicated, it was priced fairly and there were no new issues.

Transforming Nonconventional Debt: FROGs into Fixed-Rate Debt

In addition to inverse floaters, there is one other type of noncon-ventional debt that has been transformed into fixed-rate debt: FROGs. These are floating-rate notes with coupons based on the 30-year Treasury rate, which can be reset semiannually or quar-terly. FROGs are generally paired with a yield curve swap in order to produce floating-rate debt. With a yield curve swap, floating payments are exchanged at two different points on the yield curve. This debt can then be transformed into fixed-rate debt via a vanilla swap.

To see how this works, assume that a firm issues a FROG. Say, for example, that this floating-rate note (FRN) pays the 30-year Treasury rate, reset every six months (UST), minus 115 bp. The issuer enters into a yield curve swap in which he pays six-month LIBOR and receives the 30-year Treasury rate, reset every six months, less a fixed spread (say, 105 bp). This is called a yield curve swap because floating-rate payments indexed to the short end of the market are being exchanged for floating-rate payments indexed to the long end of the yield curve. The issuer has essen-tially locked in floating-rate financing as shown below:

Instrument	Action	Cash Flow
FROG (FRN)	Firm pays	UST − 115 bp
Yield curve swap	Firm receives	(UST − 105 bp)
	Firm pays	LIBOR
Synthetic floating	Net payment	LIBOR − 10 bp

UST refers to the most recent 30-year U.S. Treasury bond rate. This rate is reset every six months.

This can be converted to fixed-rate payments by means of a vanilla swap in which the issuer pays the three-year Treasury rate (T_3) + 70 bp in exchange for LIBOR.

Instrument	Action	Cash Flow
Synthetic floating	See above	LIBOR − 10 bp
Vanilla swap	Firm receives	(LIBOR)
	Firm pays	T_3 + 70 bp
Synthetic fixed	Net payment	T_3 + 60 bp

FROGs initially were created because of a need to locate counterparties for yield curve swaps. Firms were enticed to issue FROGs and swap for LIBOR funding—a transaction that generated sub-LIBOR financing for the issuer.

FROGs were very popular investments in mid-1988 as a yield curve strategy—the average spread between 30-year Treasuries and LIBOR during 1983–87 was 125 bp. At 115 basis points (10 basis points less than historical levels), these notes became very attractive. Moreover, investors who preferred or were constrained to issue short-term securities were able to obtain a short-term reset off a long-term rate—a combination not previously available. Ex-post facto, FROGs have turned out not to be attractive investments. If the yield curve had steepened, FROGs would have performed well. However, with the yield curve flattening and inverting in 1989, FROGs have performed poorly, and no new issues have come to market since late 1988.

Creating Floating-Rate Debt

We now consider funding alternatives that will enable us to create synthetic floating-rate debt. The two most common alternatives are: (*a*) a fixed-rate optionless bond plus a vanilla swap and (*b*) a callable bond plus a callable swap. Less commonly used alternatives include put bonds, used in conjunction with a putable swap, and FROGs, used in conjunction with yield curve swaps. We examine each of these in turn.

Synthetic Floating Using Vanilla Swaps
Firms with well-known names and high credit ratings can often take advantage of very inexpensive fixed-rate financing in the

Eurobond market. In fact, many of these entities are foreign banks, which would actually prefer floating-rate financing. To see how an issuer might create synthetic floating-rate assets, we start by assuming that the firm is willing to pay only 50 bp over a 10-year Treasury (T_{10}) bond rate. The swap rate is LIBOR against $T_{10} + 70$ bp. Using the swap market, the firm can create synthetic floating-rate debt at LIBOR minus 20 bp. If the firm issued the debt directly, it would issue at LIBOR. This is illustrated below:

Instrument	Action	Cash Flow
Fixed-rate bond	Firm pays	$T_{10} + 50$ bp
Swap	Firm receives	($T_{10} + 70$ bp)
	Firm pays	LIBOR
Synthetic floating	Net payment	LIBOR − 20 bp

Thus, the firm ends up paying LIBOR minus 20 bp for its funds, 20 bp less than the cost of issuing new floating-rate debt at LIBOR flat.

Transforming Callable Debt into Floating-Rate Debt

Issuers can create synthetic floating-rate financing by using a callable bond and a callable swap. The rate on this financing will often be less than on a straight floating-rate issue because the issuer is able to purchase a call option from investors (the call option that is embedded in the debt) for substantially less then the swap market is willing to pay for the call option.

The mechanics of this transaction are similar to those described in the previous section for transforming callable debt into noncallable debt. The firm issues callable debt and enters into a callable swap. This is illustrated in Exhibit 2; the difference in this case is that there is no vanilla swap.

Let us consider the payoffs of this combination under different scenarios. If rates are higher at the call date than they were at the issue date, neither the bond nor the swap will be called, and the issuer will obtain floating funding until maturity. If rates are lower at the call date than at issuance, the issuer will call the bond. The counterparty will terminate the swap. Thus, if rates go down the issuer will have floating money until the call date.

Thus, the issuer has issued floating-rate funding for a period either to call or to maturity. If issuance costs are lower, the issuer has locked in floating-rate debt for only the time until the call. If issuance costs go up, he locks in floating-rate money until maturity—a desirable situation.

Transforming Putable Debt into Floating-Rate Debt
Putable debt can be transformed into floating-rate debt by pairing a put bond with a putable swap. This is similar to transforming putable debt into optionless fixed-rate debt, as illustrated in Exhibit 3. In this case there is no need for the vanilla swap.

Let us now consider the payoffs of this combination under different scenarios. Assume a firm issues 10-year money, putable at the investor's option after Year 5. If rates turn out to be higher at the put date than at the issue date, the bond will be put, and the swap in which the issuer pays floating and receives fixed will be terminated. The issuer can raise new floating-rate money during Years 6–10 at par. Thus, the issuer has floating money over the 10-year period. If rates decline, the bond remains outstanding and the swap remains outstanding. The net result here also: floating-rate money over the 10-year period.

Transforming Nonconventional FROGs into Floating-Rate Debt
FROGs frequently are transformed into floating-rate rather than fixed-rate debt. This is done by pairing a FROG with a yield curve swap. The issuer pays the long-term Treasury rate less a spread on the FROG. Again, the long-term rate is reset every six months. The issuer then enters into a yield curve swap in which it pays six month LIBOR and receives the long-term Treasury rate, reset every six months, less a spread. To further transform the FROG into fixed-rate debt, a vanilla swap is added, as discussed in a previous section.

Creating Callable Debt

Generally, issuers who have access to the U.S. long-term fixed-rate debt markets have not found it economical to replicate callable debt. However, certain issuers, such as U.S. savings and loan associations, have been unable to borrow economically in these markets. These issuers have, on occasion, used the swap market to transform fixed- and floating-rate debt into long-term callable debt. In other instances, issuers lacking access to the corporate market prefer instead to issue debt via a medium-term note strategy, with which they can bring a small issue or an odd amount to market. (Medium term notes are noncallable.)

Long-term callable debt can be created from long-term fixed-rate debt (noncallable) by purchasing a back-end floating swaption. If rates decline, the swap will be activated and the issuer will pay floating and receive fixed. Consider an issuer of five-year noncallable debt that has purchased a back-end floating swaption for years four and five. If rates remain high, the issuer will have five-year debt. If rates decline, the issuer will have three-year fixed-rate debt.

Floating-rate debt can be transformed into fixed-rate debt via a vanilla swap. A back-end floating swaption can then be purchased to make the debt callable.

To reiterate, creating synthetic callable debt has been done primarily by issuers that do not have access to the U.S. domestic corporate debt market. This is because investors are willing to write call options at a lower price than they can be sold for in the swap market. Stated differently, the volatility that is implicit in the price of the call attached to the bond is lower than the volatility in the swaptions market.

Creating Putable Debt

We now consider a synthetic alternative to a put bond issued in the marketplace. The most common synthetic put bond is constructed as a combination of a callable bond, a back-end fixed, and a back-end floating swaption. The issuer comes to market with a callable bond. The swap counterparty has a one-time right either (*a*) to make the issuer pay the fixed rate versus receiving floating (back-end fixed swaption) or (*b*) to make the issuer receive fixed (back-end floating swaption) and pay floating.[2] The swap counterparty has purchased two options—one counteracts the embedded option on the call, and the other creates the put that is inherent in the putable bond.

---

[2] The floating rate can be either LIBOR or commercial paper.

Let us use the example of a five-year issue, callable in three years. At the end of three years the results under alternative interest rate scenarios are shown below:

Scenario	Swap	Issuer	Result
Interest rates rise higher after three years.	Issuer caused to receive fixed and pay floating for Years 4 and 5.	No action.	Issuer has ended up with three-year fixed followed by two-year floating-rate money
Interest rates are lower after three years.	Issuer caused to pay fixed and receive floating for two years.	Issuer calls issue, funds floating-rate at market.	Issuer has ended up with five-year fixed-rate money

As with a regular put bond, if rates fall the issuer has ended up with five-year fixed-rate money. If rates rise the issuer has ended up with three years of fixed funding and two years of floating funding.

The major difference between a synthetic put bond and a real put bond is that with a synthetic put bond the issuer has to raise funds in the floating-rate market if rates fall. With a real put bond the issuer has to borrow in the floating-rate market if rates rise. This is important to some issuers—such as banks and finance companies—that are more concerned about funding in a higher-rate environment than in a lower-rate environment.

Note that the attractive economics of the synthetic put bond arise because the investors can write the call option relatively inexpensively. By contrast, swap counterparties will pay full value for that call and a further significant premium for the right to buy the put.

A less commonly used variation on the synthetic put bond has been done by issuing fixed-rate noncallable debt and selling a back-end fixed swaption. Assume the debt is issued for a five-year period, and the back-end fixed swaption can be exercised at the end of Year 3. The swaption will be exercised and the issuer will have received fixed and paid floating for Years 4 and 5 if rates are lower.

This transaction could also be done by transforming floating rate debt into fixed-rate debt via a five-year swap. It could be further transformed into a synthetic put bond via a back-end fixed option.

Synthetic put bonds are more commonly based on callable debt than on optionless debt. This is because the call inherent in the bond can be purchased cheaply in the debt market and sold more extensively in the swap market. Using optionless debt, this part of the arbitrage is not present.

II. LOCKING IN THE COST OF A FUTURE ISSUANCE

While the major use of swaps centers on altering the character of a current bond issue, issuers can apply strategies involving the swap market to anticipated future issuances, as well. For example, a firm that expects rates to rise may want to lock in a fixed cost on a future issuance via a forward swap. This is sometimes also called a delayed-start swap. A firm that expects interest rates to remain steady or decline while credit spreads widen may wish to lock in a generic credit spread via a spread lock. We examine each of these in turn.

Forward Swaps

A forward swap is exactly like a regular interest rate swap transaction, except that the accruals begin on a future date—normally, the expected date of the bond issuance. A forward swap is usually used in conjunction with a floating-rate issuance in order to lock in a fixed rate.

Consider the following example. A firm enters into a three-month forward swap agreeing to pay the current five-year Treasury rate + 75 bp. In return, the firm will receive six-month LIBOR. The notional amount of the swap will be the same as that of the anticipated debt issue. In three months the firm issues floating-rate debt. Six months after the issuance, the first payments are exchanged. The firm pays the fixed rate available at the time the swap was entered into and receives six-month LIBOR. The LIBOR payment is used to pay the interest on the floating-rate debt.

The net cost of the issuance will be the fixed rate on the swap plus the difference between six-month LIBOR and the floating rate at which the firm issues its debt. If the firm issues floating-rate debt at six-month LIBOR + 25 bp, its all-in funding cost will be T_5 + the 75 bp swap spread + the 25 bp margin on the floating-rate debt. Note that the only component not locked in is the margin on the floating-rate debt.

If the firm later issues floating-rate debt off a different index from LIBOR, it can realize cost savings but will incur basis risk. If, for example, the firm issues floating-rate debt at the commercial paper rate, the cost of funds to the firm will be less than the five-year Treasury yield plus 75 bp, reflecting the fact that the commercial paper rate is below LIBOR.

Forward swaps are most attractive for issuers that like the current level of interest rates and expect a rate increase in the future, but that do not currently need funding. Entering into a forward swap locks in the rate without forcing the issuer to fund immediately.

Spread Locks

A spread lock allows an issuer to fix the credit spread without fixing the base rate. Thus, a spread lock can be viewed as a tool to hedge the general level of corporate spreads. A spread lock is most effective when a firm knows it will have to come to market within a relatively short time—two or three months.

In a spread lock, the issuer agrees to enter into a swap deal at a specified spread to Treasuries but delays fixing the absolute rate for a period ranging up to two or three months. In other words, the issuer must fix the absolute rate by the end of the period, but may choose when to fix the rate within that period. When the base rate is fixed, the prespecified swap spread is added to arrive at the fixed rate payable on the swap. If Treasury rates fall over near term, the firm is able to take advantage of the decline.

To see how a spread lock would work, assume that a firm wants a spread lock for the next two months. At the end of the two-month period—or earlier if Treasury rates look attractive in the interim—the firm issues floating rate debt and takes down the swap, in which it pays fixed and receives floating. Assume that the fixed swap spread is 80 bp and its issuing rate is LIBOR + 25 bp. The firm will, on net, pay the Treasury rate prevailing at the time the swap is taken down plus 105 bp (80 + 25).

A spread lock is typically offered at a 2–4 bp premium over the straight swap. The premium exists because the swap counterparty will short Treasury securities and invest the proceeds in short-term instruments until the swap is taken down. The negative carry during the hedge period is figured into the quoted spread. Thus, 150 bp of negative carry for two months is $0.25 per $100 par, or 2.5 bp for a seven-year issue.

A spread lock will be used if the firm expects interest rates to decline, but is concerned that credit spreads may widen. Issuers should note that the spread lock does not hedge *their* credit spread, but rather a generic credit spread.

III. ALTERING THE CASH FLOWS ON AN EXISTING LIABILITY

Issuers can also use swaps to alter the cash flow on an existing liability in a variety of ways: (*a*) by entering into a swap in order to fix the payment on an existing floating liability, (*b*) by entering into a swap in order to turn an existing fixed-payment security into a floating-rate liability, and (*c*) by entering into a forward swap in order to lock in attractive interest rates after the call date on existing debt with in-the-money call options. We discuss each of these in turn.

Fixing a Payment on a Floating-Rate Issue

A firm can convert a floating-rate issuance into a fixed-rate instrument by using a swap in which the issuer receives floating and pays fixed. The fixed rate is the then-prevailing fixed rate. Thus, when interest rate levels look attractive and seem likely to rise, a firm that initially issued floating can lock in a fixed rate through the use of the swap market.

Converting an Existing Fixed-Rate Bond into a Floating-Rate Instrument

Similarly, a firm that has initially issued fixed-rate debt can also convert that debt to floating rate through the use of the swap market. In this instance, the firm pays floating and receives fixed. If market rates have changed, the fixed rate at which the firm issued the debt is different from the prevailing fixed rate. The firm can either receive the fixed rate prevailing in the swap market, or match its own funding cost via an up-front payment if rates have declined or via an up-front receipt if rates have risen. We should note that this is *not* a way for the firm to escape high coupon debt in a declining rate environment. It is, however, a way for the firm to benefit from an expected *future* reduction in rates.

To give an example, we assume that three years ago a firm issued fixed-rate 10-year noncallable debt at 11 percent. The firm now wishes to convert this debt to floating-rate debt, in anticipation that future interest rates will be even lower than current rates. The swap market is such that the firm currently would have to pay LIBOR and receive 70 bp over the rate on seven-year Treasury notes (T_7 + 70 bp, or 9.70 percent). If the firm entered into a market swap, its cash flows would be as follows:

Instrument	Action	Cash Flow
Bond	Firm pays	11.00 percent
Swap	Firm receives	(9.70 percent)
	Firm pays	LIBOR
Synthetic floater	Net payment	LIBOR + 130 bp

Note that the firm is paying LIBOR + 130 bp. The large increment over LIBOR reflects the fact that the firm has above-market (11 percent) noncallable debt outstanding. It cannot escape this obligation. If rates decline further, however, the LIBOR financing will prove more attractive than the fixed-rate financing. If rates increase, the reverse will be true.

Alternatively, the firm could enter into an off-market swap in which it pays an up-front amount in order to pay LIBOR and receive 11 percent on the swap. The up-front payment would reflect the 130 bp per annum, capitalized into an up-front sum, as shown below.

Instrument	Action	All-in Cost per Annum
Bond	Firm pays	11.00 percent
Swap	Firm receives	(11.00 percent)
	Firm pays	LIBOR
	Firm pays $6.50 up front	130 bp
Synthetic floater	Net payment	LIBOR + 130 bp

Note the present value of the all-in costs is roughly the same if the firm accepts a market swap or an off-market swap.

If rates have risen and the issuer is convinced they have peaked, it may want to swap an outstanding fixed-rate issue into a floating-rate obligation. This allows the issuer to benefit from lower rates in the future. The issuer could opt for a swap at market rates, or opt for an off-market swap in which it accepts a below-market rate on the swap plus an up-front payment.

To give an example, let's assume that 3 years ago a firm had issued 8.00 percent debt for 10 years. In the swap market, this firm could pay LIBOR and receive $T_7 + 70$ bp, or 9.70 percent. If the firm agreed to a swap at now-current rates, its cash flows would be as follows:

Instrument	Action	Cash Flow
Bond	Firm pays	8.00 percent
Swap	Firm receives	(9.70 percent)
	Firm pays	LIBOR
Synthetic floater	Net payment	LIBOR − 170 bp

The net payment of LIBOR minus 170 bp reflects the fact that the firm had below-market debt on its books.

If the firm wanted an off-market swap, the all-in cost would be as follows:

Instrument	Action	All-in Cost
Bond	Firm pays	8.00 percent
Swap	Firm receives	(8.00 percent)
	Firm pays	LIBOR
	Firm receives $8.50 up front	(170 bp)
Synthetic floater	Net payment	LIBOR − 170 bp

In both cases, the firm's all-in cost is the same. With an off-the-market swap, the firm is compensated for accepting a below-market rate on the swap.

It is important to realize that converting fixed-rate debt to floating-rate debt should be done when rates are expected to fall. The issuer's rationale for such a move is to enable it to take advantage of further decreases in rates. Any fall or rise that has already occurred will be built into the price of the swap.

Locking in Attractive Interest Rates on Existing High-Coupon Debt

Forward swaps can be used to lock in future rates on existing callable debt. To see how this can be done, assume that a firm has 14.00 percent debt outstanding, originally issued in 1984. The debt matures in 10 years, or 1994. It is callable in 1991. If the notes were currently callable, the issuer would call the bonds and refinance with lower-cost debt. However, since the notes are not callable for some years, the company must leave the bonds outstanding until the call date and continue to pay the 14.00 percent coupon.

If the company feels that interest rates will rise by 1991 and eliminate some or all of the benefits of today's relatively low interest rates, the issuer can execute a forward swap. Essentially, this would lock in current forward rates. In other words, the firm can enter into a three-year swap two years forward in which it agrees to pay fixed and receive floating. We will assume here that the firm can lock in a 10 percent fixed rate on this swap.

This strategy leaves the company with a great deal of flexibility on the call date. If interest rates turn out to be lower than 14 percent on the call date, the firm *could* refinance on a floating-rate basis. The floating payments on the debt would be offset by payments on the swap. The firm's all-in cost would be the 10.0 percent fixed rate plus (minus) its issuing cost above (below) LIBOR.

If the firm wanted to refinance at a fixed rate, the forward swap could be sold. The cash settlement to (or by) the issuer will be equal to the present value of the difference between the forward rate swap and the market rate for new swaps with a three-year maturity. If rates turn out to be higher than 10 percent, the issuer will receive a payment. If rates prove to be lower than 10.0 percent, the issuer will pay the cash settlement from the sale of the swap.

There is a third alternative, as well. Say the firm wants to refinance with a fixed rate, but rates are lower and the issuer is reluctant to pay to buy out the forward swap. As an alternative, it could enter into an offsetting spot transaction. To see how this might work, assume the fixed rate is 9 percent, and the firm has locked in a 10 percent forward swap. The forward swap can be offset on the call date as follows:

Instrument	Action	Cash Flow
Original bond	Called	—
New bond	Firm pays	9.00 percent
Forward swap	Firms receives	(LIBOR)
	Firm pays	10.00 percent
New swap	Firm receives	(9.00 percent)
	Firm pays	LIBOR
Fixed + swap	Net payment	10.00 percent

Note that the firm has locked in the 10 percent rate. The rate on the new bond is 9.00 percent, and the 1 percent per annum loss on the forward swap is in the form of a higher net payment.

So far we have assumed that the interest rates on the call date are below 14 percent and that the issue will be called. The forward swap does not affect the company's flexibility to leave the issue outstanding if rates are above 14 percent on the call date. In this instance, if the issuer chooses to leave the issue outstanding, it could sell the forward swap. The windfall profit on the forward swap would be the difference between the then-current market rates and 10 percent for a three-year period. Thus, the forward swap locks in the intrinsic value of the call option. It does not, however, extinguish the option. And it can gain further value in the future if rates rise sufficiently.

A forward swap is useful in this context if the rates that are locked in on the swap are low, compared with an issuer's expectations about the future. If this is not the case, the issuer would want to wait before locking in rates.

CONCLUSION

In this chapter, we have examined the capital market applications of swaps. We have shown that swaps can be used to reduce the cost of a current issuance, to lock in the cost or spread on a future issuance, or to alter the cash flows on an existing liability.

Historically, most of the capital market applications of swaps have centered on reducing the cost of a current issue. Prior to the introduction of swaps, a firm had to issue debt in the ultimately desired form. There was no way to transform debt from callable to noncallable or from callable to putable.

With swaps, however, debt can be easily transformed from one form to another. Issuers can often obtain the desired form of debt synthetically at a lower cost than by a direct issuance. This is because the market allows issuers to take advantage of differential pricing between the new-issue bond market and the swap market. Call options, for example, are cheaper in the bond market than they are in the swap market. Puts are often more expensive in the bond market than in the swap market. Floating-rate issues can be less expensive than fixed-rate issues for lower-rated issuers. In addition, certain new structures can give investors their desired risk-return tradeoff while allowing the issuer to end up with what looks like vanilla debt.

Issuers can also lock in the cost of a future issuance through a forward swap. This usually is done in an environment in which rates are low, compared with historical trends, and the yield curve is relatively flat. Spread locks, another technique used relatively infrequently, can be employed to lock in generic spreads.

The swap market also allows issuers to transform floating-rate cash flows on an existing liability into fixed-rate flows. And fixed-rate flows can be transformed into floating-rate flows via swaps. An off-market swap is necessary to equate cash flows on a new swap with those on the old debt.

Finally, issuers can lock in future interest rates between the call date and the maturity date on high coupon issues that are likely to be called. Transforming the cash flows on existing liabilities is popular when interest rates are believed to be near their cyclical high or low.

We have shown that swaps are highly versatile instruments. They have transformed liability management into a more active undertaking, one that involves not only evaluating what is desirable for current issuances but also reevaluating past issuances and anticipating those of the future.

CHAPTER 8

ASSET-BASED INTEREST RATE SWAPS

Suresh E. Krishnan
Merrill Lynch Capital Markets
New York, New York

INTRODUCTION

In the early days of the swap market, swaps were predominantly used as a liability management tool. As such, they were mainly tied to the new issuance of debt securities, usually in amounts exceeding $100 million. As the market developed, many other potential uses of this flexible technique surfaced. During the last few years, investors have discovered that the technique of swapping cash flows can be applied to assets as well. This became feasible as swap warehousing became a more accepted practice and notional principal amounts on swaps declined to levels—about 5 to 10 million dollars—acceptable to institutional investors.

The variety of combinations of assets and swaps and the resultant synthetic securities are limited only by the imagination of the user. The most common form of asset swap involves the transformation of cash flows in the same currency. However, asset swaps involving currency swaps are also prevalent and can be used to change cash flows from one currency to another. In this chapter, we focus on asset-based interest rate swaps in a single-currency context.

DEFINITIONS

An interest rate swap is usually defined as a contract between two parties to exchange a series of fixed interest payments for a series of floating interest payments. These interest payments are based on a notional principal amount that is mutually agreed on between the two parties; the interest rate swap itself does not involve the exchange of principal between the swap counterparties.

An asset-based interest rate swap, sometimes simply referred to as an asset swap, refers to the combination of an asset and an interest rate swap. An interest rate swap can be used to change the complexion of an asset's cash flows. It can be used to transform a conventional fixed-rate security that produces a stream of fixed interest flows into a synthetic floating-rate security that produces a stream of floating interest flows. It can be used equally flexibly to transform a conventional floating-rate instrument into a synthetic fixed-rate instrument. In practice, asset swaps are structured and offered as a package to investors by financial institutions. The following sections describe in detail how these transformations can be achieved.

CREATING A SYNTHETIC
FIXED-RATE SECURITY

An investor wishing to own a security paying a fixed rate of interest may do so by purchasing a conventional fixed-rate security outright. Alternatively, the investor could create a synthetic fixed-rate security by buying a floating-rate instrument and combining it with an interest rate swap.

	Conventional Floating-Rate Security
Plus	**Interest Rate Swap** (Receive Fixed/Pay Floating)
Equals	**Synthetic Fixed-Rate Security**

The mechanics of this combination is illustrated in Exhibit 1. Essentially, the investor will receive interest payments from his floating-rate asset; these cash inflows are based upon a given spread over (under) the London Interbank Offered Rate (LIBOR).

EXHIBIT 1
Creating a Synthetic Fixed-Rate Security

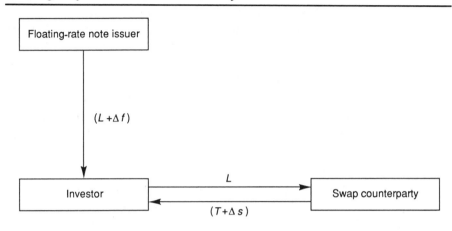

L = London interbank offered rate
T = Treasury bond yield
Δf = FRN spread over (under) LIBOR
Δb = Bond spread over T-bond yield
Δs = Swap spread over T-bond yield

Interest Flows from Investor's Perspective

Conventional FRN	Interest Rate Swap		Synthetic Fixed-Rate Security
Inflow	Outflow	Inflow	Net flow
$+ (L + \Delta f)$	$-L$	$+ (T + \Delta s)$	$(T + \Delta s + \Delta f)$

Decision Criteria

Yield on Conventional Straight Bond	$(T + \Delta b)$
Yield on Synthetic Fixed-Rate Security	$(T + \Delta s + \Delta f)$

If	Δb	Greater than	$(\Delta s + \Delta f)$	Then invest in conventional straight bond
If	Δb	Equals	$(\Delta s + \Delta f)$	Then invest in either
If	Δb	Less than	$(\Delta s + \Delta f)$	Then invest in synthetic fixed-rate security

Note: This framework assumes that the conventional fixed-rate bond and the synthetic fixed-rate bond have almost identical characteristics. Credit risk on the swap is ignored.

LIBOR is reset on a periodic basis, usually quarterly or semiannually. On the coupon payment dates, the investor makes LIBOR payments to the swap counterparty; in return, the investor receives fixed interest payments equal to the Treasury bond yield plus the swap spread. (In practice, only the net payment changes hands between the investor and the swap counterparty). As far as the investor is concerned, it now owns a synthetic security that provides a fixed stream of interest receipts. These fixed cash inflows will be equal to the sum of the Treasury bond yield, the swap spread and, the FRN spread, if any, and is known at the time the asset swap is initiated.

If we assume that the conventional fixed-rate security and the synthetic fixed-rate security have the same credit risk and that the credit risk on the interest rate swap is negligible, then the decision to invest in the straight bond or the synthetic fixed-rate bond is dependent on a comparison of their rates of return. The investor should undertake the asset swap (i.e., invest in the synthetic secu-

TABLE 1
Example of a Synthetic Fixed-Rate Security

| | | Interest Rate Swap | | Synthetic |
Time Period	Conventional Floating-Rate Note (a)	Outflow (b)	Inflow (c)	Fixed-Rate Bond Net Flow (d) = (a) + (b) + (c)
0	-100	0	0	-100
1	$+0.5L_0$	$-0.5L_0$	$+4.5$	$+4.5$
2	$+0.5L_1$	$-0.5L_1$	$+4.5$	$+4.5$
3	$+0.5L_2$	$-0.5L_2$	$+4.5$	$+4.5$
4	$+0.5L_3$	$-0.5L_3$	$+4.5$	$+4.5$
5	$+0.5L_4$	$-0.5L_4$	$+4.5$	$+4.5$
6	$+0.5L_5 + 100$	$-0.5L_5$	$+4.5$	$+4.5 + 100$
Return	LIBOR Flat	$-$LIBOR Flat	9.0%	9.0%

Cash Flows from the Investor's Perspective

Yield on a conventional 3-year fixed-rate bond of similar credit risk = 8.75%. The synthetic fixed-rate bond provides a 25 basis point pickup over the conventional fixed-rate bond.
Assumptions: Treasury yield = 8.2%, swap spread = 0.8%, return on a conventional 3-year floating-rate security = LIBOR Flat.
Notes: Time periods 0 and 1 refer to the start and end of the first six-month period, respectively. LIBOR for each period is determined at the start of the period and paid at the end of the period.

rity) only if the return on the synthetic fixed-rate security exceeds the return available on the conventional straight bond.

In the Table 1 example, we describe how a simple synthetic fixed-rate security can be created from a conventional floating-rate instrument. The three-year FRN is priced at par and pays 6-month LIBOR flat. A conventional three-year fixed-rate bond by the same issuer has a yield of 8.75 percent. The benchmark three-year Treasury bond yields 8.2 percent and the swap spread over Treasuries is 80 basis points. Therefore, the investor receives 9.0 percent from the fixed side of the swap.

The cash flows from the perspective of the investor are given in Table 1. The investor's floating-rate cash flows cancel each other, leaving only the fixed-rate cash inflows from the swap. These are received semiannually and give an internal rate of return of 9.0 percent, assuming semiannual compounding. The 25 basis point yield pickup available on the synthetic fixed-rate security makes the asset swap preferable. Note, however, that the investor has to factor in the additional credit risk on the swap, however small it may be.

CREATING A SYNTHETIC FLOATING-RATE SECURITY

An investor wishing to own a security paying a floating rate of interest may do so by purchasing a conventional floating-rate security outright. Alternatively, the investor could create a synthetic floating-rate security by buying a conventional fixed-rate instrument and combining it with an interest rate swap.

	Conventional Fixed-Rate Security
Plus	**Interest rate swap** (pay fixed/receive floating)
Equals	**Synthetic floating-rate security**

The mechanics of this combination is illustrated in Exhibit 2. Essentially, the investor will receive fixed interest payments from the fixed-rate asset. On the coupon payment dates, the investor makes fixed payments equal to the Treasury bond yield plus the swap spread to the swap counterparty; in return, the investor receives floating interest payments equal to LIBOR. As far as the investor is

EXHIBIT 2
Creating a Synthetic Floating-Rate Security

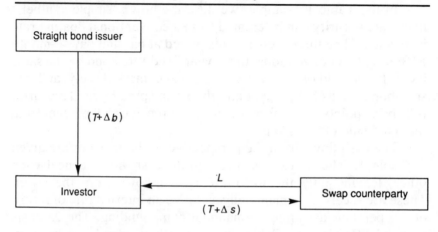

L = London interbank offered rate
T = Treasury bond yield
Δf = FRN spread over (under) LIBOR
Δb = Bond spread over T-bond yield
Δs = Swap spread over T-bond yield

Interest Flows from Investor's Perspective

Conventional Straight Bond	Interest Rate Swap		Synthetic Floating-Rate Security
Inflow	Outflow	Inflow	Net flow
$+(T + \Delta b)$	$-(T + \Delta s)$	$+L$	$(L + \Delta b - \Delta s)$

Decision Criteria

Yield on the conventional floating-rate note	$(L + \Delta f)$
Yield on the synthetic floating-rate security	$(L + \Delta b - \Delta s))$

If	Δf	Greater than	$(\Delta b - \Delta s)$	Then invest in conventional FRN
If	Δf	Equals	$(\Delta b - \Delta s)$	Then invest in either
If	Δf	Less than	$(\Delta b - \Delta s)$	Then invest in synthetic FRN

Note: This framework assumes that the conventional floating-rate note and the synthetic floating-rate note have almost identical characteristics. Credit risk on the swap is ignored.

concerned, it now owns a synthetic security that provides a floating stream of interest receipts. These floating cash inflows will be equal to LIBOR plus the spread over Treasuries for the fixed-rate bond minus the swap spread.

The decision to invest in a conventional FRN or a synthetic floating-rate note is dependent on a comparison of their rates of return. The investor should undertake the asset swap (i.e., invest in the synthetic security) only if the return on the synthetic floating-rate security exceeds the return available on the conventional FRN. Note again that these comparisons are appropriate only when the credit risks on the conventional and synthetic floating-rate securities are substantially similar and when the credit risk on the swap is quite small.

We illustrate the creation of a synthetic floating-rate security with an example (see Table 2). The yield on a conventional three-year floating-rate security is 6-month LIBOR flat. The yield on a

TABLE 2
Example of a Synthetic Floating-Rate Security

		Cash Flows from the Investor's Perspective		
		Interest Rate Swap		
Time Period	Conventional Fixed Rate Bond (a)	OutFlow (b)	Inflow (c)	Synthetic Floating-Rate Note (d) = (a) + (b) + (c)
0	−100	0	0	−100
1	+4.4	−4.3	+0.5L_0	+0.1 + 0.5L_0
2	+4.4	−4.3	+0.5L_1	+0.1 + 0.5L_1
3	+4.4	−4.3	+0.5L_2	+0.1 + 0.5L_2
4	+4.4	−4.3	+0.5L_3	+0.1 + 0.5L_3
5	+4.4	−4.3	+0.5L_4	+0.1 + 0.5L_4
6	+4.4 + 100	−4.3	+0.5L_5	+0.1 + 0.5L_5 + 100
Return	8.8%	−8.6%	LIBOR Flat	LIBOR + 20 bp

Yield on a conventional 3-year floating-rate security of similar credit risk = LIBOR flat. The synthetic floating-rate note provides a 20 basis point pickup over the conventional FRN.
Assumptions: Treasury yield = 8.0%, swap spread = 0.6%, yield on a conventional 3-year fixed-rate bond = 8.8%.
Notes: Time periods 0 and 1 refer to the start and end of the first six-month period, respectively. LIBOR for each period is determined at the start of the period and paid at the end of the period. Strictly speaking, the yield pickup will be slightly different from 20 basis points over LIBOR due to differing yield conventions used for Treasury bonds and LIBOR.

conventional three-year fixed-rate security is 8.8 percent. The three-year Treasury yield is 8.0 percent and the swap spread is 0.6 percent. The investor will receive 8.8 percent from the fixed-rate security and pay 8.6 percent to the swap counterparty. It will also receive LIBOR from the swap counterparty. The net result is that the investor will obtain LIBOR + 20 basis points for the synthetic FRN. This 20 bp pickup makes the synthetic FRN preferable to the conventional FRN if all other considerations are equal. Due to different methods used in calculating yields in the Treasury bond market and the Eurodollar market, the internal rates of return calculations have to be done on a consistent basis, where the compounding assumptions and the day count basis are made identical.

RATIONALE FOR ASSET SWAPS

Why should an investor bother with creating a synthetic security when it is easier to buy a conventional security of choice—fixed or floating—outright? The investor has to keep many considerations in mind when entering into an asset swap. They are briefly discussed in the following sections.

Windows of Opportunity

Opportunities are available from time to time that allow investors to obtain a higher yield on the synthetic security vis-a-vis the conventional security. But these opportunities are fleeting and require careful monitoring of markets. The following examples show how opportunities may arise when an asset becomes extremely undervalued due to a sell-off triggered by a particular event.

Fiasco in the FRN Market
The perpetual floating-rate note market collapsed, and its after-effects spilled over into other sectors of the FRN market in 1986 and 1987. As a result, many FRNs became undervalued and illiquid. For investors willing to take a contrarian view and a long-term perspective, asset swaps provided substantial yield pickup opportunities.

Ex-Warrant Bonds

Eurobonds with equity warrants attached were extremely popular as the stock market boomed in the mid-1980s. Japanese companies dominated the market for equity warrant issues and were able to obtain considerable savings in their cost of borrowing. Due to the increasing saturation of this market and especially following the global stock market crash, they became extremely unpopular. Some of these bonds were stripped of their warrants and the resulting low coupon bonds were then asset-swapped into attractive floating-rate instruments.

Event Risk Considerations

Many corporate bonds lost their luster when the RJR/Nabisco deal was announced in late 1988. In the aftermath of this announcement, fear of similar outcomes forced the rapid markdown in corporate bonds and demands for protection from event risk. As a result, new issues by U.S. corporations completely dried up both in the domestic market and in the Eurobond market. Spreads over Treasuries widened considerably on U.S. corporate bonds trading in the secondary market. This provided opportunities for investors to buy undervalued corporate bonds and asset-swap them.

Widening of Swap Spreads in February–March 1989

Short-term (one- and two-year) swap spreads widened dramatically and let loose a torrent of short-maturity fixed-rate bond issues, which were then swapped into floating-rate instruments. This allowed issuers to lower their borrowing costs substantially. The same phenomenon allowed investors to swap from floating-rate securities into synthetic fixed-rate securities.

Diversification of Credit Risk: Creating a Synthetic Security of the Type and Credit Risk Unavailable in the Market

Traditionally, banks have accounted for the majority of floating-rate securities issued. In the past few years concerns about safety of banks and the corresponding deterioration in bank asset quality made bank FRNs unattractive to many investors. Investors looking for floating-rate securities issued by high-quality credits found that such issues were essentially unavailable in the market. This gap in the market provided the incentive to synthetically create a high-quality floating-rate asset by buying a package of a high-quality fixed-rate security and an interest rate swap. As an added bonus, these asset swaps may at times provide returns well above LIBOR.

Portfolio Adjustments

Often investors desire to change the cash flow patterns of their asset portfolios without altering the underlying credit risk. Asset swaps allow the investor to obtain the desired cash flow patterns without having to dispose of assets from the portfolio. By attaching an interest rate swap to the underlying asset, the investor not only keeps the asset but also saves the transactions costs involved in selling the old asset and buying the new asset.

Default Risk on Underlying Security

Note that the investor is subject to the default risk of the underlying security. A default by the issuer will leave the investor without the cash flows from the bond; however, the investor is still obligated to make payments on the swap.

Credit Risk on the Interest Rate Swap

The swap carries with it the credit risk that the counterparty may default on its obligations. The investor is exposed to the risk that the swap dealer may default, while the swap dealer is exposed to the risk that the investor may default. This risk is minimal because the parties are only exposed to the net difference between the fixed and the floating payments of the swap; the risk is, therefore, only on a small percentage of the notional principal. To the extent that the investor takes on this additional credit risk on the swap, it should be compensated for the risk. The investor is therefore likely to undertake the asset swap only if the higher return on the synthetic asset compensates for this additional credit risk.

Liquidity

Lack of liquidity is the major drawback of asset swaps, which tend to have maturities of less than five years and, in general, are held until maturity. Since asset swaps are mostly built around assets with very little liquidity to start out with, this aspect should not be very surprising. In addition, unloading an asset swap involves not only selling the underlying asset but also unwinding the attached swap. Thus asset swaps tend to be less liquid than the underlying bond itself. However, the higher return available on the synthetic security takes into account the liquidity differential between the synthetic security and the conventional security.

Several methods have been devised to overcome the perception of lower liquidity. Under the first method, underlying assets and attached swaps are being offered as packages by the arranging financial institutions. Thus the resulting synthetic security itself may be bought and sold before maturity, without unwinding the swap. Even though this increases liquidity somewhat, liquidity is still dependent on the arranger's willingness to create a market in the synthetic instrument. A second approach is to launch a special purpose vehicle or entity. This special purpose entity invests in conventional securities and, through the use of swaps, converts them to synthetics. Liquidity is enhanced because the repackaged paper is backed by this special legal entity.

IMPACT OF ASSET SWAPS
ON THE PRIMARY MARKET

Asset swaps help in broadening the investor base for the primary market. For example, banks have traditionally confined their investments to floating-rate instruments in order to match their assets and liabilities. By making fixed-rate instruments available to bank investors, while at the same time achieving their floating-rate cash flow requirements, asset swaps have been able to identify a whole new class of investors.

In the same manner, asset swaps also facilitate the issuance of fixed-rate bonds by lower-rated issuers that were traditionally excluded from that market. Since investors can asset-swap these lower-rated fixed-rate bonds into floating-rate securities at margins over LIBOR, such bonds can be placed with investors more readily than in the past.

In addition, asset swaps effectively define the minimum levels below which the price of the new issue may not fall. If prices fall beyond a certain level, these new issues are likely to be asset-swapped, thus creating a demand for poorly performing new issues and keeping their prices above the floor. As a result, the asset swap market has some effect on the pricing of new bond issues, and due to the complicated web that ties together various segments of the financial market, its influence is also felt on the floating-rate note market and the syndicated loan market.

IMPACT OF ASSET SWAPS ON THE SECONDARY MARKET

Since asset swaps are usually held until maturity, this contributes to the locking up of securities for fairly long periods of time. While this can be viewed as contributing to illiquidity in the secondary market for the underlying bonds, the truth is that asset swaps are most beneficial when they are based on illiquid and underpriced bonds. Rather than hindering secondary market liquidity, asset swaps should be viewed as broadening the demand for fairly illiquid bonds.

IMPACT OF ASSET SWAPS ON THE SWAP MARKET

The traditional orientation of the swap market as a liability management tool is still very much in place, and swaps associated with new bond issues will continue to be the predominant influence on swap spreads. Since the asset swap market is still a fraction of the liability swap market, its effects on swap spreads have been fairly limited. However, if the size of the asset swap market increases in relation to the liability swap market, it is likely to exert more influence on the determination of swap spreads.

CONCLUSION

Even though it is of relatively recent origin, the asset swap market is expected to persist and grow. An outgrowth of the various applications of swaps, this market provides a valuable service to investors. Its main advantages are in the transformations of cash flows from floating to fixed, or vice versa. It is also useful in the creation of synthetic securities that are otherwise unavailable in the financial markets. Endless varieties of asset swaps can be created, and to the extent that the synthetic security fills the needs of the investor, it will remain a useful device. As the asset swap market grows in size, it is likely to have an increasing impact on the primary and secondary markets for debt issues and also on the determination of swap spreads.

CHAPTER 9

SWAPTIONS APPLICATIONS

Paul G. Cucchissi
Reto M. Tuffli
UBS Securities, Inc.
New York, New York

INTRODUCTION

Swap options, or swaptions, as they are commonly called, are one of the most innovative and rapidly growing rate risk management products to emerge in the last few years. As the name suggests, a swaption is simply an option on a swap; the buyer of a swap option has the right to start an interest rate swap with a specified fixed rate and maturity at or during a specified time period in the future. These instruments have risk and valuation characteristics very similar to those of other long-dated options. In fact, the swaption first originated as an instrument with which to arbitrage call options embedded in the fixed-income capital markets.

While the U.S. capital market continues to provide a wide variety of applications, sophisticated asset/liability managers are expanding the uses of swaptions as an integral part of their overall risk management program. Swaptions, for instance, increasingly are being considered as an alternative instrument to caps, floors, and even to generic swaps.

In this chapter we offer (*a*) a definition and description of swaptions and the swaption market; (*b*) a comparison of swaptions to other related products, such as swaps and caps; (*c*) an analysis of comprehensive transactions that contain swaptions, employing a diagrammatic framework for valuation; and (*d*) a review of the factors that influence valuation of swaptions.

DEFINITIONS AND THE MARKET

All options contain a right to buy or sell an underlying instrument or commodity at a specific strike price. For a swaption, the underlying instrument is the forward (delayed start) swap, which typically starts at the exercise date and runs to a specified maturity date. The swaption's strike price is the specified fixed interest rate of the swap (quoted as an absolute rate, not as a spread to Treasuries as is typical for generic swaps), and its value or premium is normally stated as an up-front amount, expressed as a percentage of the notional amount.

There has been considerable confusion among users and market makers regarding the correct terminology for swaptions. An identical swaption transaction may be referred to by one dealer as a call, and by another as a put. The following definitions have become the more commonly accepted and benefit from being conceptually consistent with other types of options:

Call Swaption: The right, but not the obligation, to *receive* a specified fixed rate in a swap, called the strike rate, and pay the floating rate for a stated time period, to begin at a specified future date.

Put Swaption: The right, but not the obligation, to *pay* a specified fixed rate in a swap, called the strike rate, and receive the floating rate for a stated time period, to begin at a specified future date.

European Swap Option: Exercisable at one specific point in time, typically at or shortly before the specified start date of the swap.

American Swap Option: Exercisable at any point in time during a specified period. The exercise period can be from inception until the start date of the swap. Alternatively, the period can begin at the swap start date and run to the swap maturity date.

As was noted, these definitions are consistent with standard bond option terminology. For example, a call option on a bond entitles the buyer to purchase the underlying bond at a previously stated price. The buyer will therefore have the option to begin receiving the bond coupons and principal. Similarly, the buyer of a call swaption has the right to begin receiving the fixed rate in a swap (and paying the floating rate). When bond prices rise (rates fall) a bond call option increases in value as the buyer has the right to purchase the bonds below the market price. Similarly, given a fall in rates (bond prices rise), the call swaption increases in value as the buyer has the right to begin receiving fixed in a swap at a level above the market swap rate.

Swaption structures are as varied as those available in the swap market generally. Structures can range from options to start a one-year swap in six months to 10-year options on a 10-year swap (i.e., final maturity in 20 years). Most transactions, however, are for final maturities of 10 years or less. The underlying swap can also be of the more complex, nongeneric type (e.g., amortizing, zero coupon, etc).

The floating-rate indices are predominantly LIBOR and commercial paper based, although other indices are available. The option premiums typically are paid up front, but are often structured to be paid as an annuity over the life of the transaction.

The latest 1988 survey estimated the U.S. dollar swaption market to be in excess of $40 billion, with the first half of 1989 showing continued strong growth. This is largely the result of the large volume of swaption-driven arbitrage transactions in the U.S. domestic capital markets using callable bonds. (These transactions will be discussed in greater detail in the following sections.) Swap options are also constructed on interest rate swaps denominated in foreign currencies, particularly sterling, deutsche mark, Swiss franc, and yen.

APPLICATIONS

As with other risk management products, swap options effectively can be used in three different ways: (*a*) as a means to create a speculative position, (*b*) as a hedge for an existing exposure, and (*c*) as a mechanism for creating an arbitrage.

The Speculator

Consider a pure speculator (for simplicity's sake, one having no assets or liabilities and believing rates will rise) who elects to buy a put swaption. If on the exercise date swap rates are higher than the strike rate, the speculator will exercise the right to pay fixed at the below-market swap strike rate. To lock in the gain, the speculator could then (a) sell the swap to another counterparty and receive in cash the market value of the swap or (b) enter into a reverse swap, that is, receive the fixed rate at the higher market swap rate and pay the floating rate. The latter strategy would cause the gain to be recognized over time, as the two combined swaps would generate an annuity equal to the interest differential between the two fixed rates multiplied by the notional principal of the swap. Alternatively, a gain could also be recognized prior to expiry simply by selling the put swaption. Of course, the speculator would enjoy a net gain only if the value of the swap at the time of exercise exceeded the premium paid for the option plus the forgone interest income on the premium, as would be the case with any speculative options strategy.

It can be noted from this example that a put swaption serves as a rate protection instrument analogous in many ways to an interest rate cap on floating rates. As rates rise, a put swaption becomes more valuable, as does a cap. When both instruments are "in the money," they generally pay the difference between a strike rate and the current floating rate. In fact, the main economic difference between a cap and a European swaption is that a cap is a series of individual options, one for each floating reset period, whereas a put swaption is a one-time option on a swap, which is effectively a series of forward floating-rate agreements. Clearly, however, a risk manager may choose to use either a cap or put swaption to protect against a rise in rates, and either a floor or a call swaption to protect against lower rates, depending on which product provides a better fit given the manager's views on rates, the mix of fixed-versus floating-rate liabilities, or other specific circumstances.

The Hedger

When swap options are used as hedges, they are typically structured to offset an option exposure embedded in an existing liability or asset. Consider as our hedger a finance manager who issued a bond some time ago that was puttable five years prior to final maturity. Now that the exercise date is only two years away, the manager is concerned that rates may rise. The bonds in that case would be put back to him or her by investors, and the manager would be forced to refinance at a higher interest rate for the remaining five years of the bond. He or she now elects to buy a put swaption exercisable in two years for five years, with a strike rate equal to the coupon on the bond. If swap rates are higher than the strike rate in two years, the bonds likely will be put back to the issuer. The manager can then exercise the put swaption. The fixed swap payments will replace the coupon payments formerly made on the bond. The company can now refinance with a floating rate liability, which, together with the put swaption, converts the floating-rate financing into a fixed rate equal to that of the old bond coupon.

The Arbitrager

As was noted earlier, the most frequent application of swaptions has been to arbitrage embedded capital market options, particularly those within callable bonds. A typical arbitrage of this variety consists of a finance manager purchasing an inexpensive call by issuing a callable bond in the public debt market and simultaneously selling a similar call in the form of a swaption to a swap market maker, typically a commercial or investment bank. The bond issuer receives an option premium for selling the swaption, which, for instance, is the equivalent of 20 basis points (bp) per annum over the life of the transaction, while only paying perhaps a 10 bp per annum premium over the cost of a noncall bond for the right to have a similar call feature in the bond. The issuer has thereby generated a 10 bp savings via the arbitrage. (An example of this structure will be presented later in this chapter.)

SWAPTIONS APPLIED TO CAPITAL MARKET TRANSACTIONS

As one might expect, there are numerous permutations to swaption-linked capital market transactions. Before examining specific examples, however, it is instructive to employ the use of an analytic framework for swaptions. This framework also incorporates swaps, bonds, and related products, thereby allowing the reader to examine the net results of multiproduct transactions.

Diagrammatic Framework

Payout diagrams can be used to analyze the market valuation of individual and combined transactions that contain swaptions under various interest rate scenarios. Each structure is presented on a graph such as the one below (Figure 1). The horizontal axis is a scale of bond prices or swap values that correspond to given interest rate or swap rate levels. A movement to the right along this axis indicates a decline in interest rates and an increase in bond values, whereas a movement to the left indicates a rise in rates and a decline in values.

The direction of interest rates is expressed in terms of price (bond or swap) in order to be consistent with the horizontal price scale of standard bond and stock option diagrams. The vertical axis is a scale of the payout or value of the option, swap, or bond, as applicable.[1]

Basic Bond and Swap Profiles

Figure 2 is a standard valuation profile for a bond issuer. Consider the point at which the valuation line intersects the X-axis as the rate at which the company issued debt—in this case 9 percent. Depending on the movement in rates, the issuer's position will either increase or decrease in value depending on the bond's subsequent market price movement. These movements in value are typically unrecognized by corporations from an accounting perspective, but nonetheless are real costs and benefits to a corporation from an economic, or opportunity cost, perspective. For example, if interest rates increase, the issuer's short bond position increases

---

[1] The reader should note that these payout diagrams do not reflect the true option valuation. Option values are comprised of both intrinsic and time value. A true valuation diagram would be curvilinear. To simplify, we will use linear representations that more accurately reflect the intrinsic value of the option.

FIGURE 1
Valuation or Payout Diagram

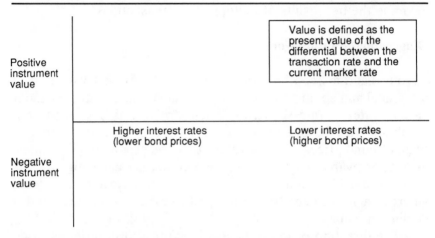

in value as it has achieved a lower cost of funds than could be attained in the current (higher rate) market environment.[2] Conversely, if rates fall, the position decreases in value. From a different perspective, the unrealized gains or losses can be thought of as the present value of the differential between the original issuance rate and the current issuing level.

Similarly, swaps can be viewed in this framework. Figure 3 shows the valuation profile of a company that enters into a swap as a payer of fixed and receiver of floating. This swap position, referred to as a short position, is quite similar to the short bond position taken by the company that issued fixed-rate debt. For example, both entities will be making fixed-rate payments over time—the swap counterparty in the form of fixed swap payments and the bond issuer in the form of coupon payments to its bondholders. Due to the similarity of the cash flows of each instrument, both positions are analogous from a valuation standpoint. As term interest rates rise, the short swap position increases in value since the fixed swap rate paid is below the current swap market level.

---

[2] The terminology *long* and *short* will be used throughout this chapter. Quite simply, the *buyer* of a financial instrument has a long position, whereas a *seller* has a short position. A company that issued debt has sold the bonds to investors and therefore, effectively, has a short bond position.

FIGURE 2
Short Noncallable Bond Position (Issue $100 MM Five-Year Note at 9 Percent)

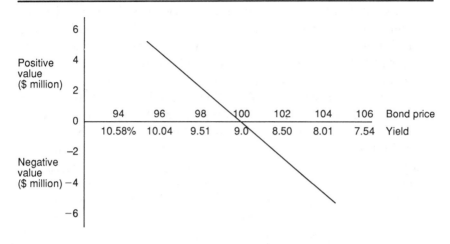

FIGURE 3
Short Swap Position (Pay Fixed on $100 MM for Five Years at 9 Percent and Receive Floating)

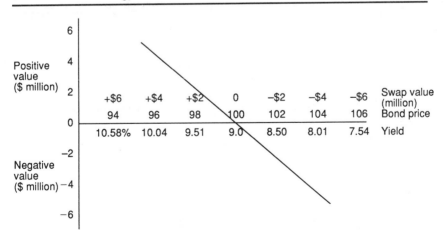

Swaption Profiles

Swaptions are now a simple extension of a plain vanilla swap. Figure 4 shows the valuation profile of a long (buy) call position, or the right to receive the fixed rate at a specified rate (and pay the floating rate). As swap rates decrease, the long call swaption increases in value as the buyer has the right to receive the fixed rate at a level above the current market swap rate. If rates increase, however, the buyer of a call swaption is holding a right that has no intrinsic value in the current swap market. As with other similar option diagrams, the gap of constant value between the X-axis and the valuation line represents the premium paid for the option. In this range of interest rates, the option has no intrinsic value and would therefore not be exercised. Since the option buyer paid a premium for the option, the net position is a loss equal to the premium. As we move horizontally to the right of the strike rate, the value on the position increases. At the intersection of the position line and the X-axis, referred to as the break-even rate, the value of the option exactly equals the premium originally paid. As

FIGURE 4
Long Call Swaption

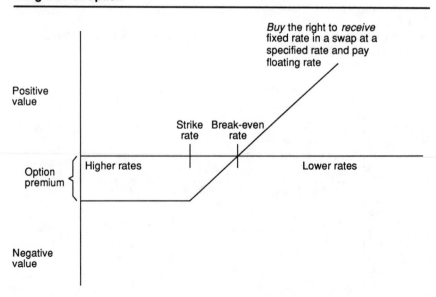

we move to the right of the break-even rate, the option value exceeds the premium originally paid, resulting in a net positive value for the position.

Figure 5 shows the valuation profile of a short put swaption, where the *counterparty* has the right to pay to the swaption seller the fixed rate in a swap at a specified rate and receive the floating rate. As market rates increase (to the left of the strike rate), the short put swaption decreases in value as the buyer has the right to pay a rate below the current market rate.

Multiproduct Transactions

These basic diagrams provide the framework for analyzing multi-product transactions that include bonds, swaps, bond options, and swaptions. By combining the individual positions on one valuation diagram, the reader will have the ability to analyze under varying interest rate scenarios the net position created. Before moving on to a complex application, let us first examine a simple combination of two positions. Figure 6 shows on the same valuation diagram a

FIGURE 5
Short Put Swaption

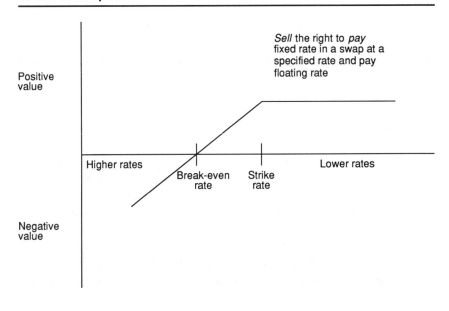

FIGURE 6
Short Five-Year Bond Position and Long Swap Position

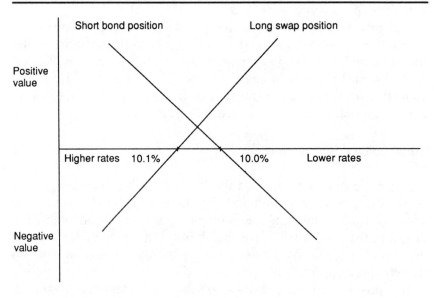

short five-year bond position issued at a 10 percent all-in cost and a long swap position at a 10.10 percent fixed payment level versus floating.

These two positions are combined additively in Figure 7 to create a synthetic floating rate position, which is insensitive to movements in term interest rates (as shown by its horizontal position).

Call Arbitrage Structure

Given this review of the various instruments, we can now analyze the typical capital market applications of a swap option. Assume, for example, ABC Corporation has the objective of achieving the most cost effective five-year fixed-rate financing. ABC chooses to issue a five-year bond callable after Year 3 and pays for this right with an additional 10 bp per annum in a yield to the investor over the cost of a straight five-year noncallable bond. Simultaneously, the issuer sells a call swaption for the equivalent of 20 bp per

FIGURE 7
Net Position—Floating Rate

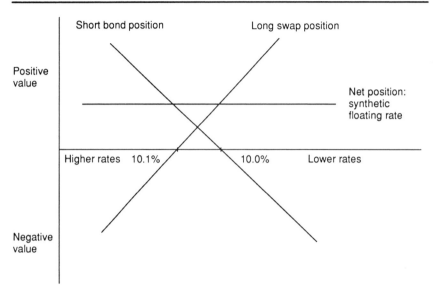

annum giving the buyer the right, but not the obligation, to receive fixed swap flows beginning in the last two years of the bond and to pay a floating rate of interest. The strike rate on the swaption is set equal to the coupon rate on the bond.

In first examining the bond, notice that the issuance of a callable bond can be broken down into two discrete components—a short noncall bond and a long call position (Figure 8).

Figure 9 depicts the net position, at the call date, created by combining the two positions, namely, that of a callable bond. In this callable bond diagram, the upward sloping line to the left of Point Y represents the positive value to the issuer of a fixed-rate bond if interest rates subsequently rise. The horizontal line to the right of Point Y represents the issuer's ability to refinance at the lower interest rates in the future. If interest rates decline, the issuer would call the bonds and refinance at a new, lower rate and thus avoid any loss in value.

The value a, shown on the vertical axis, is the premium demanded by the investor for selling the embedded call. It is equal to

FIGURE 8
Components of a Callable Bond

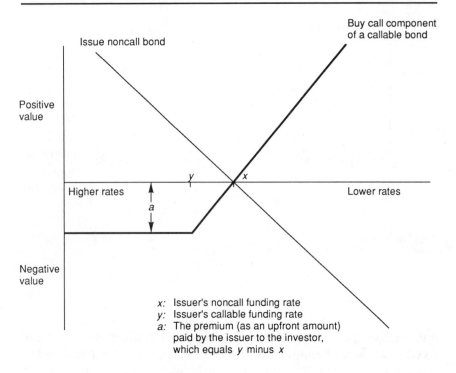

x: Issuer's noncall funding rate
y: Issuer's callable funding rate
a: The premium (as an upfront amount)
   paid by the issuer to the investor,
   which equals y minus x

the present value of an annuity Y minus X, which is the difference between the issuer's callable and noncall funding rate. Note that the net position achieved by issuing a callable bond is equivalent to a long put position. (An increase in value is recognized when rates rise, and a loss of premium occurs when rates fall.)

In Figure 10, the callable bond and the issuer's sale of a call swaption are combined on the same diagram. The net position is similar to a noncallable bond issue. As seen in Figure 11, the issuer, effectively, has sold the call option purchased from the investors and is left with a fixed-rate obligation until maturity. Note that the issuer has obtained a lower cost of financing, as illustrated by the point (Z) at which the risk profile line intersects the horizontal axis. As a result of this combined structure, ABC Corporation has obtained five-year fixed-rate financing at an all-in cost below its normal market funding rate, regardless of the future direction of interest rates.

FIGURE 9
Callable Bond Profile

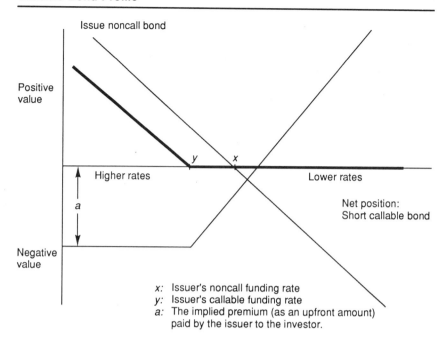

Issue noncall bond

Positive value

y   x

Higher rates   Lower rates

a

Net position:
Short callable bond

Negative value

x: Issuer's noncall funding rate
y: Issuer's callable funding rate
a: The implied premium (as an upfront amount) paid by the issuer to the investor.

FIGURE 10
Issue Callable Bond and Sell Call Swaption

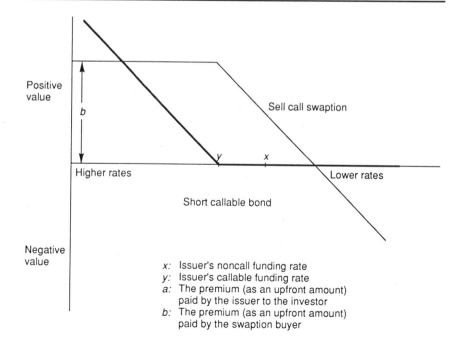

Positive value

b

Sell call swaption

y   x

Higher rates   Lower rates

Short callable bond

Negative value

x: Issuer's noncall funding rate
y: Issuer's callable funding rate
a: The premium (as an upfront amount) paid by the issuer to the investor
b: The premium (as an upfront amount) paid by the swaption buyer

FIGURE 11
Resulting Position—Synthetic Noncall Bond

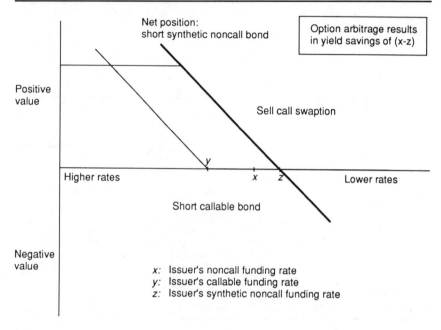

Consider the two outcomes that can exist at or after the call date. For example, if swap rates have increased in Years 4 and 5, the swaption dealer will not exercise the swap option, given that it can receive fixed in the swap market at a rate above the strike rate on the swaption. Similarly, ABC Corporation has no economic incentive to call the bonds and continues to pay fixed-rate coupons to its bondholders (Figure 12).

Conversely, if interest rates have declined below the strike rate after three years, the dealer would exercise the swaption to receive fixed-rate payments. ABC Corporation would immediately call the bonds since it must now make fixed swap payments to the swap counterparty in lieu of the fixed coupon payments to its bondholders (Figure 13). To complete the picture, the issuer must refinance its debt with a floating-rate obligation and use the swap's floating-rate inflows to service this debt. The company therefore retains its fixed-rate obligation, inasmuch as its fixed swap payments are equivalent to the original bond coupon.

FIGURE 12
Scenario Analysis—Synthetic Noncall Bond (Scenario 1: Rates Are
Higher at the End of Year 3—Swaption Not Exercised)

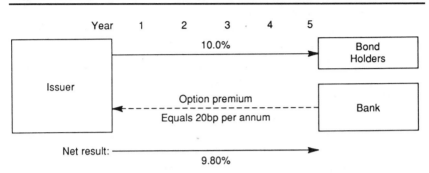

The synthetic noncall bond structure allows issuers to achieve a lower cost of financing for the five-year period due to the arbitrage of the call option market. Again, the value of the call option that issuers buy from investors of callable bonds is lower than the value of the call swaption sold in the swaption market. The premium received by the issuer for the call swaption (20 bp per annum) exceeds the premium paid for the bond call (10 bp per annum), thereby creating a 10 bp per annum arbitrage. This arbitrage

FIGURE 13
Scenario Analysis—Synthetic Noncall Bond (Scenario 2: Rates Are Lower
at the End of Year 3—Swaption Exercised)

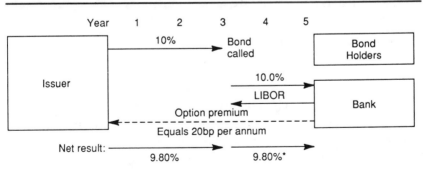

* When the bond is called assume the issuer
funds at LIBOR.

opportunity typically exists because bond investors at times undervalue the call they sell to the issuer, particularly during periods when investor demand for such options is strong relative to the available supply in the capital markets.

As was already observed, swaption transactions involve many permutations. One simple extension of the example discussed above is created by combining the synthetic fixed-rate result with a long swap position for the stated maturity of the issue—in this example five years (refer to Figure 7). These two positions combine to create a floating-rate position. Note that the profile line lies above the X-axis. This means that the issuer creates a constant positive value, thereby achieving floating-rate funds at a rate lower than would normally be available in the market. This is, of course, due to the issuer's ability to sell a call swaption for a price higher than it paid to buy the call on its bond.

Certain complicating factors must also be considered. The total arbitrage gains are affected by the issuer's future ability to refinance its obligation in the floating-rate market and by the resulting borrowing spread that is required. A future credit downgrading of a company may result in a widening of its borrowing spread to LIBOR, thereby reducing the value of the anticipated arbitrage. This type of transaction also relies upon a reasonably strong correlation between swap market and corporate bond spreads to Treasuries. If, for instance, the credit spread on an issuer's bond were to widen while swap spreads remained constant, the call swaption buyer might exercise its option at a time when it was uneconomic for the issuer to call its bonds.

Synthetic Put Bond Structure

Another application in the capital markets involves the use of a put swaption to synthetically create a puttable bond. Under such a synthetic structure, the issuer would sell a put in the form of a swaption, rather than selling a put on its bond issue to the investor. Let us diagrammatically review the structure of a synthetic 10-year bond puttable after 5 years. A corporation would issue a 10-year noncall bond and sell a put swaption giving the dealer the right to pay a fixed rate for 5 years starting in 5 years (Figure 14). The downward sloping line to the left of Point Z represents the decrease

FIGURE 14
Issue Noncall Bond and Sell Put Swaption

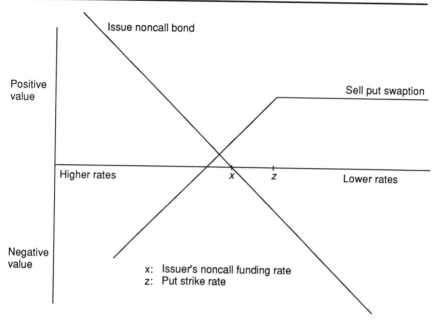

x: Issuer's noncall funding rate
z: Put strike rate

in value of the short put swaption position, given an increase in rates from the date of issue to the put date.

The decrease in value is created as higher rates prompt the swaption buyer to begin making fixed interest payments at swap rates below the current market level. For the first five years, the issuer would achieve fixed rate funding. At the end of Year 5, the combination of the noncall bond and short put swaption would produce a net valuation profile as shown in Figure 15.

Once again, two outcomes can exist at the put date. If swap rates have increased above the strike rate at Year 5 (the put date), the swaption buyer would exercise the option to pay a fixed rate of interest. The issuer therefore has been swapped into paying floating rates during a time of higher prevailing term rates (as represented by the horizontal profile line to the left of Point Z). Conversely, if rates have declined below the strike rate, the swaption buyer would not exercise the swaption, and the issuer would con-

FIGURE 15
Resulting Position—Synthetic Short Call

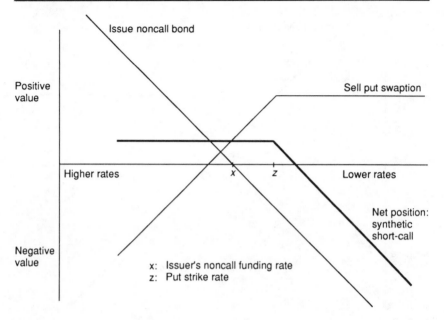

tinue to pay fixed coupons to its bondholders at a level above the current market rate (as represented by the downward sloping profile line to the right of Point Z.)

There is also a qualitative advantage to the synthetic put bond structure. Unlike the investor put bond where the issuer must refinance its borrowing if the bond is put, there is no refinancing risk in the synthetic structure since the bond remains outstanding until maturity. Note that the short bond and short put swaption positions combine to create a short call position at the put date. This synthetic structure can therefore also be produced by combining a five-year noncall bond with a short call swaption position in five years for five years. These two synthetic structures should provide similar all-in financing costs if a company's borrowing rate is at a spread to the Treasury level comparable to the spread to Treasury quoted for swaps.

One structure, however, may provide superior results if the slopes of these two curves diverge. For example, an issuer with a weak credit rating must normally pay investors a substantial spread premium to extend its bond maturity from 5 to 10 years, whereas, due to a swap's significantly lower credit exposure, the swap market demands a lower spread premium for extending maturity. The company's borrowing curve will therefore be steeper than the swap curve, making it relatively more expensive to access long-term fixed-rate funding in the capital markets. In this instance, the synthetic structure utilizing a five-year bond and a call swaption will provide superior results by allowing the issuer to access the most cost-effective market to pay fixed-rate coupons.

SWAP OPTION VALUATION

As with other options, the price of a swap option is a function of several factors, which include the strike level, time period to expiry, and rate volatility assumptions, as well as other factors unique to swap options. For a call swaption, the higher the strike rate, the greater the value of the option since the buyer has the right to receive fixed interest payments at a higher rate. Conversely, the higher the strike rate on a put swaption, the lower the option value. As with other options, swaption values increase as the time to expiry lengthens and/or as the expected yield volatility rises. In a swap option, the premium increases as the maturity on the underlying swap increases, assuming the same start date.

Intrinsic Value

As with any other option, the value of a swaption can be broken down into two components: the option's intrinsic value, if any, and its time value. The intrinsic value of any option (at, for example, the exercise date) is the amount by which the option is in the money. For a call option, the in-the-money amount, or intrinsic value, equals the market price of the underlying instrument minus the strike price, whenever the market price exceeds the strike price; for puts, it equals the strike price minus the market price, whenever the strike price exceeds the market price. For European options, the intrinsic value must be present valued to reflect its time value component, where the expiry date is at some point in the future. Quantifying the intrinsic value is fairly straightforward for many options, such as equity options, where the market price is readily observable. Consider an American call option on the stock of XYZ Corporation that has a strike of $50 and a current market stock price of $55. The intrinsic value of the call is thus $5 since the holder of the call can purchase the stock at $50 by exercising the option and then sell the stock at $55, netting a $5 profit.

For a swaption, however, the calculation of intrinsic value requires that we first establish the market rate of the underlying forward swap. Consider a European call swaption where the buyer has the right to receive the fixed swap rate, starting in three years for two years, at a strike rate equal to 10 percent. The objective is to determine the two-year swap rate which will apply for Years 4 and 5. The market forward swap rate must be calculated from the quoted market rate for spot start, generic swaps. The generic swap curve for U.S. dollar swaps is defined as Treasury yields plus swap spreads quoted by convention for maturities 2, 3, 4, 5, 7, and 10 years. A simplified generic swap curve is outlined in Table 1. From the fixed swap rates of the generic swap curve we begin by calculating the zero coupon rate for each maturity together with the series of implied forward floating rates (typically three or six months, but for purposes of simplicity one-year forwards are used).

Chapter 12 provides a review of the calculation of forward rates and zero coupon rates from a generic swap curve. This calcu-

TABLE 1
Sample Generic Swap Curve, Implied Forwards and Zeros

Maturity	Treasury Rate	Swap Spread	All-in Swap Rate	Implied One-Year Forward Rates	Implied Zero Coupon Rate
1	7.50%	100 bp	8.50%	—	8.50%
2	8.00	80	8.80	9.13%	8.81
3	8.30	75	9.05	9.62	9.08
4	8.40	72	9.12	9.37	9.15
5	8.47	70	9.17	9.42	9.21

The swap rates are quoted on an annual bond basis, for the sake of simplicity, and refer to the rate at which the dealer would pay fixed and receive floating.

lation is illustrated briefly here. Note from Table 1 that since the one-year swap rate (R_1) is also equal to the one-year zero rate (Z_1), we can imply the two-year zero (Z_2) rate from the two-year swap rate (R_2) of 8.80 percent as follows:

$$1 = \frac{R_2}{(1 + Z_1)^1} + \frac{1 + R_2}{(1 + Z_2)^2}$$

$$1 = \frac{0.088}{(1.085)} + \frac{1.088}{(1 + Z_2)^2}$$

Solving for Z_2 we get $Z_2 = 8.81^3$ percent.

Once we have the two-year zero rate, we can solve for the three-year zero rate, and so forth. We can also solve for the forward rates since zero rates are simply the product of a consecutive set of forward rates. We can compute the one-year forward rate ($_1r_2$).

Therefore,

$$(1 + Z_2)^2 = (1 + {_0}r_1)(1 + {_1}r_2)$$
$$(1.08813)^2 = (1.085)(1 + {_1}r_2)$$
$${_1}r_2 = 9.13 \text{ percent.}$$

The fixed rate for any generic swap can be thought of as the break-even rate where one should be indifferent, from a present value standpoint, between receiving the fixed swap rate (a straight annuity) or a series of implied forward rates (an annuity with differing amounts). In this technique, both the implied forward-rate cash flows and the fixed-rate cash flows must be discounted at the zero coupon rate applicable for each maturity. To calculate a forward-start swap, therefore, requires calculating the break-even fixed swap rate for the set of implied forward rates that corresponds to the period of the underlying swap (Periods 4 and 5 in our example), such that the present value of the fixed-rate flows and the reverse implied floating flows equals zero.

This technique can be applied to solve for the forward rate of our example. Note from Table 1 that the one-year forward rate for Year 3 to 4 ($_3r_4$) is 9.37 percent and for Year 4 to 5 ($_4r_5$) is 9.42 percent. From these forward rates and the corresponding zero coupon rates (Zi), we can calculate the two-year swap rate for Years 3 to 5 ($_3R_5$) as follows:

$$\left(\frac{_3R_5}{(1 + Z_4)^4} + \frac{_3R_5}{(1 + Z_5)^5}\right) - \left(\frac{_3r_4}{(1 + Z_4)^4} + \frac{_4r_5}{(1 + Z_5)^5}\right) = 0$$

$$_3R_5\left(\frac{1}{(1 + Z_4)^4} + \frac{1}{(1 + Z_5)^5}\right) = \frac{_3r_5}{(1 + Z_4)^4} + \frac{_4r_5}{(1 + Z_5)^5}$$

$$_3R_5 = \frac{\dfrac{0.0937}{(1.0915)^4} + \dfrac{0.0942}{(1.0921)^5}}{(1/(1.0915)^4 + 1/(1.0921)^5)}$$

$$_3R_5 = 9.39 \text{ percent}$$

Since the strike rate is 10 percent and the market rate for the underlying forward swap is calculated to be 9.39 percent, the swaption's intrinsic value is the rate differential of 61 bp per annum on the notional amount for two years beginning in three years (i.e., the option is 61 bp per annum in the money). This two-year annuity, starting in three years, must be present valued to calculate the swaption's current intrinsic value. To be precise, the discounting of this rate differential also should be done on a zero coupon basis, that is, using the four-year zero rate to discount the 61 bp per annum (p.a.) paid at Year 4, and the five-year zero rate for the 61 bp paid in five years.

Strike rate $\qquad$ = 10 percent p.a.
Market forward swap rate = 9.39 percent p.a.
Intrinsic value $\qquad$ = 61 bp p.a. for Years 4 and 5

Present intrinsic value $\quad = \dfrac{61 \text{ bp}}{(1.0915)^4} + \dfrac{61 \text{ bp}}{(1.0921)^5}$

$\qquad\qquad\qquad\qquad\quad$ = 82 bp

In our example, therefore, this present intrinsic value equals 82 bp multiplied by the notional amount. It can be noted that when the strike rate is set equal to the market forward swap rate, the swaption is at the money and has zero intrinsic value.

Time Value and Volatility

The time value component of a swaption, as with any other option, is the value associated with probable yield (or price) variation during the life of the option. A higher expected variance in the underlying market forward swap rate leads to a greater probability that the option will be in the money at expiry, or further in the money for an option-containing intrinsic value. A higher variance thus implies a greater option value.

The expected yield volatility, therefore, is the key variable determining the swap option's value. Several issues should be considered. First, the volatility being estimated should be the volatility of the forward swap rate, not just that of the generic swap rate associated with the swaption's final maturity. There can be significant differences between the two. Historic forward rate volatilities are not readily available, making such estimates more difficult. Second, historic Treasury yield volatility is often used as a proxy for swap volatility. Although more readily available, Treasury yield volatility does not capture the added volatility contributed by swap spreads. The additional component of swap spread volatility is an increasingly significant portion of the total volatility for swaptions. Finally, there is always the problem that historic volatility is not necessarily a good measure of future volatility, as with any other option. Despite these challenges, swaption market makers are using a variety of available information, including callable and putable corporate bonds and cap and floor volatilities to base their volatility estimates.

It should also be noted that the complexities involved in pricing swaptions require the use of more advanced options models, which include issues beyond the intended scope of this chapter. The limitations associated with the earlier options models, such as the Black-Scholes model and the binomial options models, are being addressed by market participants and academics. In particular, it is important that the swaptions models allow for discounting each probable swap rate outcome at a rate that is consistent with that outcome, rather than at a single discount rate, as with earlier models. Second, it is important that the model incorporate a consistent, arbitrage-free approach across related, longer-dated option types, such as caps and floors, and call and put swaptions.

Put-Call Parity

As with other options, there is a put-call parity relationship for swaptions that arises from the ability to create a swaption synthetically. Consider the following example. ABC Corporation buys a put swaption to pay fixed in one year for one year at a 10 percent strike. ABC's risk position can be re-created by buying a similar call swaption also with a strike of 10 percent and simultaneously entering into a one-year forward start swap as a payer of the fixed rate at 10 percent for one year. Assume ABC bought the call swaption for 90 bp up front and that this same call swaption is 50 bp in the money (i.e., it has a present intrinsic value of 50 bp). Therefore, by definition, the delayed start swap where ABC pays the fixed rate at 10 percent should also be worth 50 bp up front since the above market rate swap value is analogous to the call swaption's intrinsic value. Since the two alternatives are identical, ABC should not pay more than 40 bp up front for the purchase of the put swaption.

If, at the exercise date, swap rates are higher than 10 percent, ABC would exercise the put swaption. Alternatively, as the buyer of the call swaption, ABC would not exercise and, thus, ABC would begin to pay fixed at 10 percent under the delayed start swap. This would exactly equal its payments on the put swaption. If swap rates are lower, the put swaption will not be exercised. Alternatively, the call swaption will be exercised, but the delayed start swap will exactly offset ABC's obligations under the call swaption, thereby again equating the two results. Finally, it can be noted that when the strike rate is exactly equal to the market forward rate, the put value and call value should be identical.

SUMMARY

The development of the swaptions market has been a natural outgrowth of the important and successful role served by interest rate swaps in the arena of rate risk management generally and the capital markets specifically. Swaptions now extend the range of off-balance sheet products to include the ability to manage a wide range of fixed-income options exposures.

The use of swaptions is expected to expand further as financial managers become more familiar with analyzing the component parts of their options exposures, whether embedded or not, and become more comfortable with the mechanics and applications of the swap option itself. Utilizing the type of diagrammatic framework employed in this chapter should facilitate such analysis, particularly when considering potential risks and rewards of a complex transaction. Increased familiarity with the product by end users, together with growing trading and pricing sophistication, should lead to greater depth and liquidity in this new market.

CHAPTER 10

NON-U.S. DOLLAR INTEREST RATE SWAPS

Victoria Lasseter
Citicorp
New York, New York

INTRODUCTION

Non-U.S. dollar interest rate swaps are the same product as U.S. dollar interest rate swaps—the distinction being the currency of denomination and the related conventions of each particular capital market. Swaps are used in all major currencies (and many minor ones) for interest rate risk management and positioning in much the same way as U.S. dollar interest rate swaps. This chapter is a primer on the non-U.S. dollar interest rate swap market—its uses, its growth, and its conventions. Clearly, each currency has its own very specific interest rate swap market; hence, we do not attempt to take an in-depth look at each nondollar swap market. However, the chapter does provide an overview that we hope is helpful in relating nondollar interest rate swaps to dollar swaps.

As with dollar-denominated swaps, nondollar swaps are used primarily to change the characteristics of an exposure from fixed to floating, or vice versa (e.g., 7 percent annum fixed deutsche mark [DM] versus six-month floating DM LIBOR), or from one floating index to another (e.g., six-month DM LIBOR to six-month DM FIBOR), or from one tenor, or maturity, of a particular floating index to another (e.g., six-month DM LIBOR to three-month DM LIBOR).[1]

Non-U.S. dollar swaps are used principally by two fundamentally different groups—retail participants (generally hedgers, such as corporations) and wholesale participants (generally traders and positioners, such as banks). Both user groups may enter into a swap for a variety of reasons, but the primary ones are asset and/or liability management and interest rate positioning.

Volume in non-U.S. dollar swaps continues to grow rapidly due to the increased sophistication of the dealer community and to strengthening retail demand. Globalization of large corporations and middle market businesses, as well as the recent spate of cross-border mergers and leveraged buyouts, continues to foster very active interest in nondollar interest rate swaps and related products (e.g., cross-currency swaps, floors, ceilings, and swaptions).

The universe for nondollar swaps has expanded continually since their introduction less than a decade ago. Today, major dealers warehouse hedging instruments to manage interest rate risk in up to 15 currencies and will establish swaps on a matched basis in many others.[2] (See Table 2 for specific information on the various currencies.)

USERS OF NON-U.S. DOLLAR SWAPS

Users of swaps include participants in the retail market (i.e., manufacturing, distribution, and financial corporations) and in the wholesale market (the banks and providers of swaps to retail users). The latter also use swaps to meet their own risk management needs. Some retail customers function more as wholesalers or traders, but that is rare.

---

[1] LIBOR (London Interbank Offered Rate) is the average of eight major banks' offered rates quoted at 11:00 A.M. London time. FIBOR (Frankfurt Interbank Offered Rate) is a similar average for 12 major West German banks.

[2] These dealers may also warehouse cross-currency swaps in these same currencies. Cross-currency swaps are swaps that exchange coupon payments in different currencies.

Retail Market: Liability Management

Corporations, supranationals, and sovereigns are the major retail users of nondollar interest rate protection. As hedging tools in general have become better known and understood, financial managers have realized that hedging/managing an interest rate risk exposure is, in fact, a conservative practice and that failure to do so increases risk. This growing emphasis on hedging has been reinforced by securities analysts who view the protection as an important sign of a well-managed company. Among U.S. corporations, the primary users are multinationals whose funding decisions involve financing at the local (non-U.S.) level.

Most liability managers use interest rate swaps to convert floating-rate liabilities to fixed-rate liabilities; however, some borrow at fixed rates and convert to floating-rate debt if, for example, the yield curve is positively sloped and the borrower believes that rates will decline or remain stable, or if a floating rate better matches the maturity profile of the company's assets. The decision regarding whether, how, and when to hedge may be made at either the parent company or subsidiary level, generally depending on the degree to which the company is decentralized. An example of how such a strategy might work is presented in Figure 1. In this case, the parent company utilizes its superior ability to raise funds in the public markets to borrow on behalf of its subsidiary. Through a capital markets transaction, the parent obtains floating-rate funds to lend to the subsidiary. The subsidiary then has a floating-rate borrowing and will determine when and how to hedge this expo-

FIGURE 1
Case of an Interest Rate Swap in Parent/Subsidiary Financing

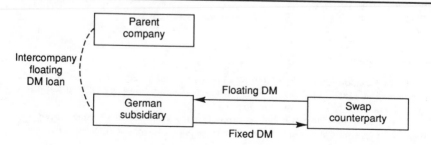

sure. Because the tenor of the intercompany loan generally closely approximates the average life of the subsidiary's assets, the subsidiary will generally enter into an interest rate swap to fix its interest rate for the term of the intercompany loan. The interest rate swap effectively locks in funds for the subsidiary, thus transferring rate risk to the swap counterparty.

Retail Market: Asset Management Applications

Investment portfolio managers have also become active participants in the nondollar interest rate swap market. These professionals are charged with overseeing the interest rate risk exposure of a portfolio that includes overseas obligations, such as non-U.S. dollar floating rate notes. Swaps may be used either on a portfolio basis or against a specific asset.

The portfolio approach involves general interest rate risk protection based on the total value and average life of the portfolio of assets, that is, on the interest rate sensitivity of the portfolio. For example, a manager with £500 million FRN (floating-rate note) portfolio that has a three-year average life might purchase a three-year interest rate swap in order to hedge £200 million of the total portfolio, protecting some of the portfolio against an adverse downward move in rates while leaving some leeway for gain if rates move favorably. (The manager might also buy an interest rate floor or use other option products.)

The specific asset swap approach actually changes the characteristics of a particular asset holding. For example, a portfolio manager may wish to purchase a floating-rate Swiss franc (SFR) bond to yield SFR LIBOR + 115 basis points (bp). There are two alternative sources of such an investment—SFR floating-rate notes (FRNs) or a fixed note swapped to floating. Often, the fixed-rate bond plus an interest rate swap will provide a higher yield, particularly when absolute swap interest rate levels are lower than the all-in rate of return on the bonds. This strategy is illustrated in Figure 2.

Often bonds and swaps are sold together as a synthetic FRN yielding LIBOR + 115 bp. The key difference between the synthetic structure and a straight FRN is that, in the synthetic structure, the bondholder may have to accept the credit risk of both the

FIGURE 2
Asset Swap

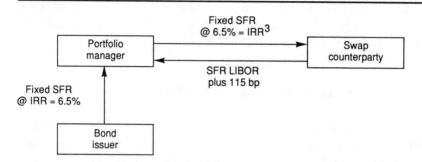

Note: IRR = internal rate of return. In this example, the offer side of the swap market is 5.30 percent. Because the dealer will receive 6.5 percent, the dealer is willing to pay the 120 bp advantage to the portfolio manager as a spread to LIBOR. The 120 bp per annum (bond basis) advantage is equivalent to 115 bp semiannual (money market basis).

bond issuer and the swap provider, as opposed to the bond issuer alone with a straight FRN.

Wholesale Market Applications

The largest group of swap users are swap traders or wholesale market makers. While largely comprised of major commercial and investment banks, this group increasingly includes corporations with a strong view on rates and a willingness to take additional risk in order to maximize returns.

Much of the liquidity of the non-U.S. dollar interest rate swap market is provided by the significant volume of wholesale trading, most of which is in the interbank swap market. The interbank swap market consists of swap dealers who are willing to take open positions in interest rate swaps. This is done for one or more of the following reasons:

- *Offsetting transactions.* Most swap books, and therefore positions, are set up primarily to support the bank's own customer, or retail, flow of demand. The dealer in effect transfers interest rate risk from the customer to the bank. In some cases, however, the bank may not wish to retain the open

interest rate risk and will look for a different counterparty—
in either the retail or professional markets—with an opposite interest rate protection need. At that time, the dealer
will enter into an offsetting transaction in order to lay off this
risk. This may be done either by establishing a new swap or
by assigning its position in the swap to the new counterparty.

- *Hedging the bank's own funding.* Interest rate swaps are
  often originated by the dealer's own treasury operations
  which seek to hedge existing interest rate exposure. In this
  case, the dealer is taking on the function more of a retail
  customer and is transferring its risk, albeit in-house, to the
  swap book. The dealer can then decide whether or not to
  offset the risk as noted above.

- *Interest rate positioning.* Given a view on the direction of
  interest rates, a dealer may take a long or short swap position, hoping to close out or offset the position at a later date
  for a profit.

- *An alternative to taking open bond positions.* Swaps have
  become an effective proxy for bonds because a fixed/floating
  interest rate swap is effectively a fixed-rate bond (long or
  short) with an associated long duration and a related floating-rate instrument (a proxy to the funding) with a very short
  duration. (See Chapter 14 for an extended discussion of the
  duration of interest rate swaps.) With interest rate swaps, a
  trader has the flexibility to take a short or long position with
  potentially less credit risk than would be incurred with the
  purchase or sale of a counterparty's corporate debt. In addition, liquidity in some foreign swap markets is actually
  greater than the liquidity in the underlying bond market and
  offers a smaller bid/asked spread and faster execution.
  Finally, unlike bonds, swaps offer traders much greater flexibility in obtaining the size, tenor, and payment streams that
  best meet their precise needs. This makes it easier to establish and liquidate positions.

Swaps may also be used as a proxy for a short bond position in
cases such as that of Germany, where it is illegal to short a government bond. In this instance the swap generally will increase in

value as interest rates rise, in the same direction, and often magnitude, as the equivalent-maturity short-bond position would in responding to rising rates. The key risk of such a proxy is the basis risk that swap rates will not move in the same direction or in the same magnitude as bond rates.

OVERCOMING ILLIQUIDITY

The non-U.S. dollar swap market has increased both in absolute size and as a percentage of the total interest rate swap market. As seen in Figures 3, 4, and 5, in 1987 the U.S. dollar market represented 79.3 percent of all interest rate swaps in terms of notional principal and declined to 72.08 percent in 1988. In terms of the number of swap contracts, the non-U.S. dollar market grew 106 percent from 1987 to 1988, whereas the U.S. market grew only 21

FIGURE 3
Interest Rate Swaps: Contracts by Currency

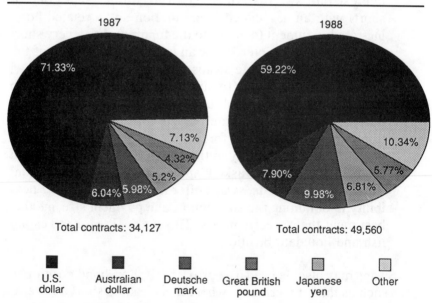

Source: International Swap Dealers Association, Inc.

FIGURE 4
Interest Rate Swaps: Notional Principal by Currency

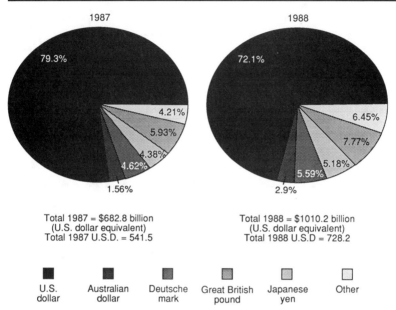

1987

79.3%

4.21%

5.93%

4.38%

4.62%

1.56%

Total 1987 = $682.8 billion
(U.S. dollar equivalent)
Total 1987 U.S.D. = 541.5

1988

72.1%

6.45%

7.77%

5.18%

5.59%

2.9%

Total 1988 = $1010.2 billion
(U.S. dollar equivalent)
Total 1988 U.S.D = 728.2

U.S. dollar	Australian dollar	Deutsche mark	Great British pound	Japanese yen	Other

Source: International Swap Dealers Association, Inc.

percent. Furthermore, as Figure 5 indicates, there was growth in notional principal in all non-U.S. dollar currencies from 1987 to 1988. The most widely traded nondollar interest rate swaps were yen, deutsche mark (DM), and sterling, with the Australian dollar, Canadian dollar, the French franc and Swiss franc markets expanding rapidly as well.

Although market expansion has increased swap market liquidity in the major currencies, some currencies remain illiquid with relatively few transactions and wide bid/asked spreads (see Table 1). Therefore, unlike the U.S. dollar market, illiquidity of the swap market may be a disincentive to undertaking certain transactions in certain currencies. This arises because the ability to exit, sell, or terminate a position at a reasonable price is critical to the risk inherent in entering into the transaction at the outset. In some cases, this problem may be resolved by hedging an exposure in one

FIGURE 5
Interest Rate Swaps: Non-U.S. Dollar Notional Principal

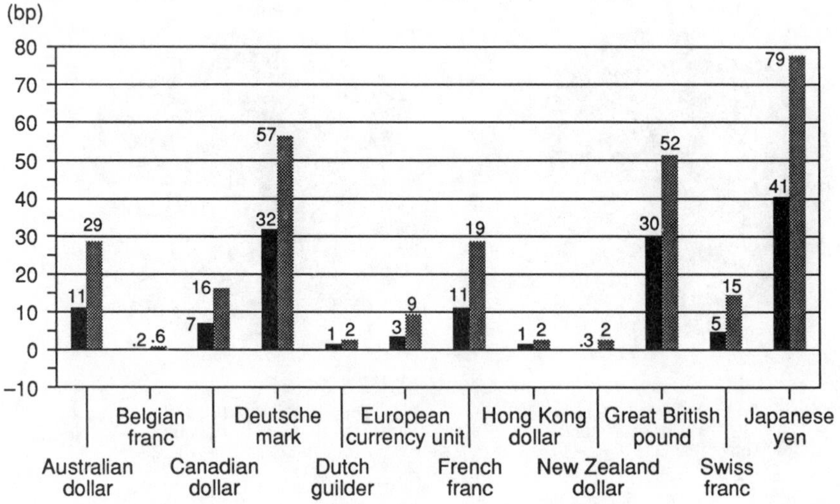

Source: International Swap Dealers Association, Inc.

currency's interest rate with an entirely different, but more liquid, related currency.

For example, a borrower who wanted to lock in an interest rate in the Dutch guilder, a currency with a less heavily traded interest rate swap market, could accomplish largely the same goal by establishing a hedge position in the more actively traded deutsche mark, so long as the currencies' interest rates and spot exchange rates were well correlated. (Again, the transactor takes significant basis risk, although a reasonable degree of correlation is likely because of their mutual membership in the European monetary union.)

The practice of such *proxy hedging* is fairly widely used by non-U.S. corporations; however, U.S. generally accepted accounting principles (GAAP) accounting precludes hedge accounting treatment for most proxy hedges, thus discouraging many U.S. transactors from engaging in these strategies.

TABLE 1
Sample Bid/Offer Spreads for Interest Rate Swaps

	3-Year (Percent)	5-Year (Percent)	10-Year (Percent)
U.S. dollar (USD)	.05%	.05%	.06%
Deutsche mark (DM)	.06	.06	.05
Japanese yen	.05	.03	.02
French franc (FFR)	.10	.10	.10
Spanish peseta (PTA)	.15	.20	—

Note: The bid/offer spreads represent the difference between the bid side and offer side of the market, as indicated by various banks or brokers. The spreads above are from September 20, 1989, and were taken from the following screens: USD-Telerate 883, DM-Reuters ICAR, Yen-Telerate 6493, FFR-Telerate 2513, PTA-Telerate 3898.

DISTINCTIONS BETWEEN CURRENCIES

When approaching the non-U.S. dollar interest rate swap market, it is important to be aware that each country has its own nuances in trading, quoting, and structuring swaps. Table 2 outlines the characteristics of the 15 most actively traded non-U.S. dollar swap markets. For each currency, it indicates the following:

- Abbreviations used to specify each currency.
- The fixed index or other pricing determinant on which the swap is based. (For example, U.S., U.K., and Canadian interest rate swaps trade as a spread to underlying governments. Most other currencies trade as an absolute rate.)
- The standard fixed-rate payment frequency.
- The floating-rate indices available and a brief description of each.
- The bases for calculating both fixed and floating rates.
- Individual currency characteristics.

ACCOUNTING AND TAX CONSIDERATIONS

Accounting and tax regulations are always under consideration and review by the relevant rule makers; therefore, any discussion here on current practice is subject to change. A related caveat is that the

TABLE 2
Interest Rate Swaps: Market Conventions

Currency	Symbols	Standard Fixed-Payment Frequency	Medium-Term Fixed Basis	Standard Floating-Rate Indices*	Floating Basis	Floating-Rate References	Comments
Australian dollar	AUD, A$, AUS	Semiannual	Act/365	A$ bank bills	Act/365	BBSW	Swaps of three years or less are quoted on a quarterly basis.
Australian shilling	AST, ATS	Annual	Act/360	VIBOR	Act/360	Reuters QQHI, Reuters QQHH	To determine VIBOR, drop the high and low rate on these pages and average the remaining six rates.
Belgian franc	BF, BFF, BFC	Annual	Act/365	BIBOR	Act/365	Reuters BELO, Telerate 3897	As of 1990, there is no longer any distinction between Belgian franc financial and convertible.
British pound (sterling)	STG, GBP, £	Semiannual	Act/365	STG LIBOR	Act/365	Telerate 3750	Spot Start in sterling means same day. LIBOR resets in sterling are done same day. Fixed STG can be quoted as a spread to British Treasury.
Canadian dollar	CAD, C$, CAN	Semiannual	Act/365	Canadian BAs	Act/365	Reuters CDOR	Fixed C$ is quoted as a spread to the Canadian Treasury. Canadian BA resets are done same day.
Danish kroner Dutch guilder European Currency Unit	DKR NLG, DFL, HFL ECU	Annual Annual Annual	30/360 30/360 30/360	CIBOR AIBO ECU LIBOR	Act/360 Act/360 Act/360	Reuters DKNH Reuters AIBO Telerate 3750	
Finnish markka	FM, FMK	Annual	30/360	HELIBOR	Act/360	Reuters SPFB	Six-month HELIBOR is most common, but 3- and 12-month have been used.
French franc	FF, FRF, FFR	Annual	30/360	FFR LIBOR, PIBOR, TAM	Act/360	Telerate 3740	Domestic FF swaps (i.e., done in France) are normally quoted against TAM. Euro FF swaps are generally done against FF LIBOR.‡
Hong Kong dollar Italian lira	HKD, H$ ITL, LIT	Annual Annual	30/360 30/360	HIBOR MIBOR ROLINT ITL LIBOR	Act/365 Act/360	Reuters HIBO Reuters ATIA, Telerate 3898, Reuters ILIR (Avg. rounded to 5 dec.)	MIBOR can be quoted either on the first day of each period or as an average of all days during the period. ROLINT is a floating rate between short- and long-term rates.§

Japanese yen	Yen, ¥	Semiannual	Act/365	YEN LIBOR	Act/360	Telerate 3750	Swaps versus yen prime exist, but they are very rare and not generally quoted.
New Zealand dollar (kiwi)	NZD	Semiannual	Act/365	NZD BBMR	Act/365	Reuters BKBM, Line "FRA"	
Norwegian krone	NKR	Semiannual	30/360	NIBOR	Act/360	Reuters NIBO	Most liquid market is in swaps less than three years and average trade size is estimated at NKR 20–25 million.
Spanish peseta	PTA, ESP, PSA	Semiannual or quarterly	Act/360	MIBOR	Act/360	Reuters FRRF, Reuters BHAX	Peseta swaps between an Spanish entity and a non-Spanish entity require approval from the Bank of Spain.
Swedish krona	SKR	Annual	30/360	STIBOR	Act/360	Reuters SIOR, Reuters SEBD	Fixed Swedish is quoted as Swedish Treasury bonds (R.O.) plus a spread. Reuters page SEBD lists spreads.
Swiss franc	SWF, SF, SFR, CHF	Annual	30/360	SWF LIBOR	Act/360	Telerte 3750	
West German mark (deutsche mark)	DM, DMK, DEM	Annual	30/360	DM LIBOR, FIBOR	Act/360	Telerate 3750, Reuters FIBO	FIBOR is mainly used for domestic transactions. It usually trades on a par with DM LIBOR.
United States dollar	US, USD, UD, U	Annual	30/360	U$D LIBOR	Act/360	Telerate 3750, Reuters LIBO	Fixed U$D is quoted as a spread to the US Treasury.

Note: This information has been obtained from sources we believe to be reliable; however, we cannot ensure the accuracy or completeness of the information.

* LIBOR London Interbank Offer Rate, BAs = Banker's Acceptances, AIBOR = Amsterdam Interbank Offer Rate, CIBOR = Copenhagen Interbank Offer Rate, FIBOR = Frankfurt Interbank Offer Rate, HIBOR = Hong Kong Interbank Offer Rate (H$), HELIBOR = Helsinki Interbank Offer Rate (FMK), MIBOR = Madrid Interbank Offer Rate (Peseta), MIBOR = Milan Interbank Offer Rate (Lire), NIBOR = Norway Interbank Offer Rate, STIBOR = Stockholm Interbank Offer Rate, VIBOR = Vienna Interbank Offer Rate, and BBMR = Bank Bills Mid Rate. (New Zealand dollar)

‡ With deregulation in France, distinctions between the "domestic" and "euro" FF markets have virtually disappeared.

§ A distinction must be made between Domestic- and Euro-Lire swaps. In the past, swaps cannot be transacted between an Italian entity and a non-Italian entity; however, those restrictions are currently being lifted.

rules are always subject to interpretation by individual accountants; hence, any transaction must be reviewed on an individual basis with the company's auditors. While this chapter does not attempt to cover all the tax and accounting rules and regulations in each country in which interest rate swaps are transacted, it will serve as a brief overview of standard U.S. practice.

Accounting

While there are currently no *authoritative* accounting rules regarding the accounting for non-U.S. dollar interest rate swaps, and therefore actual practice varies, a majority of transactors agree upon certain general guidelines:

- Swaps entered into for trading purposes should generally be marked to market, with any gains or losses treated as trading gains or losses.
- Swaps entered into for hedging purposes or as part of the overall asset/liability management of a corporation are generally not marked to market.

Many transactors agree that Statement of Financial Accounting Standards (SFAS) No. 80, "Accounting for Futures Contracts," can be interpreted to account for swaps, although they often selectively apply the criteria. SFAS No. 80 requires that the following criteria be met in order to qualify for hedge accounting: The transaction must expose the enterprise to rate risk; the transaction must reduce the risk of the transactor; and the transaction must be designated as a hedge of a specific asset, liability, firm commitment, or qualifying anticipatory transaction.

Although there is general agreement that a hedge must be identified, the criteria are not widely adhered to. This is particularly true for non-U.S. dollar swaps, since SFAS No. 52, "Foreign Currency Translation," does not include this requirement to qualify for hedge accounting. Also, the hedge designation process is often less specific for certain swaps that may be designated not as specific hedges but as an integral part of asset/liability management and, hence, not marked to the market.

Where a swap is not marked to market, the interest differential paid or received is accrued and generally recorded as interest income or expense. Also, to the extent that an entity enters into a swap in a currency other than its reporting currency, the swap may also generate a transaction gain or loss under SFAS No. 52. This would be recorded as a foreign exchange gain or loss in either income or equity, depending on the functional currency of the transacting entity.

Because of the diversity in practice, various accounting bodies are reviewing the accounting for swaps and other related financial instruments. Both the regulators and the Financial Accounting Standards Board (FASB), as part of its Financial Instruments project, are addressing the accounting for swaps and plan to propose authoritative guidance to promote greater consistency in practice. (Additional information on the accounting for interest rate swaps may be found in Chapter 22.)

Tax

The U.S. tax treatment of swap transactions will depend on whether the transaction qualifies as a full hedge, a partial hedge, or does not qualify as a hedge at all.

U.S. Tax Treatment

If a swap fully hedges a foreign currency loan or borrowing, payments made and received under the swap are fully integrated with the related loan or borrowing, and tax treatment follows accordingly. To be designated a full hedge, the swap must be entered into by the date the loan or borrowing is effective, must fully hedge all principal and interest payments made under the loan or borrowing, and must be properly identified as a hedging transaction.

If a swap is transacted to hedge a foreign currency borrowing, but all the conditions for a full hedge are not met, several rules apply. Partial hedge treatment is likely to apply, for example, where a taxpayer incurs a foreign currency borrowing and hedges the principal repayment but not the interest payments, or where the taxpayer incurs a foreign currency borrowing and hedges the interest and principal payments with a series of options. Net payments outflows are considered *interest equivalents* and are apportioned against U.S. and foreign source income as normal interest expense. Net payments *outflows* are considered interest equivalents and are apportioned against U.S. and foreign source income as normal interest expense. Net payments *inflows* are treated as U.S. source income. Also, foreign currency losses incurred on the underlying loan or borrowing will be increased or decreased by any gain or loss on the hedge, with the net amount apportioned against U.S. and foreign source income as interest expense.

Finally, payments made and received under all other swap transactions will be treated as *ordinary* income and expense and included as items of income or expense in the tax year when paid or received (the mark-to-market rules applied to foreign currency contracts do not apply to swaps).

Withholding Tax Issues

Until recently, certain swap transactions, particularly cross-currency swaps, subjected one or both of the counterparties to withholding tax. The IRS, however, recently clarified the rules such that cross-currency swaps (and nondollar interest rate swaps) are now subject to the same general rules as U.S. dollar interest rate swaps with regard to withholding taxes. Therefore, you can enter into a swap with any counterparty without regard to treaty jurisdiction. Note, however, that this does not apply to local withholding taxes for non-U.S. corporations.

LOOKING FORWARD

In the past few years, almost every innovation in the dollar-denominated interest-rate swap market has been duplicated in other currencies. Today, step-up, step-down, and zero coupon swaps are widely available. The swap is very much a customized product designed to perfectly hedge the cash flows of assets and liabilities in any currency; however, the rapid growth in demand and increasing liquidity of worldwide markets have helped to increase the commodity-like character of these products.

Today, other hedging products provide new, flexible alternatives. In addition to swaps, products like caps, floors, swaptions, and even options on swaptions are available in most actively traded currencies. As these instruments become better known and deployed, liquidity will increase in these markets as well.

As 1992 approaches and barriers to trade are being further dismantled, companies will continue to maximize financial market opportunities through cross-border expansion. These initiatives will further integrate the swap market into the most actively traded non-U.S. dollar capital markets in order to accommodate financing and investing requirements. As more currency restrictions are lifted and deregulation of capital markets continues, the number of currencies in which swaps will be transacted will increase, as will their ease of execution.

As of 1988, only about a third of the outstanding interest rate swaps have been denominated in non-U.S. dollar currencies. By the year 2000, nondollar swap transactions could account for up to 75 percent of all such transactions, should the current growth rate continue.

The burden will be on treasurers and other professionals to understand these products and to use them effectively in order to maximize returns and to protect corporate profits worldwide.

Laurence Schreiber assisted with the research for this chapter.

PART 3

VALUATION OF SWAPS

CHAPTER 11

THE INTEREST RATE SWAP MARKET: YIELD MATHEMATICS, TERMINOLOGY, AND CONVENTIONS

John Macfarlane
Daniel R. Ross
Janet Showers
Salomon Brothers Inc
New York, New York

INTRODUCTION

Since its inception in the late 1970s, the interest rate swap has developed from a negotiated device, using primarily by international banks and their corporate counterparties, into a broadly based market instrument used by virtually every type of institution.[1] The rapid growth of the over-the-counter swap market largely reflects the flexibility that it affords its participants in closing maturity, funding, and index mismatches on their balance sheets. In addition, market markers' willingness to structure swaps

---

[1] An interest rate swap is an agreement between two institutions in which each commits to make periodic interest payments to the other based on an agreed-upon notional principal amount, maturity, and either a predetermined fixed rate of interest or an agreed-upon floating money market index. No principal amounts change hands. This report will discuss only fixed-for-floating U.S. dollar interest rate swaps, although many of the principles outlined apply to other swaps as well.

that meet individual counterparty needs has further stimulated the market's growth.

The expansion of the market, however, has not come without costs. Throughout this period, the market has failed to develop a consistently used yield mathematics for swaps. This lack of consistency, along with the wide variety of swap structures, has caused specific transactions to be misunderstood and mispriced.

This report will remove the uncertainty and imprecision that have surrounded this market and explain the mathematics fundamental to its understanding. The approach that we will use follows:

- First, we will present the terminology that is most frequently used when discussing swaps.
- Second, we will describe the *generic swap,* which can serve as the basis for structuring swaps and as the cornerstone of a valuation procedure for swaps.
- Third, we will discuss complexities of swap cash flows that initially appear to make the application of traditional bond analysis difficult.
- Fourth, we will suggest a valuation methodology for analyzing a generic interest rate swap within the general bond math framework that is familiar to most market participants.
- Fifth, we will adapt our methodology for use in valuing nongeneric swaps.
- Finally, we will explore the typical nongeneric features actually found in the market and, using our methodology, describe their effect on a swap's cost or value.

Because the mathematical techniques used in this report employ only traditional bond mathematics, we hope that institutions that are presented with a swap will use this approach as a framework to analyze the swap's particular features and to assess its value.

A PRIMER ON MARKET TERMINOLOGY

Mathematics has not been the sole source of confusion for swap market participants. The lack of consistently used terminology and the fact that some terminology initially appears to be counterintuitive have left institutions unsure of how to approach the market. Thus, before we discuss mathematics, we will briefly review the following market terminology:

- The terms used when discussing the anatomy of a particular swap.
- The terms associated with positioning or making markets in swaps.
- The interpretation of market quotations for swaps.

An interest rate swap is a contract between two participants or *counterparties,* in which interest payments are made based on the *notional principal amount,* which itself is never paid or received. The fixed-rate payment in the swap (often called the fixed-rate coupon) is made by the *fixed-rate payer* to the *floating-rate payer.* Similarly, the floating-rate payment in the swap is made by the floating-rate payer (or variable-rate payer) to the fixed-rate payer. Both fixed and floating interest start accruing on the swap's *effective date* and cease accruing on the swap's *maturity date.* The *trade date* is the date on which the counterparties commit to the swap. On this date, the transaction is priced for value as of the *settlement date.*[2]

The various money market indices upon which the floating-rate payment could be based are presented in Figure 6. The floating-rate payment stream will sometimes be calculated based on the index plus or minus an agreed-upon number of basis points, known as the floating *spread.* The overall value or cost of a swap is expressed as the *all-in cost* (AIC), which will be discussed later. Although particular counterparties may supply credit enhancement devices (e.g., letter of credit, bank intermediaries, collateral, or insurance), the cost of such devices is not included in the AIC.

While the language relating to the structure of an individual swap is straightforward, the terminology associated with positioning or market making initially can appear to be somewhat confus-

---

[2] The settlement date is also the date on which any net cash payment—including any net accrued interest—changes hands. Such a cash payment could occur, for example, in secondary market or seasoned transactions, as discussed in the section on nonpar swaps. In the case of entering into a swap, the settlement date is normally the same as the effective date whether or not any cash payment occurs.

FIGURE 1
Terminology of the Swap Market

A Fixed-Rate Payer

Pays fixed in the swap
Receives floating in the swap
Has bought a swap
Is long a swap
Is short the bond market
Has established the price sensitivities of a longer-term liability and a floating-rate asset

---

A Floating-Rate Payer

Pays floating in the swap
Receives fixed in the swap
Has sold a swap
Is short a swap
Is long the bond market
Has established the price sensitivities of a longer-term asset and a floating-rate liability

---

ing. Historically, a market maker's bias has been to buy, or go long, swaps by being a fixed-rate payer.[3] A market maker who is long the swap market makes fixed-rate payments and, therefore, can be considered short the bond market (as if he had issued fixed-rate debt). This market anomaly has resulted in the widely accepted terminology shown in Figure 1.

The market convention for quoting swap levels is to quote the all-in cost (or the internal rate of return) of the fixed side of the swap versus the opposite flow of the floating index flat.[4] The swap's all-in cost can be expressed either as an absolute level on a semiannual basis or as a basis point spread to the semiannual bond equivalent of the U.S. Treasury yield curve. For an example of the latter type of quote, a seven-year LIBOR swap might be quoted to

---

[3] Given time, the market maker would sell his position to appropriate counterparties to offset these long positions. This trading strategy evolved because, initially, floating-rate payers were limited in number and relatively inflexible in accommodating various structures.

[4] The floating index *flat* means that the floating payments equal the index itself with no spread over or under the index.

a fixed-rate payer as the Treasury yield curve plus 60 basis points versus three-month LIBOR flat. This means that the fixed-rate payer could enter into a swap in which it receives three-month LIBOR flat and makes fixed payments, the internal rate of return of which equates to 60 basis points over the semiannual bond equivalent yield of the Treasury yield curve on the trade date.[5]

Market participants use several methods to define the Treasury yield curve. The most predominant methods determine at the time of execution the yield of a principal amount of Treasury securities based on the swap's notional principal amount.[6] One method defines the curve as the semiannual yield to maturity of the specific note or bond with maturity closest to that of the swap. This method, unfortunately, often results in anomalous levels because of thin trading in the particular security or because of the presence of a discount or premium in the particular security.

We believe that a better method involves using only current coupon *on-the-run* securities. If the swap's maturity is reasonably close to the maturity of such a security, then that security's yield defines the curve. If the swap's maturity lies between that of two on-the-run securities, then the curve would be defined by interpolation of the yields.[7]

THE GENERIC SWAP

Throughout the evolution of the market, we have observed one fundamental structure emerging as the point of reference against which all interest rate swaps are compared. This generic (or *plain*

---

[5] The cash flows for this internal rate of return calculation include, for analytical purposes, the price of the hypothetical fixed-rate bond and redemption of principal at maturity (see the section on valuation methodology).

[6] The price of the Treasury securities is negotiated at the time that the parties enter the swap. Market makers have historically wanted to use the bid side to determine the curve for fixed-rate payers and the offered side to determine the curve for floating-rate payers. This convention developed because a market maker selling a swap to a fixed-rate payer traditionally sold its hedge and, hence, used the bid side. Similarly, the market maker traditionally bought a hedge when buying a swap from a floating-rate payer and, thus, used the offered side.

[7] Interpolation is straight-line based on the actual number of days between the maturity of the swap and the two securities.

vanilla) swap may not be the final structure of most swaps completed, but it remains the single theme on which all of the countless swap variations are based. The generic swap, therefore, is a starting point for analysis.

The generic interest rate swap combines the characteristics of a traditional fixed-income security on the fixed-rate side with the

FIGURE 2
Terms of the Generic Swap

Terms	Definition
Maturity	1 to 15 years
Effective date	Five business days from trade date (corporate settlement). The effective date is such that the first fixed- and first floating-payment periods are full coupon periods (i.e., no long or short first coupons)
Settlement date	Effective date
	Fixed Payment
Fixed Coupon	Current market rate
Payment Frequency	Either semiannually or annually
Day Count	30/360
Pricing Date	Trade date
	Floating Payment[a]
Floating Index	Certain money market indices
Spread	None
Determination source	Some publicly quoted source, for example, the *Reuter Monitor Money Rates Service* or the *Federal Reserve Statistical Release H.15(519)*
Payment frequency	The term of the floating index itself
Day count	Actual/360 for private sector floating rate indices and actual/actual for Treasury bills
Reset frequency	The term of the floating index itself, except for Treasury bills, for which the index is reset weekly regardless of term
First coupon	Current market rate for the index
Premium or discount	None[b]
All-in-cost	Semiannual equivalent of the internal rate of return of the fixed flows versus the floating index flat[c]

[a] For details on floating-rate generic standards, see Figure 6.
[b] This means that no cash payment is made by either party on the effective date (see the section on nonpar swaps).
[c] See Footnote 5.

characteristics of a traditional floating-rate note on the floating side. These characteristics are outlined in Figure 2.

COMPLEXITIES OF SWAP ANALYSIS

Several factors complicate the analysis of cost or return of an interest rate swap within the confines of traditional bond math. Two such complications affect even the generic swap, which is the most straightforward in terms of valuation: (a) An interest rate swap involves neither an investment at settlement date nor a repayment of principal at maturity, and (b) a swap's future floating-rate payment stream is unknown. These two factors must be addressed first in setting forth a valuation technique for swaps.

Swapping Interest Payments or Swapping Securities?

The first obstacle to analyzing an interest rate swap using bond math is overcome by viewing the swap as a simultaneous exchange of two separate hypothetical securities of equal maturity. This notion holds that the fixed-rate payer has sold a hypothetical fixed-rate security to the floating-rate payer and that the floating-rate payer has sold a hypothetical floating-rate note to the fixed-rate payer. Because the par amount of both securities is the notional principal amount of the swap, a netting of the two purchase prices upon settlement and of the two principal repayments at maturity results in no net cash flow based upon principal dollars.[8]

This artificial construct allows us to look at the two securities separately for valuation purposes. Whether one thinks of a swap as an exchange of interest payments or an exchange of securities, the net cash flows of the swap are the same.

---

[8] In a generic swap the prices of the exchanged securities are equal and, thus, no net cash payment is exchanged upon settlement. In nongeneric swaps, the prices may not be equal. In such a case, the net of the two purchase prices would determine the cash payment upon settlement (see the section on nonpar swaps).

The Uncertainty of the Floating-Rate Payments

The uncertainty of the floating-rate payment stream presents a slightly more difficult problem to overcome. The fundamental question is how can one determine the market value of a swap without knowing the precise floating-rate payments. Specifically, would a technique like Simple Margin, Total Margin, Adjusted Total Margin, or Discount Margin be required?[9]

The structure of an interest rate swap, however, suggests a simple answer to this fundamental question. Unlike a true floating-rate note, a swap has two-way cash flows: fixed versus floating. This feature allows the swap market to value the relative attractiveness of a swap's floating index by bidding the accompanying fixed rate up or down. Consequently, the floating-rate note valuation techniques mentioned are not required. The value of the floating-rate security is incorporated into the fixed cost quoted versus the floating payments. Therefore, valuation questions for swaps focus on the hypothetical fixed security.

THE VALUATION METHODOLOGY FOR GENERIC SWAPS

The basic valuation method for *generic* swaps is to find the internal rate of return of the hypothetical fixed-security flows. For analytical purposes these flows, from the perspective of the fixed-rate payer, are the proceeds received from the sale of the hypothetical fixed-rate security versus an outflow of the fixed-rate payments plus the notional principal amount at maturity.[10] The internal rate of return (expressed as a semiannual bond equivalent) of the hypothetical fixed security is quoted as the all-in cost versus the floating flows that constitute the index flat.

---

[9] These tools attempt to measure a floater's return by quantifying an implicit change in the floating rate whenever the note deviates from par.

[10] The proceeds are not cash but instead are the value of the hypothetical floating-rate note received in exchange. In a generic swap the value of the hypothetical floating-rate note is par. For nongeneric swaps the proceeds are the net of the value of the floater and any cash payment on the settlement date (see the section on nonpar swaps).

THE VALUATION METHODOLOGY FOR NONGENERIC SWAPS: THE GENERIC EQUIVALENT CASH FLOW APPROACH (GECA)

The structuring of swaps to meet individual counterparty needs often results in nongeneric swaps. When a swap's floating side is not generic, merely determining the internal rate of return of the fixed side would not produce a meaningful number.[11] If the floating side could be adjusted to be generic, however, both generic and nongeneric swaps could be compared on an equivalent basis. To this end, we use the *generic equivalent cash flow approach* (GECA) to value nongeneric swaps.

Under GECA we use the following procedure in analyzing a swap:

- First, we construct the cash flows of the two securities as specified in the swap contract.
- Second, we determine whether the floating payments are generic. If they are not, we artificially adjust the floating cash flows to correspond to a stream of payments satisfying the generic standard.[12] If the floating payments must be altered, we must alter the fixed cash flows by these same dollar amounts (the *adjustment flows*) so that the swap's net cash flows remain unchanged. We will refer to these adjusted cash flows as the *analytical flows* to distinguish them from the *contractual flows*.
- The final step in the GECA process is to determine the internal rate of return (on a semiannual-equivalent basis) of the analytical fixed flows. Because the floating cash flows were adjusted to be the generic standard, this internal rate of return is the swap's all-in cost.

---

[11] The floating payments are generic if they fulfill the conditions set forth in the generic swap, namely: The payments equal the index flat; the payment frequency equals the index maturity; the reset frequency equals the index maturity (with the exception of Treasury bills, which are reset weekly); and the day-count convention is consistent with the basis on which the index is quoted (see Figure 6).

[12] For some nongeneric swaps, it is not possible to adjust the floating cash flows to the generic standard in a precise manner without knowing the level of the floating index. (For example, see the section on mismatches).

VARIATIONS ON THE GENERIC THEME

This section will discuss nongeneric swap features that often occur in the market. Where possible for each such feature, we will use our GECA methodology to describe the feature's effect on the swap's all-in cost. Because GECA requires that the floating payments be adjusted to the generic standard, our discussion will begin with nongeneric floating-payment structures. We will then consider nongeneric fixed-payment structures.

For ease of discussion, we will use a particular generic swap as an example. Then, by varying the swap's terms, we will create nongeneric swaps and discuss how these nongeneric terms affect the all-in cost.

The swap described in Figure 3 is clean analytically:

- The floating payment is the index flat.
- The floating rate is based on *Reuters*.
- The payment and reset frequencies of the floating payment are equal to the term of the index.
- There are no day-count discrepancies between payments and their standards.
- The initial floating coupon is a current rate.
- There is no premium or discount.
- The swap settles "corporate."
- There are no short or long first coupon payments.
- The swap is priced on the trade date.

Floating-Rate Variations

Spreads above or below the Floating-Rate Index
Many swaps are structured with floating-rate payments based on the floating-rate index plus or minus an agreed-upon spread. For example, a swap might be structured with a fixed-rate payment of 12.50 percent semiannual and floating-rate payment of six-month LIBOR less 25 basis points. To express this swap's AIC according to market convention against the index flat, one is tempted simply to add 25 basis points to both sides and call it 12.75 percent semiannual versus six-month LIBOR flat. Unless the fixed rate and the floating rate are calculated on the same day-count basis and paid on

FIGURE 3
Generic Swap—A Base Case Example

Notional principal amount	$10,000,000
Maturity	May 15, 1992
Trade date	May 8, 1985
Effective date	May 15, 1985
Settlement date	Effective date

Fixed Payment

Fixed coupon	12.50%
Payment frequency	Semiannual
Day count	30/360
Pricing date	Trade date

Floating Payment

Floating index	Six-month LIBOR
Spread	None
Determination source	*Reuter Monitor Money Rates Service*
Payment frequency	Semiannual
Day count	Actual/360
Reset frequency	Semiannual
First coupon	Six-month LIBOR quoted for value as of the settlement date
Premium or Discount	None
All-In cost	12.50% (semiannual) versus six-month LIBOR flat

the same frequency, however, this procedure would be inaccurate. Analyses of two different cases of this type of swap follow.

In swaps of the first case, fixed and floating payments have the same frequency. Consider our base case example described in Figure 3, with a spread under the floating index set at 25 basis points. To find the all-in cost, we use GECA. First, the floating payments are artificially altered to become LIBOR flat, and then the fixed flows are altered by the same dollar amounts.

The first floating payment covers the period from May 15, 1985, until November 15, 1985—or 184 days. An increase in the LIBOR rate by 25 basis points changes the payment by

$$0.0025 \times 10,000,000 \times 184/360 = 12,777.78.$$

In terms of the fixed-rate note, this corresponds to 25.56 basis points higher on the first coupon. On the second coupon, the in-

FIGURE 4
Effect of a Floating Spread with the Same Payment Frequencies

Contractual flows

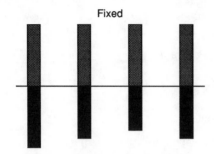

Fixed

Floating index - 25 basis points

Analytical flows

$$\text{Fixed} + \left(\frac{25}{100} = \frac{\text{Actual}}{360}\right)$$

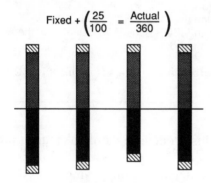

Floating index

crease is 25.14 basis points because the next period covers only 181 days. Each fixed-rate payment must be adjusted in this way to determine the precise analytical cash flows and yield of the fixed-rate note. This procedure, when completed, shows the all-in cost of this swap to be 12.7537 percent versus six-month LIBOR flat. Figure 4 depicts the contractual and analytical cash flows.

In swaps of the second case, fixed and floating payments have different frequencies. For this example, consider the generic base case swap with the floating rate changed to three-month LIBOR less 25 basis points reset and paid quarterly. As in the last example, the fixed-rate payer receives 25 basis points less on the floating payment. However, here this loss occurs quarterly instead of semiannually, which adds a compounding effect to the day-count effect of the last example. To analyze this swap structure, we must analytically add the dollar value of the 25 basis points onto the quarterly floating-rate payments to create three-month LIBOR flat and then adjust the fixed cash-flow stream by the same amounts. This procedure results in the analytical fixed-payment stream shown in Figure 5.

FIGURE 5
Effect of a Floating Spread with Different Payment Frequencies

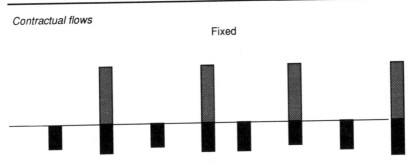

Contractual flows

Fixed

Floating index - 25 basis points

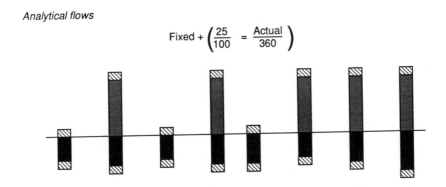

Analytical flows

$$\text{Fixed} + \left(\frac{25}{100} = \frac{\text{Actual}}{360} \right)$$

Floating index

Figure 5 illustrates the generic equivalent cash flow approach: The fixed-rate payer, essentially, makes small quarterly payments to the floating-rate payer, while the floating-rate payer analytically pays three-month LIBOR flat. This extra quarterly analytical payment increases the all-in cost of the fixed-rate payer to 12.7577 percent versus three-month LIBOR flat. The compounding effect is 0.4 basis point in addition to the 0.37-basis-point day-count effect seen in the previous example. Although both effects are small, it would be an error to ignore either one.

Mismatches

The characteristics of the floating-rate side of a generic swap are based on the cash market in the short-term instrument on which the index is based. Specifically, the swap's reset frequency and payment frequency equal the maturity of the underlying cash instrument, and the swap's floating rate accrues on a day count consistent with its form of quotation. For example, the floating rate in a generic three-month LIBOR swap resets quarterly, pays quarterly, and accrues on an actual/360 day count. The exception to this rule is a generic Treasury bill swap, which resets weekly.[13]

The flexibility of the interest rate swap market, however, often creates transactions that have floating sides that deviate structurally from the underlying cash market. Any such deviation is called a *mismatch*. We will now discuss mismatches in payment frequency, day count, and reset frequency.[14]

Payment-Frequency Mismatch.

A payment-frequency mismatch occurs when the floating-rate payment frequency does not agree with the maturity of the floating-rate index. For example, a swap in which the fixed-rate payer receives interest based on the three-month commercial paper index reset quarterly but paid semiannually is a payment-frequency mismatch swap.[15]

---

[13] While inconsistent with the cash market in bills themselves, this convention appears consistent with the structure of most bill-based floating-rate notes.

[14] One swap can possess more than one mismatch. For example, consider a swap in which three-month LIBOR is reset semiannually and paid semiannually.

[15] The receipt of a three-month index semiannually probably recurs because, for both credit and operational reasons, swap counterparties often prefer net transactions, i.e., where payment of both fixed and floating interest occurs on the same day.

In this example, the fixed-rate payer loses the compounding of interest on interest that he would have received had he invested in the underlying cash instrument. Unfortunately, the precise cost of losing this opportunity to compound is difficult to calculate. An institution presented with a payment-frequency mismatch swap must make a largely qualitative assessment of both the amount of interest available to reinvest and the rate at which it should be compounded. Because both are impossible to completely determine in advance, no methodology can quantify precisely the effect of a payment-frequency mismatch on AIC.

Although this problem is difficult to assess, it does appear to have a reasonable solution. If the accrued floating-rate interest is compounded at the next floating rate until payment of the floating interest occurs, the fixed-rate payer should be satisfied.[16] If, however, the counterparties cannot agree on this or on some other compounding arrangement, they will be forced to make a qualitative judgment about the value of the payment-frequency mismatch.

Day-Count Mismatch. The generic interest rate swap offers a day count consistent with the basis on which the floating-rate index is quoted. For example, if the certificate of deposit (CD) equivalent rate of one-month commercial paper is the basis for quoting the floating rate then the floating-rate payment should accrue according to an actual/360 day-count basis. Figure 6 outlines the most frequently used conventions.

Any inconsistencies between the swap conversion basis and the swap day count would alter the economics of the swap. Because the economic effect of a day-count mismatch varies with the absolute level of interest rates, no methodology can precisely quantify this nongeneric day-count effect. However, a counterparty can use GECA to estimate the magnitude of the day-count mismatch effect by making assumptions about the levels of the floating rate over the life of the swap.

---

[16] If there are more than two reset periods in each payment period (for example one-month commercial paper, which is reset monthly and paid semiannually), then the total accrued before a given reset period should be compounded forward through that period at that period's rate. This compounding should occur for all resets (after the first set).

FIGURE 6
Floating-Rate Generic Standards

Floating Index	Cash Market Quotation Basis	Swap Conversion Basis[a]	Swap Day Count	Payment Frequency	Reset Frequency
Treasury bills	Discount	BE	Actual/actual	Term of index	Weekly
Commercial paper	Discount	CDE	Actual/360	Term of index	Term of index
Bankers' acceptances	Discount	CDE	Actual/360	Term of index	Term of index
LIBOR	CDE	CDE	Actual/360	Term of index	Term of index
Prime	CDE	CDE	Actual/360	Quarterly	Daily
Certificates of deposit	CDE	CDE	Actual/360	Term of index	Term of index
Federal funds	CDE	CDE	Actual/360	Compounded daily to mutually agreeable frequency	Daily

[a] In the case of indices quoted on a discount basis, the actual number of days in a floating-rate period—and not a predetermined notion as to the maturity of the discount instrument—should be used when converting to a bond equivalent (BE) or CD equivalent (CDE) basis. (See the *Code of Standard Wording, Assumptions and Provisions for Swaps, 1985 Edition.*) For indices with maturities of 182 days or less, the following formulas can be used to convert between a rate quoted on a discount basis (*d*), a bond equivalent basis (*b*), and a CD equivalent basis (*c*):

$$b = \frac{365 \times d}{360 - d \times t} \qquad c = b \times \frac{360}{365}$$

where *t* is the actual number of days in the floating-rate period.

Reset-Frequency Mismatch.   A reset-frequency mismatch occurs when the reset frequency does not agree with the maturity of the floating-rate index.[17] An illustration of this nongeneric variation would be our base case example changed to require monthly resets of the six-month LIBOR index. In this revised swap, the interval between resets is shorter than the maturity of the index.

This nongeneric feature clearly changes the value of the swap. Resetting an index more frequently than its stated term ignores the fact that, by choosing a particular maturity, cash investors choose to forfeit more frequent repricing opportunities. Because the cash investor's repricing expectations are theoretically incorporated in the index, it is inappropriate to alter the reset frequency of the index without considering its impact on value.

The value of such a structure, however, depends on the investor's expectations and portfolio considerations. For example, a fixed-rate payer who wishes to match existing short-term liabilities that are reset weekly with a three- or six-month private-sector swap index might be willing to pay more for a swap with more frequent nongeneric resets than for a swap with a generic structure. Little can be done, however, to quantify the effect of this market anomaly on the pricing of interest rate swaps. Such nongeneric reset features, however, certainly deserve qualitative consideration when they appear.

Short or Long First Floating-Rate Period

A swap may trade with a first floating-rate payment period that is either shorter or longer than those in the remainder of the swap.[18] In our base case generic example, this would occur if the effective date were July 15, 1985.[19] In this case, the appropriate floating-rate index for the first floating-rate period is at issue.

---

[17] Therefore, the generic Treasury bill swap, in which the floating rate resets weekly, is a reset-frequency mismatch. The structure nevertheless is considered to be generic because it is consistent with the underlying market in bill-based floating-rate notes.

[18] This would most likely occur in the case of a secondary market trade or the sale of a seasoned swap. A *seasoned swap* is a swap held in a position by a market maker awaiting primary distribution.

[19] The trade date would be changed to July 8, 1985, to maintain corporate settlement. All other terms would remain the same.

We believe that the correct index in this example would be four-month LIBOR flat. In general, if a private-sector swap has a short or long first floating-rate period and the structure of the floating side is otherwise generic, then the index for the first period should have a maturity equal to the time from the effective date until the first reset date.[20] This structure is consistent with the cash market. Furthermore, if there is a spread over or under the regular index, then the same spread should apply to the first-period index.

The presence of a payment-frequency or reset-frequency mismatch creates problems for determining the correct index for a long or short first coupon. For example, what would be the proper short first coupon for a five-week first floating-payment period on a swap with a regular floating-rate index of three-month LIBOR reset weekly and paid quarterly? Definitive market convention has not yet been established in this area. However, the rule proposed above for use with otherwise generic swaps could be a starting point for negotiating the appropriate short or long first coupon.

Fixed-Rate Variations

Payment Frequencies
By definition generic swaps have semiannual or annual fixed-rate coupons. Although rare, other fixed-rate payment frequencies do exist. The rule for computing the all-in cost is the same whether the fixed coupons are semiannual or nonsemiannual: The AIC equals the internal rate of return (expressed on a semiannual bond-equivalent basis) of the analytical fixed flows.

For a generic (par) swap with a semiannual fixed coupon, therefore, the AIC equals the fixed-coupon rate. For an otherwise generic swap with a nonsemiannual fixed coupon, the AIC equals the semiannual equivalent of the fixed-coupon rate.

For example, if the base case example is changed to pay a 12.50 percent coupon annually, the annual yield of the hypothetical fixed-rate note becomes 12.50 percent, but the swap would be quoted at the semiannual all-in cost of 12.132 percent. If one were

---

[20] Because of the anomalies of the short Treasury bill market, Treasury bill swaps generally pay the stated index regardless of the term of the initial variable-rate period.

to structure a generic swap with a 12.50 percent semiannual all-in cost but with an annual fixed-rate coupon, the annual coupon would be 12.891 percent. (See the Appendix for conversion formulas.)

Short and Long First Fixed-Rate Period

Except when closing out an existing swap, swaps settle flat (i.e., with no accrued interest).[21] Consequently, when valuing a swap that settles on any date other than a fixed-coupon payment date, the present value calculation must incorporate a long or short first coupon period. The mathematics of this discounting is such that, on an otherwise generic swap, the all-in cost will not equal the coupon rate if the first coupon is short or long. The Appendix contains formulas for the discounting process.

Day Counts

Although the market convention is to structure swaps with fixed-rate payments accruing on a 30/360 day-count basis, other day-count methods are used. The actual/360 day count, the actual/365 and the actual/actual all appear. To determine the price or equivalent generic all-in cost for such a nongeneric swap, the GECA method is applied to the actual fixed-coupon cash flows to construct the analytical fixed flows, which then are discounted on a 30/360 basis.

Effective Date

The generic swap provides for five business days to elapse between the trade date and the effective date. (For simplicity in this discussion, assume that the effective date is the settlement date.) Any variation of this settlement period alters the economics of the swap and, therefore, requires analysis.

The impact of an accelerated or delayed effective date is the opportunity costs afforded each counterparty by entering into the swap with an irregular settlement period. One measure of this im-

---

[21] Closeouts are the termination of an existing swap between counterparties through a mutually agreeable cash payment.

pact is the difference between the fixed and floating interest that otherwise might have accrued. Typically, the two counterparties agree either to pay this adjustment on the settlement date or to amortize it over the life of the swap.

Nonpar Swaps

Thus far we have examined swaps with no net cash payment at settlement and with both hypothetical securities valued at par. At this point we will generalize the GECA methodology to incorporate cash payments and situations in which the hypothetical securities are not at par. This methodology can then be applied to analyze any swap (except those with the features mentioned above that render precise analysis impossible). Figure 7 summarizes the sequence of steps in the analysis.

It may be useful to place the previously described GECA analysis into the framework of Figure 7. Steps 1, 2, and 3 are performed in the analysis of all swaps. Thus far, in our all-in cost determinations the floating-rate note has been assumed to be at par (Step 4), and there were no cash payments. Therefore, the proceeds in Step 7 have been par, and Step 8 could be completed with 100 as the proceeds.

Even Swaps

A swap with no cash payment at the settlement date occurs when, at pricing, the value of the hypothetical fixed-rate note equals the value of the hypothetical floating-rate note received in exchange. The two securities can be equal in two situations—when they both are at par or when they both are at the same nonpar price. We call the swap situation in which both hypothetical securities are at par a *par swap*. The second situation, in which the securities have equal but nonpar prices, is called an *even swap* (see Figure 8). Note that because the hypothetical securities in a generic swap have current, regular coupons, they are at par. Therefore, generic swaps are par swaps.

Differential Swaps: Premiums and Discounts

A swap involving a cash payment at settlement occurs when the values of the two hypothetical securities are not equal at pricing.

FIGURE 7
Summary of Generic Equivalent Cash Flow Approach (GECA)

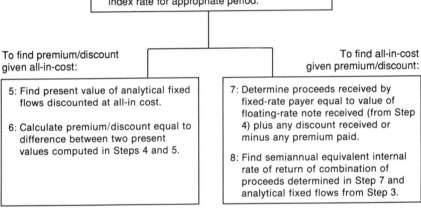

1: Determine fixed and floating contractual flows.

2: Determine adjustment flows needed to alter floating payments to generic index flat.

3: Determine fixed and floating analytical flows equal to sum of contractual and adjustment flows plus par at maturity.

4: Find present value of next analytical floating coupon plus par discounted at current market index rate for appropriate period.

To find premium/discount given all-in-cost:

5: Find present value of analytical fixed flows discounted at all-in cost.

6: Calculate premium/discount equal to difference between two present values computed in Steps 4 and 5.

To find all-in-cost given premium/discount:

7: Determine proceeds received by fixed-rate payer equal to value of floating-rate note received (from Step 4) plus any discount received or minus any premium paid.

8: Find semiannual equivalent internal rate of return of combination of proceeds determined in Step 7 and analytical fixed flows from Step 3.

FIGURE 8
Classification of Swaps by Pricing

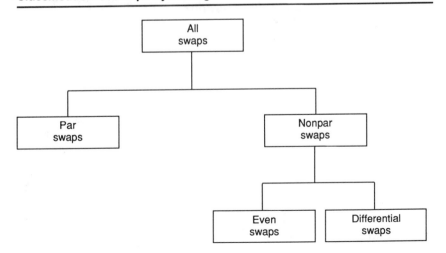

All swaps

Par swaps

Nonpar swaps

Even swaps

Differential swaps

Because the payment compensates for the difference in value of the two securities, we call this swap a *differential* swap. By swap market convention, if a counterparty makes a payment at the settlement date of a swap, then that payment is referred to as a *premium*. If a counterparty receives a payment at the settlement date, then that payment is known as a *discount*.

Although this terminology has been borrowed from the bond market, its meaning in the swap market is distinct. In the bond market, these terms refer to the difference between the price of a security and its own par value. In the swap market, these terms refer to the difference in price between the two hypothetical securities involved in a swap. In a differential swap, the cash payment is both a premium (to the party that makes the payment) and a discount (to the party that receives the payment).

Valuation of Even and Differential Swaps with GECA

The major procedural change that must be made when analyzing nonpar swaps is that we must determine the proceeds of the fixed-rate note sale. This step is not necessary in analyzing a par swap for which the proceeds are always par. In a nonpar swap, the proceeds of the sale of the hypothetical fixed-rate security are the value of the hypothetical floating-rate note received in exchange less any premium paid or plus any discount received. When solving for all-in cost, the premium or discount is known and the hypothetical floater must be valued to determine the fixed-rate payer's proceeds. Conversely, when determining the appropriate premium or discount, one must determine the value of both hypothetical securities.

Determining the Hypothetical Floating-Rate Note.
In interest rate swap analysis, the hypothetical floating-rate note paying the index flat is considered to be at par on any of its payment dates. If at some point the index flat is not deemed to be an appropriate return in the market, the swap market will revalue the fixed security to reflect new conditions. Thus, the benchmark index-flat floater will remain at par on coupon dates.

Once a coupon rate is set, however, market variations of the appropriate maturity index can cause the hypothetical security to trade above or below par.[22] For example, in a generic swap, if three-month LIBOR is 9 percent at the reset but, one month later, two-month LIBOR is at 10 percent, the flat price at the floater will be worth less than par. To determine the full price of the floating-rate note between coupon payments, determine the present value of the next coupon, which has been previously set, plus par, which is the value of the floater on the next payment date. The discount rate used is the current market rate for the appropriate maturity of the index. In the example, the appropriate discount rate is 10 percent.

Determining All-in Cost of a Nonpar Swap. To determine the all-in cost of a swap with a cash payment at settlement or with a nonpar floating-rate note, first the analytical fixed-bond flows paid versus the receipt of the generic index-flat note must be constructed using GECA (Steps 1, 2, and 3 of Figure 7). The proceeds of this hypothetical fixed-rate note are the value of the hypothetical floating-rate note plus any discount received or minus any premium paid by the fixed-rate payer. This is Step 7 of Figure 7. Then in Step 8, the all-in cost is calculated by computing the internal rate of return of the fixed-bond flows.

For example, let us alter the base case example to include a payment of 0.6 percent of the notional principal amount to the floating-rate payer on the settlement date, and let us assume that the floating-rate note has a price of 99.6; all other terms of the base case remain the same. The analytical fixed-rate security (versus six-month LIBOR flat) is a seven-year bond paying 12.50 percent semiannually with a price of 99. The semiannual all-in cost of this swap (equal to the yield on this hypothetical bond) is 12.72 percent.

Pricing Secondary Market or Seasoned Swaps with GECA

In secondary market or in seasoned-swap transactions, the terms of the fixed and floating payments have previously been negoti-

---

[22] The appropriate maturity is the period from the settlement date to the next floating-rate reset date.

ated. Current market levels determine the all-in cost. The premium or discount is the unknown. The process of determining this payment is known as *pricing* a swap.

The procedure for pricing a swap is similar to that described for determining a swap's all-in cost. Referring to Figure 7, Steps 1, 2, and, 3 are performed as before to construct the analytical flows for the two hypothetical securities. At this point each of the two component securities is priced (Steps 4 and 5). The method for pricing the floating-rate note has been described. The fixed-rate note is priced using a conventional bond math approach discounting the analytical cash flows at the all-in cost.

The difference between the prices of the hypothetical fixed-rate and floating-rate notes is the market price of the swap. If the floating security is worth more than the fixed security, then the fixed-rate payer would make a cash payment to the floating-rate payer when entering into the swap. In the same market situation, the fixed-rate payer would receive a cash payment if closing out the swap. Conversely, if the fixed security is worth more than the floating security, the floating-rate payer would make a cash payment to the fixed-rate payer when entering into the swap, or it would receive cash payment if closing out the swap. In addition to the cash payment, net accrued is also paid.

For example, suppose that the floating-rate note is worth 99 and the fixed-rate security is worth 95. The fixed-rate payer would receive a payment of four points (plus or minus the net accrued) if closing out the swap. In essence, the fixed-rate payer is repurchasing its fixed-rate security worth 95 with the floating-rate note that it holds that is worth 99. The excess of four points is returned.

CONCLUSION

As long as the interest rate swap market operates as a negotiated over-the-counter market, swap structures will vary as widely as the counterparties themselves. In our approach to interest rate swap mathematics and pricing, we do not intend to suggest that one structure is superior to another. Instead, we simply wish to establish a standard—the generic swap—against which the myriad varieties of swaps can be measured. We hope that the introduction of this standard, coupled with a fair and consistent framework for analysis of nongeneric swaps, will eliminate the uncertainty about interest rate swap mathematics. Ultimately, our goal is to increase understanding and encourage wider use of this valuable asset and liability management tool.

APPENDIX

This Appendix provides a technical description of how to price generic and nongeneric interest rate swaps using standard bond pricing methodology.[1] These procedures are based on the notion that an interest rate swap can be considered an exchange of a hypothetical fixed-income security for a hypothetical floating-rate note (see Figure 7 in the text). The Appendix will first discuss the pricing of the fixed side of the swap (including any adjustment flows required) and then describe the pricing of the floating side (which has been adjusted to the index flat). Each formula will be demonstrated through an example based on the base case generic swap set forth in Figure 3. For simplicity, the Appendix assumes that the floating rate is based on a generic LIBOR index, with a spread introduced in the appropriate examples.

Discounting Methods

The pricing of the fixed and floating sides of a swap involves present-value calculations. The discounting methods used are consistent with the pricing methods used in the corporate fixed-rate bond and floating-rate note markets, respectively. This means that the flows of the fixed-rate side of the swap, including any adjustment flows due to a spread under or over the floating index, are discounted scientifically on a 30/360 day-count basis. In contrast, the flows of the floating side, adjusted to have no spread, are discounted in a straight-line manner using the actual/360 day-count basis in the case of private-sector indices. Because the benchmark for quoting all-in cost is the index flat, spreads under the index can be thought of as payments from the fixed-rate payer to the floating-rate payer. As such, these payments (the adjustment flows) should be discounted at the fixed-rate payer's all-in cost. Only by using this convention can two swaps with the same all-in cost (one with no spread and one with

---

[1] The Appendix discusses only the pricing methodology for swaps and not the computation of a swap's all-in cost. All-in cost is determined through an internal rate of return calculation. The calculation is usually an iterative procedure that prices the swap using trial values of all-in cost until one results in the actual price.

a spread under the index and a correspondingly lower fixed-rate coupon) truly be called equivalent in terms of yield.

Pricing the Hypothetical Fixed-Rate Security

The price of the fixed-rate side of a swap can be viewed as the sum of two components: (a) the present value or full price of a fixed-rate bond (the fixed bond) based on the fixed-rate payer's contractual payments and (b) the present value of those flows necessary to adjust the floating side to the generic standard if possible (the adjustment flows). The discount rate for both present values is the swap's all-in cost, and discounting is done using methods consistent with corporate fixed-rate bond pricing.

We begin by discussing the pricing of the fixed bond in a swap with semiannual fixed payments. For such a swap, the formula for the present value of the contractual fixed-rate swap payments plus the hypothetical principal repayment at maturity is as follows:

Present value of the fixed bond =

$$
\sum_{i=1}^{n} \frac{\dfrac{C}{2}}{\left(1 + \dfrac{AIC}{200}\right)^{P_i}} + \frac{100}{\left(1 + \dfrac{AIC}{200}\right)^{P_n}} \tag{1}
$$

where n = the number of fixed coupon payments from the settlement date to maturity,

C = the fixed coupon rate (expressed as a percentage),

AIC = the all-in cost (expressed as a percentage), and

P_i = the number of whole and fractional fixed coupon periods from the settlement date to the ith fixed coupon payment date.

Using this formula to price the fixed bond in the example for May 15, 1985, settlement, at an all-in cost of 12.50 percent, we make the following calculations:

Present value of the fixed bond =

$$
\frac{\dfrac{12.50}{2}}{\left(1 + \dfrac{12.50}{200}\right)^{1}} + \frac{\dfrac{12.50}{2}}{\left(1 + \dfrac{12.50}{200}\right)^{2}} + \frac{\dfrac{12.50}{2}}{\left(1 + \dfrac{12.50}{200}\right)^{3}} + \cdots + \frac{\dfrac{12.50}{2}}{\left(1 + \dfrac{12.50}{200}\right)^{14}}
$$

$$
+ \frac{100}{\left(1 + \dfrac{12.50}{200}\right)^{14}} = 100
$$

Equation 1 applies only to swaps that have no short or long first coupons. If the first fixed coupon is short or long and the remaining fixed payments are semiannual, the following formula is appropriate:

Present value of the fixed bond =

$$\frac{\frac{C}{2} \times P_1}{\left(1 + \frac{AIC}{200}\right)^{P_1}} + \sum_{i=2}^{n} \frac{\frac{C}{2}}{\left(1 + \frac{AIC}{200}\right)^{P_i}} + \frac{100}{\left(1 + \frac{AIC}{200}\right)^{P_n}} \qquad (2)$$

If the base case swap had an effective date of April 1, 1985, with a short first coupon payment on May 15, 1985, the price of the fixed bond for settlement on April 1, 1985, at an all-in cost of 12.50 percent would be found as follows:

Present value of the fixed bond =

$$\frac{\frac{12.50}{2} \times \frac{44}{180}}{\left(1 + \frac{12.50}{200}\right)^{\frac{44}{180}}} + \frac{\frac{12.50}{2}}{\left(1 + \frac{12.50}{200}\right)^{1 + \frac{44}{180}}} + \frac{\frac{12.50}{2}}{\left(1 + \frac{12.50}{200}\right)^{2 + \frac{44}{180}}}$$

$$+ \cdots + \frac{\frac{12.50}{2}}{\left(1 + \frac{12.50}{200}\right)^{14 + \frac{44}{180}}} + \frac{100}{\left(1 + \frac{12.50}{200}\right)^{14 + \frac{44}{180}}} = 100.034$$

For swaps in which the payment frequency is not semiannual, the following generalization of Equation 2 is used to price the fixed bond:

Present value of the fixed bond =

$$\frac{\frac{C}{freq} \times P_1}{\left(1 + \frac{AIC_c}{(100 \times freq)}\right)^{P_1}} + \sum_{i=2}^{n} \frac{\frac{C}{freq}}{\left(1 + \frac{AIC_c}{(100 \times freq)}\right)^{P_i}}$$

$$+ \frac{100}{\left(1 + \frac{AIC_c}{(100 \times freq)}\right)^{P_n}} \qquad (3)$$

where $freq$ = the number of fixed-rate payments per year, and
AIC_c = the all-in cost converted to the same compounding frequency as the number of fixed-rate payments per year (expressed as a percentage).

Under market convention, the all-in cost is always quoted as a semiannual rate. To convert the all-in cost to a rate with a compounding frequency consistent with the number of fixed coupon payments per year (as required in Equation 3), use the following formula:

$$AIC_c = \left[\left(1 + \frac{AIC}{200}\right)^{\frac{2}{freq}} - 1\right] \times 100 \times freq \qquad (4)$$

For the base case swap changed to have a coupon of 12.75 percent paid annually, the two steps in computing the price of the fixed bond for settlement on May 15, 1985, at an all-in cost of 12.50 percent semiannual are the following.

First, the semiannual all-in cost is converted to its annual equivalent using Equation 4:

$$AIC_c = \left[\left(1 + \frac{12.50}{200}\right)^{\frac{2}{1}} - 1\right] \times 100 \times 1 = 12.890625$$

Then the price of the fixed bond is computed using Equation 3 as follows:

Present value of the fixed bond =

$$\frac{\frac{12.75}{1}}{\left(1 + \frac{12.890625}{100 \times 1}\right)^1} + \frac{\frac{12.75}{1}}{\left(1 + \frac{12.890625}{100 \times 1}\right)^2} + \cdots + \frac{\frac{12.75}{1}}{\left(1 + \frac{12.890625}{100 \times 1}\right)^7}$$

$$+ \frac{100}{\left(1 + \frac{12.890625}{(100 \times 1)}\right)^7} = 99.376$$

If the swap has a spread under or over the index, we must determine the present value of the adjustment flows needed to alter the floating side to the index flat. These flows correspond to the spread that accrues during each floating payment period. Since the spread accrues on the same basis as the LIBOR index (actual/360), the actual number of days in the payment period determines the size of each adjustment flow. Since the adjustment for the spread is considered part of the hypothetical fixed security, the discount rate for the adjustment flows is the swap's all-in cost. These ideas are reflected in the following formula for computing the present value of the adjustment flows:

Present value of the adjustment flows =

$$\sum_{i=1}^{n} \frac{S \times \dfrac{D_i}{360}}{\left(1 + \dfrac{AIC_c}{(100 \times freq)}\right)^{P_i}} \tag{5}$$

where n = the number of floating coupon payments from the settlement date to maturity,

S = the spread under the index (expressed as a percentage),

D_i = the actual number of days of interest accrual for the ith floating payment,

$freq$ = the number of floating-rate payments per year,

AIC_c = the all-in cost converted to the same compounding frequency as the number of floating-rate payments per year (expressed as a percentage), and

P_i = the number of whole and fractional floating coupon periods from the settlement date to the ith floating coupon payment date.

If the base case swap had a spread of 25 basis points under the six-month LIBOR index and was priced for settlement on May 15, 1985, at an all-in cost of 12.50 percent, the formulas for calculating the present value of the adjustment flows (to convert the floating side to six-month LIBOR flat) would be applied as follows:

Present value of the adjustment flows =

$$\frac{0.25 \times \dfrac{184}{360}}{\left(1 + \dfrac{12.50}{(100 \times 2)}\right)^{1}} + \frac{0.25 \times \dfrac{181}{360}}{\left(1 + \dfrac{12.50}{(100 \times 2)}\right)^{2}} + \frac{0.25 \times \dfrac{184}{360}}{\left(1 + \dfrac{12.50}{(100 \times 2)}\right)^{3}}$$

$$+ \cdots + \frac{0.25 \times \dfrac{182}{360}}{\left(1 + \dfrac{12.50}{(100 \times 2)}\right)^{14}} = 1.161$$

Because the cash flows of the hypothetical fixed-income security are the combination of the cash flows of the fixed bond and the adjustment flows, the full price of the fixed side is simply calculated as follows:

Full price of the fixed side
= present value of the fixed bond
+ present value of the adjustment flows

When computing the price of a swap being closed out in the secondary market, the settlement date of the transaction will often not be the beginning of a fixed or floating coupon period. The transaction, therefore, will involve accrued interest. A calculation of the accrued interest on the fixed side must include accrued interest on the adjustment flows to be consistent with our methodology. To compute the portion of the full price that is accrued interest, the following formulas are used:

$$\text{Accrued interest on the fixed bond} = \frac{D_F}{360} \times C \tag{6}$$

$$\text{Accrued interest on the adjustment flows} = \frac{D_A}{360} \times S \tag{7}$$

where D_F = the number of days (computed on a 30/360 basis) from the previous fixed payment[2] to the settlement date of the secondary market transaction,

D_A = the number of days (computed on an actual/360 basis) from the previous floating payment date to the settlement date of the secondary market transaction,

C = the fixed coupon rate (expressed as a percentage),

S = the spread under the index (expressed as a percentage).

If the base case swap with a spread of 25 basis points under the index were priced for a closeout in the secondary market with a settlement date of June 1, 1985, at an all-in cost of 12.75 percent, the full price and accrued interest for the fixed side would be found by applying Equations 3, 5, 6, and 7 as follows:

Present value of the fixed bond =

$$\frac{\frac{12.50}{2}}{\left(1 + \frac{12.75}{200}\right)^{\frac{164}{180}}} + \frac{\frac{12.50}{2}}{\left(1 + \frac{12.75}{200}\right)^{1+\frac{164}{180}}} + \frac{\frac{12.50}{2}}{\left(1 + \frac{12.75}{200}\right)^{2+\frac{164}{180}}}$$

$$+ \cdots + \frac{\frac{12.50}{2}}{\left(1 + \frac{12.75}{200}\right)^{13+\frac{164}{180}}} + \frac{100}{\left(1 + \frac{12.75}{200}\right)^{13+\frac{164}{180}}} = 99.409$$

---

[2] In this case (as well as in all cases that follow), if no payment has yet occurred, the number of days is counted from the swap's original effective date to the settlement date of this secondary market transaction.

Present value of the adjustment flows =

$$\frac{0.25 \times \dfrac{184}{360}}{\left(1 + \dfrac{12.75}{(100 \times 2)}\right)^{\frac{164}{180}}} + \frac{0.25 \times \dfrac{181}{360}}{\left(1 + \dfrac{12.75}{(100 \times 2)}\right)^{1+\frac{164}{180}}} + \frac{0.25 \times \dfrac{184}{360}}{\left(1 + \dfrac{12.75}{(100 + 2)}\right)^{2+\frac{164}{180}}}$$

$$+ \cdots + \frac{0.25 \times \dfrac{182}{360}}{\left(1 + \dfrac{12.75}{(100 \times 2)}\right)^{13+\frac{164}{180}}} = 1.159$$

Full price of the fixed side = 99.409 + 1.159 = 100.568

Accrued interest of the fixed bond = $\dfrac{16}{360} \times 12.50 = 0.566$

Accrued interest of the adjustment flows = $\dfrac{17}{360} \times 0.25 = 0.012$

Total accrued interest of the fixed side = 0.556 + 0.012 = 0.568

Pricing the Hypothetical Floating-Rate Note

To price the floating-rate side of a swap, we use the discounting conventions for floating-rate notes. Since the floating-rate note is assumed to have a value of par at the next payment date, the price of the floating-rate side is the present value of the next payment plus par. The discount rate used to calculate the present value should be the current market rate of the appropriate maturity index for the period from the settlement date to the next floating payment date. For example, consider a swap with a floating side that resets and pays quarterly and floats off three-month LIBOR. When priced with two months to the next floating payment, the discount rate should be the current two-month LIBOR rate. The formula for the full price of the floating-rate side, adjusted to be the index flat, is as follows:

$$\text{Present value of the floating side} = \frac{100 + ER \times \dfrac{D_{PN}}{360}}{1 + \dfrac{CR}{100} \times \dfrac{D_{SN}}{360}} \tag{8}$$

where ER = the current rate in effect for the next floating coupon payment (expressed as a percentage),

D_{PN} = the actual number of days from the previous floating payment date to the next floating payment date,

CR = the current market rate of the index for the period from the settlement date to the next floating payment date (expressed as a percentage),

D_{SN} = the actual number of days from the settlement date to the next floating payment date.

The accrued interest portion of the full price of the floating side can be calculated using the following formula:

$$\text{Accrued interest on the floating side} = \frac{ER \times (D_{PN} - D_{SN})}{360} \qquad (9)$$

To price the floating-rate side of the base case swap with a settlement date of June 1, 1985, assuming the current floating rate in effect was set at 8.9375 percent on May 15, 1985, and that the current market rate for five-and-one-half-month LIBOR is 9.00 percent, the aforementioned formulas would be applied as follows:

Full price of the floating side =

$$\frac{100 + \left(8.9375 \times \dfrac{184}{360}\right)}{1 + \left(\dfrac{9.00}{100} \times \dfrac{167}{360}\right)} = 100.377$$

Accrued interest on the floating side =

$$8.9375 \times \frac{(184 - 167)}{360} = 0.422$$

Pricing the Swap

After calculating the present values of the fixed and floating sides, we can calculate the current market price of the entire swap. Recall that we have described a swap as an exchange of two securities: a hypothetical fixed-rate note (including analytical adjustment flows) and a hypothetical floating-rate note (adjusted to the index flat). Under this notion, on closing out a swap, each party will buy back the security originally sold and sell back the other party's security originally purchased. The price of the swap will be the difference in the prices of these two securities.

Expressed as a formula, the swap's full price paid by the fixed-rate payer on closing out the swap is the following:

Full price paid by the fixed-rate payer
= full price of the fixed side − full price of the floating side

If this full price is negative, the cash payment is made by the floating-rate payer. The portion of the full price that is accounted for as accrued interest is given by this formula:

> Net accrued interest paid by the fixed-rate payer
> = accrued interest on the fixed side
> − accrued interest on the floating side

If this net accrued interest is negative, the floating-rate payer has accrued a larger interest liability than the fixed-rate payer.

Consider again the base case swap with a spread of 25 basis points under six-month LIBOR and an original floating rate set at 8.9375 percent. To close out this swap on June 1, 1985, at an all-in cost of 12.50 percent and a current market five-and-one-half-month LIBOR rate of 9.00 percent, these equations show that the fixed-rate payer would pay the floating-rate payer 0.191 percent of the notional principal amount, of which 0.146 is net accrued interest. The calculations would be as follows:

> Full price paid by the fixed-rate payer = 100.568 − 100.377
> = 0.191
> Net accrued interest paid by the fixed-rate payer = 0.568 − 0.422
> = 0.146

CHAPTER 12

INTEREST RATE SWAP
VALUATION

Benjamin Iben
General Re Financial Products Corporation
Stamford, Connecticut

INTRODUCTION

Interest rate swaps involve the exchange of interest rate payments denominated in the same currency. The basic or generic structure is a fixed/floating interest rate swap. The fixed side consists of periodic payments at a rate determined when the swap is initiated. The floating side also consists of a series of payments, but the amount of each payment is not known until the beginning of the payment period at which time the rate is set to the prevailing LIBOR rate for the period (usually three or six months). The actual payments on both sides are based on a single principal amount. This amount is not exchanged, however, and is referred to as the swap's notional principal.

In the early stages of the interest rate swap market, activity was concentrated on generic swaps. These early swaps enabled asset/liability managers to restructure their balance sheets without incurring the costs of retiring old debt and issuing new debt. Valuation of these generic swaps was straightforward and not a major

---

Much of this chapter was written while the author was employed by Manufacturers Hanover Trust Company.

issue. However, as the market grew, so did the range and complexity of available structures. Features such as front-end or back-end payments coupled with above- or below-market coupons (asset swaps), changing notional principal (amortizing swaps), and forward-start dates (forward swaps) became common.

With the addition of more complex structures, valuation was no longer so straightforward and a more comprehensive valuation methodology was needed. The work of Macfarlane, Ross, and Showers (MRS) (Chapter 11) was one of the first attempts to approach swap valuation comprehensively. The methodology MRS developed is an adaptation of the yield to maturity (YTM) approach commonly used to value bonds.

The YTM approach values all of the cash flows of a bond at a single, average rate. As a result, individual cash flows are generally mispriced using this approach, even when the underlying bond is correctly valued. This potential for mispricing became a serious drawback in a swaps market that found itself increasingly involved in the repackaging of cash flow streams, since the profitability of the repackaged flows was dependent on the accurate valuation of the individual flows. As a result, an alternative valuation methodology that accurately valued individual cash flows was needed.

One way to get around this problem is to start with the value of individual cash flows and to value streams of cash flows as the sum of the values of the individual cash flows. This approach treats each flow as a zero coupon bond with its own YTM. Given the price of any cash flow, its YTM can be calculated in the same manner as the YTM or zero coupon rate of a zero coupon bond is calculated. If zero coupon swaps for delivery at different future dates were actively traded, a yield curve or zero coupon curve could be calculated from the prices of these flows. This curve could then be used to value swaps with multiple cash flows since any difference between the price of a swap and the value of its components could be arbitraged. The zero coupon curve could thus be used to value any cash flow, regardless of the instrument to which it is attached.

In the swap market, zero coupon swaps are not actively traded; however, zero coupon swaps can be created using generic swaps. These synthetic zero coupon swaps can, in turn, be used to calculate an implied zero coupon curve. This implied zero coupon curve can then be used to determine relative value among the heterogeneous cash flow streams common in the swap market. It is this ability to consistently value irregular cash flow streams that was responsible for the rapid adoption of the zero coupon methodology by many of the major players in the swap market.

In this chapter the YTM and zero coupon approaches to swap valuation are discussed and compared. Both valuation methodologies use variations of the same basic valuation formulas, and these formulas are defined in Section 1. In Sections 2 and 3 the two alternative valuation methodologies are discussed in the framework of these basic valuation formulas. Section 4 summarizes and compares the performance of the two valuation mechanisms.

1. VALUATION FORMULAS

Two formulas relate the value of cash flows received today with cash flows received in the future. The present value (pv) of a cash flow is the value today of a flow to be received on a specific future date whereas a future value (fv) is the value at a future date of a cash flow received today and invested until that date. The interest rate to be used in both present valuing and future valuing is the rate at which funds can be invested today until the future date. The formulas for fv and pv are as follows:

$$fv(t + 1, t) = \$1 \times (1 + i) \qquad (1a)$$

$$pv(t, t + 1) = \$1/(1 + i) \qquad (1b)$$

where i = interest income (opportunity cost) from t to $t + 1$,
         t = today,
   $t + 1$ = one period in the future,
$fv(t + 1,t)$ = value at $t + 1$ of \$1 received at t and invested until
            $t + 1$, and
$pv(t,t + 1)$ = value at t of \$1 to be received at $t + 1$.

These formulas are slightly more complicated if more than one period is involved because reinvestment of interest (compounding) must be accounted for. In addition, the rate of interest available for investment in future periods is not generally the same for all periods (i.e., the yield curve is not generally flat). The valuation formulas can easily be generalized to account for these factors. The generalized formulas are as follows:[1]

$$fv(t + n,t) = \$1 \times [1 + i(t,t + 1)] \times [1 + i(t + 1,t + 2)] \cdots \tag{2a}$$

$$pv(t,t + n) = \$1/[(1 + i(t,t + 1)] \times [1 + i(t + 1,t + 2)] \ldots \tag{2b}$$

where $i(t + j, t + j + 1)$ = one period rate of interest (forward rate) available at time t for investment j periods in the future.

2. YTM APPROACH

The YTM approach values nongeneric swaps using the YTM of generic swaps. For example, all 10-year swaps are priced with the YTM of the generic 10-year swap. Swaps with odd maturities are valued by linearly interpolating in time YTMs of the generic swaps whose maturities bracket that of the odd swap.

The YTM of a fixed stream of cash flows (such as a bond or the fixed-rate side of a swap) is the single rate that when used to discount all of the cash flows in the stream returns the price of the stream. That is:

$$P = \sum_{i=1}^{n} \frac{C}{(1 + ytm)^i} + \frac{100}{(1 + YTM)^n}$$

where P = bond price (per \$100 of principal),
YTM = yield to maturity of bond (annual coupons assumed),
n = maturity of bond, and
c = annual coupon.

---

[1] This analysis assumes that the institution borrows and lends at the same rate. In practice, banks borrow at LIBID and lend at LIBOR. One approach to valuation would be to value deposits at LIBID and loans at LIBOR. This approach, however, produces inaccurate profit and loss numbers. If, for example, a bank borrows \$100 for one year at 10 percent and then lends the \$100 for 10.1 percent, it has locked in a profit of 10 bps to be received in one year. Using the bid and offer rates to value the deposit and loan, the computed profit would be zero. In order to get an accurate result, a single rate must be used to value all flows received on the same date. This rate, referred to as the midmarket rate, is the midpoint of the bid/offer rates. In the above case, the midmarket rate is 10.05 percent and the mark-to-market value of the two transactions would be 9.09 bp (i.e., the pv of 10 bp to be received in one year).

In the case of a generic swap, the flows are equal to the interest (coupon) payments plus the notional principal payment at maturity. The price of the fixed side of a generic swap is equal to its notional principal or par.[2] Since the swap is priced at par, the coupon rate is equal to its YTM.

In essence, a YTM is a weighted average rate. When the YTM approach is used, all of the cash flows of a swap are discounted at this weighted average rate instead of at their actual opportunity costs. As indicated in Equation 2b, if the yield curve is not flat, each individual flow will be mispriced; however, the sum of the pricing errors for the generic swap is zero. This means that while the YTM approach is accurate in the sense that it correctly values the generic instruments, it is not appropriate for general valuation because the value of a cash flow received in the future will depend on the YTM of the instrument to which it is attached. In fact, the pricing errors of the YTM approach are systematic. When the yield curve is upward sloping (i.e., the forward rates increase with maturity), the flows received at the beginning of the swap are undervalued since the actual opportunity cost will be less than the average opportunity cost over the entire life of the swap. On the other hand, the flows at the end are overvalued since the actual opportunity cost will be higher than the average. When the yield curve is inverted, the reverse is the case.

Another important drawback of the YTM approach is that it assumes that two swaps with the same maturity, but different coupon flows, have the same YTM when this will not be the case unless the yield curve is flat. In an upward-sloping yield curve, swaps with higher coupons will have lower yields.

These biases can be seen by comparing the values obtained using Equations 2a and 2b, which allow for variable forward rates, with those obtained using the YTM approach. Table 1 contains data for five swaps (A, B, C, D, E). The swaps in Table 1 are priced so that no arbitrages are possible among them. For example, using

---

[2] In the case of an interest rate swap, no principal payments are made. For a description of the valuation of an interest swap as the sum of a fixed rate note and a floating rate note see Macfarlane, Ross, and Showers (Chapter 11).

TABLE 1
Price Data for Five Swaps

Swap	Start Period	End Period	Coupon	Yield (Percent)	Price
A	0	1	8.0	8.00%	Par
B	1	2	10.0	10.00	Par
C	2	3	11.0	11.00	Par
D	0	3	9.57	9.57	Par
E	0	3	0	9.66	75.83

Note: All coupon payments are made at end of each period. $100 principal is paid at maturity. Swap B and C are one-period forward swaps, also known as forward rate agreements (FRAs).

Equation 2b and the opportunity costs from bonds A, B, and C, the present value of $D(PV_D)$ is as follows:

$$PV_D = \frac{\$9.57}{1.08} + \frac{\$9.57}{(1.08)(1.1)} + \frac{109.57}{(1.08)(1.1)(1.11)}$$

$$PV_D = \$8.86 + \$8.05 + 83.09$$

$$PV_D = \$100.00$$

The true value of the first coupon flow is $8.86 while the value of that same flow using D's YTM of 9.57 percent is $8.73. Thus, in this case, the YTM approach undervalues the first coupon by 13 basis points (bp) and overvalues the remaining flows by the same amount. The bias inherent in using the YTM of one bond to value another can be demonstrated by using the YTM of D to value E. Using the YTM of D (9.57 percent), the value obtained is $76.02 whereas the true value (obtained using Equation 2b) is $75.83.

The potential for bias is, however, especially great when YTMs are used to calculate forward rates. A forward rate (fr) is the rate, available today, for investment at a future date. For example, the forward rate starting n periods in the future and ending in $n + 1(fr[n,n + 1])$ is the rate that could be obtained today for investment from n to $n + 1$. This rate can be obtained by comparing the future value of a flow received today and invested for n periods with the future value of the same flow invested for $n + 1$ periods.

The formula corresponding to this is

$$fr(n,n + 1) = fv(t,t + n + 1)/fv(t,t + n). \qquad (3)$$

Thus, in order to correctly calculate forward rates, a valuation methodology must be able to correctly value individual cash flows. Accurate forward rate calculation is particularly important in the swap market because forward rate agreements (FRAs) are among the most actively traded swap products. An FRA is an agreement between two counterparties where one party agrees to receive at an agreed rate over a forward period and pay the LIBOR rate prevailing at the beginning of that period. In general, only the difference in the two rates is actually paid.

As was shown earlier, the YTM approach does not price individual cash flows accurately. Using the YTMs of Swaps A and D to calculate future values, the forward rate for Period 3 is 10.82 percent, whereas the true forward rate (obtained from Swap C) is 11 percent. This 18 bp pricing error is quite significant in a market with bid/offer spreads of 10 bp or less. This type of pricing error can be avoided by using the zero coupon approach to valuation.

3. ZERO COUPON APPROACH

A zero coupon rate (zero rate) is just the YTM of a zero coupon bond. The zero rate for a zero coupon bond maturing in n periods with price (or present value) p and face value (or future value) f is

$$z[n] = (f/p)^{1/n} - 1. \qquad (4)$$

As this formula indicates, $z[n]$ is the per period rate of return of an n period investment. This return, unlike that of coupon bearing bonds, is locked in since it does not involve reinvestment risk.

An alternative way to lock in an n period return is to make n period investments at the current forward rates. Since the returns to both strategies are locked in, absent transaction costs, the return to each of these two strategies must be equal. That is:

$$z[n] = [1 + i(t,t + 1)] \times [1 + i(t + 1,t + 2)] \ldots$$
$$[1 + i(t + n - 1,t + n)]^{1/n} - 1 \qquad (5)$$

Thus, a zero rate may be calculated either from the price of the appropriate zero coupon bond or from a series of forward rates.

Each flow on a coupon bearing bond can be viewed, in turn, as a zero coupon bond. That is, the value of each flow is determined by discounting it at the appropriate zero rate. If the bond's price is different from the value of its components, then arbitrage profit can be earned. As a result, the zero coupon approach accurately prices each flow on a bond as well as the bond as a whole.

The market in zero coupon swaps is not active and zero coupon prices are not generally observable. However, a similar arbitrage can be done among coupon-bearing swaps, and implied zero rates can be calculated from a series of generic swap rates using a technique called *bootstrapping*. The first step in this procedure is to calculate the one-year zero rate ($z[1]$) using the one-year swap rate ($c[1]$). Given an annual payment frequency, and the fact that the generic swap will be priced at par, the one-year zero rate can be calculated as follows:

$$1 = \frac{1 + c[1]}{1 + z[1]} \tag{6}$$

The one-year zero and the two-year swap rate ($c[2]$) are then used to calculate the two-year zero rate ($z[2]$) using the following relationship:

$$1 = \frac{c[2]}{1 + z[1]} + \frac{1 + c[2]}{(1 + z[2])^2} \tag{7}$$

This process is then continued to calculate an entire zero rate curve (zero curve). Table 2 contains a zero curve calculated from a swap yield curve by bootstrapping.

In the examples in Table 2, the frequency assumed for coupon payments corresponds exactly to the frequency of the generic swap quotes. In this case, no interpolation is necessary to calculate

TABLE 2
Zero Rate Curve Derived from Swap Yield Curve

Maturity	Swap Rate	Zero Rate
1	10.00	10.00
2	11.00	11.06
3	12.00	12.17
4	12.50	12.73
5	13.00	13.35

the zero rates to the maturity of each of the generic swaps, and there is an exact formula for calculating the n period zero rate, given that the zero rates for all preceding periods are known. That formula is as follows:

$$z[n] = \left[\frac{1 + C[n]}{1 - C[n] \sum_{i=1}^{n-1} \left(\frac{1}{1 + z[i]} \right)^i} \right]^{1/n} - 1 \qquad (8)$$

where $z[i]$ = ith period zero rate and
$\quad c[n]$ = n year swap rate.

The zero rates for all other dates must be calculated by interpolating the zero rates calculated from the generic swaps. Linear interpolation of zero rates is one reasonable approach.

The actual payment frequency for generic interest rate swaps in a particular market may, however, be semiannual or quarterly. Since generic swap rates are generally available only at annual intervals, the bootstrapping methodology must be modified. One way to do so is to assume that the zero curve between the maturity of any two generic swaps is linear. Given this assumption, the zero rate at each maturity can be calculated iteratively. The exact procedure for doing this is presented in the Appendix.

Once a zero coupon curve is calculated, the same valuation formula can be used for all swaps, regardless of the coupon frequency or basis of the instruments used to derive it. The simplest way to do this is to assume a single basis for all zero rates when calculating the zero curve. This basis is then appropriate when using the zero curve. In fact, once the zero curve is calculated, no more reference to the generic swaps that created it is necessary since the curve already incorporates all of the pricing information contained in the generic swaps.

Given the zero curve, the only information necessary to value a deal is the cash flow schedule. Table 3 provides an example of the cash flow schedule of five-year amortizing swap paying annual coupons of 12.13 percent. The swap's notional principal in the first year is $100 million. The notional principal declines $20 million in each successive year. This swap is equivalent to a series of five swaps, maturing in 1, 2, 3, 4, and 5 years, and each with a notional principal of $20 million. The coupon rate is set such that the value of the combined swap (using the zero rates in Table 2) is $100

TABLE 3

	Year				
	1	*2*	*3*	*4*	*5*
Swap 1	22,426	—	—	—	—
Swap 2	2,426	22,426	—	—	—
Swap 3	2,426	2,426	22,426	—	—
Swap 4	2,426	2,426	2,426	22,426	—
Swap 5	2,426	2,426	2,426	2,426	22,426
Combined swap	32,130	29,704	27,278	24,852	22,426
pv of combined flows	29,209	24,082	19,328	15,191	11,985

Note: All flows are in thousands of dollars.

million, the initial notional principal. The counterparty that would receive the fixed payments would be likely to attempt to receive a higher rate, while the counterparty making the fixed payments would attempt to negotiate a lower rate.

Since the zero rates are arbitrage based, the value of any cash flow to be received is unaffected by the instrument to which it is attached. As a result, the zero coupon approach consistently prices all types of swaps, regardless of the complexity of the cash flows. There are, however, limitations on the valuation precision possible using zero rates derived from generic swap rates. Two limiting factors are (*a*) the length of intervals between maturities of observed swap rates and (*b*) the liquidity of generic swaps.

The length of the intervals between the maturities of observed swap quotes determines the amount of interpolation necessary to calculate a zero curve. The greater the intervals, the more interpolation is necessary. Generally, the maturities of observed swap rates differ by at least one year. Interpolation error is particularly important for maturities greater than five years. The liquidity of the generic swaps determines the quality of the price information incorporated in them. The less liquid the underlying swaps, the less reliable the pricing information.[3]

---

[3] Measurement error is generally most significant for pricing FRAs using implied zero rates because forward rates are very sensitive to changes in zero rates. As a result, a small error in a zero rate may cause a large error in a forward rate. Potential errors can be reduced by smoothing the zero curve.

Since a zero rate is equivalent to the return on a series of one-period investments at the available forward rates, observed forward rates can be used to calculate a zero coupon curve. One approach would be to calculate zero rates from FRA quotes. It might prove difficult to obtain accurate FRA quotes for all maturities on a timely basis. The Eurodollar (ED) futures contracts traded on the Chicago Mercantile Exchange, like FRAs, settle against LIBOR. Thus, an ED futures contract and a three-month FRA settling on the same date will settle at the same rate, and the two instruments will (absent transactions costs and credit considerations) trade at the same rate. As a result, the ED futures market provides a means for readily observing forward rates at three-month intervals. Currently, trading is limited to 12 contracts. Thus, the zero curve out to three years can be calculated from Eurodollar futures. The basic formula to calculate a zero rate from a series of Eurodollar futures prices is as follows:[4]

$$z[j] = \left[\left(1 + r[1] \times \frac{91}{360}\right)\left(1 + r[2] \times \frac{91}{360}\right) \cdots \right.$$

$$\left. \left(1 + r[j] \times \frac{91}{360}\right)\right]^{\frac{365}{91 \times j}} - 1 \tag{9}$$

where $z[j]$ = zero rate to end date of jth futures contract,
$r[i]$ = Eurodollar rate implied by ith futures price ($p[i]$), and
$p[1]$ = price of nearby futures contract.

Since the forward rates are observed at three-month intervals, the need to interpolate is minimized. Also, the impact of errors in the measurement of input prices is minimized. This methodology essentially uses the Eurodollar futures curve as a proxy for the swap curve. Thus, the accuracy of the curve derived is dependent on the extent to which the two curves coincide.

The Eurodollar futures curve (the zero curve derived from futures) is a good proxy for the swap curve because a series of

---

[4] This formula assumes that futures contracts mature every 91 days and each year has 365 days.

Eurodollar futures positions can closely replicate the coupon flows on a swap. In essence, an ED futures contract is, like an FRA, a one-period swap. Thus, combining flows on a series of ED futures contracts essentially creates a multiperiod swap. Since the expiration dates of the ED futures contracts will not generally match exactly with the payment dates of a generic swap, the arbitrage between swaps and ED futures is not exact. The closer the maturity dates of the ED futures contracts match the payment dates on generic swaps, the closer the futures curve is to the swap curve. Table 4 contains the one-, two-, and three-year swap rates on May 30, 1989, and the same rates implied by the futures curve.

On May 30, the rates implied by the ED futures curve were 4 bp above the midmarket swap quote. This is a typical swap/ED futures spread. In this case, it would probably be better to receive fixed in the ED futures market and pay fixed in the swap market. The ED futures curve would then correspond to the offer curve.

The zero coupon curve obtained from futures can be used in conjunction with medium term swap rates (i.e., those swaps that mature after the end date of the last ED futures contract currently traded) to calculate a complete zero coupon curve. If, however, the ED futures curve is not in line with the swap curve, the forward rates between the last zero rate produced from futures and the first zero rate produced from swaps may be anomalous. That is, any differences between the zero curve derived from the short-term swap market and that derived from futures will have a disproportionate effect on the forward rates in the transition period between the short-term and medium-term curves when ED futures and swap-based zero rates are spliced together. This effect can be

TABLE 4
Term Swap Rates and Rates Implied by
Futures Curve

Maturity	Rate Implied by Futures Curve	Midmarket Swap Quote
1 year	9.54	9.50
2 year	9.43	9.39
3 year	9.43	9.39

greatly reduced by relaxing the assumption that the zero curve should value each generic instrument exactly.

4. SUMMARY

As the previous discussion has indicated, there are a number of important criteria to consider when choosing among valuation methodologies. There are, however, three requirements of any methodology used as a general swap valuation mechanism. The first is that it accurately values generic swaps. The accurate valuation of generic swaps is important both because generic swaps make up a large portion of deals and because they are used as a benchmark for the valuation of nongeneric swaps. The second is that it consistently values all cash flows regardless of the instrument to which they are attached. This requirement ensures that all instruments are priced consistently. The third requirement is that the methodology identifies arbitrage opportunities among instruments. This requirement is necessary both to take advantage of arbitrage opportunities and to avoid being arbitraged. Table 5 summarizes the performance of the YTM and zero coupon methodologies using these three criteria.

The zero coupon approach satisfies all three requirements, whereas the YTM approach only satisfies the first. The zero coupon approach has another important advantage over the YTM approach: flexibility. Although calculating a zero coupon curve requires a modest amount of computation, once the zero curve is calculated, all cash flows are valued in the same manner. As a

TABLE 5
YTM and Zero Coupon Methodologies Compared

	Methodology	
Criteria	YTM	Zero Coupon
Accurately prices generic swaps	Yes	Yes
Consistently values all cash flows regardless of the instrument to which they are attached	No	Yes
Identifies arbitrage opportunities among instruments	No	Yes

result, no adjustments to the zero coupon methodology are required in order to value new instruments. However, since the YTM approach is instrument specific, the YTMs of existing instruments are not accurate for valuing new instruments with different cash flows. Given these advantages it is not surprising that the zero coupon approach has become the standard methodology for swap valuation.

APPENDIX: MODIFIED BOOTSTRAPPING

The bootstrapping methodology can be used to calculate a zero curve from a series of generic swap quotes regardless of the frequency of coupon payments of the swaps. However, if the frequency of coupon payments does not correspond to the frequency of quotes (e.g., the maturity gap between swap quotes is annual while the generic swaps pay semiannual coupons), the bootstrapping methodology must be modified so that the number of known variables (market quotes) equals the number of unknown variables. One way to do this is to assume that the zero rates between the maturity dates of adjacent generic swap quotes all lie on a line. Given this assumption, the bootstrapping equation is:

$$1 = \sum_{i=1}^{2(j-1)} \frac{C[j]/2}{(1 + z[i])^{i/2}} + \frac{C[j]/2}{(1 + 0.5 \times z[zJ] + 0.5z[zJ - 2])^{\frac{2J-1}{2}}} + \frac{1 + C[j]/2}{(1 + z[zj])^J}$$

where $c[j]$ = swap rate of generic swap maturing in j years and
$z[i]$ = annual zero rate maturing in $i/2$ years.

CHAPTER 13

WHAT DRIVES INTEREST RATE SWAP SPREADS?

Ellen Evans
Gioia Parente Bales
Salomon Brothers Inc
New York, New York

Although much has been written about the mechanics of the interest rate swap market, the major influences on the level and direction of swap spreads have not been fully analyzed.[1] Therefore, market participants have found it difficult to predict the performance of interest rate swaps in different market environments. In this chapter, we analyze the primary influences on interest rate swap spreads by identifying the relationships between the swap and related financial markets.

- At shorter maturities, interest rate swaps are priced relative to the implied yield on a strip of Eurodollar futures contracts for the same maturity: The two instruments create the same interest rate profile.
- Further out on the yield curve—at maturities between 3 and 10 years—the demand and supply for swaps are more closely related to spreads in fixed-income markets. At these maturities, swaps are used to create synthetic assets and

---

[1] For a complete discussion of the mechanics of the market, see Chapter 11.

liabilities that must be compared with alternative securities in traditional financial markets. Since 1984, swap spreads have generally hovered within the range defined by AA- and A-rated new-issue spreads in the domestic and international bond markets.

• Several other factors also affect the relative supply of fixed- and floating-rate payers in the swap market, shifting swap spreads within these bounds or, on occasion, outside of the bounds. The overall direction of interest rates and the shape of the Treasury yield curve are significant: Swap spreads have tended to widen in Treasury rallies and narrow in setbacks. In addition, technical factors affecting the hedging costs of swap dealers periodically influence overall market rates.

INTRODUCTION

An interest rate swap is an agreement between two parties to exchange interest payments of differing character based on a notional principal amount for a specified period. In general, no principal is exchanged, up front or at maturity. In the most common type of interest rate swap, one counterparty makes payments based on a fixed rate of interest, while the other party's payments are referenced off a floating-rate index: Three- or six-month LIBOR is the floating-rate index used in nearly 90 percent of these transactions, although some swaps are based on Treasury bill and commercial paper rates. The price of a fixed-floating swap is quoted as a spread over the U.S. Treasury benchmark for the maturity of the swap against the floating-rate index flat. In a second type of swap transaction—a basis swap—each counterparty makes payments based on a floating-rate index and receives payments based on another floating-rate index. The reference floating-rate indexes in the most common type of basis swap are LIBOR and the Federal Reserve AA Composite commercial paper rate. The price on this type of swap is quoted as a spread over one of these reference indexes versus the other index flat.

Since its inception in the early 1980s, the interest rate swap market has grown in size and importance in the domestic and international capital markets. Increasingly, financial managers—from a wide range of institutions—are utilizing interest rate swap agreements as part of overall asset/liability management strategies.

Interest rate swaps have become an important tool for restructuring liabilities to meet specific preferences and needs. For example, issuers have secured cost-effective funding by borrowing in markets where they enjoy relative cost advantages and, in turn, using the swap market to obtain the interest rate exposure that is ultimately desired—either fixed or floating rate. Indeed, swap-driven issuance has become an important source of primary market supply: A large proportion of the new Eurodollar straight bonds issued in the past few years were ultimately converted into floating-rate liabilities through the swap market. Other borrowers have used interest rate swaps to alter the interest rate exposure on liabilities previously incurred.

In addition, asset-based interest rate swaps—in which an investor swaps the interest rate exposure on attractively priced mortgage, Eurodollar straight, floating-rate note (FRN), high-yield, or real estate securities—have often generated returns far above those available for comparable credits on traditional investment vehicles. In some cases, a large volume of similarly structured securities—such as ex-warrant bonds and outstanding FRNs—have been swapped, repackaged, and then reoffered to the primary market. Market participants have also entered into interest rate swap agreements on an outright basis purely as asset substitutes, without first purchasing underlying securities to fund the swap.

The increased utilization of interest rate swaps in an asset/liability context has caused the volume of swap agreements to soar: According to the International Swap Dealers Association (ISDA), the notional volume of U.S. dollar interest rate swaps transacted in the first quarter of 1987 was more than $57 billion—an increase of roughly 44 percent over the 1986 period. The notional volume of outstanding interest rate swaps reached $313 billion at year-end 1986. The introduction of innovative swap products such as options on swaps has further enhanced the flexibility of the product, while the development of the secondary market, in which swap positions are reversed or unwound, has spurred additional growth.

FUNDAMENTAL DETERMINANTS OF SWAP SPREADS

Interest rate swaps are priced relative to other funding and invest-ment vehicles that achieve essentially similar results. At shorter maturities, swaps mimic interest rate futures contracts: Both are used to manage interest rate risk on assets and liabilities. At longer maturities, interest rate swaps are used to create synthetic assets or liabilities as alternatives to traditional fixed- and floating-rate instruments.

Primary Influence at Shorter Maturities—The Eurodollar Futures Market

Spreads on LIBOR-based shorter-dated swaps—those with matu-rities of three years or less—are determined largely by hedging costs in the Eurodollar futures market.[2] Eurodollar futures con-tracts can be used to hedge the exposure on short-term floating-rate assets or liabilities—that is, to lock in a fixed rate. A series of these futures contracts for different maturities therefore creates the same effect as an interest rate swap. For example, a borrower wishing to fix the exposure on a two-year liability indexed to LIBOR could either enter into a two-year interest rate swap to pay fixed and receive floating LIBOR payments, or, alternatively, the issuer could sell a series of Eurodollar contracts matching the pay-ment dates on the underlying liability. In either case, the borrower has effectively locked in fixed-rate financing: If LIBOR rises, higher financing costs are offset either by higher floating-rate pay-ments in the swap or by gains realized on the futures contracts. Commercial banks—which generally tend to be active participants in short-term financial markets—dominate the shorter-dated swap

---

[2] Until recently, the effect of Eurodollar futures prices was most pronounced in maturities of two years or less. However, in July 1987, the maturity of Eurodollar futures contracts traded on the Chicago Mercantile Exchange was lengthened to three years. The influence of this market on interest rate swap spreads now extends to three-year maturities, to the extent permitted by the liquidity of the longer-dated Eurodollar futures contracts. Swap spreads at this maturity are also influenced by corporate borrowing costs as described in the following section.

FIGURE 1

Two-Year Interest Rate Swap Spreads versus Synthetic Spreads Available in the Eurodollar Futures Market[a]

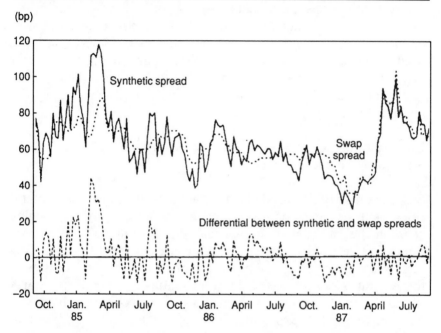

(bp)

[a] The synthetic spread is the fixed rate created with a strip of Eurodollar futures contracts (closing prices) expressed as a spread over U.S. Treasuries. Transaction costs are not included. Both swap and synthetic spreads represent midmarket levels.

market. This largely reflects the extensive exposure to LIBOR on their balance sheets.

Because LIBOR-based interest rate swap contracts perform much the same function as a strip of Eurodollar futures contracts, the two instruments are similarly priced. Figure 1 compares two-year LIBOR-based swap spreads with the synthetic fixed rate into which a LIBOR liability could be hedged using Eurodollar futures contracts (expressed as a spread over U.S. Treasuries).[3] Although

---

[3] The interest rate swap spreads quoted in this report are exclusively those of the Salomon Brothers group. Therefore, these rates may differ from those of other market makers. The spreads are indicative quotes for the bid side of a generic LIBOR-based swap (that is, the

the differential between these spreads was as wide as 40 basis points at the beginning of 1985, the two series have differed by an average of less than 1 basis point over the entire period. Furthermore, the differential on any given date may reflect measurement errors that result from minor differences in the time of day at which swap and synthetic spreads have been priced.

As shorter-term swap spreads respond directly to fluctuations in Eurodollar futures prices, they tend to reflect changes in the differential between government and bank borrowing rates. The sharp rise in short-dated swap spreads in mid-1987 mirrored the widening in the spread between implied yields on the Treasury bill and Eurodollar futures contracts—the TED spread: Two-year swap rates rose by roughly 50 basis points, as the TED spread on the near futures contract approached 175 basis points, its widest level since autumn 1984.[4]

Primary Influences at Longer Maturities—The Corporate Bond Market

Longer-dated interest rate swaps—with maturities of three years or longer—are also priced relative to rates available in other markets, although the alternatives at maturities greater than three years differ significantly from those available in the short-dated market. Interest rate futures contracts do not exist at longer maturities, and the longer-dated, over-the-counter forward market is relatively illiquid. Instead, longer-dated swaps are priced relative to rates in the traditional fixed- and floating-rate financing markets—that is, the cost of corporate borrowing.

Since the early 1980s, the majority of typical interest rate swap counterparties have been corporations, sovereigns, and financial institutions, which access the interest rate swap market to raise relatively cheap fixed- or floating-rate funds. In one example of a

---

counterparty receives fixed-rate payments from Salomon Brothers), unless otherwise noted. Swap spreads are generally not adjusted for the quality of the counterparty. Instead, lower-quality counterparties must typically provide some form of credit enhancement.

[4] For a more comprehensive discussion of the spread between U.S. Treasury bills and LIBOR, see *The TED Spread—Outlook and Implications* by Nancy J. Kimelman and Gioia M. Parente (New York: Salomon Brothers Inc, July 15, 1987).

FIGURE 2
Five-Year Interest Rate Swap Spreads versus New Eurodollar Bond
Spreads over U.S. Treasuries

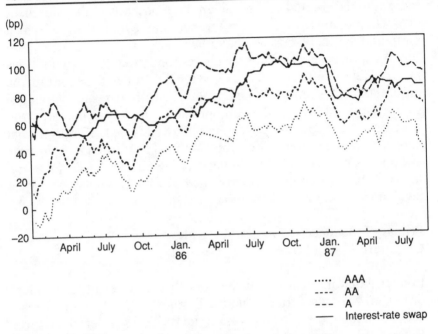

classic swap, a highly rated corporate or sovereign borrower raises funds in the U.S. domestic or Eurodollar bond market and swaps interest rate payments with a lower-rated counterparty that has raised funds in the international banking markets. *Typically, fixed-rate bond markets have tended to require a wider quality spread between higher- and lower-rated counterparties than is typical of floating-rate markets.*[5] Although the highly rated issuer borrows more cheaply than does the lower-rated issuer in both markets, the former participant generally enjoys a greater advantage in the bond market. Conversely, the lower-rated issuer faces less of a quality

---

[5] Many reasons for this relative borrowing cost differential have been proposed, including relatively greater risk aversion among investors in the bond markets and differences in information across markets. Some of these factors suggest only temporary arbitrage opportunities, while others will persist. Thus, the incentives for swap transactions are not likely to disappear.

differential in the floating-rate market. If each borrower raises funds in the market in which it has a *relative* advantage, the resultant interest rate payments can be swapped to achieve cheaper funding for both.

To date, the primary incentive for swap counterparties has been the arbitraging of funding rates. Thus, swap rates have been influenced primarily by yield movements in public debt markets such as the U.S. domestic corporate, Yankee, and Eurodollar bond markets. As Figures 2 and 3 show, swap spreads are roughly equivalent to the level of investment-grade corporate spreads over U.S. Treasuries. *More specifically, swap spreads have almost consistently remained in a 20- to 30-basis-point range defined by AA- and A-rated spreads.*

This relationship makes intuitive sense because many counterparties enter into swaps to obtain cheaper funding: The synthetic fixed rate attained by the fixed-rate payer—usually the lower-rated

FIGURE 3
Ten-Year Interest Rate Swap Spreads versus New Domestic Industrial Spreads over U.S. Treasuries

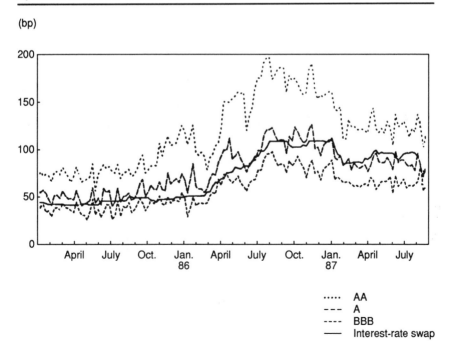

(bp)

..... AA
--- A
---- BBB
— Interest-rate swap

counterparty—must be lower than the rate available to that counterparty in the bond market. Similarly, the synthetic rate obtained by the floating-rate payer—usually the higher-rated counterparty—must be lower than the costs achieved in the traditional floating-rate market. *This implies that the lower bound of swap spreads is the spread over U.S. Treasuries paid by an AA-rated counterparty in the bond market plus the spread under LIBOR available to the same issuer in the traditional floating-rate market. Similarly, the upper bound is the fixed rate achieved by an A-rated counterparty adjusted for its costs in the traditional floating-rate market.* (See the Appendix to this chapter for a more detailed development of the boundary conditions.) Although adjustments for floating-rate financing costs make the bounds more precise, indicative corporate bond spreads, as illustrated in Figures 2 and 3, serve as a close approximation.

Synthetic funding achieved through the swap market, on occasion, has been substantially below what could be attained in traditional markets for the same maturity. For most of 1986, top-quality borrowers were able to create synthetic floating-rate funding at spreads of more than 50 basis points below LIBOR for five- to seven-year maturities, while the lowest spreads achieved by these types of issuers in the Eurodollar FRN market were only 15–25 basis points below LIBOR. Similarly, in the first half of 1986 the fixed rate paid in a swap ranged between 10–30 basis points below what was paid by A-rated borrowers in the bond market. BBB-rated credits have an even greater incentive than do A-rated issuers to swap into fixed-rate debt. However, these issuers, as well as other institutions with lower credit ratings, must often provide some form of credit enhancement, which raises the cost of synthetic debt.

The savings provided by synthetic funding may be even greater for counterparties willing to assume rollover risk. In some instances, commercial paper issuers have been able to swap one-month, AA-rated paper into three-year, fixed-rate funding averaging 15 basis points below AA-rated bond spreads (see Figure 4). In this transaction, however, the issuer remains exposed to an increase in the rate at which it issues commercial paper versus the Federal Reserve AA Composite commercial paper rate received in the swap.

FIGURE 4

Three-Year Synthetic Fixed-Rate Debt versus New-Issue Eurodollar and Domestic Corporate Bonds, Spreads over U.S. Treasuries

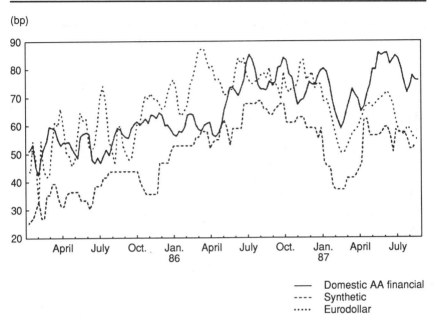

(bp)

Assumes the borrower issues commercial paper at the one-month Federal Reserve AA Composite rate and swaps into fixed-rate debt for a three-year maturity.

THE SHAPE OF THE SWAP SPREAD CURVE

Since autumn 1984—the earliest period for which swap spread data are available—the interest rate swap market has been characterized by four distinct periods. Each of these periods is defined by shifting trends in the level of corporate spreads at different maturities. Figure 5 displays the swap spread curve, commonly referred to as the swap yield curve, typical of each of these periods. Figures 6–8 illustrate the historical movement of three- to seven-year interest rate swap spreads based on the most common floating-rate reference rates—LIBOR, Treasury bills, and commercial paper. As demonstrated, swap spreads mirror the changing shape of the corporate spread curve.

FIGURE 5
Swap Spread Curve

(bp)

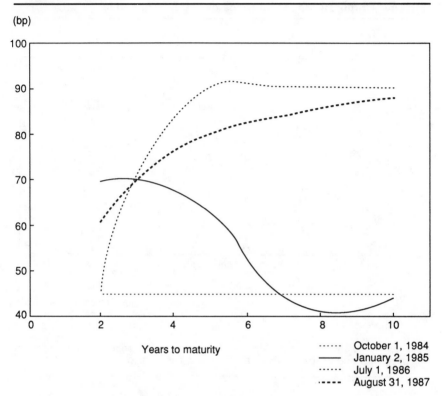

Years to maturity

...... October 1, 1984
——— January 2, 1985
······ July 1, 1986
·---- August 31, 1987

From the third quarter of 1984 through early 1986, swap spread curves based on all the floating-rate indexes were negatively sloped—for the first and only time since the inception of the swap market (see Figure 5). Across all swap markets, three-year rates exceeded those posted at the five-year maturity by as much as 20 basis points, while seven-year spreads almost consistently fell below the five-year levels by the same margin (see Figures 6–8). Similarly, the Eurodollar bond spread curve was negatively sloped during most of the period. Three-year spreads exceeded those at the 10-year maturity by an average of 20 basis points. The domestic corporate spread curve over Treasuries, however, was generally positively sloped.

At the end of the first quarter of 1986, spread relationships were entirely reversed. Five- and seven-year swap spreads rose by

FIGURE 6

Interest Rate Swap Spreads over U.S. Treasuries versus Six-Month LIBOR

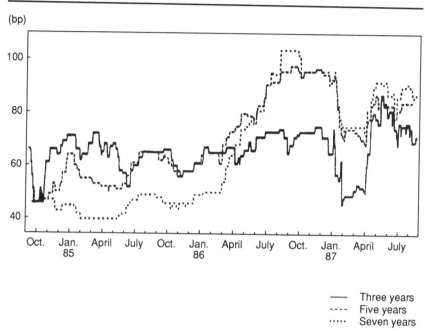

as much as 40 basis points to the 90- to 100-basis-point level—their historical high—while three-year spreads remained relatively constant. As a result, LIBOR-, Treasury bill-, and commercial paper–based swap spread curves—which had all been sharply inverted—flattened and then gradually steepened. Likewise, corporate spreads rose across the board, as investors became more sensitive to the hazards of event risk. In addition, corporate spreads rose proportionately more at longer maturities as the volume of refundings increased and issuers refinanced a large volume of securities in the primary market. At the same time, investors required higher yields on bonds with call options. Longer-maturity spreads in both the swap and corporate bond markets remained at these relatively high levels through the end of 1986.

The third period, from January 1987 through the close of the first quarter, witnessed the most dramatic movement of swap spreads to date. In a two-week period, swap spreads—which typi-

FIGURE 7
Interest Rate Swap Spreads over U.S. Treasuries versus Three-Month Treasury Bills

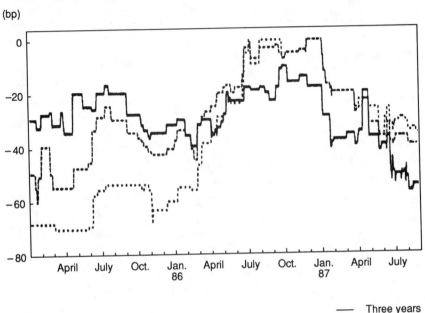

Three years
Five years
Seven years

cally exhibit very low volatility—declined by as much as 20 basis points across the maturity spectrum, maintaining the steepness of the yield curve. Five- and seven-year LIBOR-based spreads moved in tandem, falling below the 80-basis-point level, and three-year spreads sunk to 45 basis points—the lowest level posted at this maturity. Corporate spreads also plunged in this quarter in response to lower interest rate volatility and a significant tightening in the supply of corporate bonds.

Since the beginning of the second quarter of 1987, spreads have risen across the maturity spectrum. LIBOR-based swap spreads at maturities of five years or more have increased by roughly 15 basis points to levels just under the historical highs posted in the fall of 1986. However, three-year swap spreads jumped by twice as much, significantly flattening the curve. Longer-maturity swap spreads now exceed those at the three-year maturity by only 15 basis points—the smallest differential since the

FIGURE 8

Interest Rate Swap Spreads over U.S. Treasuries versus One-Month Commercial Paper.†

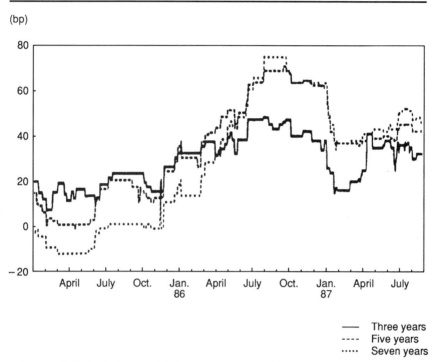

(bp)

	Three years
----	Five years
.....	Seven years

† One-month Federal Reserve AA Composite commercial paper rates.

curve became positively sloped at the beginning of 1986. These same patterns were seen in the domestic and international bond markets. In the domestic market, spreads were generally higher as investors shunned fixed-rate issues in the face of markedly higher Treasury yields. International investors also became increasingly nervous about the value of the U.S. dollar.

OTHER INFLUENCES ON INTEREST RATE SWAP SPREADS

Other factors also affect the relative supply of fixed- and floating-rate payers in the interest rate swap market, thereby influencing the level of swap spreads. While the impact of many of these factors is short-lived, some have been important enough to shift swap spreads either *within* the bounds defined by corporate spreads or, on occasion, outside these bounds. Thus, the boundary conditions set by new issue A- and AA-rated corporate spreads are not restrictive. Spreads are also influenced by factors such as the absolute level and shape of the U.S. Treasury yield curve, the volume of asset-based swaps, and technical factors that affect swap dealers.

The Relationship between the Interest Rate Swap, Corporate and U.S. Treasury Markets

The overall direction and shape of the Treasury yield curve affect swap spreads to the extent that they influence interest rate expectations and therefore the desired mix of interest rate exposure. Because most swap transactions have been liability based in the past, one might expect that the supply of fixed-rate payers would decline when interest rates are expected to fall or the yield curve is expected to flatten, thereby driving swap spreads lower. Conversely, if interest rates were expected to rise or the yield curve were expected to steepen, borrowers would prefer to be fixed-rate payers—locking in the relatively low interest cost and, thus, pushing spreads higher.

It is difficult to measure the interest rate expectations of market participants. *However, historical data on changes in the absolute levels of rates show that swap spreads often move inversely to Treasuries: Swap spreads have tended to widen in rallies and narrow in setbacks.* This relationship is also exhibited in corporate bond markets at least initially following a significant move in Treasuries. To demonstrate these relationships, Figure 9 shows interest rate movements of U.S. Treasuries, Eurodollar, and domestic corporate bonds and interest rate swaps during distinct bull and bear market periods since autumn 1984. Swap spreads widened or showed no change as interest rates declined in six of eight bull markets during this period. Eurodollar and domestic corporate bond spreads widened in all of the bull market periods.

This inverse relationship between swap spreads and Treasury yields also reflects the relatively low volatility of interest rate swap spreads. Since late 1984, swap spreads have moved, on average, by less than 1½ basis points for every 10-basis-point movement in Eurodollar bond spreads at the five-year maturity. At 10 years,

FIGURE 9

Comparison of Recent Interest Rate Differentials in the U.S. Treasury, Eurodollar, and Domestic Corporate Bond Markets and the Interest Rate Swap Market

Period	Type of Market	Change in U.S. Govt Yields		Change in Euro$ Bond Yields		Change in Dom Corp Bond Yields		Change in Euro$ Bond Spreads vs Govts		Change in Dom Corp Bond Spreads vs Govts		Change in Interest Rate Swap Spreads vs Govts	
		5 Yr	7 Yr	5 Yr	7 Yr	5 Yr	7 Yr	5 Yr	7 Yr	5 Yr	7 Yr	5 Yr	7 Yr
3 Oct 84 to 5 Nov 84	Bull	−116 bp	−113 bp	−64 bp	−75 bp	−75 bp	−53 bp	52 bp	38 bp	13 bp	33 bp	3 bp	1 bp
29 Jan 85 to 22 Feb 85	Bear	71	82	34	40	44	56	−37	−42	−24	−17	−2	−2
15 Mar 85 to 19 Apr 85	Bull	−96	−85	−91	−87	−92	−79	5	2	4	6	−1	0
5 Jul 85 to 2 Aug 85	Bear	69	65	51	45	69	71	−18	−20	0	5	4	2
2 Aug 85 to 23 Aug 85	Bull	−40	−46	−35	−34	−41	−34	5	12	−1	13	0	0
6 Sep 85 to 1 Nov 85	Bull	−55	−57	−38	−25	−29	−49	17	32	26	7	−6	−2
6 Dec 85 to 27 Dec 85	Bull	−60	−63	−49	−54	−11	−42	11	9	49	21	3	3
10 Jan 86 to 28 Feb 86	Bull	−104	−121	−69	−80	−85	−84	35	41	20	37	1	4
18 Apr 86 to 30 May 86	Bear	112	118	95	98	65	57	−17	−20	−4	−31	−1	−7
30 May 86 to 18 Jul 86	Bull	−99	−99	−75	−79	−65	−11	24	20	34	88	11	14
29 Aug 86 to 19 Sep 86	Bear	68	72	56	42	29	14	−12	−30	−39	−58	−2	−2
9 Jan 87 to 13 Feb 87	Bear	25	24	10	8	14	5	−15	−16	−12	−19	−8	−8
13 Mar 87 to 24 Apr 87	Bear	128	129	124	125	119	96	−4	−4	−9	−34	15	17
22 May 87 to 19 Jun 87	Bull	−55	−47	−48	−57	−42	−23	7	−10	13	24	−6	−10
10 Jul 87 to 31 Jul 87	Bear	22	23	18	23	12	−2	4	0	−19	−36	0	0

swap spreads have moved by 5 basis points for every 10-basis-point change in Eurodollar bond spreads. The comparison of standard deviations shows the same difference between swap and Eurodollar bond markets: The standard deviation of swap spreads at both 5- and 10-year maturities has been fairly stable at two basis points, while the standard deviation of Eurodollar bond spreads has averaged eight basis points.[6] Swap spreads at maturities of under three years have tended to be somewhat more volatile than longer-term spreads. Short-dated swaps are priced closely in relation to the implied yield on a strip of Eurodollar futures contracts, which trade in liquid, highly sensitive markets. Longer-dated swaps, on the other hand, are priced relative to a variety of fixed-income spreads, which tend to be more stable.

Asset-Based Interest Rate Swaps

An increasing number of swap market participants use the agreements to change the interest rate exposure on assets, as well as liabilities. The volume of these transactions—which involve the creation of synthetic assets through the purchase of securities and the simultaneous execution of swaps—has often been large enough to affect swap spreads. The attractiveness of asset-based transactions, and thus their potential influence on swap spreads, depends largely on the investment opportunities available in traditional fixed- and floating-rate markets. Three common examples of asset-based transactions are discussed below: risk-controlled arbitrage by thrift institutions, the creation of Eurodollar synthetic floating-rate instruments, and the creation of Eurodollar synthetic fixed-rate instruments.

Risk-Controlled Arbitrage by Thrift Institutions
One of the most popular applications of interest rate swaps has been a form of risk-controlled arbitrage in which fixed-rate mortgages are converted to synthetic floating-rate investments. U.S. thrift institutions—which often have short-term liabilities in the form of deposits and long-term assets in the form of fixed-rate

---

[6] Moving 20-day standard deviation.

FIGURE 10
**Risk-Controlled Arbitrage Using Benchmark Coupon GNMAs[a] and
Interest Rate Swaps**

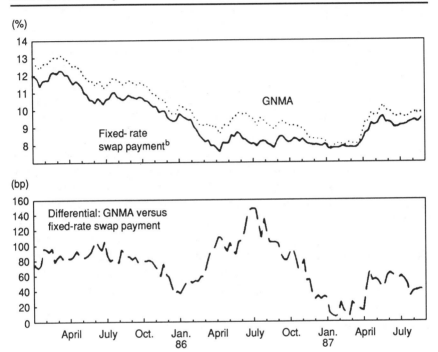

[a] Yields of benchmark coupon GNMAs are based on Salomon Brothers' long-term projected prepayment rate, which assumes interest rates remain unchanged from current levels.
[b] Ten-year Treasury plus the 10-year swap spread.

mortgages—use swaps to manage this asset/liability mismatch and thereby reduce their exposure to fluctuations in interest rates.[7] In a typical transaction, a thrift purchases a mortgage security and enters an interest rate swap agreement as the fixed-rate payer. Figure 10 illustrates one example involving the swapping of benchmark

---

[7] Applications of the interest rate swap market for thrift institutions are discussed in detail in *Constructive Use of Fixed-Rate Mortgages—Arbitrage Opportunities for Financial Institutions* by Michael Waldman (New York: Salomon Brothers Inc, May 1985).

coupon Government National Mortgage Association (GNMA) securities. The extent to which the yield on the mortgage security exceeds the fixed rate payable on the 10-year swap translates into a spread over their funding costs. The thrift is able to lock in this spread regardless of interest rate movements, subject, of course, to changes in the prepayment rates on the underlying mortgages.

Thrift institutions completed the greatest volume of these risk-controlled arbitrage transactions in the first half of 1985, when the differential between the yield on the mortgage security and the fixed rate paid in the swap hovered around 80–100 basis points. The resultant strong demand for swaps contributed to a notable increase in swap spreads from AA- to A-rated new-issue spreads during this period. In July 1986, this risk-controlled arbitrage generated a spread of 150 basis points, yet thrift activity in the swap market declined: Thrift institutions had recently experienced the effects of unexpectedly high prepayment rates, which consequently limited their interest in this type of risk-controlled arbitrage. During most of 1987, risk-controlled arbitrage using interest rate swaps has been relatively light: The differential between the yield on benchmark coupon GNMAs and the fixed rate paid in the swap has averaged only 40 basis points, while thrifts have generally aimed to achieve a spread of at least 75 basis points.

Creation of Synthetic Eurodollar Floating-Rate Investments

An increase in the supply of fixed-rate payers also occurs when attractive synthetic floating-rate investments are available through the swap market. For example, at the end of the first quarter of 1986, an investor could create a high-yielding, floating-rate security by simultaneously purchasing a swap—thus becoming the fixed-rate payer—and a high-quality U.S. corporate Eurodollar bond.[8]

---

[8] For a complete discussion of this investment opportunity, see *Fixed-Income Investment Opportunities: Create High-Yielding Eurodollar Floating-Rate Notes Through Asset-Based Interest Rate Swaps* by Gioia M. Parente (New York: Salomon Brothers Inc, April 23, 1986).

This investment paid as much as 20 basis points over LIBOR in April 1986—an attractive level compared with spreads for comparable credits available in the Eurodollar FRN market (see Figure 11). Although interest rate swap spreads were wide at this time—the five- and seven-year maturities had hit record highs for the period—they had widened by a smaller magnitude than those in other fixed-income markets. Therefore, investors could purchase Eurodollar securities at relatively wide spreads to the U.S. Treasury curve and swap the interest payments to create a floating-rate asset. The extent to which the fixed rate paid on the swap—Treasuries plus the swap spread—was lower than the yield on the Euro-

FIGURE 11
Creation of Synthetic Floating-Rate Notes through the Interest Rate Swap Market

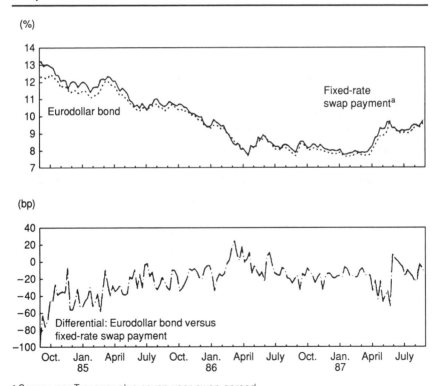

[a] Seven-year Treasury plus seven-year swap spread.

dollar bond, enhanced the attractiveness of the asset-based swap for the fixed-rate payer.

The rush of fixed-rate payers into the swap market to capitalize on this investment opportunity early in 1986 contributed to a change in the relationship between swap spreads and corporate spreads. By July 1986, swap spreads had shifted from the level of AA-rated corporate spreads—where they had traded for six months—to A-rated levels.

A more recent example of the creation of Eurodollar floating-rate instruments is the repackaging of Eurodollar bonds initially issued with equity warrants attached. Once the equity warrants are detached, the remaining low-coupon bond is swapped to a floating-rate asset, either on an individual basis or as part of a pool of similarly structured securities. Approximately $2 billion of these securities have been reoffered to the market since January 1987.

Creation of Synthetic Eurodollar Fixed-Rate Investments

The unprecedented setback in the Eurodollar FRN market at the beginning of 1987 created a significant opportunity for investors to create high-yielding synthetic fixed-rate assets through the purchase of cheap floating-rate instruments and the simultaneous sale of interest rate swaps. These synthetic fixed-rate instruments paid more than 70 basis points over the Treasury yield curve, in contrast to the roughly 50 basis points on traditional Eurodollar straight bond investments for comparable credits.[9] Although interest rate swap spreads had declined by record amounts in early 1987—thus, lowering the fixed rate received in the swap—spreads in other fixed-income markets had narrowed more dramatically. This transaction, although not widely exploited, increased the supply of floating-rate payers and thus contributed some downward pressure on swap spreads.

---

[9] For a complete discussion of this investment opportunity, see *Fixed-Income Investment Opportunities: Use Cheap LIBOR-Based Floating-Rate Notes and Interest Rate Swaps To Create High-Yielding Fixed-Rate Instruments* by Gioia M. Parente (New York: Salomon Brothers Inc, March 5, 1987).

Hedging Costs

One of the more important technical factors to influence the swap market is the hedging costs faced by swap dealers. A swap dealer typically hedges the interest rate risk on a swap—at least temporarily—in the U.S. Treasury and government repurchase markets before matching the position with an offsetting swap. For example, when a dealer enters into a swap to make fixed- and receive floating-rate payments, the dealer, generally, hedges the interest rate mismatch by purchasing a U.S. Treasury security with the same maturity as the swap contract and financing the purchase in the short-term collateralized reverse repurchase market. The difference between the LIBOR payment received in the swap and the repurchase rate represents positive carrying costs for the dealer. As positive carrying costs rise, the dealer is willing to offer more for an offsetting swap. On the other side of the market, a swap dealer making floating and receiving fixed payments uses short Treasury positions and repurchase agreements (repos) as a hedge. In this case, the LIBOR-repo spread represents negative carry for the dealer. Swap spreads tend to rise as the LIBOR-repo spread increases in order to compensate for the higher financing costs incurred by the dealer.

CONCLUSION

Interest rate swaps have assumed a greater role in financial markets as the creation of synthetic securities—in both an asset and liability context—has become more common. A clear understanding of the determinants of interest rate swap spreads is crucial to market participants assessing the relative advantages of these synthetic instruments versus the more traditional vehicles directly available in the securities markets. Furthermore, the ability to gauge swap performance in different interest rate environments and effectively time swap transactions facilitates the efficient management of swap portfolios. The analytical framework presented in this report will be even more important as the interest rate swap market becomes increasingly complex and additional derivative products are developed.

APPENDIX: BOUNDARY CONDITIONS FOR INTEREST RATE SWAP SPREADS

Boundary conditions for interest rate swap spreads are determined by prices in alternative financial markets. For example, suppose that a highly rated borrower issues fixed-rate debt in the bond market and simultaneously enters into an interest rate swap with the same maturity to make floating-rate and receive fixed-rate payments. This transaction makes sense for the issuer only if the resultant floating-rate borrowing cost is lower than that available in the traditional floating-rate markets. In other words, if

$$[T + A] - [(T + S) - (LIBOR)] \leq LIBOR - a$$

where A = fixed-rate spread over U.S. Treasuries paid by the higher-rated counterparty on traditional straight bond financing,

a = floating-rate spread under LIBOR typically paid by the higher-rated counterparty on traditional floating-rate financing,

S = swap spread over U.S. Treasuries, and

T = yield on U.S. Treasuries.

Rearranging terms, we get

$$LIBOR - [(T + S) - (T + A)] \leq LIBOR - a$$
$$LIBOR - [S - A] \leq LIBOR - a$$
$$[S - A] \geq a, \text{ or}$$
$$S \geq a + A. \qquad (1)$$

Similarly, an issuer will consider synthetic fixed-rate debt—a floating-rate note coupled with a swap in which the issuer makes fixed- and receives floating-rate payments—only if it results in cheaper fixed-rate funding than is available to the same issuer in bond markets. In other words, the fixed-rate payer enters into the swap only if

$$[LIBOR - b] + [(T + S) - LIBOR] \leq T + B.$$

Or,

$$T + S - [LIBOR - (LIBOR - b)] \leq T + B$$
$$T + S - b \leq T + B$$
$$S - b \leq B$$
$$S \leq B + b \qquad (2)$$

where B = fixed-rate spread over U.S. Treasuries paid by the lower-rated counterparty on traditional straight bond financing and b = floating-rate spread under LIBOR typically paid by the lower-rated counterparty on traditional floating-rate financing.

Together, these two conditions imply that the following inequality must hold if the swap is to be written:

$$a + A \leq S \leq B + b \qquad (3)$$

In other words, the bounds for swap spreads are determined by borrowing costs in alternative fixed- and floating-rate markets. The lower bound is the spread over U.S. Treasuries paid by the higher-rated counterparty in fixed-rate markets plus the spread under LIBOR available to the same issuer in the traditional floating-rate markets. Similarly, the upper bound is the fixed rate achieved by the lower-rated counterparty plus the spread under LIBOR available to the same issuer in the traditional floating-rate markets.

This analysis also highlights the conditions under which interest rate swaps provide an effective arbitrage across credit markets. Swaps enable market participants to lower borrowing costs or increase yields when the quality spread in the fixed-rate market is at least as large as the quality spread in the floating-rate market, or

$$B - A \geq a - b. \qquad (4)$$

CHAPTER 14

THE DURATION OF A SWAP

Laurie S. Goodman
Eastbridge Capital
New York, New York

Many financial firms face interest rate risk. In the natural course of doing business, they match long-term assets against shorter-term liabilities or, less frequently, shorter-term assets against longer-term liabilities. As interest rates rise (fall), firms that have pursued the first (second) course of action can suffer large losses. But a firm can make a conscious decision to correct this interest rate mismatch. In order to do so, the firm must first be able to measure the extent of the mismatch.

The most commonly used technique for measuring the degree of interest rate mismatch on a firm's balance sheet is to measure the price responsiveness of the assets to a small change in interest rates and subtract the price responsiveness of the liabilities to the small change in interest rates. The most commonly used measure of the price responsiveness of a position is technically known as *modified duration,* but is usually referred to as *duration.* Modified duration is defined as the percent change in price of the position divided by the change in interest rates. Thus, if interest rates went up by 10 basis points (bp) and the value of $100 of assets went down to 99.50—a .5 percent decline—the modified duration of the assets would be 5(.5/.1). Similarly, if we knew the duration of the assets was 5, and the firm had $100 of assets, a 10-basis-point rise in rates would cause a $.50 drop in value. Thus, if we know the modified duration of the assets, the amount of the assets, the modified duration of the liabilities, and the amount of the liabilities, we know the extent of the interest rate mismatch.

Once the firm has measured its mismatch, it must choose tools to neutralize the effect of the interest rate mismatch. Interest rate swaps are an important tool in this interest risk management process. As such, the duration, or interest rate sensitivity, of these instruments needs to be well understood. That is, once the firm has determined its basic mismatch, it must determine how many swaps it would need to hedge this position. In this chapter, we show that, although there is no notional exchange of principal, the interest rate sensitivity of a swap can be computed as if there is. In other words, a swap in which a firm promises to pay the floating rate of interest and receive a fixed rate of interest can be looked at as a short position in a floating-rate note and a long position in a fixed-rate bond. When looked at in this manner, most of the price sensitivity of the instrument comes from the fixed side. Equivalently, a swap transaction can be viewed as swapping a stream of payments. Considered thus, most of the price sensitivity comes from the floating-rate side. This perhaps unexpected implication will be made clear in the discussion that follows.

A SWAP POSITION IS EQUIVALENT TO A POSITION IN A FLOATING-RATE NOTE AND A BOND

Assume one party promises to pay the floating rate of interest and receive a fixed rate of interest. In a flat 10 percent yield curve environment, the payments on a five-year swap with a semiannual reset are as follows:

	Payment	Pay Floating	Received Fixed
Year 1	1	-5	$+5$
	2	$-fl_2$	$+5$
Year 2	3	$-fl_3$	$+5$
	4	$-fl_4$	$+5$
Year 3	5	$-fl_5$	$+5$
	6	$-fl_6$	$+5$
Year 4	7	$-fl_7$	$+5$
	8	$-fl_8$	$+5$
Year 5	9	$-fl_9$	$+5$
	10	$-fl_{10}$	$+5$

Thus, the first floating payment is fixed until the reset at the end of six months.

We now show that the cash flows of this position are equivalent to a short position in a floating-rate note and a long position in a fixed-rate bond:

	Payment	Short an FRN	Long a Fixed-Rate Bond
Year 1	1	−5	+5
	2	$-fl_2$	+5
Year 2	3	$-fl_3$	+5
	4	$-fl_4$	+5
Year 3	5	$-fl_5$	+5
	6	$-fl_6$	+5
Year 4	7	$-fl_7$	+5
	8	$-fl_8$	+5
Year 5	9	$-fl_9$	+5
	10	$-100-fl_{10}$	+105

The last payment nets out to $5-fl_{10}$—exactly the same as swapping a stream of payments.

Conversely, a swap position in which a firm promises to pay a fixed rate of interest and receive a floating rate of interest is equivalent to being short a fixed-rate bond and long a floating-rate note. This can be easily seen by laying out the cash flows as above.

Since the cash flows are the same, we would expect the price sensitivity, or duration, to be the same.[1] The next section shows that this is in fact the case.

PRICE SENSITIVITY OF A SWAP

We can compute the price sensitivity of a swap, viewing the swap either as a long/short position or as an exchange of annuity payments. We first look at the price sensitivity of a position in which

---

[1] While the interest rate sensitivity of the two positions is the same, the credit risk is not. If you had issued a floating-rate note and used the proceeds to purchase a bond that did not pay the promised cash flows, you would still be obligated to noteholders for principal repayment.

you are short a floating-rate note and long a bond. We look at the swap immediately after its inception, assuming both securities pay semiannually. Thus, there is six months to the reset of the floating side. If interest rates change by 10 basis points, the change in the value of the positions is as follows:

	Five-Year Bond Position (Long)	FRN Position (Short)	Net Value (Long Minus Short)
Original value	100	100	0
Value after a 10 basis point increase	99.615	99.952	−.337
Net change	−.385	−.048	−.337

The decrease in the value of the fixed-rate bond is the decrease associated with holding a 10.0 percent coupon if rates increase to 10.1 percent. The decrease in the value of the floating-rate note reflects the fact that the floating-rate note would sell at par if the first semiannual interest payment were $5.05. In fact, the first payment is $5.00. This $.05 must be discounted back to the present. Having made the calculation, we find $.05/(1 + .101/2) = .048. Thus, the FRN position is worth a bit less than par.

The net value of the position is the value of the long position minus the value of the short position. Consequently, the decrease in the value of the position is $.337. Note that most of the price sensitivity is on the fixed side, as the fixed side has the price action of a five-year bond. The floating side has the small price change of a six-month security.

If we look at a swap as swapping payments, the overall price sensitivity is the same, as shown above, but most of the price action comes from the floating side. Assume that interest rates jump 10 basis points. All floating payments except the first must be $.05 higher than otherwise.

To calculate the value of the original payment stream, we discounted the old payments at 10 percent. The new payments were discounted at 10.1 percent. The present value of the new payments is $.243 higher than that of the old payments. Thus, the floating payments actually *increase* in value as interest rates rise, as shown in the table on the next page. In a floating-rate note, this is offset by the decreased present value of the principal repayment.

	Payment	New Payment	Old Payment
Year 1	1	5	5
	2	5.05	5
Year 2	3	5.05	5
	4	5.05	5
Year 3	5	5.05	5
	6	5.05	5
Year 4	7	5.05	5
	8	5.05	5
Year 5	9	5.05	5
	10	5.05	5
	Present value	38.852	38.609

In a floating-rate note, this is offset by the decreased present value of the principal repayment.

The semiannual fixed payments are the same $5 as before. They are discounted at a rate of 10.1 percent instead of 10 percent. The old present value of the payments was $38.609. The new present value is $38.515. Thus, the present value of the payments drops by .094.

In this case we are long the fixed payments, short the floating payments. The net change in price can be summarized as follows:

	Five-Year Fixed Payments (Long)	Five-Year Floating Payments (Short)	Net Value (Long minus Short)
Original value	38.609	38.609	0
Value after 10-bp increase in rates	38.515	38.852	−.337
Net change	−.094	+.243	−.337

Thus, the change in price is exactly the same as before. However, the price action comes from the floating side rather than the fixed side.

The implication of this analysis is that, for hedging purposes, it is unnecessary to look at a swap as exchanging two annuity streams, where the price sensitivity calculation is not intuitively obvious. We can instead look at a swap as being long one instrument and short another. The price sensitivities of the long and short securities can be easily calculated.

Duration is often used as a measure of the price sensitivity that results from changes in interest rates.[2] It is defined as the percent change in price of a security that is associated with a change in yields. Duration is measured in years. Thus, a security with a six-year duration will be twice as price sensitive as a security with a three-year duration.

The duration of a security is given by Equation 1.

$$D = \frac{-\Delta P/P}{\Delta r} \qquad (1)$$

where D = the duration of the security,
P = the price of the security, and
r = the interest rate.

Thus, the duration of the fixed-rate security is 3.85 years: $-(-.385/100/.001)$. The duration of the floating rate security is .48 years: $-(-.048/100/.001)$. The duration of the interest-rate swap position is given by Equation 2.

$$D_S = \frac{D_X P_S - D_G P_S}{P_S} = D_X - D_G \qquad (2)$$

where D_S = the duration of the interest-rate swap position,
D_X = the duration of the fixed-rate instrument position,
D_G = the duration of the floating-rate instrument position, and
P_S = the notional amount of the swap.

That is, the duration of the short position is subtracted from the duration of the long position. In our example above, the duration of the swap position is 3.37 years.

Note that a swap position in which you pay floating and receive fixed has a positive duration. A swap position in which you receive floating and pay fixed has a negative duration; that is, it increases in value as rates rise.

For an asset-liability hedge, the swap position must neutralize the asset-liability mismatch on a firm's balance sheet. The mismatch is the price responsiveness of the assets—or their duration times the market value, less the price responsiveness of the liabil-

---

[2] The measure of duration used in this paper is modified duration, as opposed to Macauley duration. Modified duration can be multiplied by $(1 + r/2)$ to give Macauley duration.

ity—or their duration times the market value. Thus, the size of a swap position necessary to neutralize a given asset-liability mismatch can be

$$O = D_A V_A - D_L V_L + D_S V_S \qquad (3)$$

where D_A = the duration of the assets,

   D_L = the duration of the liabilities,

   D_S = the duration of the swap,

   V_A = the value of the assets,

   V_L = the liabilities, and

   V_S = the notional amount of the swap position.

Solving Equation 3 for $D_S V_S$ we obtain the following:

$$D_S V_S = D_L V_L - D_A V_A \qquad (4)$$

If liabilities have a shorter dollar-weighted duration than assets, a firm would want to add a swap position with a negative duration. That is, it would like to receive floating-rate payments and make fixed-rate payments in order to offset its balance sheet mismatch. A firm could achieve this result with a swap of any maturity. The longer the maturity, the less the notional amount of swap needed to accomplish the desired hedge. However, once an initial hedge is set up, it must be altered over time as the durations of the assets, liabilities, and swaps change. In the next section, we examine how the duration of a swap is affected by the passage of time.

THE DURATION OF A SWAP OVER TIME

The passage of time will affect the net duration of a swap as well as the net duration of the assets and liabilities. In the case of a swap, the same principles for computing duration apply that were introduced in the previous section—the net duration is simply the duration of the fixed-rate side less the duration of the floating-rate side (for a payer of floating), or the duration of the floating-rate side less the duration of the fixed-rate side (for a payer of fixed).

The passage of time affects a fixed-rate bond because the amount of time to the final maturity changes and because the time to the next coupon payment changes. The passage of time affects a floating-rate note because the time shortens to the next coupon payment and hence to the next reset. As a result of these effects, the duration of a swap remains constant between resets, provided interest rates remain unchanged.

To make this point, let us consider the five-year fixed-rate bond discussed earlier. We consider this bond immediately before the first reset. Since the bond purchase price includes the accrued coupon, the security would cost $105.00 ($100 plus $5 to compensate the seller for the coupon it would not be receiving). To calculate duration, we assume a 10-basis-point increase in rates occurs. A 10 percent 4.5-year bond would be priced at $99.645 plus the $5 accrued interest. Thus, the price declines by $.355. The duration is 3.38 years. It is the percent decline in initial value [(.355/105) × 100] divided by the percent increase in yield (.1). More simply, we can express this as the change done in Equation 1—.355/105/.001. Looking at the duration immediately before each reset, we obtain a declining pattern as follows:

Time to Maturity	Duration in Years	Change in Duration
4.5 years	3.38	—
4.0	3.07	.31
3.5	2.75	.32
3.0	2.41	.34
2.5	2.06	.35
2.0	1.69	.37
1.5	1.30	.39
1.0	.88	.42
.5	.45	.43
0	0	.45

Note as the time to maturity gets shorter, the duration declines more rapidly. The duration of the bond immediately before each reset is equivalent to the duration of a swap at this point, as the duration of the floating-rate side is zero immediately prior to its coupon reset. From Equation 2 we know the duration of a swap is equal to the duration of the fixed-rate side less the duration of the floating-rate side.

Now let us consider the duration of a swap at two other points—immediately after a reset and halfway between resets. Immediately after the floating rate is set, the fixed-rate side has a duration of a 10 percent five-year par bond. That is, a 10-basis-point increase in rates would cause the price of the bond to fall to $99.6148—a price change of $.3852. This translates into a duration of 3.852 years (.3852/100/.001). The floating-rate side has a duration of .476 years. That is, a 10-basis-point rise in rates would cause a price change of $.0476. Duration is then calculated as .0476/100/.001. Thus, the net duration is 3.376 years—3.38 years rounded to two decimal points.

Consider now the duration midway through the reset period—when there are 4.75 years until maturity. If there were a 10-basis-point rise in rates, the value of the bond immediately before the reset would be $99.645 plus the $5 accrued interest. This must be discounted back at the new interest rate for one half a period [1 + (.101/4), or 1.02525]. The value of the bond is $102.068 ($104.645/1.02525) midway through the period. If there had been no change in rates, the bond would sell for $102.439 ($105/1.025) midway through the period. This $.371 price difference translates into a duration of 3.62 years—approximately halfway between 3.85 and 3.38 years. Thus, duration declines approximately linearly between coupon dates. The duration profile for the fixed side of a swap or a fixed rate bond is shown in Exhibit 1.

The duration of the floating rate side of a swap also declines approximately linearly between resets. We know the initial duration is .476 immediately after a reset. It is zero immediately before the next reset. If rates go up 10 basis points midway through the period, the holder of the floater should receive $5.025 (5 × ½ + 5.05 × ½) rather than $5. Thus, the change in the price of the FRN, discounted, would be $.0244. The duration would be .0244/102.5/.001, or $.238. Exhibit 1 shows that the duration of a floater (the lines at the bottom of the graph that move from a maturity of 5 to 4.5 years, 4.5 to 4 years, etc.) also declines roughly linearly between coupon dates.

We saw in the section on price sensitivity of a swap that the duration of a swap involves subtracting the duration of the floating-rate side from the duration of the fixed-rate side. Thus, the duration of a swap remains constant for the time between resets. That is, the durations of the fixed-rate side and the floating-rate side decline equally. This is shown clearly by the dotted lines in Exhibit 1. At any point in time the duration of a swap will be the duration of a fixed-rate bond immediately prior to the next reset.

EXHIBIT 1
The Duration of a Swap over Time

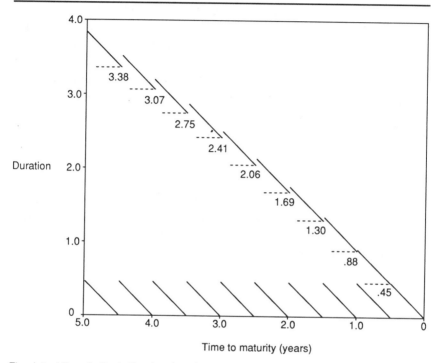

Time to maturity (years)

The dotted lines indicate the duration of a swap during each time period. The duration of the interest rate swap is the duration of the fixed-rate side less the duration of the floating-rate side.

SUMMARY

In this chapter, we have shown that for the purposes of assessing interest rate risk, an interest-rate swap in which one party pays a floating rate and receives a fixed rate can be looked at as short position in a floating-rate note and a long position in a fixed-rate bond. That is, the cash flows and the price sensitivity are identical whether the swap is looked at as a two-bond position (long a fixed-rate bond, short a floater) or as an exchange of interest payments. In the former case, most of the price action comes from the fixed-rate side; in the latter case, it comes from the floating-rate side.

Given this analysis, it is relatively easy for a firm to compute the size of a swap necessary to eliminate a firm's interest rate mismatch. Assume, for example, a firm has $100 million in assets, $90 million in liabilities. The assets have a duration of five years and the liabilities have a duration of one year. The firm has decided to use a new 5-year swap—with a duration of 3.38 years to close the interest rate gap. The firm needs the dollar duration of the swap to equal −$410 million ($1 \times 90 - 5 \times 100$). Thus, the firm must enter into $121.3 million of swaps (4.10/3.38) in which they receive floating and pay fixed. Fewer swaps would be needed if the firm selected a 10-year swap instead of a 5-year swap.

We have also shown that the duration of a swap is affected by the passage of time. At any point in time, the duration of a swap will be the duration of a fixed-rate bond with a maturity equal to the time from the next reset to the maturity of the swap. As time passes, the duration of the assets and liabilities will also change. The firm will most likely have to rebalance its hedge periodically. In doing so, it will want to take into account the duration of its outstanding swap position.

PART 4

CONCEPTUAL RELATIONSHIPS

CHAPTER 15

THE PORTFOLIO APPROACH TO SWAPS MANAGEMENT

Lee M. Wakeman
Continental Bank
Chicago, Illinois

1. INTRODUCTION

Most papers written to date on the subject of swaps have concentrated on securities analysis in that they have focused on the individual instruments (e.g., interest rate swaps, basis swaps, fixed currency swaps, currency coupon swaps, zero swaps, etc.). This chapter attempts to complement this approach by focusing on the portfolio management aspects of the swaps products.

In Section 2, the basic forms of swap transactions are defined, and the concepts of a swap as either two bonds or a portfolio of forward contracts are explained. Section 3 discusses the evolution of the role of the intermediary, from the initial role as a broker—finding counterparties to match custom-tailored swaps without

This paper was first presented at the European Portfolio Managers' meeting at INSEAD in May, 1986. Since some of the material in the original paper ("An Analysis of Swaps Transactions" and "The Rationale for Swaps") has already been published, it has been dropped from this revised version, which concentrates on the zero coupon curve approach to pricing any arbitrary swap and to managing the risk of a portfolio of such swaps. In revising this paper in 1989, I have attempted to remain faithful to the original, and have noted, where appropriate, the inclusion of any insights garnered since 1986. The approach described in this paper was first used at Citicorp International Bank Ltd., London in 1984/1985, and its successful implementation owes much to Pratap Sondhi and David Pritchard of Citicorp and Professor Stephen Schaefer of the London Business School.

credit or market exposure—to the current role as a *warehouse* manager, that is, accepting a swap contract without an immediately available matching counterparty. This acceptance of exposure has led to the development of techniques, such as using government securities and financial futures, to hedge the market exposure of the inventoried swaps.

The techniques for hedging swap risk discussed in Section 3 are tailored to the individual swap, and a warehouse is viewed as a collection of swaps, to be hedged individually without consideration of the other swaps in the warehouse. By 1986 only a few intermediaries in the swaps market had taken the next step—hedging the warehoused swaps as a single entity. This portfolio approach to managing a *book* of swaps is detailed in Section 4, which also discusses the application of the *dedicated portfolio* and *immunized portfolio* hedging strategies to a portfolio of swap transactions.

These techniques are similar to those used in the management of pension fund and insurance company portfolios, and Section 5 concludes the paper with a discussion of the potential for swaps products to enhance portfolio performance.

2.   AN ANALYSIS OF SWAPS TRANSACTIONS

Generally, a company will enter into a swap transaction in order to exchange one pattern of future cash flows for another, more preferred pattern. The diversity of swap products currently available can be encompassed by variations in the two basic elements of a swap—the nature and timing of the exchanged cash flows. To illustrate this point, first consider a currency swap.

2.1   Currency Swaps

In a currency swap, the counterparties agree on the nature of the cash flows to be exchanged (setting both the principal amounts in each currency and the appropriate interest rates) and on the timing of these cash flows (detailing both the final maturity at which the principal amounts will be exchanged and the intermediate dates on which the interest payments in each currency will be made). The cash flows from a standard fixed currency swap are illustrated in

FIGURE 1
Cash Flows to a Company Receiving Fixed Swiss Francs and Paying
Fixed Dollars in a Fixed Currency Swap

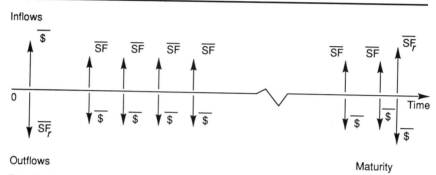

The short arrows represent the payment of interest at the fixed dollar rate ($) and the receipt of interest at the fixed Swiss franc rate (SF). The long arrows denote the initial exchange of principal (which need not occur) and its reexchange at maturity.

Figure 1. This type of swap is often used by a U.S. company which is simultaneously issuing a Swiss franc bond.

A first glance at Figure 1 suggests that this swap can be viewed as though the U.S. company buys a Swiss franc bond and issues a U.S. dollar fixed-rate bond. The swap thus converts the Swiss franc liability into a fixed-rate dollar obligation.

Since the company has agreed to pay, on each payment date, a given amount of U.S. dollars and to reçeive a fixed amount of Swiss francs, a second glance at Figure 1 should convince the reader that this currency swap can also be viewed as a series of forward foreign exchange contracts. The only difference between a currency swap and a portfolio of foreign exchange contracts is that the agreed exchange rate in a currency swap is the current spot rate, rather than the forward rate used in a forward foreign exchange contract. This exchange-of-cash-flows approach to swaps allows a swap to be decomposed into a series of forward contracts, and thus can simplify the evaluation and pricing of unusual swaps.

Using the current spot rate as the contract rate, then, implies that, for currencies that have different zero coupon interest rate curves, the company receiving the low-coupon currency (in this example, Swiss francs) will tend to make a series of net payments in the earlier years and receive a relatively large net payment at

FIGURE 2

Present Value of Expected Net Payment Flows for a $100 Currency Swap in Which the Company Receives Swiss Francs and Pays U.S. Dollars

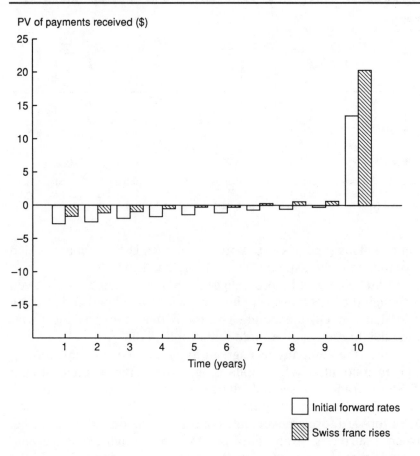

maturity. This pattern of expected net payments is set out in Figure 2. As can be seen in this figure, the present value in dollars of the company's net outflows decreases and of its net inflows increases when the Swiss franc strengthens, just as one would expect for a series of regular forward foreign exchange contracts.

A simple variant of the above swap is the currency coupon swap, which can be used by the U.S. company to convert the Swiss franc obligation to a floating-rate (LIBOR-based) dollar obligation.

FIGURE 3
Cash Flows to a Company Receiving Fixed Swiss Francs and Paying
Floating Dollars in a Currency Coupon Swap

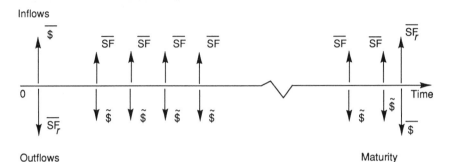

The short arrows represent the payment of interest at the floating dollar LIBOR rate ($\tilde{\$}$) and the receipt of interest at the fixed Swiss franc rate ($\overline{SF}$). The long arrows denote the initial exchange of principal (which need not occur) and its reexchange at maturity.

Again, this swap can be viewed either as a combination of a Swiss franc bond and a U.S. dollar floating-rate note or as a portfolio of forward FX (foreign exchange) contracts where the dollar payments are not fixed in advance but set by the LIBOR rate as it evolves through time.

2.2   Interest Swaps

Interest rate swaps were introduced after currency swaps, but now account for the majority of swaps completed worldwide. They are especially popular in the domestic United States market, where they have been used both by industrial corporations and by savings and loan institutions to create a more even balance between fixed- and floating-rate liabilities. Analytically, an interest rate swap can be viewed as a simplified currency coupon swap (in that both sides of the swap are denominated in the same currency). As illustrated in Figure 4, the primary difference is that the initial and final exchanges of principal are absent because they are of the same amount in the same currency.

A simple variant of the above is the basis rate swap, in which the cash flows are denominated in the same currency, but both interest rates are floating. A typical basis rate swap permits a company to change its basis for calculating cash flows from one stan-

FIGURE 4

Cash Flows to a Company Receiving Fixed Dollars and Paying Floating Dollars in an Interest Rate Swap

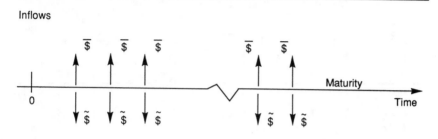

Inflows

Outflows

The arrows represent the receipt of interest at a fixed dollar rate ($\overline{\$}$) and the payment of interest at a LIBOR-based rate ($\tilde{\$}$).

dard (ex. the one-month commercial paper rate) to another (ex. the three-month LIBOR rate), and again allows the company to obtain a more preferred pattern of future cash flows.

3. HEDGING AN INTEREST RATE SWAP

Initially, swaps were arranged transactions. Having ascertained the requirements of one counterparty, the intermediary would attempt to find a counterparty that was willing to match both the nature and the timing of the proposed transactions's cash flows. Since there are several diverse elements involved in detailing an exactly offsetting transaction, as was mentioned in Section 2, the intermediary might have to conduct a considerable search before an appropriate match was found. Further, the proposed terms of the swap might have to be modified before a swap agreement acceptable to both counterparties was concluded.

Because interest rate swaps are denominated in only one currency, there are fewer potential mismatches than is the case for currency swaps. Furthermore, swap intermediaries soon discovered that there was a far larger number of companies—banks, savings and loans, industrial corporations, real estate corporations, etc.—interested in U.S. dollar–denominated interest rate swaps than in currency swaps.

The combination of a simple product, the large number of companies that could benefit from interest rate swaps, and the increased customer awareness of these available benefits, led to a veritable explosion of the dollar-denominated interest rate swap market in the 1980s.

This increased flow of transactions soon convinced intermediaries that, even if a matching counterparty could not be immediately found, a swap between the intermediary and one counterparty need only be held in inventory—warehoused—for a relatively short time before an offsetting swap could be arranged which matched the initial swap.[1] Increasing competition soon forced intermediaries to write swaps contracts as counterparties, taking both credit risk (which stays with them until the termination of that contract) and market risk (movements in the swaps yield curve over time). This market risk can then either be matched against offsetting positions internally (e.g., one commercial bank books its swaps into its funding book) or hedged with government securities or financial futures until a matching swap removes the first swap from the warehouse. Hedging of this market risk is the subject of the following sections.

3.1   The Hedged Instrument

In Section 2, we saw that a currency swap can be viewed either as a combination of two bonds or as a portfolio of forward foreign exchange agreements, and that an interest rate swap can be analyzed as a simplified currency coupon swap. This implies that we can hedge interest rate swaps using either of two equally valid approaches: the bond/floating-rate note (FRN) approach, which will be described in this section, or the portfolio of forward rate

---

[1] *Matched* in this context means that if the intermediary is paying the fixed rate in one swap and receiving the fixed rate in a second swap whose maturity and payment dates are relatively close to those of the first swap (e.g., within 5 or 10 business days), these two swaps are considered matched up to the smaller of the two nominal principal amounts involved and are removed from the warehouse. The remaining portion of the swap on the higher nominal principal amount is retained in the warehouse until another match is obtained.

FIGURE 5

Decomposition of an Interest Rate Swap into Offsetting Fixed-Rate and Floating-Rate Loans for a Company Receiving Floating Dollars and Paying Fixed Dollars

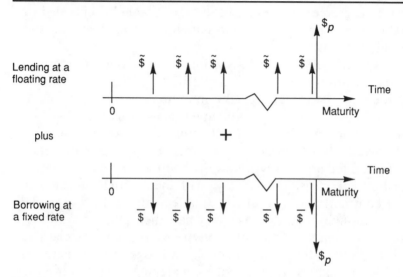

The short arrows represent the payment and receipt of interest, and the long arrows represent the payment of principal at maturity.

agreements (FRAs) approach, which is described in the following chapter.[2]

In Section 2.2, an interest rate swap was analyzed as a simplified currency coupon swap wherein the principals were not exchanged at the maturity of the swap because they were the same amount and denominated in the same currency. It is helpful, however, if we do not net out these equal and offsetting principal payments due at maturity. Then, as illustrated in Figure 5, we can decompose an interest rate swap into offsetting fixed-rate and floating-rate loans of equal maturity. Thus, the present value (PV) of the swap to the receiver of the fixed-rate interest can be expressed as

$$PV \text{ (swap)} = PV \text{ (bond)} - PV \text{ (floating-rate note)}$$

---

[2] Both Citicorp, London, and Chemical Bank, New York, were using the bond/FRN approach in 1985. I switched to the FRA approach when I started the interest rate caps desk at Chemical in May 1986 because it fitted more naturally with the Chicago futures contracts I was using as hedges.

and the swap's value to the payer of the fixed-rate interest as

$$PV \text{ (swap)} = PV \text{ (floating-rate note)} - PV \text{ (bond)}.$$

At origination, the value of a swap is approximately zero, but this is not necessarily true over the life of the swap. The interest rate set on the fixed-rate side of the swap can, in the above context, be viewed as the coupon on a corporate bond of equivalent maturity. By contrast, the interest rate set on the floating-rate side of the swap can be viewed as the short-term interest rate (set at x basis points above or below LIBOR) on a floating-rate note. If the term structure of interest rates is upward sloping, we would expect the difference between the coupon of the fixed-rate bond and the interest rate set on the floating-rate note to be initially positive. This difference would decrease over time and become sufficiently negative so that the present value at the initiation of the swap of all these different payments would net to zero.[3]

In the short-run, the market risk of a swap transaction predominates, and the main concern is how to hedge against moves in the swaps yield curve whilst the swap is in the warehouse. But since an interest rate swap can be viewed as offsetting fixed-rate and floating-rate loans, the problem of hedging against changes in value of the swap can be decomposed into two simple problems— hedging the fixed side of the swap and hedging the floating side of the swap.

3.2   Hedging the Fixed Side of the Swap

Assume that the intermediary has entered into a swap transaction as a payer of the fixed rate. Then, following Figure 4, the intermediary has incurred a fixed-rate annuity as an obligation. The first step, following Figure 5, is to add a zero coupon bond obligation at the maturity of the swap and thus create a normal coupon Eurodollar bond obligation to be hedged.

---

[3] This implies that the credit exposure of the two counterparties to the swap will not be equal. In this example, counterparty default will cause lower losses to the floating-rate payer than to the fixed-rate payer. Thus, in an upward-sloping term structure environment, a lower-rated counterparty will create greater credit exposure problems if it is the receiver of the fixed rate in an interest rate swap.

The hedging of this synthetic Eurobond can be done using Treasury futures contracts, but maturity mismatches and the additional risk created by cash/futures basis volatility have led most dollar warehouse managers to use the Treasury bond market to hedge the fixed side of their swaps.[4]

In the above example, the intermediary would hedge the synthetic Eurobond by either investing in or contracting to repurchase the appropriate amount of a similar-maturity Treasury bond. Two practical questions are then raised:

1. How similar in maturity should the Treasury bond be?
2. What is the appropriate amount to be invested in this bond?

The first question is best answered by comparing two alternative hedging instruments—an *off-the-run* (thinly traded) Treasury issue whose maturity matches that of the swap, and an *on-the-run* (very liquid) Treasury issue whose maturity differs from that of the swap by several months. The added liquidity and the fact that the on-the-run issue is used as a pricing reference rate consistently outweigh the marginal disadvantage of not matching the cash flows more exactly, and it is rare for off-the-run issues to be used.[5]

Given that the choice of an on-the-run issue as the hedging vehicle normally precludes the dedicated cash flow hedging approach, the question of how much to invest in the hedging vehicle is usually answered by using the *immunized* (duration-matched) hedging approach.

To illustrate, let the price of a T period maturity Treasury bond be given by

$$P_g = \sum_{t=1}^{T} \frac{C_t}{(1 + r_T)^t}$$

and its duration be given by

---

[4] 1989: I want to differentiate between information in the original paper (1986) and information made available between 1986 & 1989: Hence "1989:" The combination of increased liquidity in the 5- and 10-year bond futures contracts and increased emphasis on the capital adequacy implications of cash bond positions has led to an increased use of the futures contracts.

[5] The use of an off-the-run issue is normally associated with a warehouse manager's view on the expected relative short-run performance of that issue compared with the nearby on-the-run issue.

$$D_g = \left\{ \sum_{t=1}^{T} \frac{tC_t}{(1 + r_T)^t} \right\} \Big/ P_g$$

where C_t = the coupon in periods 1, 2, . . . $T - 1$ and the coupon plus principal in period T and

r_T = the government par yield for period T.

Then the price sensitivity of the bond with respect to changes in the term structure at period T is given by the following:

$$\frac{\Delta P_g}{\Delta r_T} = - \sum_{t=1}^{T} \frac{tC_t}{(1 + r_T)^{t+1}}$$

$$= \frac{-D_g P_g}{(1 + r_T)}$$

where $D_g/(1 + r_T)$ is known as the *modified duration* of the bond.

Applying the same reasoning to the modified fixed-rate side of a swap, with maturity τ, we have

$$P_s = \sum_{t=1}^{\tau} \frac{C_t}{(1 + r_\tau + s_\tau)^t}$$

and

$$D_s = \sum_{t=1}^{\tau} \left\{ \frac{tC_t}{(1 + r_\tau + s_\tau)^t} \right\} \Big/ P_s$$

where s_τ = the swap spread over the government par yield at maturity τ.[6]

If we then assume that the swaps spread over Treasury, s_τ, is independent of the level of the term structure, r_τ, we can write the price sensitivity of the fixed-rate side of an interest rate swap as follows:

$$\frac{\Delta P_s}{\Delta r_\tau} = \frac{-D_s P_s}{(1 + r_\tau + s_\tau)}$$

---

[6] Since the swap market quotes both bid and asked prices for a swap, there is some question as to how this spread should be measured. One approach is to use the rate midpoint between the bid and the asked yields. The alternative approach is to use the yield which the market would charge the warehouse to close out the position—in this example, since the intermediary is paying the fixed rate on the original swap, the bid rate at which the market would pay the fixed rate in a matching swap is used. The difference in the resulting price sensitivity calculation is quite small.

Then, for a given notional amount of the swap, N_s, we can find the notional amount of the hedge instrument, N_g, to be used to equate the sensitivity to changes in the term structure of the total values of the fixed side of the swap and the Treasury hedge instrument:

$$\frac{\Delta P_g}{\Delta r_T} N_g = \frac{\Delta P_s}{\Delta r_\tau} N_s$$

Solving for N_g gives the following:

$$N_g = \frac{N_s D_s P_s}{D_g P_g} \times \frac{(1 + r_T)}{(1 + r_\tau + s_\tau)}$$

When the maturity mismatch is quite large, as in the case of an 8- or 9-year interest rate swap, the warehouse manager may decide to bracket the swap by using two hedge instruments; in this case, the 7- and 10-year on-the-run issues. For this example, a simple solution to the hedging problem is given by solving the two simultaneous equations which equate modified duration and present value for N_7 and N_{10}, the amounts to be invested in the two hedging government bonds.[7]

$$\frac{D_s P_s}{(1 + r_\tau + s_\tau)} \times N_s = \frac{D_7 P_7}{(1 + r_7)} \times N_7 + \frac{D_{10} P_{10}}{(1 + r_{10})} \times N_{10}$$

$$N_s P_s = N_7 P_7 + N_{10} P_{10}$$

In solving for the amount of the hedge instrument required, we made two simplifying assumptions which can cause some errors in hedge performance. The first assumption is that movements in the government term structure are restricted to parallel shifts in the maturities of the swap and the hedge instrument. Specifically, the hedge instrument's sensitivity is measured with respect to changes in the yield curve at maturity T, r_T, and the swap's sensitivity is measured with respect to changes in the term structure at maturity τ, r_τ. The hedge will therefore only be correct if

$$\Delta r_T = \Delta r_\tau.$$

---

[7] 1989: A more efficient hedge is given by using equations that equate the first derivatives (modified duration) and the second derivatives (convexity). The present value equation was used rather than the second derivative equation at Citicorp, London, in 1984–1985 for managerial accounting reasons.

To the extent that changes in the interest rates at the two maturities are not equal, there will be residual price volatility.[8] In practice, the discrepancy in maturities is usually sufficiently small for this problem to be minor, but can be significant in the longer maturities where the maturity gaps between the hedging instruments (5-, 7-, and 10-year Treasury bonds) become quite large.

The second assumption leading to residual risk is that changes in the price of the swap are only caused by changes in the government term structure at time τ, r_τ. More completely, the change in price of this synthetic Eurobond is given by

$$dP_s = \frac{\Delta P_s}{\Delta r_\tau} \times dr_\tau + \frac{\Delta P_s}{\Delta s_\tau} \times ds_\tau + \frac{\Delta P_s}{\Delta s_\tau} \times \frac{\Delta s_\tau}{\Delta r_\tau} \times dr_\tau$$

where we assume that the swap spread at maturity τ, s_τ is affected by the government yield at that maturity, r_τ.[9]

The Treasury bond hedges against movements in the yield curve at maturity τ, dr_τ, but does not hedge against movements in the swaps spread at maturity τ, ds_τ.[10] If a warehouse's inventory is approximately equally split between swaps in which the intermediary is paying the fixed rate and swaps in which the intermediary is receiving the fixed rate, the warehouse will be reasonably well self-hedged against movements in the swap spread.[11] If the warehouse becomes imbalanced, it is then exposed to changes in the swaps spread. For example, in the spring of 1986, the swap spread at most maturities widened quite drastically, and this caused problems for

---

[8] This problem of differing price sensitivities is actually more subtle in that, even if the maturity of the hedge matches that of the swap exactly, there will still be residual risk if the cash payments on the hedge do not exactly match the cash payments on the swap. In this case, the hedge is generally correct only for parallel shifts in the entire yield curve. This problem is related to the phenomenon that two U.S. Treasury bonds, maturing on exactly the same day, may have considerably different yields to maturity without being mispriced. This point is covered in Section 4.2 in discussing the zero yield curve concept.

[9] 1989: Empirically, the swap spread appears to be positively correlated to the level of treasury yields at 2 years, approximately independent at 3 and 4 years, slightly negatively correlated at 5 years, more negatively correlated at 7 years, and even more negatively correlated at 10 years.

[10] This problem is analogous to using Treasury instruments to hedge positions in Eurobonds.

[11] To the extent that the correlation of the swap spreads at different maturities is not perfect, an evenly balanced swaps portfolio will still have residual swaps spread risk.

several warehouses that had booked a one-sided flow of new deals in this period.[12]

Initial research by Cornell finds a positive correlation between the swaps spread and the spread between the three-month T-bill and LIBOR rates.[13] This suggests that the swap spread could be potentially hedged using the TED spread in the T-bill and Eurodollar futures markets, but to date few warehouse managers have considered the correlation sufficiently high to warrant the costs involved in setting up TED hedges. The general response of warehouse managers to this problem has been to modify their price quotes so as to discourage new swaps that exacerbate an imbalance problem and to encourage new swaps that mitigate the problem.

3.3 Hedging the Floating Side of a Swap

In order to hedge the fixed-rate side, we added offsetting cash flows equal to the nominal principal amount of the swap. As can be seen in Figure 5, this converts the floating-rate annuity side of the swap into a floating-rate note (FRN). Before the interest rate on a floating-rate note for the next payment period (usually six months) is set—at LIBOR $\pm$ x basis points—the value of a floating-rate note remains approximately constant (assuming no changes in the risk of the instrument that render x an inappropriate risk premium). This occurs because changes in the value of the zero coupon bond component almost completely offset changes in the value of the floating rate annuity.[14] Therefore, for hedging purposes, an FRN at issue has the same response to changes in the term structure of interest rates as a cash receipt on that date.

But once an FRN is issued, the amount to be paid as interest on the first payment date (normally in six months' time) is known with certainty, and the interest rate will only be reset on that payment date, when the FRN will be "reissued." Thus, after issue and

---

[12] There was an even more pronounced upward shift in the latter half of October 1989.

[13] B. Cornell, "Pricing Interest Rate Swaps: Theory and Empirical Evidence," working paper presented at the New York University Conference on Swaps and Hedges, March 14, 1986.

[14] The same result obtains throughout the life of the FRN if the interest rate is reset continuously.

between payment dates, an FRN has the same response to changes in the yield curve as a cash flow—equivalent in amount to the principal plus the agreed interest—on the next payment date.

Mathematically, if we value the remaining flows on an FRN with principal P one period before maturity, just before the last LIBOR fixing (and ignoring the payment being made on the previous fixing), we know that the cash flow at maturity will be

$$P \times (1 + \tilde{L}_{T-1,T} \times (\text{actual days}_{T-1,T}/360))$$

and the value at this time of this cash flow will be

$$\frac{P \times (1 + \tilde{L}_{T-1,T} \times (\text{actual days}_{T-1,T}/360))}{1 + \tilde{L}_{T-1,T} \times (\text{actual days}_{T-1,T}/360)}.$$

Thus, for valuation purposes, we can replace the payment of the principal and interest at time T with the payment of the principal at time $T - 1$. Then, if we value this revised principal payment, plus the interest payment due to be made at $T - 1$, just before the LIBOR fixing at time $T - 2$, the present value of this cash flow at time $T - 2$ will be as follows:

$$\frac{P \times [1 + \tilde{L}_{T-2,T-1} \times (\text{actual days}_{T-2,T-1}/360)}{1 + \tilde{L}_{T-2,T-1} \times (\text{actual days}_{T-2,T-1}/360)}$$

Continuing recursively, we arrive at the time t

$$\frac{P \times [1 + \bar{L}_{0,1} \times (\text{actual days}_{0,1}/360)]}{1 + \tilde{L}_{t,1} \times (\text{actual days}_{t,1}/360)}$$

where $\bar{L}_{0,1}$ is the LIBOR rate set at the first fixing and t ranges from 0 to 1.

Thus, at a maximum, an FRN's price sensitivity is equivalent to a newly issued six-month note, and at a minimum, to a note maturing on that day.

We can then conclude that a warehouse with a series of interest rate swaps in inventory will, on the floating side, exhibit the same price sensitivity as a portfolio containing both long and short positions in three- and six-month notes maturing at differing times in the next six months.

Two general approaches are usually taken to hedging this position. The first is to consider such a portfolio to be essentially *self-hedging* in the sense that the sensitivity of each swap FRN is relatively low (because of the maximum six-month maturity) and

that normally there is a reasonable balance in the warehouse between swaps in which the intermediary is receiving the floating rate
and swaps in which the intermediary is paying the floating rate.[15]
The alternative approach is to explicitly recognize the floating-rate
side of the warehouse inventory as a portfolio of short-maturity
investments and include it in the intermediary's position.

3.4 Summary

In the preceding sections we have shown how the fixed- and floating-rate annuities that constitute an interest rate swap can be re-
constituted, for hedging purposes, as a synthetic Eurodollar
coupon bond and a synthetic Eurodollar floating-rate note, respectively. The synthetic Eurobond is then hedged with a Treasury
Bond of appropriate maturity, whilst the FRN is either hedged with
Eurodollar futures contracts or left unhedged. This last action, in
conjunction with the hedging of the synthetic Eurobond with a
Treasury bond, has led to a misperception of swaps hedging that is
quite widespread. Specifically, the statement is made that we only
hedge the fixed side of the swap, and let the floating side take care
of itself. In reality, as can be seen by comparing the cash flows in
Figure 4 with those in Figure 5, the *coupons* on the Treasury bond
hedge the *fixed rate annuity,* which is one side of an interest rate
swap. The *zero-coupon bond,* which constitutes the Treasury
bond's principal at maturity, hedges the *floating rate annuity,*
which is the other side of the swap, by converting the annuity into
a floating-rate note, which is far less volatile.[16]

---

[15] Given the recent history of high volatility at the short end of the yield curve, the
increasing size of warehouse inventories could cause problems if a warehouse becomes one-
sided. In these circumstances, recourse is usually made to the Eurodollar futures market to
hedge the risk. 1989: In fact, several warehouses have suffered considerable losses on the
floating side of their books in the last few years when they failed to properly hedge a one-
sided book.

[16] Consideration of the fixed-rate flows in Figure 5 would show that a bond of maturity T is
hardly a good hedge for a T-period annuity paying an amount almost equal to the coupon on
the bond. Further, consideration of how volatile the value of a floating-rate annuity can be
should convince the reader of the inadvisability of leaving such instruments unhedged.

4. THE PORTFOLIO APPROACH
TO HEDGING SWAPS

The individual swap hedging approach discussed in Section 3 implies that, for every swap inventoried in an intermediary's warehouse, a separate hedging transaction must be undertaken. Further, since the hedge ratio is generally set using the modified duration immunization approach detailed in the previous section, each hedge must be rebalanced over time since both changes in the yield curve and the passage of time affect duration-derived hedge ratios. Thus, warehoused swaps require that the warehouse manager incur the transaction costs involved in installing, rebalancing, and removing separate hedges. To the extent that two or more swaps in the warehouse have similar maturities, the transaction costs involved in hedging the swaps can be lowered if the swaps are treated as a group. If the maturities of two offsetting swaps, although insufficiently close to qualify as matching, are similar (e.g., five years versus five and one quarter years), hedging the net exposure would involve far smaller transaction costs. Further, to the extent that these transaction costs have a fixed-cost component, hedging the net exposure of two similar maturity swaps that are not offsetting will also reduce transaction costs for the warehouse managers. So one incentive to hedge the warehoused swaps as a portfolio, rather than as individual transactions, is to save on the transaction costs involved in initiating and rebalancing holdings of the hedge instruments.[17]

If the warehoused swaps are treated not only as a single portfolio but also as a portfolio of cash flows, another advantage becomes apparent—the lack of the requirement that swaps be matched and removed from the book. In the warehouse approach, most accounting systems do not recognize the profit for accounting purposes of an inventoried swap until it is matched with an offsetting swap and removed from the book. Thus incentives are created:

---

[17] Under the portfolio approach, the addition of a new swap to the warehouse may lead to only one transaction—the removal of an existing hedge position.

1. To provide potential counterparties to warehoused swaps with more favorable prices for an offsetting swap that matches the maturity of one of the inventoried swaps.
2. To shun deals having low probability of being matched and removed from the warehouse. Known in the vernacular as *nonvanilla* deals, these are swaps in which the pattern of cash flows does not fit the standard pattern of equally sized and equally timed cash flows.

The application of the portfolio management concept to swaps implies that swaps may stay in the portfolio throughout their lives—and this requires that the accounting system used recognizes the profit potential of one swap from its initiation. The emphasis on cash flow also removes the stigma from swaps with unusual patterns of cash flows—either in timing and/or in amount—and opens the way to book amortizing swaps, project-finance swaps, zero swaps, and "crazy" swaps (swaps where the timing and amounts swapped are tailored to the particular, unusual requirements of the counterparty).

Operating a swaps portfolio management hedging system requires the portfolio manager to

1. Establish which cash flows are to be hedged.
2. Determine which interest rates will be used to discount these cash flows.
3. Calculate the volatility of these interest rates.

At the conclusion of this process, the manager can determine the volatility of the swaps portfolio and then establish what the impact of adding various hedge instruments would be on the resulting portfolio's volatility. At this point, the manager can then decide the degree of residual risk to which the portfolio of swaps should be hedged, and evaluate the impact on the portfolio of a potential new swap. The modules needed to undertake this process are presented in the next four sections.

4.1 The Cash Flow Module

Following Figure 4, the actual dates and amounts of the cash flows involved in the swap are first established. For operational purposes, this provides the basic information required to answer the question, Who pays whom how much on what day? For hedging purposes, the next step is to add the notional principal amount to both sides of the swap, creating the synthetic FRN and the synthetic Eurobond discussed in Figure 5 of Section 3. For nonvanilla swaps, this may take some care, working backwards from the maturity of the swap to create the relevant set of FRNs. The general approach used is to create a series of vanilla swaps, of different maturities, whose combined fixed cash flows duplicate the fixed cash flows of the nonvanilla swap. Then for each of these vanilla swaps, the notional principal is added, and the resulting synthetics are added to the portfolio.[18]

At this point, it is usual to pass the two sides of the swap into the relevant portfolios. In the case of interest rate swaps, the synthetic Eurobond would be added to the fixed dollar portfolio and the synthetic FRN to the floating dollar portfolio. Similarly, a fixed currency swap would be broken down, for hedging purposes, into two synthetic Eurobonds and added to the appropriate currency portfolios.[19]

At this point, we will concentrate on hedging the fixed dollar portfolio, but the general techniques apply to other currency portfolios. (And it should be remembered from Section 3 that in hedging the synthetic Eurobond, we are actually hedging most of the risk of the floating-rate side of the swap as well.)

4.2 The Discount Rate Module

Contrary to widespread opinion, the yield to maturity for a Eurobond of given maturity is generally not the appropriate discount rate for a zero coupon bond of equal risk and maturity. In fact, it is quite simple to show, for U.S. government securities, that pricing government zeros (known as *strips*) using the par yield curve would lead to arbitrage profits unless the par yield curve is horizon-

---

[18] One early "wedding cake" swap required a total of 17 vanilla swaps to mimic its performance. The valuation problems caused by marking these swaps to market using the par yield curve strengthened my belief in the zero curve, and the accounting problems caused by trying to keep track of all these artificial swaps led me to the floating-rate agreement approach described in Chapter 16.

[19] Citicorp, a leading proponent of this system, runs books in U.S. dollars, Canadian dollars, sterling, deutsche marks, French francs, Swiss francs, ECUs, and yen.

tal.[20] The reason for this, as shown by Schaefer, is that the par yield at a given maturity, y_t, is a weighted average of the zero yields at each of the coupon payment dates, $z_1, z_2, \ldots, z_t$.[21] Specifically y_t is given by the following equation:

$$\sum_{t=1}^{T} \frac{C_t}{(1 + z_t)^t} + \frac{100}{(1 + z_T)^T} = P = \sum_{t=1}^{T} \frac{C_t}{(1 + y_T)^t} + \frac{100}{(1 + y_T)^T}$$

Thus, if the zero yield curve slopes upwards, the par yield at a given maturity will lie below the zero yield at that maturity, and vice-versa if the zone curve slopes downwards.[22]

Given that the appropriate cash flows for a swap were identified in the previous section, and are equivalent to zero coupon Eurobonds, the next step is to convert the available yield curves—the par Treasury curve and the par swaps curve (quoted as a spread over the par Treasury curve)—to the zero yield curve required to obtain the current value of these future cash flows.

The usual approach is to reverse the causality so that given a series $y_1, y_2, \ldots, y_t$, we can obtain the relevant series $z_1, z_2, \ldots, z_t$. One simple method of doing this is to "bootstrap" your way up the curve. To do this, we first start with the one-period par yield, y_1 (the logic of this argument applies equally well to both the Treasury and swaps par curves), and note that for a one-period bond, the equation can be written as follows:

$$\frac{C_1 + 100}{1 + z_1} = P_1 = \frac{C_1 + 100}{1 + y_1}$$

Therefore, for the first period, $z_1 = y_1$. We can now progress to the two-period bond. For this, the equation becomes

$$\frac{C_2}{1 + z_1} + \frac{C_2 + 100}{(1 + z_2)^2} = P_2 = \frac{C_2}{1 + y_2} + \frac{C_2 + 100}{(1 + y_2)^2}.$$

---

[20] The ability to exploit such arbitrage profits is currently somewhat limited by the difficulties encountered when attempting to short sell strips or the equivalent "CATS" and "TIGERS."

[21] S. M. Schaefer, "The Problem with Redemption Yields," *Financial Analysts Journal* 33 (July/August 1977).

[22] The analogy to the interrelationship between the marginal cost curve (the zero curve) and the average cost curve (the par curve) in basic microeconomics is quite close, and the conditions under which the zero and par curves will intersect are similar to those governing the crossing of the marginal and average cost curves.

Since we know C_2, y_2, and z_1, we can solve for z_2. We then repeat this process for longer maturities, bootstrapping our way along the curve.

A problem arises, however, when there is a gap in the par yield curve figures provided. In order to match the pattern of coupon payments (semiannual in the United States), there should be par yields available every six months. This problem is reasonably manageable at shorter maturities, where there are only 12 months between maturities quoted, but becomes quite difficult at longer maturities, where the gap grows to three or more years between quotes. One alternative is to first extrapolate the zero curve outward to the next quoted maturity from its last observation using smoothed curves for the discount factor (i.e., the present value of a dollar received at maturity t) and the forward rate (the implied six-month rate at maturity t). A value for the par bond of that maturity is then calculated using these estimates and compared with the actual price. A reiterative process then begins that adjusts the estimated discount factors whilst maintaining the smoothness of both the discount factor and forward rate curves until the difference between the model's price and the actual bond price is reduced to an acceptably small level.[23] Since the zero curve estimates made for the middle maturities will also affect the estimation of the zero coupon curve at longer maturities, the process of adjusting only the nearby estimates can lead to errors, but in practice these tend to be small.[24] Another alternative is to broaden the set of bonds used to calculate the zero curve. This approach can be used to complement the extrapolation method, but must be used with some caution since the pricing of off-the-run issues can include nontrading errors and illiquidity discounts.

More sophisticated approaches ranging from the spline regression methods of Vasicek and Fong to the linear programming for-

---

[23] 1989: It continues to surprise me how often the smoothed zero curves produced by some available software programs do not produce smooth forward curves, but rather excellent imitations of a roller coaster track.

[24] It is rare, at the conclusion of this exercise, for the model's price of a U.S. Treasury bond to differ from the actual price by more than $.30 per $100. This compares very favourably indeed with using the yield to maturity of one Treasury bond to calculate the price of another Treasury bond with equal maturity.

mulation of Schaefer are available, but are beyond the scope of this chapter.[25]

4.3   The Valuation Module

In Section 4.1, a swap was analyzed as a series of future cash flows, the present value of which can be determined by discounting those cash flows at the appropriate zero coupon yield determined in Section 4.2.

Generally, for a straightforward interest rate swap, the swap's par curve can be used to price a potential swap because this par curve is generally correct for valuing the pattern of cash flows that constitute the fixed side of an at-market vanilla swap.[26] But the par curve approach breaks down when the pattern of cash flows from the swap become more complex. Thus, to value an amortizing swap using the par curve approach, the swap must be decomposed into a series of vanilla swaps. When the swap becomes slightly more complex, with either nonregular flows or a mismatch in cash flows (as for example in a zero swap), the par curve approach becomes almost impossible to use, and intermediaries must either refrain from participating in such swaps or—far more profitably— turn to the cash flow/zero coupon discount rate approach, which allows an intermediary to price any arbitrary set of cash flows involved in a tailor-made swap (such as a project-finance–related swap).

One presentational problem arises when an intermediary uses this approach. Conceptually, the warehouse may have projected cash inflows or outflows on each of the next 2,500 or more business days (swaps with maturities beyond 10 years, although rare, do exist and can be expected to become more popular as the Euro-markets accept extensions in the maturity of new issues). In order to simplify the valuation and hedging of this swaps portfolio, the

---

[25] O. A. Vasicek and H. G. Fong, "Term Structure Modelling Using Exponential Splines," *Journal of Finance* 37 (1982), pp. 339–48; S. M. Schaefer, "Tax-Induced Clientele Effects in the Market for British Government Securities: Placing Bounds on Security Values in an Incomplete Market," *Journal of Financial Economics* 10 (1982), pp. 121–59.

[26] The par curve approach, by its very definition, misvalues any off-market swap if the curve is not horizontal out to that maturity.

cash flows can be adjusted to a common grid of maturities spanning the maturities of the swaps.[27] Thus, for example, grid dates could be chosen as three-month periods starting from today and ending at the period immediately following the maturity of the longest swap in the book. An alternative approach would be to use shorter periods (daily, then weekly, then monthly) between grid dates in the near future, and longer periods (six months, annually, etc.) between grid dates in the more distant future. In either method, cash flows that are widely dispersed at a multitude of points in time can be concentrated for analysis at a few points in time.

A simple way of accomplishing this allocation is to ensure that the method chosen maintains both the cash flows and the net present values involved. Thus, for any cash flow at time t, C_t, there will be two cash flows, at the grid point immediately preceding time t, $C-$, and at the grid point immediately following time t, $C+$, whose values are obtained from the following set of simultaneous equations:

$$C_t = C- + C+$$

and

$$\frac{C_t}{(1 + z_t)^t} = \frac{C-}{(1 + z_t^-)^{t-}} + \frac{C+}{(1 + z_t^+)^{t+}}$$

The resulting grid of amalgamated cash flows is simpler to present and to analyze and mimics the value of the portfolio of cash flows.[28]

4.4 The Hedging Module

Given the wide range of cash flow dates involved in a swaps portfolio and the limited range of maturities available in on-the-run Treasury issues, the portfolio manager is immediately forced to

---

[27] This approach is used to analyze prices in the U.K. government bond (*gilts*) markets by S. D. Hodges and S. M. Schaefer, "A Model for Bond Portfolio Improvement," *Journal of Financial and Quantitative Analysis* 12 (1977), pp. 243–60.

[28] 1989: For managerial accounting reasons, cash value and present value equations were used in the original formulation. Obviously, a better hedge would be created by using first and second derivative equations.

turn from the concept of dedicated cash flow hedging to the looser concept of immunized cash flow hedging of the fixed-rate side of the swaps portfolio.

Given the cash flows and the zero coupon yield curve, it is remarkably simple to calculate the modified duration of the swaps portfolio and to then create a hedge portfolio with an approximately equal and offsetting price sensitivity.

But at this point, the assumption made in Section 3.2 which allowed us to use an instrument of one maturity to hedge a synthetic Eurobond of another maturity, becomes important. For a single-instrument hedge of a synthetic Eurobond with a Treasury bond, the mismatch of cash flows is quite small, and the assumption of parallel shifts in the yield curve is therefore relatively innocuous. But once we are attempting to hedge a portfolio of arbitrary cash flows, the probability of severe mismatches of cash flows between the swaps portfolio and the hedging portfolio becomes quite large, and the residual risk caused by nonparallel changes in the yield cure quite significant. To illustrate this point with an admittedly extreme example, imagine that a long position in a portfolio of synthetic Eurobonds with maturities in the 5–7-year range was hedged with a short position in the 20-year T-bond futures contract. Then, if the yield curve arched, with the yield at 7 years rising and the yield at 20 years falling, the futures contract position would exacerbate the losses suffered by the portfolio rather than hedge them.

One way to handle arbitrary changes in the term structure is to consider the cash flows at the grid points in the fixed swaps portfolio as zero coupon securities, and assess their volatilities. For a single cash flow at time t, we know that its duration equals its maturity, and we can therefore, following Section 3, write the price sensitivity (return) of this synthetic zero as

$$\frac{\Delta P_t}{P_t} = \frac{-t}{(1 + r_t + s_t)} \times \Delta r_t$$

and its volatility as

$$\sigma^2 \left(\frac{\Delta P_t}{P_t} \right) = \frac{t^2}{(1 + r_t + s_t)^2} \sigma^2 (\Delta r_t). \tag{1}$$

We have, in this equation, expressed the volatility of the component of the fixed rate swap portfolio at maturity t in terms of the volatility of the Treasury zero rate at that maturity t. Therefore, following the approaches used to assess the volatility of an equity portfolio pioneered by Markowitz and Sharpe, we can calculate the volatility of the swaps portfolio. These approaches require us to calculate the correlations between the rates at different maturities on the Treasury zero curve. Before moving on to the details of this approach, it seems appropriate to note that the duration immunization model—with its assumption of parallel shifts in the yield curve—is a special case of this approach since it presumes that interest rates are perfectly positively correlated.

The calculation of portfolio volatility must be done quite often—at any time when the warehouse manager is considering the impact on the portfolio's risk of a new deal (and thus what price to quote) and at the regular period set by management for auditing purposes (usually daily). There is, therefore, a premium on simplicity, and it is this desire for simplicity that leads to the use of index models (a la Sharpe's single-index model for equity returns).

A simple index model for measuring portfolio risk is the two-factor model developed by Stephen Schaefer at the London Business School.[29] In this model, the change in zero coupon yield at any maturity t is give by

$$\Delta r_t = \alpha_t + \beta_t \Delta r_{10} + \gamma_t \Delta u_1 + \varepsilon_t \qquad (2)$$

where Δr_{10} = change in yield of a long maturity zero instrument (in our example, the 10-year zero).

Δu_1 = change in the yield spread between a short maturity zero (in our example, the one-year zero) and the long zero. The correlation of r_{10} and u_1 is either assumed to be zero or u_1 is constructed (by using the residual from a regression of the 1-year zero on the 10-year zero) so that the correlation is zero.

ε_t = unexplained residual—the maturity specific nonsystematic risk.

Then, substituting Equation 2 into Equation 1 gives us

$$\sigma^2 \left(\frac{\Delta P_t}{P_t} \right) = \frac{t^2}{(1 + r_t + s_t)^2} \times [\beta_t^2 \sigma^2 (\Delta r_{10}) + \gamma_t^2 \sigma^2 (\Delta u_1) + \sigma^2 (\varepsilon_t)]$$

---

[29] This model is similar in concept, although differing in details, from the model used by Citicorp Investment Bank.

where the covariance terms drop out since Δr_{10}, Δu_1, and ε_t are all uncorrelated by either assumption or construction. For another maturity, t^*, we have a similar equation, and we also know that the covariance between the change in values at the two maturities t and t^* is given by

$$\sigma \left(\frac{\Delta P_t}{P_t}, \frac{\Delta P_t^*}{P_t^*} \right) = \frac{t}{(1 + r_t + s_t)} \times \frac{t^*}{(1 + r_t^* + s_t^*)}$$

$$\times [\beta_t \beta_t \times \sigma^2(\Delta r_{10}) + \gamma_t \gamma_t \times \sigma^2(\Delta u_1) + \sigma(\varepsilon_t)\sigma(\varepsilon_{t^*})\rho(\varepsilon_t, \varepsilon_{t^*})]$$

where $\rho(\varepsilon_t, \varepsilon_{t^*})$ is the correlation coefficient between the maturity-specific risks.

Given a series of historically derived data on zero coupon yields, Equation 2 can be run for all relevant maturities, establishing the regression coefficients at different maturities; and after the covariance matrix of the ε_t's has been calculated, the covariance matrix of price volatilities can be established.

Then, since we have both this matrix and the present value of the synthetic cash flows at the various maturities, the portfolio's volatility can be calculated thus:[30]

$$\sigma^2(\text{Portfolio}) = \sum_{t=1}^{T} \sum_{t^*=1}^{T} P_t P_{t^*} \sigma \left(\frac{\Delta P_t}{P_t}, \frac{\Delta P_{t^*}}{P_{t^*}} \right)$$

Given that the volatility of a portfolio of swaps can be measured, the manager of a swaps warehouse is in a position to establish how the volatility would change if a new swap or hedge instrument were added and thus decide both how to price new swaps (the price would reflect the swap's impact on the portfolio's volatility) and to what degree the portfolio should be hedged.

4.5 Summary

In this section, we have shown how swaps, rather than being treated as individual transactions for valuation and hedging purposes, can be treated as components in a portfolio of swaps, lead-

---

[30] For completeness, changes in the swap's spread over the relevant Treasury, which also affect the value of the portfolio, should be modeled and included. This requires estimating the swap's spread variance–covariance matrix in a manner similar to that used for the ε_t's.

ing to more accurate valuation and hedging. Specifically, the future cash flows from a warehouse of swaps can be identified and managed as a portfolio of zero coupon bonds. This allows the warehouse manager to value any arbitrary cash flow swaps, to identify future cash flow mismatches in the swaps warehouse, to determine the risk of such mismatches, and to manage that risk to an acceptable level. This approach also allows the manager to determine the risk contribution (increasing or decreasing) of any new swap and quote a price that reflects this marginal risk.[31]

5. SWAPS AND PORTFOLIO MANAGEMENT

In Section 4, a portfolio of swaps was decomposed into the component cash flows, and then managed as a portfolio of synthetic zero coupon bonds, ranging in maturity from less than one month to more than 10 years. The appropriate zero coupon yield curve was used to value these synthetic bonds, and modern portfolio theory provided the model for assessing the risk (standard deviation) of this portfolio at any point in time.

Using this technique, the portfolio manager can simulate a range of hedges and assess the hedging costs and residual volatility of each. At one extreme, the synthetic zero coupon portfolio can be left unhedged, and at the other, the portfolio can be almost completely hedged using dedicated cash flow techniques. The manager can observe any cash flow mismatches and the resulting volatility of a duration-immunized portfolio and can then—if necessary—rehedge the portfolio to reduce the magnitude of those cash flow mismatches that most threaten duration immunization's assumption of parallel shifts in the yield curve.

The foregoing discussion has suggested that modern portfolio theory can be used to extend the range of hedging techniques available for managing bond portfolios and has illustrated this approach utilizing a portfolio of dollar interest rate swaps.[32] The other pur-

---

[31] This is entirely analogous to the portfolio risk/beta approach used by many equity portfolio managers.

[32] The same technique can be, and is, applied to swap portfolios in other currencies, although incompleteness in the relevant government bond markets causes valuation and hedging problems.

pose of this chapter is simple—to suggest that both interest rate and currency swaps are viable instruments and that both asset- and liability-based swaps are interesting weapons to add to the armory of the international portfolio manager. For example, they can be used to create bond-like exposure to a certain currency without requiring an attendant investment in either equities or bonds denominated in that currency. They are an efficient means of accomplishing major rebalancings of a portfolio between currencies and can be an important instrument in reducing a portfolio's exposure to regulations in countries of interest.

The swaps market is growing fast, and although it is still somewhat illiquid, there are significant opportunities for international portfolios—with cash flows denominated in a wide range of currencies—to participate in this market.[33]

BIBLIOGRAPHY

Cornell, B. "Pricing Interest Rate Swaps: Theory and Empirical Evidence." Working paper presented at the New York University Conference on Swaps and Hedges, March 14, 1986.

Frydl, E. J. "Some Regulatory Implications of Swaps." Working paper presented at the New York University Conference on Swaps and Hedges, March 14, 1986.

Hodges, S. D., and S. M. Schaefer. "A Model for Bond Portfolio Improvement." *Journal of Financial and Quantitative Analysis* 12, 1977, pp. 243–60.

Levich, R. "On the Microeconomics of Swaps and Hedges." Working paper presented at the New York University Conference on Swaps and Hedges, March 14, 1986.

McCulloch, J. H. "Measuring the Term Structure of Interest Rates." *Journal of Business* 44, 1971, pp. 19–31.

Schaefer, S. M. "The Problem with Redemption Yields." *Financial Analysts Journal* 33, July/August, 1977.

Schaefer, S. M. "Measuring a Tax Specific Term Structure of Interest Rates in the Market for British Government Securities." *Economics Journal* 91, 1981, pp. 415–38.

[33] 1989: There is evidence of increasing use of currency swaps by global portfolio managers, but I do not believe that the opportunities have yet been fully explored.

Schaefer, S. M. "Tax-Induced Clientele Effects in the Market for British Government Securities: Placing Bounds on Security Values in an Incomplete Market." *Journal of Financial Economics* 10, 1982, pp. 121–59.

Smith, C. W.; C. W. Smithson; and L. M. Wakeman. "The Evolving Market for Swaps." *Midland Corporate Finance Journal* 3, no. 4, 1986, pp. 20–32.

Vasicek, O. A., and H. G. Fong. "Term Structure Modelling Using Exponential Splines." *Journal of Finance* 37, 1982, pp. 339–48.

CHAPTER 16

INTEGRATING INTEREST RATE DERIVATIVE PRODUCTS

Lee M. Wakeman
Continental Bank
Chicago, Illinois

Reto M. Tuffli
UBS Securities, Inc.
New York, New York

INTRODUCTION

In the early 1980s, when swap arrangers first considered un-matched interest rate swaps, the question arose, How do we hedge an unmatched deal against interest rate risk until we find a suitable counterparty with whom to match this warehoused deal?[1] The initial approach, following the experience gained in the already developed currency swap market, was to model an interest rate swap in terms of two products that were already well understood—bonds and floating rate notes. As can be seen in Figure 1, adding the notional principal of the swap to both sides of the transaction at maturity converts the fixed side of a swap into a bond and the floating side of the swap into a floating-rate note whose first coupon

---

[1] An *unmatched* swap is one in which a financial intermediary has entered into a swap with a counterparty without having arranged an offsetting swap with another counterparty. For example, an intermediary that agreed to receive fixed for three years versus six-month LIBOR on $50,000,000 would then have an unmatched position until it could find a swap in which it paid fixed versus six-month LIBOR for approximately three years to offset the original swap.

FIGURE 1

Decomposition of an Interest Rate Swap into Offsetting Fixed-Rate and Floating-Rate Loans for a Company Receiving Floating Dollars and Paying Fixed Dollars

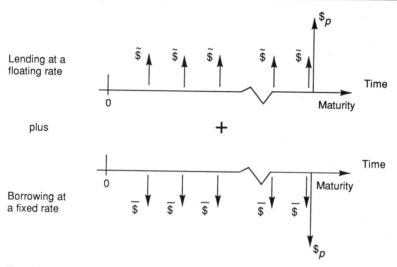

The short arrows represent the payment and receipt of interest and the long arrows represent the payment of principal at maturity.

has been set. The fixed side of the swap can then be hedged (albeit with residual basis risk) with government bonds and bond futures, using modified duration to determine the appropriate bond position,[2] and the floating side of the swap can be hedged with futures or floating rate agreements.

This bond/modified duration approach has met with sufficient success over the last few years to become widely accepted as a basis for both hedging swaps books and setting risk limits for swap groups. But the bond/duration approach has several problems. Theoretically, it assumes parallel shifts of the zero yield curve, which is inconsistent with both the historical evidence and the implied volatility curve in the LIBOR options market.[3] Practically,

---

[2] See Chapter 15, "The Portfolio Approach to Swaps Management," for further details.

[3] Most swap portfolio hedgers have by now switched from calculating par yield curve duration to calculating the more accurate zero yield curve duration; see Chapter 12 for further details.

considerable manipulation of the uneven cash flows involved in an accreting and/or amortizing swap is required to fit these swaps into the bond/duration framework; and conceptually, futures, FRAs, and options do not easily fit into this framework.

An alternative approach, more recently developed, is to consider each fixing of the swap as a separate hedging problem and to hedge each fixing with Chicago Eurodollar futures contracts. As trading volume in these contracts has increased and contracts have become available in the third (and then fourth) year, more and more short-term swaps are hedged using Eurodollar futures.

So the situation can arise where a bank has a long-term swaps desk that is hedging with government bonds, a short-term swaps desk hedging with Eurodollar futures, and an interest rate options desk hedging with Eurodollar futures and options.

If swaps and bonds can be placed in the same conceptual framework as futures and options, interest rate derivative products could be hedged in a single, integrated book. The purpose of this chapter is to show how each of these instruments can fit into a simple forward curve framework. Given this framework, all these interest rate derivative products can be hedged in one book, using this forward curve methodology.

HEDGING DERIVATIVE PRODUCTS

In addressing the problem of hedging a derivative product portfolio, we should seek the answers to these questions:

1. What variables affect the present value of this portfolio?
2. How do we measure the influence of these variables, either alone or together, on the portfolio's value?

The concept underlying the hedging strategy is then quite simple: Break down each product into its constituent elements and identify the factors affecting the value of these elements. We start with the simplest product: a Eurodollar futures contract.

Eurodollar Futures Contract

A futures contract on LIBOR from time t to $t + 3$ months is marked to market daily and therefore its present value (PV) is given by

$$PV \text{ (futures)} = \text{principal} \times (\text{strike price} - \text{LIBOR}_{t,t+3}) \times \frac{90}{360}.$$

The only variable in this equation that affects this present value is the three-month LIBOR annualized rate at time t. If you are long a $1,000,000 futures contract, and the futures price rises from 92.00 to 92.01, then the estimated LIBOR rate falls from 8.00 percent to 7.99 percent and the present value of the futures contract rises by

$$\$1,000,000 * .01/100 * 90/360$$

or $25. (In the Eurodollar pits, being long one Eurodollar futures contract is described as having a $+1$ *Delta* position.) The next simplest product is the forward rate agreement.

Forward Rate Agreement (FRA)

Like a futures contract, the payment on a FRA is a function of the difference between the appropriate LIBOR rate at time t and the strike price. But unlike a futures contract, a FRA is not settled at full value on a daily basis but is assumed to pay out at time t. So the present value of the FRA is given by

$$PV \text{ (FRA)} = \frac{\text{principal} \times (\text{LIBOR}_{t,t+\tau} - \text{strike price}) \times \dfrac{\text{days}_{t,t+\tau}}{360}}{\left(1 + \text{LIBOR}_{t,t+\tau} \times \dfrac{\text{days}_{t,t+\tau}}{360}\right) \times (1 + z_t)^t}$$

where z_t is the appropriate zero rate for discounting LIBOR cash flows from time t to the present.

The first point to note is that unlike a futures contract, the impact of a change in the appropriate LIBOR rate at time t is not a constant, but is a decreasing function of the maturity, t, of the FRA. If the number of days in the period is 90, the numerator for a one-basis-point increase in the appropriate LIBOR forward rate is $25.00 ($1,000,000 \times .01/100 \times 90/360). But because the payoff occurs in the future, the present value of the change can be considerably less than $25.00. Figure 2 illustrates the effect, as of June 1988, of an increase in the LIBOR forward rates on the value of a three-month FRA starting in March 1991. Because the FRA payout is almost three years in the future, the effect on the present value of the FRA of a one-basis point increase in the three-month LIBOR rate in March 1991 is not $25 but rather $19.20. Furthermore, the

FIGURE 2

**Effect of Changes in the LIBOR Forwards Rates on the Value of a
Three-Month FRA (Starting March 18, 1991)**

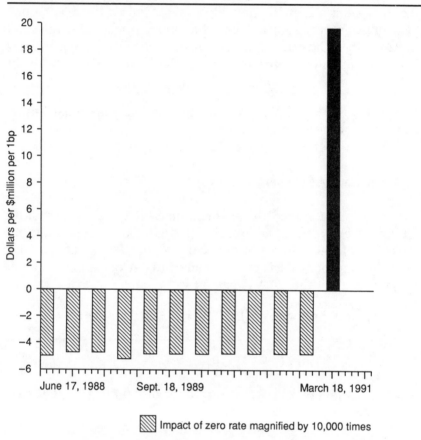

☒ Impact of zero rate magnified by 10,000 times

impact is not linear, as is the case for a futures contract, but is
convex: Decreases in the LIBOR rate have an increasing impact
and increases in the LIBOR rate have a decreasing impact on the
FRA's present value. This occurs because the formula for the
present value of an FRA includes a term in the denominator discounting the payment by the LIBOR rate for that period. So even
though the numerator is the same whether LIBOR rises 100 basis
points from 9 percent to 10 percent or falls 100 basis points to 8
percent ($25 × 100), the present value differs because the increase

of \$2,500 will be discounted by 1.10 and the decrease of \$2,500 will be discounted by 1.08. (This same phenomena is known as the *convexity* of a bond.)

The second point to note is that the present value of the FRA is a function of the zero rate, z_t. If z_t increases, the present value of the FRA decreases. We could keep track of both the LIBOR forward rates and zero rates, but to simplify, we note that, as illustrated in Figure 3, any zero rate can be modeled, in an arbitrage-free context, as a geometric combination of the previous zero rate and forward rate:

$$(1 + z_t)^t = (1 + z_{t-\tau})^{t-\tau} \times \left(1 + \text{LIBOR}_{t-\tau,t} \times \frac{\text{days}_{t-\tau,t}}{360}\right)$$

Working iteratively back towards the present, we can then say that the zero rate is a geometric combination of forward rates between 0 and time t:

$$(1 + z_t)^t = \left(1 + f_{0,1} \times \frac{d_{0,1}}{360}\right) \times \left(1 + f_{1,2} \times \frac{d_{1,2}}{360}\right)$$

$$\times \ldots \times \left(1 + f_{t-1,t} \times \frac{d_{t-1,t}}{360}\right)$$

From this, we can see that the present value of the FRA is slightly negatively affected by increases in any of the forward rates

FIGURE 3
Relation between Forward Interest Rates and Zero Interest Rates

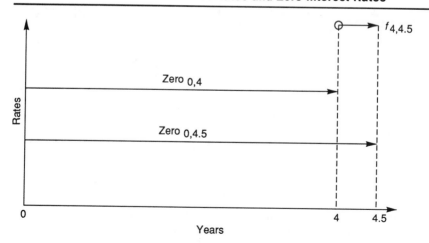

between 0 and time t. So, rather than keeping separate track of the forward rate and zero rate effects, we can combine them and present them in the same format, in Figure 2. (The negative, zero rate impacts have been magnified by 10,000 in order to be seen on the same scale as the positive LIBOR impact.)

We can see from this figure that while the present value of the FRA increases by $19.20 for a one-bp increase in the three-month LIBOR forward rate on March 18, 1991, it is slightly negatively affected by increases in any of the three-month LIBOR forward rates before March 18, 1991 (approximately .05¢ for each one-bp increase).

To summarize, the variables affecting the value of any given FRA are first, the appropriate maturity LIBOR forward rate on the FRA's settlement date (this sets the amount to be paid), and second, the collection of LIBOR forward rates from today to the settlement date (these affect the present value of the FRA), and third, time.

Interest Rate Swap

Normally, when we purchase a strip of FRAs, the strike price is separately set for each FRA so that each FRA has a present value of zero. But now imagine that we purchase the same strip, but set a common strike price for all the FRAs. By appropriate selection of the strike price, we can ensure that although the present value of each FRA is no longer zero, the sum of the present values of the strip of FRAs is zero. Given the upward sloping forwards curve starting at 7.9 percent and finishing at 9.5 percent illustrated in Figure 4, the choice of a constant strike price of approximately 9 percent for each of the eight FRAs produces the expectation of three negative cash flows followed by five positive cash flows, with the sum of their present values being equal to zero. Then imagine that instead of making a discounted payment on the settlement date of an FRA, we make an undiscounted payment on the (later) maturity date. Because the settlement date payment is discounted by the LIBOR rate for the period from the settlement date to the maturity date, the present value of the discounted payment equals the present value of the undiscounted payment. What we have now

FIGURE 4

Four-Year Interest Rate Swap as a Collection of Eight FRAs under Alternative Interest Rate Scenarios

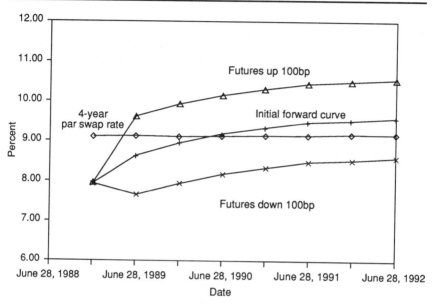

Note: Because the floating rate for the first payment was set at the initiation of the swap, the magnitude of the first cash flow is unaffected by changes in the futures/forwards curve.

created with this *single strike price/payment in arrears* strip of FRAs is a simple interest rate swap.

So we can conclude that the cash flows illustrated in Figure 4 are exactly equal to those for a four-year interest rate swap. Further, when we move the forward curve up or down 100 basis points, as shown in Figure 4, we can see that although the first payment is fixed because the first LIBOR has already been set, the other seven cash flows change quite dramatically, and that the present value of the swap is very much affected by changes in the forward rates. Since we can now model a swap as a portfolio of off-market FRAs, we can conclude that, as illustrated in Figure 4, the variables affecting the present value of a swap are just those variables that affect the present value of a FRA—the collection of

LIBOR forward rates between now and the swap's maturity, and time.

Interest Rate Cap

An interest rate cap can be viewed as a portfolio of call options on interest rates. For each of these options, the terminal wealth condition at maturity t for a LIBOR option can be written as

$$C_t = \max \left[\frac{\text{principal} \times (\text{LIBOR}_{t,t+\tau} - \text{strike}) \times \dfrac{\text{days}_{t,t+\tau}}{360}}{(1 + \text{LIBOR}_{t,t+\tau} \times \dfrac{\text{days}_{t,t+\tau}}{360})} ; 0 \right]$$

where the discounting term reflects the fact that the option payment, if any, is made not on the settlement date of the option but one period later. If we use the Black options-on-futures model to price this option, we see that the following variables affect the present value of the cap:

1. The LIBOR forward rate at time t.
2. The volatility of the LIBOR forward rate.
3. Time.
4. Either the collection of government forward rates between today and the maturity of the option (if the Black-Scholes riskless hedge concept is followed exactly, the appropriate discount rate used to calculate the option's present value is the government zero rate), or the similar collection of LIBOR forward rates (if discounted by the appropriate risky discount rate).

At this point, we've seen that futures, FRAs, swaps, and caps share a sensitivity to the LIBOR forward curve. Since these products are affected by the same fundamental factors, they can be hedged together, rather than in separate books, against changes in the LIBOR forwards curve.

Government Bond and Bond Futures

At the shorter end of the maturity spectrum (less than or equal to three years), the Eurodollar futures contracts provide the easiest hedging vehicle, but at the longer end, we have to turn to government bonds and bond futures to hedge the derivative products book. The question then arises, How do we fit a bond into the forward curve model we have developed? The answer is quite simple: we use, in reverse, the swap modeling approach discussed in Section 1. There we noted that receiving fixed on a swap is equivalent to going long a bond and short a floating-rate note:

$$\text{Swap (receive fixed)} = \text{bond} - \text{FRN}$$

Reversing this, we can model the bond in terms of a swap and an FRN:

$$\text{Bond} = \text{swap (receive fixed)} + \text{FRN}$$

But we already know that we can model a swap as a portfolio of FRAs, so that receiving fixed on a swap can be considered as selling a strip of FRAs. Further, the present value of the FRN at time t is given by

$$PV \text{ (FRN)} = \frac{\text{principal} \times \left(1 + \text{LIBOR}_0 \times \dfrac{\text{days}_{0,\tau}}{360}\right)}{\left(1 + \text{LIBOR}_{t,\tau} \times \dfrac{\text{days}_{t,\tau}}{360}\right)}$$

where LIBOR_0 is the floating rate set at the beginning of the period. By inspection, we can see that the present value of this FRN is also only affected by the current LIBOR rate and time. So we can model changes in the price of a government bond as being caused by changes in the collection of government forward rates between today and the maturity of the bond.

At this point, we can summarize the products' factor sensitivity in Table 1.

TABLE 1
Factors Affecting the Value of LIBOR-Based Derivative Products

	LIBOR Forwards Curve	LIBOR Volatility Curve	Time	Government Forwards Curve
Futures	*			
FRAs	*		*	
Swaps	*		*	
Caps	*	*	*	*
Government bonds			*	*

HEDGING RISK

As mentioned in the Introduction, many swap portfolio managers have borrowed the concept of modified duration from government desks to hedge their books. But an examination of the factors listed in Table 1 suggests that in order to hedge an integrated derivative products group, we should borrow the hedging concepts developed for futures and options books.[4]

In such books, the sensitivity of the portfolio to changes in the forwards rates is measured in terms of *delta* (the change in value of the instrument or portfolio for a one-basis-point change in the forward interest rate) and *gamma* (the change in the delta for a one-basis-point change in the forward interest rate);[5] the sensitivity of the portfolio to changes in the volatility is measured in terms of *vega* (the change in value of the instrument or portfolio for one basis point of change in the volatility); and the sensitivity of the portfolio to time is measured in terms of *theta* (the change in value of the instrument or portfolio for a one-day change in time to maturity).

We can illustrate this analysis of the sensitivity of a derivative product portfolio in Figure 5, which depicts the response of such a portfolio to a 100-basis-point change in the LIBOR forwards rate for each month from June 1988 to June 1997. For example, if the LIBOR forwards rate in December 1988 rose by 100 bp, the portfolio would lose almost $700,000. Such a delta maturity map allows the portfolio manager not only to see the overall response of the portfolio to a parallel shift in the forward curve (the portfolio's duration) but to see the influence of each part of the yield curve on the portfolio. Thus, Figure 5 shows that the depicted portfolio has a reasonably small and balanced exposure to changes in the forwards curve at longer maturities, but that the portfolio has a large and unbalanced exposure to changes in the forwards curve in the first two years. The sum of the deltas in Figure 5 (equivalent to the

---

[4] For more details, see, for example, Chapter 5 in M. Desmond Fitzgerald, *Financial Options* (London: Euromoney Publications, 1987).

[5] Since the response of most derivative products to changes in the forwards rates are nonlinear, the first derivative (the delta) can change as the forward rates change. The second derivative (the gamma) indicates how this change takes place and provides a measure of the stability of the delta hedge.

FIGURE 5

Time Distribution of the Effect of a 100-BP Change in the LIBOR Forward Curve on the Value of a Derivative Products Portfolio

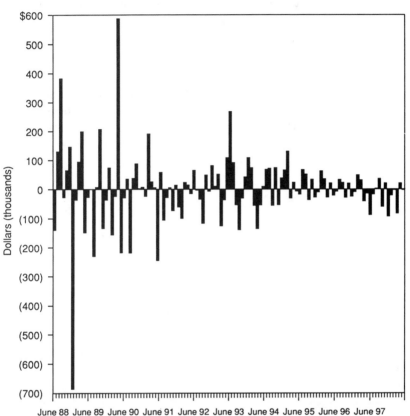

June 88 June 89 June 90 June 91 June 92 June 93 June 94 June 95 June 96 June 97

portfolio's modified duration) is approximately − $100,000, but that number obscures the important information that this portfolio is very susceptible to twists in the first two years of the forwards curve.

IMPLICATIONS

When computation costs were high, it was entirely appropriate to seek mathematically derived measures that approximated the portfolio's behavior. Now that computational costs are considerably lower, it makes sense to also use simulation techniques, especially when dealing with disaster scenarios that entail significant moves in the underlying variables. Time-based simulation, which answers questions such as What happens to this portfolio if, in six months time, the yield curve inverts and volatility increases? will play an increasing role in helping management assess the risks inherent in the portfolio.

Looking ahead, recent experiments with three-dimensional graphs and contour maps lead us to believe that maturity maps will eventually be replaced by response surfaces that map the value of the portfolio over wide ranges of the relevant variables, making it easier for senior management to assess the portfolio's riskiness and answer *what if* questions both accurately and quickly.

CHAPTER 17

LINKAGES BETWEEN INTEREST RATE SWAPS AND CROSS-CURRENCY SWAPS

Carl A. Batlin
Manufacturers Hanover Trust Company
New York, New York

INTRODUCTION

Swap transactions, through which two parties agree to trade periodic interest payments that differ by the basis on which they are calculated, fall into two general categories: interest rate swaps and cross-currency swaps. The most common structure employed in both types is the exchange of fixed-rate payments, in which the interest rate is fixed over the life of the transaction, for floating-rate payments, in which the interest rate is reset periodically according to some short-term index, such as six-month LIBOR. In the case of an interest rate swap, both sides are denominated in the same currency (often U.S. dollars, but several nondollar currencies as well), so payments are simply calculated by multiplying each interest rate (fixed or floating) by the same notional principal amount. The additional complication in a cross-currency swap is that the two sets of payments are denominated in different currencies (almost always fixed-rate foreign currency payments in exchange for U.S. dollar LIBOR payments), so an initial spot exchange rate must also be specified to determine the notional principal amounts on both sides of the swap for payment calculation purposes. In addition, the final payment typically includes the reexchange of these principal amounts—a practice that would be an unnecessary formality in the context of an interest rate swap.

Because they require the exchange of fixed contractual payments, swaps create gains or losses in market value when interest rates and/or exchange rates change. This property makes these instruments useful to firms whose balance sheets contain financial assets and liabilities. Indeed, firms enter into swaps either (*a*) to alter the exposure (in terms of the potential gain or loss) of their balance sheets to changes in interest rates and/or exchange rates or (*b*) to enhance the yields of their assets or reduce the costs of their liabilities while leaving their overall exposure unchanged. The first use (exposure alteration) enables firms to act on their expectations about future interest rate and/or exchange rate changes by either reducing their exposure (hedging) or increasing it (speculation). In either case, whether the augmented balance sheet (with the addition of the swap) produces a gain or a loss depends on the extent to which the firm's interest rate and/or exchange rate expectations are indeed realized. In contrast, the second use (yield enhancement/cost reduction) is more of an arbitrage operation, whose profitability depends only on interest rate discrepancies between the cash market, where the underlying assets and liabilities are priced, and the swap market. Both purposes make use of the exposures swaps create, but before analyzing the nature of these exposures, it is helpful to specify the mechanics of how swaps accomplish these purposes.

HOW INTEREST RATE SWAPS ARE USED

With interest rate swaps, firms can either lengthen the maturities of their assets or liabilities by transforming them from a floating-rate to a fixed-rate basis, or they can shorten them by changing fixed-rate assets or liabilities into floating-rate ones. As Table 1 shows, the position that a firm should take on a swap (i.e., either to pay the fixed rate and receive the floating rate or to receive the fixed rate and pay the floating rate) depends on whether the underlying instrument whose exposure it wants to alter is an asset or a liability.

TABLE 1
Appropriate Interest Rate Swap Positions to Alter Existing Exposures

Desired Effect	Underlying Instrument	
	Asset	Liability
Lengthen maturity	Receive fixed rate	Pay fixed rate
Shorten maturity	Pay fixed rate	Receive fixed rate

Furthermore, firms can enhance asset yields or reduce borrowing costs by combining interest rate swaps with assets or liabilities whose effective maturity is different from that which is desired, to create the synthetic equivalent of desired assets or liabilities. Whether this synthetic combination involves the lengthening of a floating-rate asset or liability to a fixed-rate one or the shortening of a fixed-rate asset or liability to a floating-rate one depends on two factors: (*a*) whether the cash instrument involved is an asset or a liability and (*b*) whether the fixed rate that firms can pay or receive in the swap market (i.e., the swap rate) is higher or lower than the fixed rate at which firms can borrow or lend in the cash market (i.e., the cash rate), as Table 2 shows.

Note that Tables 1 and 2 together imply the straightforward conclusion that firms should receive the fixed rate on the swap when that fixed rate exceeds the fixed rate available in the cash market, and they should pay the fixed rate on the swap when that fixed rate is lower than what they would be required to pay in the cash market.

TABLE 2
Appropriate Interest Rate Swap Operation to Enhance Yields or Reduce Costs

Market Condition	Underlying Instrument	
	Asset	Liability
Swap rate > cash rate	Lengthen maturity	Shorten maturity
Swap rate < cash rate	Shorten maturity	Lengthen maturity

HOW CROSS-CURRENCY SWAPS ARE USED

In the case of cross-currency swaps, firms can, in addition, alter their exposure to changes in exchange rates through changing the denomination of their existing assets or liabilities by swapping them into foreign currencies and out of U.S. dollars, or out of foreign currencies and into U.S. dollars. Whether they should achieve the desired objective by receiving the foreign currency interest and principal cash flows and paying the U.S. dollar cash flows in the swap, or by paying the foreign currency cash flows and receiving the U.S. dollar cash flows depends, analogously to the interest rate swap case, on whether the instrument whose denomination they want to transform is an asset or a liability, as Table 3 shows.

Moreover, asset yield enhancement or borrowing cost reduction can be achieved by combining cross-currency swaps with underlying assets or liabilities in an undesired denomination to create the synthetic equivalent of assets or liabilities in the desired denomination. Similar to the use of interest rate swaps for this purpose, the question of whether the synthetic combination requires the swapping of a U.S. dollar asset or liability into a foreign currency denomination, or the swapping out of an underlying instrument in a foreign currency into one in U.S. dollars depends, as Table 4 shows, on two factors: (a) whether the transformation involves an asset or a liability and (b) whether the fixed foreign currency interest rate that firms can pay or receive in the cross-currency swap market is higher or lower than the fixed rate at which firms can borrow or lend in the foreign currency's cash market.

TABLE 3
Appropriate Cross-Currency Swap Positions to Alter Existing Exposures

	Underlying Instrument	
Desired Effect	Asset	Liability
Swap into foreign currency	Receive foreign currency	Pay foreign currency
Swap out of foreign currency	Pay foreign currency	Receive foreign currency

TABLE 4
**Appropriate Cross-Currency Swap Operation to Enhance Yields or
Reduce Costs**

| | Underlying Instrument | |
Market Condition	Asset	Liability
Swap rate > cash rate	Swap into foreign currency	Swap out of foreign currency
Swap rate < cash rate	Swap out of foreign currency	Swap into foreign currency

As with interest rate swaps, Tables 3 and 4 jointly imply that it is profitable to receive the foreign currency rate on the swap when that rate exceeds the rate available in the cash market, but it is appropriate to be a foreign currency rate payer on the swap when that swap rate is lower than the rate required in the foreign currency's cash market.

INTEREST RATE SWAP EXPOSURE

The decision rules described above are operable because a particular swap position—whether to pay or receive the fixed rate on an interest rate swap or the foreign currency rate on a cross-currency swap—creates a reliable exposure to changes in interest rates and/or exchange rates. To facilitate the analysis of these exposures, we will assume that payments generated by both sides of the swap (fixed rate and floating rate) are reinvested and compounded forward, and that a single net payment is made at the maturity of the swap. This structure, known as a zero coupon swap, or bullet swap, creates the same exposures as normal coupon-paying swaps but allows the mathematical representation of these exposures to be done more clearly. Accordingly, our approach in what follows will be to elucidate the nature of swap exposures generally through an examination of the determinants of the gains or losses from the bullet payment of a zero coupon swap.

In an interest rate swap, a fixed-rate payer under these circumstances would receive a payment that resulted from compounding together all the short-term rates that were set at the reset dates and would make a payment that resulted from compounding the fixed rate over the life of the swap. The net payment received, then, at the maturity of the swap (per dollar of notional principal) would therefore be

$$(1 + {_0R_1})(1 + {_1R_2}) \ldots (1 + {_{n-1}R_n}) - (1 + {_0R_n})^n \qquad (1)$$

where ${_tR_{t+i}}$ is the notation for an i-period interest rate set at time t and maturing at time $t + i$. In this case, the fixed-rate payer would receive the compounded effects of n one-period (short-term) rates and would pay the original n-period fixed rate prevailing at time 0, compounded over the n periods. Note that at the inception of the swap (time 0) only the first short-term rate (${_0R_1}$) and the fixed rate (${_0R_n}$) are known. The fixed-rate payer, therefore, (*a*) gains from the swap if the future short-term rates, together with the initial short-term rate, compound together to a larger amount than the original fixed rate and (*b*) loses if the compounded short-term rates wind up compounding to a lower amount than the fixed rate. The payment to a fixed rate receiver, incidently, is the negative of the fixed rate payer's payment. The fixed rate receiver, therefore, gains if compounded short-term rates are less than the fixed rate and loses if they are higher.

An alternative way of characterizing the exposure of an interest rate swap lies in the fact that the fixed rate can be reexpressed as

$$(1 + {_0R_n})^n = (1 + {_0R_1})(1 + {_0F_{1,n}})^{n-1} \qquad (2)$$

where ${_0F_{1,n}}$ is the $n - 1$ period forward interest rate implied in the yield curve at time 0 (in the relationship between ${_0R_n}$ and ${_0R_1}$) for a rate to be set at time 1 and maturing at time n. By using Equation 2, a transformation of the fixed rate payer's gains or losses in Equation 1 can be expressed as the following:[1]

---

[1] To derive Equation 3, first express Equation 1 as the ratio of the floating-rate payment to the fixed-rate payment, rather than the difference, so that the fixed-rate payer's gains (losses) are represented by a ratio greater (less) than unity. Then, after substituting Equation 2, taking the logarithm of the gain/loss ratio, and using the fact that the logarithm of 1 plus a small number can be approximated by the number itself, a simple rearrangement of terms produces the expression in Equation 3.

$$\frac{1}{n-1}(_1R_2 + {_2R_3} + \ldots + {_{n-1}R_n}) - {_0F_{1,n}} \qquad (3)$$

This expression states that a fixed-rate payer gains from rising short-term rates and loses from falling short-term rates, while a fixed-rate receiver is in the reverse position. Moreover, the breakeven condition for both parties occurs when the average future short-term interest rate equals the forward rate implied in the yield curve at the inception of the swap. As a result, a fixed-rate payer in a swap can be characterized as a short bond position (a long-term borrower), while a fixed-rate receiver is equivalent to a long bond position (a long-term investor).

CROSS-CURRENCY SWAP EXPOSURE

Linkage with U.S. Dollar Interest Rate Swaps

Although analysis of the exposure created by a cross-currency swap is, of necessity, more complex, the problem can be simplified by making use of the two normal linkages that tie standard cross-currency swaps (in which fixed-rate foreign currency payments are exchanged for U.S. dollar LIBOR payments) to interest rate swaps. As Figure 1 shows, the first of these linkages is that a standard cross-currency swap can be replicated by a U.S. dollar interest rate swap and a cross-currency swap in which fixed-rate U.S. dollar payments are exchanged for fixed-rate foreign currency payments.

Since the fixed-rate U.S. dollar cash flows in the U.S. dollar interest rate swap cancel with those in the fixed-fixed cross-currency swap, the two transactions together are equivalent to the standard cross-currency swap. The implication is that the exposure created by a standard cross-currency swap is the sum of the exposures of a U.S. dollar interest rate swap (already analyzed as the exposure of a long or short U.S. dollar bond position) and a fixed-fixed cross-currency swap. It is to an analysis of the exposure of this latter swap transaction that we now turn.

In a fixed-fixed cross-currency swap, a fixed interest rate $_0R_n^{US}$ is established for the U.S. dollar side of the swap, a fixed interest rate $_0R_n^{FC}$ is determined for the foreign currency side of the swap, and an initial spot exchange rate S_0 is set for making the foreign

FIGURE 1
Replication of a Standard Cross-Currency Swap with a U.S. Interest Rate Swap and a Fixed-Fixed Cross-Currency Swap

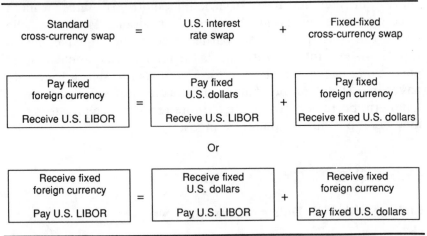

currency value of the notional principal consistent with the U.S. dollar value. If we express exchange rates as the number of U.S. dollars per unit of the foreign currency (i.e., higher values reflect a stronger foreign currency and a weaker U.S. dollar, while lower values represent the reverse), the original U.S. dollar notional principal is translated into the foreign currency equivalent by dividing it by S_0. Then, after principal and interest are compounded at the foreign currency interest rate, the amount is reconverted into U.S. dollars at maturity by multiplying by the spot exchange rate prevailing at that time, S_n, to net the foreign currency payment of the swap with the U.S. dollar payment. Accordingly, the net receipt at maturity in U.S. dollars for the foreign currency payer in a zero coupon, or bullet, fixed-fixed cross-currency swap (per U.S. dollar of notional principal) would be

$$(1 + {_0}R_n^{US})^n - (1 + {_0}R_n^{FC})^n \, S_n/S_0 \tag{4}$$

Naturally, the net payment received by the foreign currency receiver is simply the negative of Equation 4.

Since the two fixed interest rates and the initial spot exchange rate are known at the inception of the swap, the only variable that determines the gains or losses to the two parties is the value of the spot rate at maturity. As Equation 4 makes clear, a foreign currency payer gains when the foreign currency weakens (the U.S. dollar strengthens) and loses when the reverse occurs. The foreign currency receiver, on the other hand, gains when the foreign currency strengthens (the U.S. dollar weakens) and loses under the reverse circumstances. It is notable that the foreign currency payer creates a fixed-rate U.S. dollar asset and foreign currency liability, while the foreign currency receiver creates a fixed-rate foreign currency asset and U.S. dollar liability through the swap. Since the holder of the foreign currency liability (the foreign currency payer) gains if the value of the foreign currency subsequently weakens, while the holder of the foreign currency asset (the foreign currency receiver) gains if the value of the foreign currency subsequently strengthens, the rule for gaining from fixed-fixed cross-currency swaps is to borrow in overvalued currencies (i.e., create liabilities in currencies that subsequently weaken) and lend in undervalued currencies (i.e., create assets in currencies that subsequently strengthen).

There is another way of shedding light on the exposure created by a fixed-fixed cross-currency swap. Consider a forward foreign exchange transaction, in which parties can trade currencies for forward delivery at prices available today. If $_0F_n$ represents the forward exchange rate (in number of U.S. dollars per unit of foreign currency) available at time 0 for delivery at time n, at maturity, when the contract can be reversed in the spot exchange market, the gain or loss per U.S. dollar to the seller of forward foreign currency and buyer of forward U.S. dollars is

$$_0F_n - S_n. \tag{5}$$

The gain or loss to the buyer of forward foreign currency and seller of forward U.S. dollars is the negative of Equation 5. As Equation 5 indicates, sellers of forward foreign currency gain if the foreign currency weakens and the U.S. dollar strengthens and lose if the reverse occurs, while buyers of forward foreign currency gain if the foreign currency strengthens and the U.S. dollar weakens and lose under the opposite circumstances. In both cases, the initial forward exchange rate (generally different from the spot rate S_0 available at that time) is the break-even rate to which the future spot exchange rate S_n must be compared to determine gains or losses.

Next, consider the determinants of the forward exchange rate $_0F_n$. If interest rates in two currencies differ, arbitrageurs try to borrow at the low rate, convert the funds into the other currency in the spot exchange market, and invest the proceeds at the high rate. If, at the same time, they could contract at the forward exchange rate to profitably reconvert the investment returns at maturity and retire the debt, the operation would permit riskless arbitrage profits, which is generally not possible. The Interest Rate Parity Theorem, which formalizes this logic, implies that the forward exchange rate must satisfy the following relationship:

$$_0F_n = S_0 \left(\frac{1 + {_0R_n^{US}}}{1 + {_0R_n^{FC}}}\right)^n \tag{6}$$

Loosely speaking, Equation 6 states that the forward premium or discount $(_0F_n/S_0)$ is offset by the interest rate differential $[(1 + {_0R_n^{US}})/(1 + {_0R_n^{FC}})]^n$.

Now, if Equation 6 is used in Equation 4, the gain or loss to the foreign currency payer in a zero coupon (or bullet) fixed-fixed cross-currency swap can be reexpressed as

$$\frac{(1 + {_0R_n^{FC}})^n}{S_0} (_0F_n - S_n). \tag{7}$$

Since this gain or loss is directly proportional to the gain or loss accruing to the seller of forward foreign currency in Equation 5, it is apparent that the exposure created by a fixed-fixed cross-currency swap is equivalent to that inherent in a forward foreign exchange transaction. That is, the foreign currency payer is short forward foreign currency and long forward U.S. dollars, while the foreign currency receiver is long forward foreign currency and short forward U.S. dollars. As Equation 7 makes clear, this implication is self-evident in the case of a zero coupon fixed-fixed cross-currency swap. More generally, though, for a coupon-paying fixed-fixed cross-currency swap, each contractual future cash flow created by the two fixed interest rates and the initial spot exchange rate can be viewed as an individual bullet swap and is thus also equivalent to a forward foreign currency position. The entire coupon-paying fixed-fixed cross-currency swap can therefore be characterized as a strip, or sequence, of forward foreign exchange positions for delivery at regular future intervals.

Linkage with Foreign Currency Interest Rate Swaps

The second linkage tying standard cross-currency swaps to interest rate swaps is depicted in Figure 2, which shows that a standard cross-currency swap can be replicated by a foreign currency interest rate swap and a cross-currency swap in which floating rate U.S. dollar payments (e.g., U.S. LIBOR) are exchanged for floating rate foreign currency payments (e.g., foreign currency LIBOR). Since the foreign currency LIBOR cash flows in the foreign currency interest rate swap cancel with those in the floating-floating cross-currency swap, the two transactions together reduce to the equivalent of a standard cross-currency swap. The exposure created by a standard cross-currency swap is therefore the same as the sum of the exposures created by a foreign currency interest rate swap (equivalent to that of a long or short foreign currency bond position) and a floating-floating cross-currency swap.

The only difference between the floating-floating cross-currency swap and the fixed-fixed cross-currency swap is that the interest rates on each side of the floating-floating swap are reset

FIGURE 2

Replication of a Standard Cross-Currency Swap with a Foreign Currency Interest Rate Swap and a Floating-Floating Cross-Currency Swap

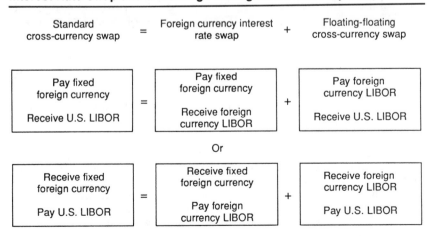

each period. As a result, the foreign currency payer in a floating-floating zero-coupon (or bullet) cross-currency swap (per U.S. dollar of notional principal) would receive at maturity

$$(1 + {}_0R_1^{US})(1 + {}_1R_2^{US}) \ldots (1 + {}_{n-1}R_n^{US})$$
$$- (1 + {}_0R_1^{FC})(1 + {}_1R_2^{FC}) \ldots (1 + {}_{n-1}R_n^{FC})S_n/S_0 \qquad (8)$$

where ${}_tR_{t+1}^{US}$ and ${}_tR_{t+1}^{FC}$ denote the U.S. dollar and foreign currency one-period interest rates, respectively. Correspondingly, the foreign currency receiver would receive the negative of Equation 8. In contrast to the net receipt of the fixed-fixed cross-currency swap in Equation 4, movements in future U.S. dollar and foreign currency short-term interest rates, as well as the previously described movements in the spot exchange rate, influence the gain or loss to the two parties at maturity. Specifically, widening U.S. dollar–foreign currency short-term interest rate differentials favor the foreign currency payer and hurt the foreign currency receiver, while narrowing differentials have the reverse effect.

There is also an analogy in the floating-floating cross-currency swap to the equivalence between a fixed-fixed cross-currency swap and a forward exchange position. To see this relationship, the spot exchange component of Equation 8, S_n/S_0, must first be expressed in its equivalent form,

$$\frac{S_n}{S_0} = \frac{S_1}{S_0} \cdot \frac{S_2}{S_1} \ldots \frac{S_n}{S_{n-1}}. \qquad (9)$$

Furthermore, from the Interest Rate Parity Theorem in Equation 6, the relationship between any one-period forward exchange rate ${}_tF_{t+1}$ and the relevant spot exchange rate S_t and one-period interest rates is given by

$$_tF_{t+1} = S_t \left(\frac{1 + {}_tR_{t+1}^{US}}{1 + {}_tR_{t+1}^{FC}}\right). \qquad (10)$$

Then, by using Equations 9 and 10, a transformation of the foreign currency payer's gains or losses in Equation 8 can be expressed as the following:[2]

---

[2] To derive Equation 11, first express Equation 8 as the ratio of the U.S. dollar payment to the foreign currency payment. Next, substitute Equation 9 for the S_n/S_0 component, and use Equation 10 to substitute for each $1 + {}_tR_{t+1}^{US}$ component. Then, after canceling the common $1 + {}_tR_{t+1}^{FC}$ and S_t terms, take the logarithm of the resulting ratio and use the earlier approximation regarding the logarithm of 1 plus a small number to produce Equation 11.

$$\frac{{}_0F_1 - S_1}{S_1} + \frac{{}_1F_2 - S_2}{S_2} + \cdots + \frac{{}_{n-1}F_n - S_n}{S_n} \qquad (11)$$

In comparing Equations 11 and 7, it is apparent that the foreign currency payer in both a floating-floating cross-currency swap and a fixed-fixed cross-currency swap have short forward foreign currency and long forward U.S. dollar exposure, while the foreign currency receiver in both swaps has the opposite exposure. The difference between the two types of swaps lies in the nature of their equivalent forward exchange contracts: The fixed-fixed cross-currency swap contains long-dated forward exchange exposure incurred at the inception of the swap for delivery at maturity or, more generally, when the swap's cash flows are received (i.e., in a coupon-paying fixed-fixed cross-currency swap, the swap's cash flows would be replicated by a strip of a long-dated forwards). In contrast, the floating-floating cross-currency swap contains short-dated forward exchange exposure incurred on a rolling basis as the swap ages. In other words, because the floating-floating cross-currency swap's future cash flows are not known until the beginning of each payment period, when the two interest rates are reset, the equivalent forward exchange positions are a series of new contracts undertaken at fixed intervals during the swap's life. Thus, a strip of long-dated forwards consists of n contracts entered into at time 0 with different delivery dates (and therefore different maturities), at forward prices that are known at time 0 (i.e., ${}_0F_1, {}_0F_2, \ldots, {}_0F_n$). In contrast, a program of rolling short-dated forwards consists of n one-period contracts entered into at different times, at prices that are (with the exception of the first) unknown at time 0 (i.e., ${}_0F_1, {}_1F_2, \ldots {}_{n-1}F_n$). Clearly, if the realized short-dated forward exchange rates happen to average together to equal the relevant long-dated forward exchange rate, the gain or loss associated with a long-dated forward exchange position will equal the gain or loss that materializes from rolling a series of comparable short-dated forward exchange contracts. Alternatively stated, if the forward interest rates implied in the fixed rate of a fixed-fixed cross-currency swap happen to predict perfectly the realized short-term interest rates that are reset over the life of a floating-floating cross-currency swap, the gain or loss from the fixed-fixed cross-currency swap will equal that of the floating-floating cross-currency swap. Of course, such an event could only occur by chance.

SUMMARY

In summary, the exposure of a standard cross-currency swap can be characterized as the sum of the exposures of either (*a*) a U.S. dollar interest rate swap and a strip of long-dated forward exchange contracts or (*b*) a foreign currency interest rate swap and a program of rolling short-dated forward exchange contracts. These relationships are illustrated in Figure 3, where the points of the triangle represent the three types of standard fixed-floating swaps, and the sides of the triangle indicate the types of forward exchange contracts needed to link together the pairs of standard swap transactions.

Consequently, the foreign currency payer in a standard cross-currency swap has the exposure of either (*a*) a short U.S. dollar bond (i.e., gains when short-term U.S. dollar interest rates rise and loses when they fall) *plus* a short foreign currency position in a

FIGURE 3
Fixed-Floating Swap Triangle

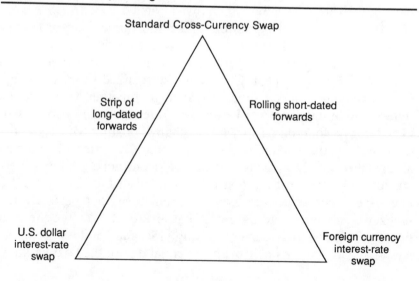

strip of long-dated forward exchange contracts (i.e., gains when the foreign currency weakens and the U.S. dollar strengthens, and loses when the reverse occurs) **or** (*b*) a short foreign currency bond exposure *plus* a short forward foreign currency exposure in a program of rolling forward exchange contracts. In contrast, the foreign currency receiver is effectively long a bond (U.S. dollar *or* foreign currency) *and* long the forward foreign currency (a strip of long-dated contracts *or* a program of rolling short-dated contracts).

CHAPTER 18

SWAP RATIONALIZATION: EQUIVALENCE OF SHORT-DATE AND LONG-DATE INTEREST RATE SWAP STRATEGIES

Samuel C. Weaver
Hershey Foods Corporation
Hershey, Pennsylvania

A financial manager must decide how to finance the expansion of the company while at the same time revisiting the efficiency of past financing decisions. Should the firm's growth be financed with debt or equity? Should the debt be short-term debt, intermediate-term notes, or a plain chocolate, traditional long-term bond?

The matching concept is a principle tenet that has provided a foundation for financial theory for decades. The theory is simple: Match the maturity of the debt to the maturity of the underlying asset. However, throughout the past decade, this principle has come under closer scrutiny due to

- Increased emphasis on debt financing.
- Significantly increased interest rate volatility.
- More sophisticated interest rate forecasting.
- Recognized debt market opportunities that may accommodate differing costs of a particular type of debt depending on the borrower.
- An exploding financial services industry.

- The advent of innovative financial instruments such as interest rate futures, options, and swaps.
- Rapid technological changes that make assets functionally valueless within a significantly shorter economic life than was originally estimated.
- Marketable portfolios of separable companies acquired in the megamerger market of the 1980s that lead to sometimes unpredictable cash flow generation that could be applied to reduce enormous amounts of debt.

No longer can the matching concept be blindly and irresponsibly applied. A company's debt portfolio demands as much management attention as its asset portfolio. The maturity profile of outstanding debt and the market's implied interest rates are key factors in liability management. In addition, an extension of the analysis of variable-rate versus fixed-rate debt leads to considerations regarding the use of a strip of short-date swaps versus a long-date swap to obtain the desired structure.

This chapter examines the conditions that have an impact on the choice of a debt-financing portfolio strategy involving a strip of short-date interest rate swaps versus the choice of an alternative strategy involving a long-date swap. Swaps facilitate the conversion of fixed-rate debt to floating-rate debt or floating-rate to fixed-rate debt. A swap is a convenient management tool that provides the flexibility to convert debt from one position to the other and is identical to altering the interest payment—fixed rate to floating rate, and vice versa. A swap can be implemented at the inception of debt borrowing or throughout the life of an existing borrowing.

It turns out that any rational choice between a series of short-date swaps or forward contracts (i.e., variable-rate financing) and a long-date swap (i.e., fixed-rate financing) will relate necessarily to expectations regarding future short-term interest rates. In the final analysis, the appropriate decisions will be revealed to the marketplace, and actual decisions will generate gains or losses to the extent that their underlying expectations are fulfilled or matched in the marketplace.

We begin by examining the term structure of interest rates and developing the crucial role played by implied forward rates or expectations. Armed with this background, the main issues of establishing conditions under which the choice of a strip of short-date swaps dominates a long-date swap, or vice versa, are addressed. The final section presents a summary of the main points of the discussion.

TERM STRUCTURE: THEORY AND IMPLICATIONS FOR SWAPS

The theory of the term structure of interest rates deals with the relationship between the yield to maturity on identical securities (e.g., same coupon, default risk, tax treatment) and their time to maturity. The yield curve is the graphical counterpart of the term structure. Typical patterns of the yield curve are upward sloping, downward sloping, flat, or humped. In this section, however, our main interest lies in investigating the analytical underpinnings of the term structure.

Implied interest rates, or the market's forward interest rate expectations, are the infrastructure underlying the theory of the term structure of interest rates. Said differently, implied interest rates are the forward one-period (i.e., annual) interest rates implicit in an observed multiperiod interest rate. That is, a two-year rate can be separated into a one-year rate and an implied forward rate from the end of year one to the end of year two. This concept is necessary to an examination of the relationship between short-date and long-date contracts.

EVALUATION OF A SHORT-DATE STRATEGY

To place the concept of implied rates in context, suppose that a borrower wants to borrow funds for two years and has numerous alternatives. Keep in mind that this problem is analogous to choosing a long-date swap or a strip of short-date swaps to accomplish a given strategy: hedge, speculation, or arbitrage. Furthermore, this presentation can be extended to the mirror-image of this transaction, the investor's perspective.

Specifically, suppose the borrower narrows its choice to two alternatives: (a) to borrow for two years via a zero coupon instrument that returns an annual interest rate of 8.5 percent or (b) to borrow its required amount for one year in an 8 percent bank loan and at the end of the first year to reborrow for the second year at the then prevailing one-year interest rate. This second alternative is identical to a short-date swap or variable-rate financing.

If the first alternative is accepted, so that $1,000 is financed for two years at 8.5 percent, the borrower will be required to pay $1,177 at the end of the second year, based on annual compounding as follows:

$$FV = PV (1 + i)^n \qquad (1)$$

where

FV = future value at the end of period n,
PV = present value at the beginning,
i = stated interest rate, and
n = number of years of investment.

Or, specifically:

$$\$1,177 = \$1,000 (1 + .085)^2$$

On the other hand, rolling the loan over in sequential one-year loans assures the borrower of nothing more than at the end of one year the amount of the loan will have increased by 8 percent to $1,080 (in accordance with Equation 1). The question facing the borrower is, What will be the annual interest rate from the end of the first year to the end of the second year (denoted as i_{1-2})? To answer this question, Equation 1 must be rearranged to allow for differing annual interest rates:

$$FV = PV (1 + i_{0-1}) (1 + i_{1-2}) \qquad (2)$$

Or, specifically:

$$FV = \$1,000 (1 + .08) (1 + i_{1-2})$$

The following table presents the results of three different refinancing rates (i_{1-2}) and the associated future costs of the initial $1,000 financing, assuming an 8 percent return in the first year of the two-year debt horizon:

Refinancing Rate (i_{1-2})	Value at the End of Two Years
8%	$1,166
9%	1,177
10%	1,188

If the investment community, borrowers and investors, thought the annual interest rate at the end of the first year would be only 8 percent, (a) all borrowers would follow a rollover strategy rather than a two-year financing, and (b) everyone with a two-year investment horizon would invest in a two-year investment rather than rolling over a one-year investment at an expected 8 percent reinvestment rate. This situation would put upward pressure on two-year security prices and downward pressure on one-year security prices, altering the stated interest rate relationship of 8 percent for a one-year investment and 8.5 percent for a two-year investment.

Conversely, if the market expected the annual interest rates to increase next year to 10 percent, two-year borrowing would best suit the borrower while the rollover strategy would be more attractive for the investor. Again, the buying and selling pressure would alter the current stated interest rate relationships until the 10 percent expectation would be fully reflected in the current one-year and two-year interest rates.

INTEREST RATE EXPECTATIONS

Clearly, with the given structure of interest rates (one-year, 8 percent; two-year, 8.5 percent) in the example, the borrower and investor would be indifferent regarding the choice between an instrument of two years or an instrument for one year at 8 percent that would be reissued for the second year at 9 percent. Given these stated rates, the market expects the second year's one-year interest rate to be 9 percent. Furthermore, as illustrated in the previous example, when long-term financing cost (investment return) is equal to the return implied in the rollover strategy (assuming reissuance at the expected interest rate), there is no immediate market pressure to adjust existing interest rates. This result—the market's expectation, or implied interest rate—can be derived by equating the future values of the two strategies as in Equation 3:

Period n financing = rollover strategy for n periods.

$$PV (1 + i)^n = PV (1 + i_{0-1})(1 + i_{1-2}) \cdots [1 + i_{(n-1)-n}]. \quad (3)$$
$$(1 + i)^n = (1 + i_{0-1})(1 + i_{1-2}) \cdots [1 + i_{(n-1)-n}].$$

Or, specifically, for the two-period investment in the example,

$$(1 + .085)^2 = (1 + .08)(1 + i_{1-2})$$
$$1.177 = 1.08\,(1 + i_{1-2})$$
$$1.09 = 1 + i_{1-2}$$
$$.09 = i_{1-2}$$
$$9\% = i_{1-2}$$

The example suggests that by observing multiple-period interest rates, it is possible to derive the market's expectations for future single-period interest rates. These expected future rates are described as implied rates. The risk that the bond issuer (or investor) faces is that these expectations may not be realized. In the example, if the actual future one-period interest rate (i_{1-2}) would have been only 8 percent, the rollover strategy would have been more (less) advantageous to a borrower (investor), providing a total terminal cost (return) of $1,166. On the other hand, if the actual future one-period interest rate (i_{1-2}) would have been 10 percent, then the longer-term strategy of financing for two years at 8.5 percent would have been more (less) advantageous to a borrower (investor), providing a total terminal cost (return) of $1,177.

MULTIPLE-PERIOD INTEREST RATE EXPECTATIONS

As demonstrated above, the market's implied forward annual interest rate, or expected interest rate, can be determined via the relationship between a one-year and two-year bond's yield to maturity. In more general terms, any one-year implicit forward rate can be derived from two long rates with adjacent terms to maturity.

Table 1 illustrates this concept. Given the term structure of interest rates detailed under the "Yield to Maturity" heading, a one-year implied interest rate for the final year of a three-year rollover strategy can be observed by employing Equation 3:

Three-year actual yield = (two-year actual yield) (one-year implied yield)
$$(1 + .088)^3 = (1 + .085)^2 (1 + i_{2-3})$$
$$1.2879 = 1.1772\,(1 + i_{2-3})$$
$$.094 = i_{2-3}$$
$$9.4\% = i_{2-3}$$

TABLE 1
Implied Interest Rates

Year	Yield to Maturity	One-Year		Two-Year		Three-Year		Four-Year	
		Period	Rates	Period	Rates	Period	Rates	Period	Rates
1	8.00%	i_{1-2}	9.00%	i_{1-3}	9.20%	i_{1-4}	9.34%	i_{1-5}	9.38%
2	8.50%	i_{2-3}	9.40%	i_{2-4}	9.50%	i_{2-5}	9.50%		
3	8.80%	i_{3-4}	9.60%	i_{3-5}	9.55%				
4	9.00%	i_{4-5}	9.50%						
5	9.10%								

The implied one-year interest rate from Year 2 to Year 3 is 9.4 percent. Said differently, a two-year financing with an 8.5 percent yield followed by a one-year rollover with a cost of 9.4 percent is equivalent to a three-year financing with 8.8 percent yield. In both cases the cost is $1,288 in total.

In more general terms Equation 3 can be rewritten to determine any set of market expectations from any point in the future, for example, the two-year interest rate one-year from now. To solve this problem more directly, Equation 3 can be rewritten as

$$i_{t-n} = \sqrt[(n-t)]{\frac{(1 + i_{0-n})^n}{(1 + i_{0-t})^t}} - 1 \tag{4}$$

where t = intermediate time period, and
$n-t$ = implied interest rate term to maturity.

Although Equation 4 is not intuitive, a simple detailed example can clearly illustrate its use. In this case, based on Table 1, the market's implied, or expected, two-year interest rate one year from now can be calculated by focusing on the three-year and one-year bonds as follows:

$$i_{1-3} = \sqrt[2]{\frac{(1 + .088)^3}{(1 + .080)^1}} - 1$$

$$i_{1-3} = \sqrt[2]{\frac{(1.2879}{1.08}} - 1$$

$$i_{1-3} = \sqrt[2]{1.1925} - 1$$
$$i_{1-3} = 1.0920 - 1$$
$$i_{1-3} = .0920$$
$$i_{1-3} = 9.2\%$$

The "Two-Year" implied interest rate columns of Table 1 illustrate the other potential two-year rates that exist within a five-year financing horizon.

Equation 4 could also be employed to develop three-year and four-year expected interest rates. For example, from Table 1, a borrower with a five-year financing horizon is indifferent between a straight five-year debt instrument at 9.10 percent or a one-year borrowing at 8.00 percent with a subsequent reissuance in one year of a 9.38 percent four-year bond.

TABLE 2
Expected Cost of Financing

Years of Actual Interest Rates	Years of Implied Interest Rates				
	0	1	2	3	4
1	$1,080	$1,177	$1,288	$1,412	$1,546
2	1,177	1,288	1,412	1,546	
3	1,288	1,412	1,546		
4	1,412	1,546			
5	1,546				

Note: The total term of the financing is equal to the years of actual interest rates plus the years of implied interest rates. For example, a four-year financing can be accomplished via a four-year actual financing with no rollover or a two-year actual financing with a 2-year rollover. Both strategies are expected to cost $1,412.

As illustrated on Table 2, any possible combination of actual borrowings and rollover strategies is expected to cost the same. For instance, a five-year financing is expected to cost $1,546 whether it is done as a five-year borrowing, a one-year financing followed by a four-year financing, or any combination as extracted from Table 2:

Actual	Implied	Cost (Using Equation 2)
i_{0-1}	i_{1-5}	$1,546
i_{0-2}	i_{2-5}	$1,546
i_{0-3}	i_{3-5}	$1,546
i_{0-4}	i_{4-5}	$1,546
i_{0-5}	N/A	$1,546

$$FV = \$1,000 \ (1 + i_{0-1}) \ (1 + i_{1-5})^4$$
$$= 1,000 \ (1 + .08) \ (1 + .0938)^4$$
$$= 1,546$$

Further illustrations can also be seen from Table 2.

EXPECTATIONS AND NONTRADITIONAL YIELD CURVES

To this point, the chapter has been centered on traditionally shaped yield curves. That is, as illustrated in Table 1, an upward-sloping yield curve has been used to develop the theory of implied interest rates. This application is not unique to traditional yield curves. It is extended below to the nontraditional yield curves that have dominated 1988 and 1989.

Equations 3 and 4 are applicable in this situation and were used to derive the expected, or implied, interest rates in Tables 3, 4, and 5.

Table 3 presents expected interest rates that underlie an inverted yield curve. An inverted yield curve is characterized by a higher cost for short-term funds than for long-term funds. As illustrated, rates drop from 9.25 percent (with a one-year maturity) to 8.85 percent (with a five-year maturity).

In this case, a financial manager that needs to borrow money for two years is neutral between a two-year note at 9.10 percent or a one-year note (at 9.25 percent) followed by a one-year rollover at 8.95 percent (i_{1-2}). Similarly, if the borrower is considering a three-year financing, it is indifferent between a three-year financing at 9.00 percent or a one-year note (at 9.25 percent) followed by a two-year rollover at 8.88 percent (i_{1-3}) or a two-year note (at 9.10 percent) followed by a one-year rollover at 8.80 percent (i_{2-3}).

After discerning the market's implicit expectations for future interest rates, and if the financial manager projects lower rates than the market's expectations, a rollover strategy would be the preferred strategy. On the other hand, if the borrower believes that interest rates will rise above the implied interest rates, then an opportunity exists to lock in the cost of financing via a long-date financing.

In the case of a flat yield curve (Table 4), the expectations as estimated by the market at that time are constant. In this case, the yield curve is flat at 9 percent, and expectations are also flat at 9 percent. The financial manager needs to compare the direction of interest rate forecasts versus the steady chart pointed out by the market's expectations. If the borrower's expectations are for declining (increasing) interest rates, a rollover (long-date) financing strategy is the most advantageous.

On occasion the yield curve becomes humped. That is, interest rates rise over the intermediate term and then decline. Such an example is demonstrated on Table 5. Notice, in this particular case, that expected interest rates also rise and then decline.

TABLE 3
Implied Interest Rates (Inverted Yield Curve)

Year	Yield to Maturity	One-Year Period	Rates	Two-Year Period	Rates	Three-Year Period	Rates	Four-Year Period	Rates
1	9.25%	i_{1-2}	8.95%	i_{1-3}	8.88%	i_{1-4}	8.78%	i_{1-5}	8.75%
2	9.10%	i_{2-3}	8.80%	i_{2-4}	8.70%	i_{2-5}	8.68%		
3	9.00%	i_{3-4}	8.60%	i_{3-5}	8.63%				
4	8.90%	i_{4-5}	8.65%						
5	8.85%								

TABLE 4
Implied Interest Rates (Flat Yield Curve)

Year	Yield to Maturity	One-Year Period	Rates	Two-Year Period	Rates	Three-Year Period	Rates	Four-Year Period	Rates
1	9.00%	i_{1-2}	9.00%	i_{1-3}	9.00%	i_{1-4}	9.00%	i_{1-5}	9.00%
2	9.00%	i_{2-3}	9.00%	i_{2-4}	9.00%	i_{2-5}	9.00%		
3	9.00%	i_{3-4}	9.00%	i_{3-5}	9.00%				
4	9.00%	i_{4-5}	9.00%						
5	9.00%								

TABLE 5
Implied Interest Rates (Humped Yield Curve)

Year	Yield to Maturity	One-Year		Two-Year		Three-Year		Four-Year	
		Period	Rates	Period	Rates	Period	Rates	Period	Rates
1	8.70%	i_{1-2}	9.10%	i_{1-3}	9.15%	i_{1-4}	8.97%	i_{1-5}	8.83%
2	8.90%	i_{2-3}	9.20%	i_{2-4}	8.90%	i_{2-5}	8.73%		
3	9.00%	i_{3-4}	8.60%	i_{3-5}	8.50%				
4	8.90%	i_{4-5}	8.40%						
5	8.80%								

EVALUATION OF THE FINANCIAL STRATEGY

The purpose of the previous section was to delineate the market's implied, or expected, interest rates under a variety of term structures of interest rates. If the market's expectations come to fruition, as was assumed, the borrower is neutral as to its financing strategy. Unfortunately, a borrower's vision is not always 20/20. At the time of implementing a financial strategy, the financial manager should compare his or her interest rate forecast against the market's expectations. If a borrower analyzes the market's expectations and formulates a set of lower interest rate projections as the view of future rates, there is an opportunity to more advantageously finance via a rollover strategy or short-date swap. On the other hand, if the financial manager's expectations are for higher rates than the market's expectations, then the financial manager is faced with an opportunity to raise funds more advantageously via a long-term debt instrument including a long-date swap. Personal expectations must be compared to the market's expectations.

Only after the strategy is completed will the financial manager know the degree of success or failure. Comparing the placement of a four-year debt instrument with four annual rollover financings under differing realized annual interest rates provides the evaluation of the strategy on an after-the-fact basis.

The following information was taken from Table 1 and serves to illustrate the foregoing strategies compared to alternative hypothetical realized results:

| | | | Realized Results | | |
Year	Long-Date Strategy	Implied Rates	Rates Decline	Rates Increase	Rates Fluctuate
1	9.00%	8.00%	8.00%	8.00%	8.00%
2	9.00%	9.00%	8.50%	9.50%	9.45%
3	9.00%	9.40%	8.90%	9.90%	9.20%
4	9.00%	9.60%	9.10%	10.10%	9.40%
Cost of $1,000	$1,412	$1,412	$1,392	$1,431	$1,412

As we discussed throughout this chapter, if the financial manager employs a rollover or short-date swap strategy and the market's expectations are realized, the resulting cost of the borrowing

($1,412) is the same as that with a long-date debt instrument. Note that by invoking a four-year debt instrument the interest rate is locked in at 9.00 percent each year.

If the interest rate declines while the borrower is involved with a short-date swap or rollover program, it benefits as noted above. However, if rates increase and the borrower holds to the short-date swap or rollover strategy (because personal expectations are for declining interest rates), the financial manager realizes a higher cost of borrowing. In this case, the cost of financing is $1,431, or $19 more than the four-year debt instrument or long-date swap.

The final column highlights the fact that in a period of fluctuating interest rates, the financial cost of a short-date swap may be the same as the long-date swap without the implied interest rates being realized. In this case, Year 2 had an actual interest rate that was higher than the implied rate, while Years 3 and 4 had an actual interest rate that was lower than implied. In the end, both strategies resulted in an actual cost of $1,412. The final cost is determined via the compounding of the actual interest.

As stated previously, swaps facilitate the conversion of fixed-rate debt to floating-rate or floating-rate to fixed-rate debt. Because a swap can be implemented at the inception of debt borrowing or throughout the life of existing borrowing, a swap is a convenient technique of altering between variable- and fixed-rate financing as the financial manager's views change relative to the market's implied forward rates.

In the final analysis, the value of a short-date swap or a long-date swap financing strategy is seen clearly after the fact. At the time of implementation, the financial manager must understand the market's interest rate expectations, compare those to personal interest rate forecasts, and put in place an appropriate financial strategy. This strategy must be continually reevaluated as the term structure and personal forecasts of interest rates change.

SUMMARY

This chapter has investigated the conditions under which financial managers would prefer, prospectively, a strip of short-date swaps (i.e., variable-rate financing) or a long-date swap (i.e., fixed-rate financing).

The theory of the term structure of interest rates has been reviewed because it provides the theoretical framework for understanding this decision. Armed with this background, some of the basic conditions necessary for either strategy to be dominant were discussed. Of course, the actual behavior of the interest rates will tell us in hindsight which strategy resulted in larger gains (or lower losses).

The question, which is the central point of this chapter, is why a borrower should utilize a short-date swap or a long-date swap. When is a short-date swap preferred? In light of the previous discussion, it becomes apparent that the firm will be better off with the short-date swap if, and only if, personal forecasts of interest rates are below the market's expectations and these forecasts are realized:

Personal interest rate forecasts $<$ market's expectations

and

Realized interest rate $<$ market's expectations

The firm is clearly worse off if it locks itself into a short-date swap and short-term rates climb above the implied rate.

Two final refinements must be mentioned before concluding this chapter:

- Cost of short-date swap.
- Hedging variable interest rate exposure.

When implementing a short-date swap, the financial manager needs to adjust his or her personal interest rate forecast to accommodate transaction costs. This may be reflected as additional borrowing (lump-sum) or as additional required basis points if the swap is implemented.

Finally, a short-date swap may provide opportunities to arbitrage mispricing in the derivative interest rate markets (i.e., futures and options). Careful management and use of these tools offer hedging potentials that could accent the anticipated benefits of short-date swaps while alleviating the risk of volatile interest rates.

In sum, interest rate expectations play a key role, as anticipated, in the choice between a strip of short-date swaps (i.e., variable-rate financing) and a long-date swap (i.e., fixed-rate financing). In addition, this decision is clear-cut only when the financial manager's personal interest rate forecasts are above or below the implied rates during the periods encompassed by the swap. The true test of performance results comes with time and only if the manager's expectations were superior to the market's expectations when compared to the realized interest rates.

Financial managers, of course, must make decisions with incomplete information. The discussion in this chapter should make apparent that understanding the structure of interest rates is necessary for implementing intelligent swap strategies.

CHAPTER 19

A SWAP ALTERNATIVE: EURODOLLAR STRIPS

Ira G. Kawaller
Chicago Mercantile Exchange
New York, New York

Whether for trading or risk-management purposes, managers may choose between interest rate swaps and strips of Eurodollar futures contracts to meet certain of their objectives. Both allow the conversion of a floating-rate exposure to a fixed rate, or vice versa, thereby increasing or decreasing sensitivity to forthcoming interest rate changes. In the case of the swaps, however, the precise fixed rate in question is readily identifiable. For interest rate strips, on the other hand, the ultimate outcome is more obscure and somewhat uncertain. This chapter is designed to provide a methodology for making direct comparisons between Eurodollar strips and interest rate swaps, to ease the task of identifying the more attractively priced instrument. A brief description of swaps and strips precedes the presentation of the methodology.

SWAPS

The standard, or plain vanilla, swap agreement is summarized in Figure 1. Here, two counterparties enter into a contract whereby A calculates an interest rate expense obligation based on a floating

This chapter is largely based on a prior published work: "Interest Rate Swaps versus Eurodollar Strips," *Financial Analysts Journal*, September–October 1989.

FIGURE 1
Plain Vanilla Swap

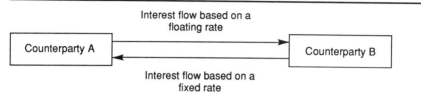

interest rate benchmark, and B calculates an obligation based on a known fixed rate. Clearly, the amount of the interest expense for which A is responsible will rise in a rising rate environment and fall with declining rates. In contrast, B's obligation is constant, based on the stated, notional amount specified by the swap agreement and the contractually determined fixed interest rate. The swap requires periodic interest payments whereby the net, or difference, between the two interest obligations is passed from the party with the greater obligation to the party with the lesser obligation.

Consider the case where A agrees to pay B based on the London Interbank Offered Rate (LIBOR) on three-month Eurodollar deposits, and B agrees to pay A based on a fixed money market rate of 10 percent.[1] Assume a notional amount of $100 million for the swap and quarterly interest payments. With each fixing of LIBOR, A establishes its forthcoming interest obligation. For example, if LIBOR were equal to 10 percent at the first rate setting, no cash adjustment would be made by either party; if LIBOR were 11 percent, counterparty A would pay B $250,000 [($100 million × .11 × ¼) − ($100 million × .10 × ¼)]; and if LIBOR were 9 percent, counterparty B would pay A $250,000 [($100 million × .09 × ¼) − ($100 million × .10 × ¼]. The same process would continue for the term of the contract, following each quarterly reset of LIBOR.

---

[1] Often, the terms of the swap will relate the fixed rate to some benchmark (e.g., 300 basis points above five-year U.S. Treasury securities). This practice allows a general swap agreement to be worked out where the pricing details will reflect market conditions at the time the deal is signed.

Assuming both A and B had no exposure to interest rates prior to executing the swap contract, the swap would expose A to the risk of higher short-term rates and the opportunity of lower rates; B's exposure would be the opposite. Often, however, counterparties will use swaps as an offset for preexisting exposures. In the first case the swap is being used as a trading vehicle, and in the second it is being used as a hedge.

EURODOLLAR STRIPS

The Eurodollar futures contract sets rates on Eurodollar time deposits, commencing on a specific forthcoming date—the third Wednesday of March, June, September, or December, depending on the contract expiration month. Operationally, future prices are derived by subtracting an interest rate (in percentage points, carried to two decimal places) from 100. Therefore, as interest rates rise, futures prices will fall, and vice versa. As the face amount of the Eurodollar futures contract is $1 million and its maturity is three months, every basis point move in the futures price (yield) translates to a value of $25.[2]

For example, a price move from 91.27 to 91.30 (three basis points) will cause the long-position holder to receive $75 per contract, reflecting the $25 value of a basis point noted above. For the short position, that price move will require a payment of the same amount. In practice, the broker facilitates these cash flows; and to protect itself from the contingency of a default on the part of the customer, the broker will require *initial margin,* which is simply a collateral obligation sufficient to cover the potential of one day's exposure.

In general, movements in the Eurodollar futures market will be closely correlated to yield movements in the underlying Eurodollar time deposit market, though changes will not be precisely equal over any given period of time.

As long as one maintains the futures position—either long (hoping the market will rise in price, decline in yield) or short

---

[2] $1,000,000 \times .0001 \times 90/360 = \$25$.

(hoping the market will decline in price, rise in yield)—the participant will be obligated to mark the contract to market on a daily basis and make daily cash settlements for any change in value. This obligation can be terminated at any time by simply trading out of the position (i.e., making the opposite transaction to the initial trade). Upon the expiration of the contract, any participant still maintaining contracts will have a final mark-to-market adjustment, with the final settlement price based on an average derived from a survey of London bankers who report their perception of the cash market three-month Eurodollar offered rate to the Chicago Mercantile Exchange at the time of the survey.

Strips of Eurodollar futures are simply the coordinated purchase or sale of a series of futures contracts with successive expiration dates. The objective of employing a strip is to lock in a rate of return for a term equal to the length of the strip. For example, a strip consisting of contracts with four successive expirations would lock up a one-year term rate; eight successive contracts would lock up a two-year rate, etc. As is the case with swaps, futures strips may be used either to take on additional interest rate risk in the hopes of making trading profits or as an offset, or hedge, to an existing exposure. A buyer of a Eurodollar futures strip would be equivalent to a fixed-rate receiver on an interest rate swap, and a seller of a Eurodollar futures strip would be equivalent to a fixed-rate payer on an interest rate swap.

CALCULATING STRIP YIELDS

In calculating the yield that is implied in a strip of Eurodollar futures contracts, two questions arise. First, what is the term interest rate that can be expected to result from employing a strip of Eurodollar futures? And, second, how should the hedge be constructed to achieve this rate? In fact, the answer depends on the objectives of the strip creator vis-a-vis the decision on how to treat accruing interest. That is, creation of a synthetic zero coupon fixed-income security would require one particular hedge construction, while creation of a synthetic coupon-bearing security would require another. To understand all the various alternatives, we start with the case of the zero coupon strip. This methodology is then adopted for the other, perhaps more typical, case.

Consider the problem of creating a one-year zero coupon strip, when four successive contract expirations would be used. Assume the prices for these contracts are 92.79, 92.51, 92.27, and 92.05, respectively. Under these conditions, the hedger would have four hedgeable events designed to lock up rates of 7.21 percent (100 − 92.79) in the first quarter, 7.49 percent (100 − 92.51) in the second quarter, 7.73 percent (100 − 92.27) in the third quarter, and 7.95 percent (100 − 92.05) in the fourth quarter. The number of contracts required for the hedge is determined by first determining principal plus interest at the end of each quarter. Assume the number of days in each of the quarter are 91, 91, 91, and 92, respectively. If so, at the end of the first quarter the principal plus interest would be calculated by multiplying the starting principal by the first futures' interest rate (7.21 percent) by 91/360.[3] This end-of-quarter value would become the amount to be hedged to the second quarter, etc. Table 1 assumes an initial value of $100 million.

The number of contracts required is found by taking the value of a basis point for each quarter's opening principal (that is, the prior quarter's ending principal plus interest) divided by $25, or the value of the basis point per futures contract. The actual hedge ratio would have to be rounded to a whole number, of course, as futures cannot be bought or sold in fractional units. The calculations are shown in Table 2.

Moving from the specific example to the general methodology, we incorporate the concept of the bond-equivalent yield, which can be derived for a strip of virtually any length (up to the maximum number of quarterly expirations available) from the following formula:

$$
\left(1 + RF1\,\frac{DQ1}{360}\right)\left(1 + RF2\,\frac{DQ2}{360}\right)\left(1 + RF3\,\frac{DQ3}{360}\right)
$$
$$
\cdots \left(1 + RFN\frac{DQN}{360}\right) = (1 + Reff/P))^{N \times P/4} \quad (1)
$$

---

[3] The denominator 360 reflects the convention that LIBOR is quoted as a money market rate, counting the actual number of days during the period in the numerator.

TABLE 1
Strip Hedge Objectives

Quarter	Amount Hedged	Quarterly Futures Interest Rate	Days per Quarter	Principal plus Interest (End of Quarter)
1	$100.00 million	7.21%	91	$101.82
2	101.82	7.49	91	103.75
3	103.75	7.73	91	105.78
4	105.78	7.95	92	107.93

RF1, RF2, RF3, and *RFN* are the respective annual futures rates (100 minus the appropriate futures prices, expressed as decimals); *DQ1, DQ2, DQ3,* and *DQN* are the days in each of the three month periods beginning with the third Wednesday of the respective futures' expiration months;[4] *N* is the number of quarters in the strip; *Reff* is the effective annual bond equivalent yield for the strip; and *P* is the number of periods per year for which compounding is assumed.

TABLE 2
Calculating Hedge Ratios

Quarter	Hedge Ratio Calculations*
1	[$100.0 million × (.0001) × 91/360] /$25 = 101 contracts
2	[$101.82 million × (.0001) × 91/360] /$25 = 103 contracts
3	[$103.75 million × (.0001) × 91/360] /$25 = 105 contracts
4	[$105.78 million × (.0001) × 92/360] /$25 = 108 contracts

* This hedge construction implicitly assumes that the rate on the Eurodollar strip will move point for point with the rate on the exposed instrument. Clearly, this assumption may be modified by simply adjusting the hedge ratios by a factor designed to take into account the expected relative rate change.

---

[4] One should measure the number of days in the quarter by counting from the calendar day of the third Wednesday of the expiration month to that same calendar day, three months later (e.g., March 17 to June 17, which measures 92 days).

The left-hand side of Equation 1 shows the effect of borrowing (or lending) for each quarter at the interest rate designated by the appropriate futures contract. The right-hand side incorporates the effective yield that would be required to generate the same principal plus interest by the end of the term. In all cases, effective yields are approximations, as the periods covered by the futures contracts may either overlap or have gaps.[5] Despite the fact that futures expire quarterly, one may calculate an effective term rate assuming any compounding frequency. Most likely, the choice of P would reflect the compounding assumptions implicit in the fixed-rate quotation of an instrument to which the strip yield may be compared.

Returning to the conditions in the above example where a one-year strip was arranged with contracts priced at 92.79, 92.51, 92.27, and 92.05, respectively, the target one-year return is 7.93 percent.[6] To demonstrate the robustness of this hedge, two extreme cases are shown. End-of-quarter balances are found by investing the initial $100 million at the spot LIBOR, but adjusting the ending principal plus interest by the gains or losses on that quarter's hedge. Such practice is consistent with the accounting tradition of allocating hedge results to the quarter for which the hedge is designed. On a cash flow basis, however, hedge gains and losses for all contracts are generated daily with the variation margin adjustments. Returns calculated from actual cash flows, therefore, would differ from the calculations shown.

In the first case (Table 3) it is assumed that LIBOR immediately skyrockets to 15 percent and remains there, following the

---

[5] That is, the value date of Eurodollar futures contracts is always the third Wednesday of the contract month, and the underlying instrument is the three-month deposit that would mature three months later, on the same calendar day. That maturity day, however, may not coincide with the value date of the subsequent futures. For example, the value date of the March futures might be March 18, while the value date of the June futures might *not* be the 18th. If the third Wednesday of June were earlier, the cycle would result in some overlap of the hypothetical deposits. On the other hand, if the value date were later, the cycle would result in some gaps.

[6] This result follows from an ending principal plus interest of $107.93 million, one year after an initial principal of $100 million. It assumes $P = 1$.

TABLE 3
Case 1: Interest Rates Rise to 15 Percent

Quarter	Futures results*
1	101 contracts × (85.00 − 92.79 × $2,500 = −$1.97 million
2	103 contracts × (85.00 − 92.51 × $2,500 = −$1.93 million
3	105 contracts × (85.00 − 92.27 × $2,500 = −$1.91 million
4	108 contracts × (85.00 − 92.05 × $2,500 = −$1.90 million

Quarter	End of Quarter Balances
1	$100 million $(1 + .15^{91}/_{360})$ − $1.97 million = $101.82 million
2	$101.82 million $(1 + .15^{91}/_{360})$ − $1.93 million = $103.75 million
3	$103.75 million $(1 + .15^{91}/_{360})$ − $1.91 million = $105.78 million
4	$105.78 million $(1 + .15^{92}/_{360})$ − $1.90 million = $107.93 million

* As prices are reflective of percentage points, rather than basis points, the multiplier becomes $25 × 100, or $2,500. Positive values indicate gains; negative values indicate losses.

initiation of the hedge. Thus, all futures are liquidated at 85.00. In the second case (Table 4) it is assumed that LIBOR drops to 2 percent and remains there; thus, all futures are liquidated at 98.00. Both cases result in identical ending balances, demonstrating the robustness of the hedge.

TABLE 4
Case 2: Interest Rates Decline to 2 Percent

Quarter	Futures results
1	101 contracts × (98.00 − 92.79 × $2,500 = −$1.32 million
2	103 contracts × (98.00 − 92.51 × $2,500 = −$1.41 million
3	105 contracts × (98.00 − 92.27 × $2,500 = −$1.50 million
4	108 contracts × (98.00 − 92.05 × $2,500 = −$1.61 million

Quarter	End of Quarter Balances
1	$100 million $(1 + .02^{91}/_{360})$ + $1.32 million = $101.82 million
2	$101.82 million $(1 + .02^{91}/_{360})$ + $1.41 million = $103.75 million
3	$103.75 million $(1 + .02^{91}/_{360})$ + $1.50 million = $105.78 million
4	$105.78 million $(1 + .02^{92}/_{360})$ + $1.61 million = $107.93 million

REAL WORLD CONSIDERATIONS

Despite the apparent precision shown, it should be recognized that the analysis assumes perfect convergence between LIBOR and the Eurodollar futures rate each time a futures contract expires or is liquidated. In fact, a nonzero basis at the time of hedge liquidations could alter the results.[7] The size of this effect, of course, depends on the magnitudes and directions of the basis upon liquidation. For the long strip (that is, where the futures contracts are originally purchased), a desirable liquidation basis is one where LIBOR is higher than the rate implied by the futures contract. An undesirable basis upon liquidation is one where LIBOR is below the futures rate. For the short strip, the opposite characterizations apply. A worthwhile exercise assumes a worst-case basis, based on possible adverse market conditions that might apply when the futures contracts are liquidated.[8]

Returning to Case 1 as an example, and assuming a long strip were created with LIBOR at 15 percent, assume the worst case of futures liquidation at 84.75, or a rate of 15.25 percent for each futures contract. The worst-case projected results differ from the previous results because of the somewhat greater futures losses in each quarter—the differences equaling the number of contracts for that quarter's hedge times 25 basis points times $25 per basis point, as shown in Table 5.

Because of the greater futures losses, a return of 7.65 percent results, rather than a bond-equivalent yield of 7.93 percent as initially targeted. Given the subjective nature of the estimate of the worst case circumstance, however, a more judgmental approach may be incorporated at this stage. The above calculation demonstrates that the adverse basis of 25 basis points at each hedge liquidation lowers the perfect convergence target by 28 basis points (7.93 percent − 7.65 percent)—just about one for one. Importantly, the magnitude of this anticipated liquidation basis is

---

[7] The basis is the difference between the spot market price (or rate) and the futures market price (or rate).

[8] The existence of gaps or overlaps due to the futures expiration cycle can be considered as a special case contributing to this risk.

TABLE 5
Worst-Case Scenario

Quarter	Futures results
1	101 contracts × (84.75 − 92.79 × $2,500 = −$2.03 million
2	103 contracts × (84.75 − 92.51 × $2,500 = −$2.00 million
3	105 contracts × (84.75 − 92.27 × $2,500 = −$1.97 million
4	108 contracts × (84.75 − 92.05 × $2,500 = −$1.97 million

Quarter	End of Quarter Balances
1	$100 million (1 + .15⁹¹⁄₃₆₀) − $2.03 million = $101.76 million
2	$101.76 million (1 + .15⁹²⁄₃₆₀) − $2.00 million = $103.62 million
3	$103.62 million (1 + .15⁹¹⁄₃₆₀) − $1.97 million = $105.58 million
4	$105.58 million (1 + .15⁹²⁄₃₆₀) − $1.97 million = $107.65 million

judgmentally determined, and in many cases this actual outcome would likely be substantially smaller than that just shown. For example, this effect could be virtually negligible in the case where hedges are scheduled for liquidation at or near futures' expiration dates. It should also be realized that the basis conditions upon the hedge liquidation may be favorable, in which case the hedge performance would be better than that indicated by the perfect convergence calculation.

EXTENSIONS AND REFINEMENTS

When considering the strip as an alternative to another fixed-income security, one should try to arrange the strip so it mirrors the cash flow properties of the competing instrument as closely as possible. As an example, if the alternative to the strip is a two-year swap where the fixed payments are scheduled semiannually, the strip should be formulated to replicate semiannual cash disbursements.

To clarify the process, think about the two-year fixed-income obligation as if it were a series of four six-month zero coupon strips, where the bond-equivalent yield of each six month strip would be calculated and implemented as explained in the previous section. The effective rate for the whole two-year period would reflect compounding of all substrip segments. The appropriate general formula follows:

$$(1 + BEY1/P)^t(1 + BEY2/P)^t \cdots (1 + BEYK/P)^t = (1 + R/P)^{Kt} \quad (2)$$

where $BEYi$ = the bond-equivalent yield of the ith substrip,

P = the assumed number of compounding periods per year,

t = length of each substrip in compounding periods,

K = the number of substrips,

R = the annualized yield to maturity.

For illustrative purposes, consider the prices in Table 6 relevant to the above synthetic two-year semiannual-coupon fixed-income construction.

Days per quarter are counted rigorously, from the third Wednesday of the expiration month to that calendar day three months later, and the two-quarter strip yields are calculated using the methodology of Equation 1.[9] Next, using the bond-equivalent yield from Table 6 and incorporating equation (2), one can find the annualized yield to maturity R. In this case R = 9.18 percent.

The final step needed to realize this outcome is to set up the hedge properly. As this synthetic construction is designed to mimic a security with semiannual coupons, the amount to be hedged in the first, third, fifth, and seventh quarter will be the notional amount of the deal. Assuming a $100 million deal, given the respective days in each of these quarters, the hedge ratios are 100, 100, 102, and 100 contracts, respectively (see Table 7). For the remaining quarters (two, four, six, and eight) the calculation takes the original notional amount plus the interest income from the prior quarter, based on that quarter's futures rate. That is, the hedge ratio for the second quarter depends on the futures rate locked up in the first quarter, the hedge ratio for the fourth quarter depends

---

[9] P of Equation 1 is assumed to reflect semiannual compounding for these calculations.

TABLE 6
Futures Prices and Board Equivalent Yields (BEYs)

Contract Expirations	Futures Price	Days per Quarter	BEY Two-Quarter Strips
1	91.22	90	
2	91.34	92	8.91
3	91.21	90	
4	91.04	92	9.08
5	90.87	92	
6	90.90	91	9.37
7	90.82	90	
8	90.75	91	9.37

on the third quarter's futures rate, and so on. These calculations are shown in Table 7.

As was the case with the zero coupon strip construction, the actual outcomes may differ somewhat from the calculated target due to rounding errors and the prospect of imperfect convergence. Thus, we should give appropriate allowance for some deviation from these calculations when determining whether or not to choose a strip as the preferred transaction vehicle. With these considerations in mind, failure to choose the alternative with the more

TABLE 7
Hedge Construction: $100 Million with Semiannual Coupons and Two-Year Maturity

Quarter	Hedge Ratio	
1	$100 million $\times$ .0001 $\times$ 90/360/25 =	100
2	$100 million $\times$ (1 + .0878 $\times$ 90/360) $\times$ .0001 $\times$ 92/360/25 =	104
3	$100 million $\times$ .0001 $\times$ 90/360/25 =	100
4	$100 million $\times$ (1 + .0879 $\times$ 90/360) $\times$ .0001 $\times$ 92/360/25 =	104
5	$100 million $\times$ .0001 $\times$ 92/360/25 =	102
6	$100 million $\times$ (1 + .0913 $\times$ 92/360) $\times$ .0001 $\times$ 91/360/25 =	103
7	$100 million $\times$ .0001 $\times$ 90/360/25 =	100
8	$100 million $\times$ (1 + .0918 $\times$ 90/360) $\times$ .0001 $\times$ 91/360/25 =	103

(most) attractive yield necessarily leaves money on the table and thus reflects a suboptimal market decision.

STRIPS VERSUS SWAPS

It should be clear from the above discussion that the Eurodollar strip may substitute for interest rate swaps in certain cases. It may not be suitable to make the substitution in all cases, however. Specifically, the primary constraint is the length of the futures expiration cycle. Currently, the Eurodollar expirations extend for four years, suggesting that Eurodollar strips may best be used in conjunction with or in place of relatively short-term interest rate swaps (i.e., swaps with less than a four-year term). For longer terms, one might be tempted to take temporary futures positions in available expirations and then roll these trades into the appropriate month, once they become available for trading. This strategy, however, may be somewhat risky, as the relative prices in place at the time of the roll will vary with changing yield curve positions. Importantly, this risk may also turn out to be an opportunity, as the outcome may yield more, rather than less, desirable results.

Aside from the pure price considerations, some other institutional aspects of future versus swaps should be appreciated by potential users:

1. Being a principal-to-principal transaction, swaps can be tailored to meet the individual needs of the counterparties, reflecting very specific timing and exposure characteristics. In contrast, Eurodollar futures are standardized with respect to both timing and dollar values.
2. The arrangement of a swap involves a single transaction at its inception. Futures require periodic subsequent transaction as well. That is, at each rate-fixing date, those contracts designed to hedge that specific exposure need to be liquidated or offset. Thus, futures require more ongoing maintenance and managerial effort than do swaps.
3. A secondary managerial difference deals with cash flow

characteristics of the two alternatives. The daily marking to market, required by futures but not by swaps, may result in cash inflows or outflows with associated profit and tax implications. The former case enhances the economics of the deal, while the latter case detracts.[10] Additionally, the harder to measure managerial costs of handling this cash flow obligation are associated with futures but absent for swaps.

4. Bid-Ask spreads will vary in the swap market, depending on the identity of the counterparty. Greater acceptance in the marketplace will mean more liquidity and thus tighter spreads. In contrast, standardization of the Eurodollar futures allows for significantly tighter bid-ask spreads.

5. Each swap deal requires a separate settlement and documentation for each counterparty. Thus, the first deal with any new counterparty requires substantial preliminary work and legal attention. For futures, once the broker/customer agreement is signed, the whole market becomes accessible, virtually instantaneously.

6. With futures, buying and selling (or initiating and liquidating) positions is equally easy, with no market penalty or widening of bid-ask spreads associated with an offsetting transaction. The same statement may not be the case with swaps. Reversing a swap will typically require some accommodation by the counterparty, for which there will likely be a market impact.

7. With a swap on the books, the rise of default is everpresent, and the cost of nonperformance may be considerable. In contrast, with exchange-traded futures, the credit exposure rests with the clearing house, and daily marking to market and cash settlement practices serve to virtually eliminate the kind of counterparty risk associated with swaps.

---

[10] A process called *tailing* can be implemented to mitigate this effect. See Chicago Mercantile Exchange strategy paper by I. G. Kawaller, "Hedging with Futures Contracts: Going the Extra Mile."

CONCLUSION

Though swaps and Eurodollar strips each have their own special features or characteristics, they are perhaps more similar than they are different. Each can be used to convert a fixed-rate exposure to floating, or vice versa; each can be used for trading or hedging purposes; and each can serve as an offset, or hedge, for the other. The most intelligent use of the markets, therefore, allows for using the two markets, choosing the more attractive, whenever the need exists.

Constructing Eurodollar strips requires a certain amount of care and tailoring in order to make proper comparisons with alternative instruments. Inappropriate yield calculations and improper hedge implementation obviously could cause either the incorrect choice or unexpected results. Whenever employing a strip, one should try to match the cash flow provisions of the competing alternative instrument as closely as possible. The payoff for correctly making this calculation and implementing it properly is achieving incrementally superior returns. Certainly, choosing the more attractively priced alternative will necessarily enhance performance.

PART 5

PERIPHERAL ISSUES

CHAPTER 20

INTEREST RATE SWAP CREDIT EXPOSURE AND CAPITAL REQUIREMENTS

Larry D. Wall
Federal Reserve Bank of Atlanta
Atlanta, Georgia
John J. Pringle
University of North Carolina at Chapel Hill
James E. McNulty
Florida Atlantic University
Boca Raton, Florida

Interest rate swaps have become an important tool for managing corporate interest rate risk. However, both participants in a swap take on potential credit risk, the risk that the other side of the swap will be unable to make the promised payments. Financial intermediaries are participants in the swap market in part to control their own interest rate risk but also to help reduce the costs of credit evaluation for nonfinancial users of swaps.[1] Financial intermediaries can reduce the costs of credit evaluation by standing between two swap users, thus eliminating the need for the users to evaluate each other's credit quality. Most of the swap volume at major

---

[1] L. D. Wall and J. J. Pringle, "Alternative Explanations of Interest Rate Swaps: A Theoretical and Empirical Analysis," *Financial Management*, Summer 1989, pp. 59–73, find that 109 of the 250 firms disclosing the use of interest rate swaps in their financial statements are either commercial banks or thrifts.

international commercial banks has been a result of the banks providing swaps as a product to large institutional customers.

The regulators of depositories have noted the growth of the swap market and have become concerned about the effect of interest rate swaps on depositories' interest rate and credit risk. Swaps may increase or decrease depositories' overall interest rate risk, depending on the position taken by the depository (fixed-rate payer versus floating-rate payer), the duration of the firm's assets, and the duration of its liabilities. Swaps unambiguously increase the credit riskiness of a depository. The credit losses may occur when the other party defaults on a swap that has positive market value to the depository.

The principal concern of central banks and other commercial bank regulators has been on the effect of swaps on the credit riskiness of banks. The regulators' concern about credit risk is reflected in plans for risk-based capital regulation, which were recently adopted in Basle by the central banks of 12 major industrial countries.[2] The U.S. thrift regulatory agencies have focused primarily on the potential for swaps to reduce thrifts' interest rate risk. In 1986 the Federal Home Loan Bank Board provided reductions in required capital to thrifts that controlled their asset-liability gap, and it is currently proposing greater integration of capital requirements with a measure of interest rate risk.

This chapter (a) analyzes both the interest rate and credit risk associated with swaps and (b) considers treatment of swaps by bank and thrift regulators, including recently announced capital requirements.

RISKS ASSOCIATED WITH SWAPS

Interest rate swap contracts are subject to several types of risk. Among the more important are interest rate, or position, risk and credit risk. Interest rate risk arises because changes in market

---

[2] The framework was approved by the Group of Ten countries (Belgium, Canada, France, the Federal Republic of Germany, Italy, Japan, the Netherlands, Sweden, the United Kingdom, and the United States) together with Switzerland and Luxembourg.

interest rates cause a change in a swap's value. Credit risk occurs because either party may default on a swap contract. Both participants in a swap are subject to each type of risk.

Interest Rate Risk

As market interest rates change, interest rate swaps generate gains or losses that are equal to the change in the replacement cost of the swap. These gains and losses allow swaps to serve (*a*) as a hedge that a company can use to reduce its risk or (*b*) as a speculative tool that increases the firm's total risk. A swap represents a hedge if gains or losses generated by the swap offset changes in the market values of a company's assets, liabilities, and off-balance sheet activities such as interest rate futures and options. However, a swap is speculative to the extent that the firm deliberately increases its risk position to profit from expected changes in interest rates.

The determination of whether and how to use a swap is straightforward for a firm that is a user, one which enters into a swap agreement solely to adjust its own financial position.[3] First, the company evaluates its own exposure to future changes in interest rates, including any planned investments and new financings. Then, it makes a judgment on the future levels and volatility of interest rates. Firms wishing greater exposure to market rate changes enter into swaps as speculators. Alternatively, if less exposure is desired, the company enters into a swap as a hedge.

The problem facing a dealer—a firm that enters into a swap to earn fee income—is more complicated. A dealer may enter into a swap to hedge changes in market rates or to speculate in a manner similar to users. However, a dealer may also enter into a swap to satisfy a customer's request even when the dealer wants no change in its interest rate exposure.[4] In this case, the dealer must find some way of hedging the swap transaction.

---

[3] This analysis does not consider the use of the futures, forwards, and options markets. See C. W. Smithson, "A LEGO® Approach to Financial Engineering: An Introduction to Forwards, Futures, Swaps, and Options," *Midland Corporate Finance Review* 4 (Winter 1987), pp. 16–28, for a discussion of the various financial instruments that may be used to control interest rate risk.

[4] The dealer may also enter into a swap for a customer even though the dealer desires a change in exposure in a direction opposite to the swap.

FIGURE 1
Interest Rate Swap with a Dealer

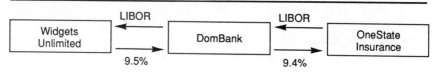

The simplest hedge for one swap transaction by a dealer is another swap transaction whose terms are the exact opposite of the first swap. An example of this arrangement is given in Figure 1, in which the dealer's promised floating-rate payments of LIBOR to Widgets Unlimited is exactly offset by OneState's promise to pay LIBOR. Similarly, the fixed payments to OneState Insurance are covered by Widget's promised fixed payments, and, the dealer, DomBank, is left with a small spread. This combination of swaps is referred to as a *matched pair*. Two problems arise from relying on matched pairs: (*a*) The dealer is exposed to interest rate changes during the time needed to find another party interested in a matching swap, and (*b*) the dealer may be relatively better at arranging swaps with fixed-rate payers and, thus, have problems finding floating-rate payers to execute the matching swap (or vice versa).

An alternative to hedging one swap with another swap is to rely on debt securities, or on futures or options on debt securities, to provide a hedge. In Steven D. Felgran's example, a dealer agrees to pay a fixed rate and receive a floating rate from a customer.[5] The dealer uses the floating-rate receipts to support a bank loan, which is then used to purchase a Treasury security of the same maturity and value as the swap. Any gains or losses on the swap are subsequently offset by losses or gains on the Treasury security. Felgran does note one problem with using Treasury securities to hedge a swap: The spread between them and interest rate swaps may vary over time.[6] According to Felgran, dealers are unable to hedge float-

---

[5] "Interest Rate Swaps: Use, Risk, and Prices," *New England Economic Review*, November/December 1987, pp. 22–32.

[6] Indeed, some variation in the spread should be expected since the Treasury yield curve incorporates coupon interest payments and principal repayments at the maturity of the security, whereas the swap contract provides only for periodic interest payments.

ing-rate payments perfectly. Sources of risk include differences in payment dates and floating-rate reset days, disparities in maturity and principal, and *basis risk,* that is, the risk associated with hedging floating payments based on one index with floating payments based on another index.

Using the futures market to hedge swaps also entails certain drawbacks. Lee M. Wakeman points to the "additional risk created by the cash/futures basis volatility."[7] He also notes that matching the fixed-rate payments from a swap with the Treasury security of the closest maturity may not be optimal when the Treasury security is thinly traded. As an alternative he suggests that on-the-run (highly liquid) Treasury issues be used for hedging. The investment amount and type of issues to be used may be determined by applying a duration-matching strategy. Still, this approach is unlikely to eliminate interest rate risk for the swap dealer since duration matching provides a perfect hedge only under very restrictive assumptions.

Credit Risk

Aside from interest rate and basis risk, both interest rate swap participants are subject to the risk that the other party will default. The maximum amount of the loss associated with this credit risk is measured by the swap's replacement cost, which is essentially the cost of entering into a new swap under current market conditions with rates equal to those on the swap being replaced.

A simple example can demonstrate the credit risk of swaps. Suppose that Widgets Unlimited agreed to pay a fixed rate of 9.5 percent to DomBank, and in return Widgets would receive LIBOR on a semiannual basis through January 1994. If the market rate on new swaps maturing in January 1994 subsequently fell to 8 percent, the swap would have positive value to DomBank. However, if Widgets defaults, Dombank could lose this value and may have to pay an up-front fee to entice a third party to enter into a swap whereby DomBank receives its contractual fixed rate of 9.5 per-

---

[7] "The Portfolio Approach to Swaps Management," unpublished working paper, Chemical Bank Capital Markets Group, May 1986, p. 15.

cent. DomBank will suffer a credit loss if Widgets becomes bankrupt while the rate is 8 percent and pays only a fraction of its obligations to creditors. On the other hand, if the rate on swaps maturing in January 1994 rises to 10.5 percent and DomBank defaults, Widgets may suffer a credit loss.

This example demonstrates that both parties to an interest rate swap may be subject to credit risk at some time during the life of a swap contract. However, only one party at a time will be subject to credit risk. If rates in the example fall to 8 percent, the floating-rate payer, DomBank, can suffer credit losses, but Widgets is not exposed to credit risk. That is, the swap has negative value to Widgets when the market rate is 8 percent; Widgets would be happy to drop the swap agreement if DomBank were to go bankrupt. In practice, though, Widgets is unlikely to gain from DomBank's failure because DomBank's successors will attempt to recover the value of the swap as a part of a bankruptcy proceeding.[8]

One way of reducing the credit risk associated with swaps is for one or both parties to post collateral. Some swaps provide for collateral but most do not. According to Felgran (see note 5 above), swap collateralization is of uncertain value because such documentation has yet to be adequately tested in court. Moreover, some parties that would be happy to receive collateral are themselves reluctant to post it when swap rates move against them. Certain commercial banks in particular have a strong incentive to avoid collateralization. Such institutions take credit risks in the ordinary course of business and are comfortable with assuming

---

[8] Swap contracts may provide for payments in default in one of two ways: (a) one-sided payments in which only the defaulting party is liable or (b) mutual payment where either party may be liable depending on the market value of the swap at the time of default. S. K. Henderson recommends the mutual payment option in "Exposures of Swaps and Termination Provisions of Swap Agreements," in *Swap Finance*, vol. 2, (London: Euromoney Publications Limited, 1986), pp. 125–41. He suggests that the one-sided payment provisions increase the risk that the bankruptcy court will rule that the default provisions of a swap contract contain penalty aspects that are against public policy and, therefore, are unenforceable. See also S. K. Henderson and A. C. Cates, "Termination Provisions of Swap Agreements under U.S. and English Insolvency Laws," in *Swap Finance*, vol. 2, ed. Boris Antl (London: Euromoney Publications Limited, 1986), pp. 91–102, for a discussion of terminating a swap under the insolvency laws of the United States and the United Kingdom.

credit risk on interest rate swaps. Investment bankers, on the other hand, are typically at risk for only short periods of time with their nonswap transactions and are not as experienced in evaluating credit risk. Thus, the continued presence of credit risk in the swap market strengthens the relative competitive position of commercial banks.

Empirical Research on Credit Risk

Several simulation studies have explored the magnitude of the credit risk associated with individual swaps or matched pairs of swaps. Most of these studies have found the risk to be relatively small. Marcelle Arak, Laurie S. Goodman, and Arthur Rones examined the credit exposure—or maximum credit loss—of a single interest rate swap to determine the amount of a firm's credit line that is used by a swap.[9] They assumed that short-term rates follow a random walk with no drift; in other words, the change in short-term rates does not depend on the current level of, or past changes in, short-term rates. After the swap begins, the floating-rate component of the swap is assumed to move one standard deviation each year in the direction of maximum credit exposure. The standard deviation of interest rates is calculated using 1985 data on Treasury issues. For these data, their results suggest that until the swap matures, the maximum annual credit loss on swaps is likely to be between 1 and 2 percent of notional principal.

J. Gregg Whittaker investigated the credit exposure of interest rate swaps in order to develop a formula for swap pricing.[10] Using an options pricing formula to value swaps and assuming that inter-

---

[9] "Credit Lines for New Instruments: Swaps, Over-the-Counter Options, Forwards, and Floor-Ceiling Agreements," in *Conference on Bank Structure and Competition* (Chicago: Federal Reserve Bank of Chicago, 1986), pp. 437–56. One way that banks typically limit their risk to individual borrowers is to establish a maximum amount that the organization is willing to lend to the borrower, called the borrower's credit line. The amount of a credit line used by a loan is the principal of the loan; however, the amount of the line used by a swap is less clear since a swap's maximum credit loss is a function of market interest rates.

[10] "Pricing Interest Rate Swaps in an Options Pricing Framework," working paper RWP 87-02, Federal Reserve Bank of Kansas City, 1987.

est rates follow a log-normal distribution and volatility amounts to one standard deviation, Whittaker found that the maximum exposure for a 10-year matched pair of swaps does not exceed 8 percent of the notional principal.

The Federal Reserve Board and the Bank of England studied the potential increase in credit exposure of a matched pair of swaps.[11] The study's purpose was to develop a measure of the credit exposure associated with a matched pair of swaps that is comparable to the credit exposure of on-balance sheet loans. The results were used to help determine the regulatory capital requirements for interest rate swaps. The joint central bank research assumes that, for regulatory purposes, the swap's credit exposure should be equal to its current exposure, that is, the replacement cost plus some surcharge to capture potential increases in credit exposure. The investigation uses a Monte Carlo simulation technique to evaluate the probabilities associated with different potential increases in credit exposure.[12] Interest rates are assumed to follow a log-normal, random-walk distribution, with the volatility measure equal to the 90th percentile value of changes in interest rates over six-month intervals from 1981 to mid-1986.[13] The credit exposure of each matched pair is calculated every six months and the resulting exposures are averaged over the life of the swap. At the 70 percent confidence level, they find the potential increase in credit exposure will be no greater than 0.5 percent of the notional principal of the swap per year; at the 99 percent confidence level, they find the credit risk exposure to be no greater than 1 percent of the notional principal.[14]

Terrence M. Belton followed this line of research in analyzing the potential increase in swap credit exposure, but he used a differ-

---

[11] See also M. Muffet, "Modeling Credit Exposure on Swaps," in *Conference on Bank Structure and Competition* (Chicago: Federal Reserve Bank of Chicago, 1987), pp. 473–96.

[12] The Monte Carlo technique involves repeated simulations wherein a key value, in this case an interest rate, is drawn from a random sample.

[13] The study defined the 100th percentile as the largest observed change.

[14] See C. W. Smith, C. W. Smithson, and L. M. Wakeman, "Credit Risk and the Scope of Regulation of Swaps," in *Conference on Bank Structure and Competition* (Chicago: Federal Reserve Bank of Chicago, 1987), pp. 166–85, for a critical analysis of the Federal Reserve and Bank of England study.

ent method of simulating interest rates.[15] Belton estimated a vector autoregressive model over the period from January 1970 to November 1986 to estimate seven different Treasury rates. (Vector autoregressive models estimate current values of some dependent variables—in this case, interest rates at various maturities—as a function of current and past values of selected variables. Belton used current and past interest rates as explanatory variables.) Changes in the term structure were then simulated by drawing a set of random errors from the joint distribution of rates and solving for future values at each maturity. In effect, Belton's procedure allows the historical shape of the yield curve at historical changes in its level and shape to determine the value of various interest rates in his stimulations. Belton's analysis differs from prior studies in that he used stochastic, or random, default rates rather than focusing exclusively on maximum credit exposure. His results imply that the potential increase in credit exposure of swaps caused by rate changes can be covered by adding a surcharge of 1 to 5 percent of the notional principal to the current exposure for swaps with a maturity of 2 to 12 years.

While the foregoing analyses suggest several ways of estimating the increased credit exposure associated with matched pairs of swaps these approaches might not be completely applicable to banks' swap portfolios. Starting with the assumption that banks use matched pairs of swaps and that the swaps are entered into at market interest rates, the fixed rate on the matched pairs will change over time as interest rates move up and down. Larry D. Wall and Kwun-wing C. Fung pointed out that if rates have fluctuated over a certain range, a bank may have credit exposure on some swaps in which it receives a fixed rate and on others in which it receives a floating rate.[16] In this case, an increase in rates generates an increase in the credit exposure of swaps in which the bank receives a floating rate, but also causes a decrease in the exposure

---

[15] "Credit Risk in Interest Rate Swaps," working paper, Board of Governors of the Federal Reserve System, April 1987.

[16] "Evaluating the Credit Exposure of Interest Rate Swap Portfolios," working paper 87-8, Federal Reserve Bank of Atlanta, December 1987.

of swaps in which the bank receives a fixed rate. Similarly, a decrease in rates will increase the exposure on the swaps in which the bank receives a fixed rate and decrease exposure on those in which the bank receives a floating rate.[17]

In a more empirical vein, Kathleen Neal and Katrina Simons simulated the total credit exposure of a portfolio of 20 matched pairs of interest rate swaps.[18] The initial portfolio was generated by originating one pair of five-year swaps per quarter from the fourth quarter of 1981 through the fourth quarter of 1986 at the prevailing interest rate. For the period 1987 through 1991, the interest rates were generated randomly, based on the volatility observed in historical rates.[19] The maturing matched pair was dropped each quarter from the sample, and a new five-year swap was added to the portfolio at the simulated interest rates. After running several thousand simulations, and assuming a portfolio of interest rate swaps with a notional principal of $10 million, Neal and Simons found the average maximum credit loss to be $185,000 and the 90th percentile exposure, $289,000.

No single correct approach is available to determine the expected credit exposure on an interest rate swap. The results may be influenced by the assumptions that are made about the distribution of future interest rates. However, as indicated here, several studies using different methodologies have reached the conclusion that the maximum exposure on a matched pair of swaps is unlikely

---

[17] Consider two matched pairs of swaps. For the first matched pair the bank agrees to two swaps: (a) The bank pays a fixed rate of 11 percent and receives LIBOR on the first swap, and (b) the bank pays LIBOR and receives 11 percent. For the second matched pair the bank pays and receives a 9 percent fixed rate for LIBOR. Assume that the notional principal, maturity, and repricing interval of all swaps are equal. If the current market rate for swaps of the same maturity is 10 percent, the bank has credit exposure on the 9 percent fixed-rate swap in which it pays a fixed rate of interest and has credit exposure on the 11 percent fixed-rate swap in which it pays a floating rate of interest. If the market rate on comparable swaps increases to 10.5 percent, credit exposure increases on the 9 percent swap in which the dealer pays a fixed rate, and it decreases on the 11 percent swap in which the dealer pays a floating rate. Given the assumptions of this example, the change in exposure is almost zero when the market rate moves from 10 percent to 10.5 percent.

[18] "Interest Rate Swaps, Currency Swaps, and Credit Risk," *Issues in Bank Regulation,* Spring 1988, pp. 26–29.

[19] The paper does not explain how swap replacement values and interest rate volatility were calculated.

to exceed a small fraction of the swaps' notional principal. Moreover, the analysis of a single matched pair may overstate the expected exposure of a swap portfolio. Therefore, additional simulations of portfolio risk may be appropriate to determine the exposure of swap dealers. Dominique Jackson has reported that a survey of 71 dealers showed that 11 firms had experienced losses with "total write-offs accounting for $33 million on portfolios which totaled a notional (principal) of $283 billion."[20]

REGULATION AND THE SWAP MARKET

Thrifts

Thrifts, of course, have traditionally had mismatched maturities and a need to hedge their interest rate risk.[21] However, most hedging techniques were not specifically authorized by regulation until the early 1980s. In 1981, thrifts were specifically authorized for the first time to use futures and options to control their interest rate risk. Futures, however, turned out to be a poor instrument for hedging for many thrifts. The reasons for this are examined briefly in order to illustrate how swaps came to be encouraged by thrift regulators as an alternative way of controlling interest rate risk.

Using financial futures for hedging interest rate risk for a thrift requires taking a short position in the futures market in order to protect the institution if interest rates should go up. What happened between 1982 and 1986, of course, was that interest rates fell substantially. As a result, many thrifts experienced huge losses on their hedge positions.

Even the most well-constructed short hedge in the financial futures market will produce hedge losses if interest rates come down. These hedge losses are the natural consequence of the hedge positions that have been previously established to produce the hedge gains that are supposed to protect the institution if rates

---

[20] "Swaps Keep in Step with the Regulators," *Financial Times,* August 10, 1988, p. 22.

[21] The discussion of thrift regulation is based in part on J.E . McNulty, "Interest Rate Risk: Lessons Learned and Questions Unanswered," *Journal of Retail Banking,* Fall 1987, pp. 29–34.

rise. Futures positions, of course, have to be marked to market daily (swaps do not). While thrifts, like most financial institutions, follow book value accounting practices, market losses on futures positions have to be recorded as losses immediately (although they are normally deferred over the remaining time to maturity of the instrument being hedged). Market gains on the hedged assets on the other side of the balance sheet would not qualify for similar treatment. In addition, the margin calls create an immediate cash outflow for the thrift.

The combination of large deferred losses and cash outflows as a result of *declining* interest rates created tremendous psychological problems for an industry that had just experienced huge realized losses because of the *rising* interest rates of the 1979–82 period. These losses convinced many boards of directors, as well as many regulators, that hedging in the futures market is not an appropriate activity for the institutions for which they are responsible.[22] In addition, continued management of futures positions requires a level of expertise that many thrifts do not possess. The fact that Treasury bill futures contracts extend only two years forward also makes the futures markets difficult to use for institutions that want to hedge their long-term liability costs.

The interest rate swap market became a natural place where thrift financial managers could turn to avoid these problems. Statements by thrift regulators that cash market hedging, such as interest rate swaps and interest rate caps, was more suitable for thrifts than futures hedging provided another stimulus to the use of swaps to manage the interest rate risk of thrift institutions. With swaps, of course, margin calls do not exist and other problems such as basis risk are more manageable. As a result of these developments, many thrift financial managers became much more comfortable with swaps than with other hedging techniques.

The suitability of swaps for hedging mortgage portfolios has also been confirmed by research. Robert Crane and Peter Elmer simulated the performance of a number of asset and liability struc-

---

[22] While the official regulatory attitude toward futures has not changed since the early 1980s, many, if not most, regional thrift regulatory officials do not have a favorable attitude toward futures for the reasons mentioned here.

tures for a financial institution under 1,500 different interest rate scenarios.[23] The strategy that performed best on a risk-return basis was to fund fixed-rate assets (in this case, 15-year mortgages) with deposits that had been extended in maturity using interest rate swaps. In fact, swaps performed so well in these simulations that they reduced the risk of 15-year fixed-rate mortgages below that of a strategy based on adjustable-rate lending.

Maturity Matching Credit

One regulatory development that had an important effect on the growth of the swap market was the *maturity matching credit,* which was instituted by the Federal Home Loan Bank Board in 1987. The maturity matching credit gave thrifts a reduction in their required capital if their asset-liability gap was between 15 percent and 25 percent of assets. Institutions whose cumulative one- and three-year gaps were both below 15 percent would qualify for a credit equal to 2 percent of assets. Thus, a thrift that would otherwise have been required to hold capital equal to 5 percent of assets could lower its requirement to 3 percent.[24] This was one of the earliest forms of formal risk-based capital requirements in the United States in the 1980s. For thrifts that were not sufficiently well capitalized, the maturity matching credit provided a strong incentive to hedge. Since swaps are the most popular hedge vehicle for thrifts, this regulation gave a further boost to thrift participation in the swap market.

Table 1 illustrates how a swap would enable a thrift to qualify for the maturity matching credit. This hypothetical institution has total assets of $100 million, $70 million of which has a maturity over three years. The thrift has $10 million in short-term assets and $40 million in short-term liabilities. This makes its one-year asset-liability gap of a negative $30 million, or 30 percent of assets. Because both its one- and three-year gaps are in excess of 25 percent of assets, the institution would not qualify for the maturity

---

[23] Adrift in FRMs,'' *Secondary Mortgage Markets,* Fall 1986, pp. 2–7.

[24] Institutions whose gap ratios were between 15 and 25 percent of assets received partial credit on a sliding scale.

TABLE 1

Gap Analysis: First Federal Savings and Loan Association (Maturity or Time to Repricing)

	Under One Year	One to Three Years	Over Three Years	Total
Before Hedging				
Assets	10	20	70	100
Liabilities				
and net worth	40	30	30	100
GAP (A − L)	−30	−10	40	
Cumulative GAP	−30	−40	0	
After Hedging				
Assets	10	20	70	100
Liabilities				
and net worth	40	30	30	100
Adjustment of				
liabilities				
for hedging*	−25	0	+25	0
Liabilities				
after hedging	15	30	55	100
GAP (A − L)	−5	−10	15	
Cumulative GAP	−5	−15	0	

* The Hedge is a twenty-five-million-dollar interest rate swap that converts variable-rate liabilities into fixed-rate liabilities.

matching credit and would be required to hold capital at 5 percent of assets.

By entering into a $25-million interest rate swap as the fixed-rate payer, the institution would be able to lower both its one-year and three-year gaps to a level that would qualify for the full 2 percent credit. The swap extends the maturity of the short-term liabilities (most likely deposits or repurchase agreements) beyond three years. This is shown in the items for "adjustment of liabilities for hedging" as a reduction of short-term liabilities of $25 million and an increase in long-term liabilities of the same amount. This lowers the one-year gap to a negative 5 percent of assets and the three-year gap to a negative 15 percent of assets.

A survey by Craig Ruff of southeastern thrifts done in mid-1989 showed that the thrifts that were most likely to have engaged in hedging were those whose net worth ratios were between 3 and 6 percent of assets, precisely the type of thrift that would benefit from the maturity matching credit.

Additional Regulatory Initiatives

Further encouragement for the use of swaps by thrifts will no doubt result from two Federal Home Loan Bank Board (FHLBB) regulatory initiatives in 1989. One, known in the industry as Thrift Bulletin 13, set out specific responsibilities for management and boards of directors for the control of interest rate risk. Thrift Bulletin 13 requires each insured thrift's board of directors to set specific limits on the institution's exposure to changes in interest rates. These exposure limits are to apply to (*a*) the percentage change in net interest income and (*b*) the percentage change in the market value of the net worth of the institution. Thrift Bulletin 13 also requires each institution over $500 million in assets to perform a regular simulation analysis to estimate its exposure to changes in interest rates.

The philosophy behind this regulation is to treat the board of directors as the first line of defense against excessive interest rate risk. Most thrifts continue to have a large amount of interest rate exposure, although it has declined since 1984 when the FHLBB first began to measure it. It is inevitable that when boards of directors see precise numerical estimates of the amount of interest rate exposure at their institution, and are asked to approve it, they will force management to restructure the balance sheet or engage in off-balance sheet hedging. As noted earlier, the simplest and most popular form of hedging for thrifts is swaps.

The risk-based capital proposal, also initiated in 1989, bases thrift capital requirements on the sensitivity of the market value of the net worth of the institution to changes in interest rates. Specifically, it states that thrifts need to hold, as one part of a three-part capital requirement, one half of the change in the market value of net worth resulting from a 200-basis-point change in interest rates.[25] Institutions with large amounts of interest rate risk will

---

[25] There is also a credit risk component similar to that used for commercial banks, and a collateralized borrowing requirement.

thus need to hold more capital. An alternative to holding more capital would be, again, to hedge the interest rate risk using swaps.

Commercial Banks

The regulation of commercial bank participation in the swap market proceeded in a different direction. Commercial banks frequently take some interest rate risk, but they have historically been far less exposed to interest rate changes than most thrifts. The bank regulators' primary concern has been with the credit risk being taken by commercial banks. Although the regulators had shown increasing concern, swaps were not formally considered by U.S. regulators until 1986. For example, the capital regulations adopted in the United States in 1981 and still in effect through 1989 applied only to on-balance sheet assets. However, in 1988 an agreement on new procedures for evaluating capital, sometimes called the Basle Agreement, was reached by the Group of Ten countries, plus Luxembourg and Switzerland. The new standards provide for the inclusion of off-balance sheet activities and provide for weighting a bank's on- and off-balance sheet activities based on their credit riskiness. Interest rate risk is not explicitly incorporated into the capital guidelines.

Definition of Capital
The agreement defines two types of capital: core (Tier 1) capital and supplementary (Tier 2) capital. Core capital consists of the book value of common and perpetual preferred equity, minority equity interest in consolidated subsidiaries, and retained earnings less goodwill. Supplementary capital includes items such as general loan loss reserves, mandatory convertible debt, perpetual debt, subordinated debt, and limited-life preferred stock. Total capital is the sum of core and supplementary capital.

The capital standards become fully effective at the end of 1992. At that time banks will be required to maintain a ratio of total capital to risk-weighted on- and off-balance sheet items of at least 8 percent. At the end of 1992 banks will also be required to have a core capital ratio of at least 4 percent. Transitional arrangements provide for banks to achieve at least a 7.25 percent total capital ratio by the end of 1990, with Tier 1 elements of capital totaling at least 3.25 percent.

Risk Weighting

On-balance sheet assets are assigned to various risk categories, and weights are assigned to each category. Assets with virtually no credit risk, such as cash and central government securities from OECD countries, are assigned a zero weight (i.e., they require no capital). Other assets, such as most bank certificates of deposit, receive a 20 percent weight. Home mortgages receive a 50 percent weight. Assets of normal credit risk are assigned a 100 percent weight. The assets in this category include claims on the private sector, fixed assets, and real estate.

Off-balance sheet items are first converted into credit-risk equivalent values based on the type of instrument. For example, a credit conversion factor of 100 percent is applied to such direct credit substitutes as standby letters of credit. These are then generally multiplied by the weights applicable to the counterparty for an on-balance sheet transaction.

Exposure Calculation Methods

The credit conversion of swaps may proceed in one of two ways. The *current exposure* method places most of the weight on the current mark-to-market value of the swap. The *original exposure* method assigns an exposure based on the swaps' maturity and does not take account of subsequent changes in market value. A majority of the Group of Ten supervisors favored the current exposure method, but the agreement allows supervisors to choose either procedure. The Basle Agreement also allows the bank regulators to permit individual banks to choose which method to adopt, with the understanding that once a bank chooses the current exposure method, it cannot switch back to the original exposure method.

The current exposure approach divides the credit risk component of a swap into two parts: the actual current exposure and the potential for a future increase in exposure depending on interest rate changes. The actual current credit exposure is set equal to the mark-to-market value of the swap if the swap has positive value to the bank (the net present value of the net swap payments is positive to the bank). If the swap has negative value to the bank, then the bank is not currently subject to credit risk, and the value of the current exposure is set equal to zero. The potential increase in credit exposure due to interest rate changes is equal to 0.5 percent of the notional principal of the swap for swaps that mature in more than one year. If the swap matures in one year or less, then the potential increase in exposure is set equal to zero.

An example of the computation of the credit equivalent amount is provided in Table 2. Both of the first two swaps mature in under one year. Hence, their potential exposure is set equal to zero and only their current exposure is considered. The first swap has a positive replacement cost of $10,000 and hence has a credit equivalent exposure of $10,000. The second swap has a negative replacement cost (i.e., the bank would receive a payment for entering into a swap with the same terms as the second swap). As indicated above, the regulations do not count negative replacement cost, hence this swap has a credit equivalent exposure of zero. The third swap illustrates the calculation of credit equivalent exposure for a swap with negative replacement cost and more than one year to maturity. In this case the credit equivalent amount is equal to the potential exposure of the swap. Swaps 4 and 5 illustrate that the potential conversion factor is not influenced by the remaining maturity for swaps under the current exposure method because any increase in replacement cost will be reflected in higher current exposure when the swap is next valued for capital adequacy purposes.

The original exposure method is less accurate but is computationally easier. This approach may also be more consistent with the rest of the risk-based standards in that it avoids the mark-to-market element. This method sets the credit exposure equal to the notional principal of the swap multiplied by a conversion factor that depends on each swap's maturity. The agreement permits each regulator to choose whether the conversion factors will be based on the original maturity of the swap or its residual maturity. The conversion factor for swaps maturing in under one year is 0.5 percent. An additional 1.0 percent is added to the conversion factor for each additional year.

Interest rate and foreign exchange contracts, including interest rate swaps, are treated differently from other off-balance sheet

TABLE 2
Calculation of Credit Equivalent Amounts for Interest Rate Swaps under Risk-Based Capital Guidelines (Current Exposure Method)

| | | Potential Exposure | | | + | Current Exposure | | = | |
Swap Number	Remaining Maturity	Notional Principal (Dollars) ×	Potential Exposure Conversion Factor	Potential Exposure (Dollars)		Replacement Cost[a]	Current Exposure (Dollars)[b]		Credit Equivalent Amount (Dollars)
1	six months	5,000,000	0	0		10,000	10,000		10,000
2	six months	5,000,000	0	0		−5,000	0		0
3	four years	10,000,000	.005	50,000		−200,000	0		50,000
4	four years	10,000,000	.005	50,000		150,000	150,000		200,000
5	seven years	5,000,000	.005	25,000		325,000	325,000		350,000

[a] These numbers are purely for illustration.
[b] The larger of zero or positive mark-to-market value.

activities after a credit equivalent amount is calculated. The credit equivalent amounts of such contracts are all multiplied by a 50 percent credit risk weighting, regardless of the credit risk of the counterparty. This weighting reflects the judgment of the regulators that most of the participants in the swap market are first-class names. The Basle Agreement notes, however, that the credit risk weighting on swaps could be raised if the average credit quality of banks' swap counterparties deteriorates or if swap loss experience increases.

Netting of Swap Payments

Important elements in determining a bank's capital requirements for its swap portfolio are contractual agreements to net swap payments across multiple swaps between two parties. The Basle Agreement generally permits banks to net contracts subject to novation. Novation occurs when swaps payable in the same currency and at the same time are automatically amalgamated and only a single net payment is made. Netting by novation may be phased in, however, in individual countries where national bankruptcy laws allow liquidators to unbundle transactions within a given period under a charge of fraudulent preference.[26] The agreement does not permit netting where the contracts are merely subject to closeout clauses. That is, where the outstanding obligations on all swaps are accelerated and netted to determine a single exposure when one of the participants is wound up; for example, in a court finding of bankruptcy. The supervisors approve of these clauses but contend that they have not yet been adequately tested in the courts. Netting of these contracts may be permitted in the future in those jurisdictions where the netting is upheld in the courts.

Coverage of the Basle Agreement

One important limitation of the Basle Agreement is that the capital standards do not necessarily apply to firms that are not regulated by one of the respective central banks. For example, U.S. invest-

---

[26] Fraudulent preference exists if a debtor transfers property without a fair consideration in exchange.

ment banking and insurance companies are not regulated by the Federal Reserve and, hence, are not bound by the swaps capital regulation. Joanna Pitman has discussed the competitive implications of exempting some swap dealers from the capital regulation.[27]

CONCLUSION

The market for interest rate swaps began as an unregulated market. However, regulation has increased with the growth of the market and the increase in our understanding of the risk implications of swaps. One of the effects of interest rate swaps is to alter the interest rate exposure of swap participants. United States thrift regulators have recognized the potential for altering rate risk and have incorporated the effect of swaps on interest rate risk into both their current and proposed regulations. Another way in which swaps can affect the risk of a financial intermediary is by increasing its credit risk, the risk that the other party to a swap will default. The bank regulators of the Group of Ten countries together with Switzerland and Luxembourg have responded to the concerns about credit risk by including swaps in their risk-based capital plan, sometimes referred to as the Basle Agreement. The bank regulators' plan does not take explicit account of interest rate risk, and, therefore, the plan does not consider the effect of swaps on banks' interest rate exposure. However, both bank and thrift regulations may well become more sophisticated over time as our understanding of swaps develops.

BIBLIOGRAPHY

Arak, Marcelle; Laurie S. Goodman; and Arthur Rones. "Credit Lines for New Instruments: Swaps, Over-the-Counter Options, Forwards, and Floor-Ceiling Agreements." In *Conference on Bank Structure and Competition*. Chicago: Federal Reserve Bank of Chicago, 1986.
Belton, Terrence M. "Credit Risk in Interest Rate Swaps." Working paper, Board of Governors of the Federal Reserve System, April 1987.

---

[27] Swooping on Swaps," *Euromoney,* January 1988, pp. 68–80.

Crane, Robert C., and Peter J. Elmer. "Adrift in FRM's." *Secondary Mortgage Markets,* Fall 1986, pp. 2–7.

Federal Reserve Board and Bank of England. "Potential Exposure on Interest Rate and Exchange Rate Related Instruments." Staff paper, 1987.

Felgran, Steven D. "Interest Rate Swaps: Use, Risk, and Prices." *New England Economic Review,* November/December 1987, pp. 22–32.

Henderson, Schuyler K. "Exposures of Swaps and Termination Provisions of Swap Agreements." In *Swap Finance,* vol. 2, ed. Boris Antl. London: Euromoney Publications Limited, 1986.

Henderson, Schuyler K., and Armel C. Cates. "Termination Provisions of Swap Agreements under U.S. and English Insolvency Laws." In *Swap Finance,* vol. 2, ed. Boris Antl. London: Euromoney Publications Limited, 1986.

Jackson, Dominique. "Swaps Keep in Step with the Regulators." *Financial Times,* August 10, 1988, p. 22.

McNulty, James E. "Interest Rate Risk: Lessons Learned and Questions Unanswered." *Journal of Retail Banking,* Fall 1987, pp. 29–34.

Muffet, Mark. "Modeling Credit Exposure on Swaps." In *Conference on Bank Structure and Competition.* Chicago: Federal Reserve Bank of Chicago, 1987.

Neal, Kathleen, and Katerina Simons. "Interest Rate Swaps, Currency Swaps, and Credit Risk." *Issues in Bank Regulation,* Spring 1988, pp. 26–29.

Pitman, Joanna. "Swooping on Swaps." *Euromoney,* January 1988, pp. 68–80.

Ruff, Craig. "Off-Balance-Sheet Hedging Activity: Fourth District Thrifts," *Review,* Federal Home Loan Bank of Atlanta, September 1989.

Smith, Clifford W.; Charles W. Smithson; and Lee Macdonald Wakeman. "Credit Risk and the Scope of Regulation of Swaps." In *Conference on Bank Structure and Competition.* Chicago: Federal Reserve Bank of Chicago, 1987.

Smithson, Charles W. "A LEGO® Approach to Financial Engineering: An Introduction to Forwards, Futures, Swaps, and Options." *Midland Corporate Finance Review* 4 (Winter 1987), pp. 16–28.

Wakeman, Lee Macdonald. "The Portfolio Approach To Swaps Management." Working paper, Chemical Bank Capital Markets Group, May 1986.

Wall, Larry D., and Kwun-wing C. Fung. "Evaluating the Credit Exposure of Interest Rate Swap Portfolios." Working paper 87-8, Federal Reserve Bank of Atlanta, December 1987.

Wall, Larry D., and John J. Pringle. "Alternative Explanations of Interest Rate Swaps: A Theoretical and Empirical Analysis." *Financial Management,* Summer 1989, pp. 59–73.

Whittaker, J. Gregg. "Pricing Interest Rate Swaps in an Options Pricing Framework." Working paper RWP 87-02, Federal Reserve Bank of Kansas City, 1987.

CHAPTER 21

ASSESSING DEFAULT RISK IN INTEREST RATE SWAPS

Raj Aggarwal
John Carroll University
Cleveland, Ohio

This chapter examines the nature of default risk in swap agreements. It shows that procedures for the assessment of such risks should account not only for the credit risks of the swap counterparties and the risks due to changing market conditions but also for the costs and fees associated with a swap replacement and the risks due to the considerable legal and regulatory uncertainties still surrounding swaps. Unfortunately, current swap risk assessment procedures seem to ignore these latter costs and risks. This chapter presents a procedure to calculate swap risks that includes an assessment of these additional costs and risks.

INTRODUCTION

Transactions in the market for interest rate and cross-currency swaps have grown greatly in recent years. According to the International Swap Dealers Association (ISDA) the total volume of such swaps outstanding at the end of 1988 was $1.2 trillion.[1] It has been estimated that 30 to 40 percent of all primary capital market

---

[1] See "A Little Local Difficulty," *The Economist,* March 18, 1989, p. 84.

transactions involve some type of swap.[2] This percentage increases with the size of the financing, and among some participants in the capital markets, swaps have become so ubiquitous that financing that does not involve swaps is considered unusual enough to require an announcement that swaps were not involved. Nevertheless, swaps are still considered to be relatively new instruments that exploit market imperfections, and the economics of their pricing is not yet entirely clear. For example, there is some evidence that swap pricing does not reflect credit risks accurately.

Further, since the swap market began with transactions between major companies and financial institutions and such participants still account for most of the volume, there have been very few defaults and still fewer court cases to test and resolve murky areas in swap agreements. In spite of the swap market's large size, write-offs in swaps had amounted to only about $35 million until the end of 1988.[3] The rules governing the accounting and reporting of swap agreements are also unclear and inconsistent, limiting the informational role of market forces. These legal and economic uncertainties, naturally, have raised concerns among regulators and policymakers responsible for the safety and soundness of financial systems.[4]

While corporations and financial institutions have found swaps very useful, relatively little attention has been paid to the analysis and commercial and policy implications of defaults in swap transactions. Further, current procedures for swap risk assessment seem to ignore the costs and fees associated with a swap replacement and the legal and institutional risks surrounding swap agreements. The purpose of this chapter is to correct this neglect, examine the nature of default risk in swap transactions, and present a comprehensive procedure for its assessment.

---

[2] See Michelle Calarier, "Swap's Judgment Day," *United States Banker,* July 1987, pp. 16–20.

[3] As reported in Lisabeth Weiner, "Survey Shows Losses Are Low in Swap Market" *American Banker* 153, no. 2, (July 20, 1988), pp. 2 and 23, and cited in "Swap Galore," *The Economist,* August 5, 1989, p. 54. A similar figure of $33 million is reported in Dominique Jackson, "Swaps Keep in Step with Regulators" *Financial Times,* 10 August 1988, p. 22.

[4] See, for example, note 2 above, and Ron Cooper, "Still Plenty Room to Grow," *Euromoney,* October 1988, pp. 35–38.

The next section starts with a brief exposition of the economic framework useful in assessing swap risks. Next, the institutional, legal, market structure, and pricing risks in swap transactions are discussed. The section ends with the presentation of an equation for swap exposure that consolidates all of these factors. The chapter concludes with some observations concerning, and implications of, the swap risk assessment procedure presented here.

RISKS IN SWAP TRANSACTIONS

There are many reasons for undertaking swaps. Swaps allow parties to raise money in markets where they have the greatest advantage and the lowest effective cost, swapping the proceeds for the type of capital actually needed.[5] Thus, swaps seem to take advantage of market segmentation and other imperfections caused by differential information and institutional restrictions.[6] Such arbitrage-related advantages should, in theory, become smaller or disappear with increased volume in the swap markets[7]—however, that hypothesis is at variance with the facts. Thus, other reasons have been advanced for the continuing growth of the swap market. For example, swaps are said to reduce financing costs by taking advantage of the differences in agency costs between long- and short-term debt,[8] and to allow borrowers to fix the risk-free rate

---

[5] For a more detailed discussion of swaps and the swap market, see, for example, Boris Antl, ed., *Swap Finance* (London: Euromoney Publications Limited, 1986); Carl R. Beidleman, *Financial Swaps* (Homewood, Ill.: Dow Jones-Irwin, 1985); Bank for International Settlement (BIS), *Recent Innovations in International Banking* (Basel, Switzerland: Author, 1986); R. W. Folks and Raj Aggarwal, *International Dimensions of Financial Management* (Boston: PWS-Kent Publishers, 1988) and Smith, C. W., Jr. C. W. Smithson and D. S. Wilford, *Managing Financial Risk* (New York: Harper & Row, 1990).

[6] James Bicksler and Andrew H. Chen, "An Economic Analysis of Interest Rate Swaps," *Journal of Finance* 41, no. 3 (July 1986), pp. 645–55.

[7] Stuart M. Turnbull, "Swaps: A Zero Sum Game," *Financial Management* 16, no. 1 (Spring 1987), pp. 15–21.

[8] Larry D. Wall and John J. Pringle, "Alternative Explanations of Interest Rate Swaps: A Theoretical and Empirical Analysis," *Financial Management* 18, no. 2 (Summer 1989), pp. 59–73.

while allowing the credit risk premium to fluctuate from period to period.[9]

Many of these contentions await empirical confirmation, and the economic rationale for interest rate swaps is still not completely clear. This lack of clarity regarding the economic bases of swaps adds to the legal and regulatory uncertainty surrounding swaps to further reduce the ability of market forces to accurately determine swap prices. Thus, it is unclear whether swaps are priced appropriately or, for example, whether they reflect default risk accurately. Consequently, any explicit assessment of swap risks should account for these uncertainties.

Changing interest rates and market conditions alter the value of a swap. For example, the value of the stream of fixed interest payments required by a swap agreement increases with a rise in market interest rates, while the opposite is true for the counterparty committed to make floating interest payments. A decline in interest rates produces the opposite effects. Such a decline in market interest rates decreases the value of a swap for the counterparty with the commitment to make the fixed-rate payments, while it increases the value of the swap to the counterparty committed to make the floating-rate payments. The credit worthiness of the swap counterparty that faces adverse changes in swap values may influence the riskiness of a swap agreement to the party that enjoys the increase in swap value.

In addition, the riskiness of swap agreements is also influenced by the nature and structure of the swap market and by legal and regulatory aspects of swap agreements. Thus, it is important to understand how swap market structure and its legal and regulatory aspects influence default risks in swaps.

In order to assess default risk in swap transactions, it is important to first estimate what constitutes default. Further, as indicated above, risks in swap transactions are also influenced by the credit worthiness of the counterparties and by the political risks that arise

---

[9] Marcelle Arak, Arturo Estrella, Laurie S. Goodman, and Andrew Silver, "Interest Rate Swaps: An Alternative Explanation," *Financial Management* 17, no. 2 (Summer 1988), pp. 12–18.

due to changes in taxes and government regulations. Moreover, the assessment of default risk in swap transactions involves an assessment of the monetary amount at risk and of the pricing and liquidity risks that arise from changes in market conditions and swap pricing spreads over Treasury rates of similar maturity.

Market, Legal, and Regulatory Aspects of Swaps

This section reviews the still-evolving nature of swap market institutions. It is shown that the considerable legal and regulatory uncertainties associated with swap transactions should be reflected in procedures for swap risk assessment.

Default Definition
A swap agreement is considered to be in default when there is nonpayment even after the expiration of the grace period (if any). Most swap agreements also specify that default occurs if it is discovered that there has been incorrect representation of any material aspect, if there is other failure to perform, if there is a change in ownership of either counterparty or a guaranteeing entity, or if there is cross-default on another contract among the parties to the swap agreement.

Most swap agreements have evolved to fairly standard 10- to 12-page contracts with standard wording, assumptions, and provisions covering definitions developed by the International Swap Dealers Association.[10] Most swaps are governed by master agreements that cover the general conditions common to all swaps between two counterparties. However, the standard swap agreement formats do not cover credit-related issues. Further, while the basics of swap agreements have been fairly standardized, swaps are still evolving and becoming more of a traded instrument. Liquidity of swaps has been enhanced by requiring collateral from the weaker parties, such as thrifts, and, in some swap agreements, by modifying the agreement and including a transferable right to call for margin in case of doubt in the ability to pay.

---

[10] For details see International Swap Dealers Association, *Code of Standard Wording, Assumptions, and Provisions for Swaps* (New York: Author, 1985).

Settlement options in case of default are generally influenced by "fault" clauses in the swap agreement. For example, settlement may be based (*a*) on agreement value based on a specified method of assessing the replacement cost of the swap, (*b*) on another formula based on equivalent financing, or (*c*) on other calculations and negotiation. Similarly, because of the growth of a secondary market in swaps, the swap agreement may specify conditions for the voluntary premature termination of the swap agreement. Such premature termination may involve the exchange of a fixed lump sum or an amount based on prespecified calculation procedures.[11]

Legal Risks

The assessment of risks inherent in a swap agreement is further complicated by the fact that there have been very few defaults to date in the swap markets. Of the defaults that have occurred, many have been settled directly by the counterparties or their intermediaries, and hence even fewer swap agreements have been tested in the courts than might otherwise be the case. Also, the legal status of any collateral posted against a swap has not yet been tested in the courts. For example, such collateral posted by thrifts may be valueless given the prior claims of deposit insurance agencies in the event of a default.[12] The legal status of cross-border swap agreements are further complicated by international differences in contract and insolvency laws. Thus, the legal status of a number of aspects of swap agreements remains murky and uncertain.[13]

In a lawsuit related to two $20 million swaps made in 1984 between Life Savings of Rockford, Illinois, and Homestead Savings of Burlingame, California, a U.S. Federal Court in Illinois ruled in 1987 that swap contracts made over the telephone are binding. However, it should be noted that Life Savings had failed,

---

[11] See Schuyler K. Henderson and Armel C. Cates, "Termination Provisions of Swap Agreements under U.S. and English Insolvency Laws," in *Swap Finance,* vol. 2, ed. Boris Antl (London: Euromoney Publications Limited), pp. 91–102.

[12] For details, see, for example, Rodney R. Peck, "Collateralisation of Swap Transactions," in *Swap Finance,* vol. 2, ed. Boris Antl (London: Euromoney Publications Limited, 1986), pp. 163–76.

[13] The same point has been made by other writers. See, for example, Daniel P. Cunningham and William P. Rogers, Jr., "The Status of Swap Agreements in Bankruptcy," memorandum, Cravath, Swaine and Moore, 1988.

and the swap dispute was inherited by the Federal Savings and Loan Insurance Corporation (FSLIC), which in an earlier S&L takeover had already stated that swap deals made over the phone are binding.[14]

There are also many legal uncertainties surrounding bankruptcy clauses in swap agreements that give swap counterparties the ability to prevent the swap from becoming a part of the assets being managed by the bankruptcy trustee. In this connection, it should be noted that the superior court in Delaware ruled in February 1989 (civil action number 88C-NO-80) that Drexel Burnham could use a bankruptcy default clause in the swap agreement to terminate its swap with MCorp after MCorp had declared that it was suspending payments on its debt and preferred stock but before MCorp had filed for bankruptcy.

Another set of cases related to swap agreements are pending on the court docket in the United Kingdom. A number of municipalities in the United Kingdom have engaged in swap transactions whose volume far exceeds their outstanding debt. United Kingdom municipalities accounted for a third of all interest rate swaps involving the British pound. For example, the municipality of Hammersmith had a total outstanding debt of about 350 million pounds while its swap commitments involved 5 billion pounds in notional amount. While it is clear that United Kingdom municipalities have the authority to engage in swap transactions designed to hedge interest rate risk for their debt, their authority for engaging in these excessive volumes of swaps is the issue being tested in the courts. In February 1989, the appropriate government minister in the United Kingdom declared such authority to be ultra vires, causing the municipalities of Blackburn, Hammersmith and Fulham, Harlow, Ogwr, and Southwark to default on their swap agreements.[15]

---

[14] See, for example, John Morris, "A Swap over the Phone Is Binding," *Euromoney,* April 1987, p. 27.

[15] For details of these cases see, for example, note 1 above; John Dizard, "The Swap Market Shrugs off Its First Defaults" *Corporate Finance,* May 1989, pp. 29–30; Colin Paul, "Legal Risk Involved in the Swaps Market," *Financial Times,* March 15, 1990, p. 12; and Neil Wilson, "Portfolio of Trouble," *The Banker,* August 1989, pp. 9–13.

Market Structure–Related Risk Asymmetry

Potential risks in swap transactions tend to differ between the floating- and fixed-rate sides of a swap. The floating-rate payers in a swap, which are usually the largest firms and banks, multinational corporations, and government agencies, are very good credit risks and have high credit ratings, compared with most fixed-rate payers. Since only the relatively creditworthy floating-rate payers in a swap suffer a loss in the value of their swaps if interest rates rise, fixed-rate counterparties are largely shielded from the usual problems brought about by higher rates. On the other hand, the less-creditworthy fixed-rate payers in a swap may face resistance when attempting to roll over their underlying floating-rate liabilities at higher rates, thus increasing their chance of default.

Market Structure and Pricing of Swap Credit Risks

The market for swaps is characterized by the dominating presence of financial intermediaries as swap brokers and originators. There is some evidence that credit risks are not reflected adequately in the pricing of swaps. The typical financial institution that deals in swaps quotes prices that are jointly determined by its swap, credit, and relationship departments. Each of these departments has its own interest at stake—the swap department seeks income, the credit department seeks to limit exposure in accordance with approved credit lines, and the relationship department seeks to attract customers to the institution's broad line of financial products. The results of this organization is that swaps are, first and foremost, a competitive instrument and are marketed and priced accordingly. Though swap credit officers make the credit risk assessment, and the relationship officer influences the desirability of dealing with the client, they do not usually pass on any credit risk premiums explicitly through to the quoted price of the swap.

A survey of 20 leading swap dealers conducted by Steven D. Felgran revealed that none of them consistently and methodically included the credit risk premium in the quoted price.[16] Instead, if

---

[16] "Interest Rate Swaps: Use, Risk, and Prices" *New England Economic Review*, November–December 1987, pp. 22–32.

the swap officer could not cover the credit risk premium at the prevailing swap price in the market, the deal was not done.

This survey indicated that a range of counterparties of varying but acceptable creditworthiness are all charged the same price. The results is that some swap transactions are priced too high while others are priced too low, as relatively good credits subsidize relatively bad ones. For example, two fixed-rate payers of differing creditworthiness might both be quoted an asking price of Treasury plus 60 basis points, while risk-based pricing would require spreads of, perhaps, 57 and 63. In effect, the better credit pays an additional three basis points in order to lower the lesser credit's price.

However, the survey also found that the more aggressive swap dealers have attempted to differentiate their products in order to raise their prices and profits and better cover their credit risks. By creating market niches, dealers can create demand for their customized swaps and get away from the competitive pricing demanded by the market. By strengthening customer relationships, dealers can charge the prices needed to protect themselves against customer defaults. Nevertheless, this survey found that even when above-market prices were charged, dealers did not distinguish between different credit risks.

Credit risks in swaps are much lower than in loans of comparable size and maturity because the principal in a swap is not exposed, swap cash flows are proportional to differences in interest rates and not to their absolute value, and swaps are exposed only if their value to the weaker counterparty is negative. While credit risk in swaps appears to be lower than that in comparable loans, swap dealers still face credit risk and must include appropriate credit risk premiums in their prices. Dealers that properly price their swaps would be able to build up capital reserve positions that would shield them from the effects of occasional defaults. If credit risks were underestimated, dealers could possibly underprice their swaps, thereby accepting a level of risk larger than that justified by the return. On the other hand, dealers that overestimate their risks might charge prices in excess of marginal costs for the level of risk they are taking. The existence of underpricing or overpricing depends both on the accuracy of credit risk assessment and on the state of competition in the swap market.

Risks due to Accounting and Reporting of Swaps

Rules governing accounting and reporting of swap transactions are currently unclear, inconsistent, and variable internationally. For example, in the United States, the accounting treatment of swaps depends on differentiating swaps according to their purpose. Swaps that have been undertaken as speculative investments must be marked to current market value daily. On the other hand, swaps undertaken as hedges may be carried at cost or at market and may be amortized and accorded the same accounting treatment as the position being hedged. Unfortunately, the method for ascertaining which swaps are considered as hedges is not completely clear or consistent. According to Statement of Financial Accounting Standards (SFAS) No. 52, foreign currency swaps are hedges only if they hedge a specific, identifiable exposure, whereas according to SFAS No. 80, interest rate swaps are hedges only if they hedge the overall exposure of the whole entity. Further, if swaps are considered not to be material, they need not be disclosed specifically.

Partially because of this lack of clarity and inconsistency in accounting standards, there is wide diversity in practice in how swaps are accounted for and reported.[17] This lack of accurate and consistent accounting information greatly limits the role of market forces and prices in managing and assessing swap risks.

Country or Regulatory Risks

Because of the high degree of competition among swap market makers, it has been contended that swaps may be systematically underpriced with regard to their risks. Because of this inaccurate market assessment of swap transactions, because swaps can be and often are used to circumvent government controls and regulations, and because moral hazard may lead to an overuse of swaps among financial institutions that are provided government deposit insurance, governments have generally attempted to regulate the use of swaps by financial institutions. While there has been a wide

---

[17] See, for example, BIS, *Recent Innovations in International Banking,* 1986; H. Bierman, "Accounting for Interest Rate Swaps," *Journal of Accounting, Auditing, and Finance* 2 (Fall 1987), pp. 396–408; and Keith Wishon and Lorin Chevalier, "Interest Rate Swaps— Your Rate or Mine," *Journal of Accountancy,* September 1985, pp. 63–84.

range of governmental response to the growth of the swap market, most governments have required at least increased disclosure of swap transactions undertaken by financial institutions. As an example, U.S. banks must disclose the notional amounts of their swap agreements to the Federal Reserve System. Unfortunately, however, call reports on swap transactions filed by U.S. banks exclude affiliates and subsidiaries and are not suitable for aggregation and assessment of overall swap risk.

In addition, the United States and 10 other large countries have agreed to impose by 1992 a minimum capital requirement (as a percent of assets) that would include a proportion of swap agreements in the asset base. The asset equivalent of a swap agreement for this purpose has been defined as half of the replacement cost plus 0.25 percent of the notional amount of a swap. Some governments impose withholding taxes and fees on swap transactions, and some governments require government approval for swap transactions. Changes in government control and regulation of swap transactions constitute an additional source of risk to participants in the swap markets in particular and to financial markets in general.

Changes in government rules and regulations regarding cross-border payments can also generate payment and settlement risks in swap agreements. Settlement risk can be minimized by agreeing on specific payment procedures that take into account the time zones and payment conventions in the countries and locations of each party to the swap agreement. Naturally, these latter risks are of little direct concern to participants in swap agreements between counterparties in the same country.

Swap Risks and Changes in Market Rates

This section provides a brief review of the procedures suitable for assessing and calculating swap risks associated with changes in market interest rates. As discussed earlier, changes in interest rates influence the market values of swaps. Further, replacement values of swaps must also account for fees and other costs associated with such replacements.

Pricing Risks

Swap prices are quoted as a spread over a fixed rate versus a given floating-rate index, e.g., seven-year Treasury plus 60 basis points versus six-months LIBOR. These quoted swap spreads depend on the cost of hedging these transactions that are faced by market makers and on the balance between the supply of and demand for swaps. Bid-ask spreads in swap prices change with market activity and competition among dealers.

The normal interest rate basis for swap prices is the simple interest CD equivalent, as in the prime rate, federal funds rate, or LIBOR. Other interest rate bases, such as the discount rate as used in T-bills, bankers acceptances, commercial paper, or repurchase agreements, must be converted to CD equivalent for use in swap pricing. Swap pricing includes the assumption that the payment frequency and reset are generally the same as the term of the floating index used, with only a few exceptions such as quarterly for the prime rate and daily for the fed funds rate.[18]

In summary, pricing risk in swaps depends on market forces and how they change over the life of the swap contract. Generally, because swaps involve a periodic exchange of net payments, credit and price risks in swaps are less than those in forward contracts of the same maturity but more than those in futures contracts, as the latter are marked to market daily. While some of these credit and price risks can be hedged, they generally cannot be eliminated completely.

Amount at Risk

As the principal, or notional amount, is not usually traded in most swap transactions, it is not exposed to default risk in interest rate swaps. As most swaps involve an agreement only to exchange a net stream of future cash flows, the present value of such net payments represents the gross amount at risk. The net amount at risk in a swap agreement is the difference between the present value of the stream of future cash flows agreed upon in the original

---

[18] For details see, for example, Bidyut Sen, "The Price of Swaps," in *Swap Finance*, vol. 2, ed. Boris Antl (London: Euromoney Publications Limited, 1986), pp. 79–86.

swap transaction, and the present value of the stream of future cash flows that would be necessary if the original swap agreement had to be replaced by a new swap agreement at currently prevalent terms and conditions including any fees, bid-ask spreads, and other expenses associated with such a replacement. This exposure may indeed be positive or negative, and, as explained below, it changes over time not only because of changes in market conditions but also because of changes in credit, tax, and reporting conditions of the participants.

Calculation of Replacement Costs of Swaps

Both counterparties generally cannot lose in a swap transaction at the same time. The loss (or gain) in the event of default depends on which of the counterparties has failed and on the direction of interest rate movements. An increase in market interest rates causes the value of the swap to the fixed-rate payer to rise and the value of the swap to the floating-rate payer to fall, and a decrease in market interest rates has the opposite effects.

As discussed above, the replacement cost of a swap depends on a number of factors. For example, a dealer would be subject to a loss in the event of default by a floating-rate payer if the dealer had originally swapped fixed payments at 8.5 percent for six-month LIBOR and interest rates had since risen. If the default occurred when an equivalent swap would cost 10.0 percent, and assuming the contract still had six years to run, the actual loss would be 1.5 percent per year for six years, or a present discounted value of about 6.65 percent of the notional principal if we ignore the fees and other transactions costs associated with a swap replacement. If the original floating-rate payer did not actually default at this time, the expected loss could be measured as a fraction of the loss due to the need for replacement, depending on the floating-rate payer's credit rating. Thus, if the interest rate risk continued to be 6.65 percent and if the credit rating spread reflecting default risk were 150 basis points over comparable Treasury rates, the expected loss due to credit risk would be 9.975 basis points ($0.0665 \times 0.015 = 0.0009975$), or 0.0009975 of the notional principal.

The measurement of expected loss due to credit risk is more complex than this example would indicate. The credit risk of each swap is determined by the credit rating of each counterparty, the sensitivity of the swap's value to changes in interest rates, the volatility of interest rates, the slope of the yield curve, the frequency of payments, the swap's maturity, whether some performance bond is posted, and by the fees, bid-ask spreads, and other costs associated with the replacement of a swap. The credit risk faced by the fixed-rate payer compared with that faced by the floating-rate payer is particularly influenced by the gap in the yield curve between their relative positions. The appropriate discount rate used for valuing each future cash payment in a swap should reflect yields on zero coupon bonds with equivalent maturities and portfolio risks, as discussed in detail in Chapter 12.

The measurement of current default risk is only a partial clue to potential future risk, which depends on actual interest rate changes and is subject to changes in the credit rating of each counterparty. In particular, an unexpected deterioration in a counterparty's credit increases the risk of default. Certain credit enhancements such as collateral are of uncertain value since most swap documentation has not yet been tested in court actions.

The potential future risk of a swap transaction should not simply be viewed as its replacement cost under some worst-case scenario. Instead, the potential future risk should be treated as the expected replacement cost given an entire range of interest rates and credit ratings. It should be recognized that over the life of a swap, the potential risk could equal any one of a number of values with varying probabilities, but that default is unlikely unless interest rates move against the counterparty. Therefore, the expected replacement cost of a swap is properly measured as the weighted average of all possible replacement costs, using the probabilities of adverse interest rate movements as weights.

A number of writers have estimated the size of the replacement costs of swaps based on various assumptions about the nature of the future movements in interest rates. For example, Marcelle Arak, Laurie S. Goodman, and Andrew Rones assume that interest rates follow a random walk with no drift and that interest rates change by one standard deviation per year to increase swap exposure.[19] They estimate that swap exposure amounts to between 1 and 2 percent of the notional amount for each year of the swap agreement. J. Gregg Whittaker assumes a log-normal distribution and volatility of one standard deviation to estimate the exposure of a pair of matched 10-year swaps to be less than 8 percent of the notional amount.[20] The joint Federal Reserve and Bank of England study similarly estimates credit exposure to be no greater than 1 percent of the notional amount per year.[21] Terrence M. Belton uses a vector autoregressive procedure to estimate interest rates at various maturities and assumes stochastic default to arrive at an estimate of 1 to 5 percent of the notional amount for swaps with maturities of 2 to 12 years.[22]

It should be noted that these preceding estimates focus primarily on changes in the market value of a swap because of changing market conditions and ignore the fees and other costs associated with a swap replacement. These estimates also ignore the considerable legal uncertainties and institutional risks currently associated with swaps. The next section presents a swap risk formula that overcomes these shortcomings.

A Comprehensive View of Swap Risks

As the preceding discussion indicates, swap risks depend not only on the credit worthiness of the counterparties, on changes in market interest rates, and on the replacement fees and costs; but because the swap market and its institutions are still evolving, swap risks also depend on legal and regulatory risks. Thus, in calculating the expected costs of swap replacement, the present value of interest rate differences must be augmented by the fees and other costs associated with replacement and by the expected costs due to the

---

[19] "Credit Lines for New Instruments: Swaps, over-the-Counter Options, Forwards, and Floor-Ceiling Agreements," in *Conference on Bank Structure and Condition* (Chicago: Federal Reserve Bank of Chicago, 1986), pp. 437–56.

[20] "Interest Rate Swaps: Risk and Regulation" *Economic Review,* Federal Reserve Bank of Kansas City, (March 1987), pp. 3–13.

[21] "Potential Exposure on Interest Rate and Exchange Rate Related Instruments," staff paper, Federal Reserve System, 1987.

[22] "Credit Risk in Interest Rate Swaps," working paper, Board of Governors of the Federal Reserve System, 1987.

legal, regulatory, and country risks that would be faced in case of default. These relationships can be summarized as follows:

$$\text{Probability of non-payment} = P_{cd}$$
$$\text{Total replacement cost} = ECPV + ERFC + P_{lrc} \times CLRC$$

Combining these two relationships, we obtain

$$ERC = P_{cd}(ECPV + ERFC + P_{lrc} \times CLRC)$$

where

ERC = expected replacement cost and exposure of a swap,
P_{cd} = probability of credit condition–related default,
P_{lrc} = probability of legal, regulatory, and country risks,
$ECPV$ = expected changes in the present value of a swap,
$ERFC$ = expected swap replacement fees and other costs,
$CLRC$ = costs of legal, regulatory, and country problems.

Most current literature on the assessment of swap defaults has focused fairly narrowly on the somewhat complex procedures used to calculate the expected changes in the present or market value of a swap, $ECPV$. As suggested in the literature, future cash flows associated with a swap must be estimated under a range of possible future interest rates for each period during the maturity of the swap. Further, as discussed earlier, it is important that the discount rates used to evaluate the present value of the future cash flows associated with a swap reflect yields on zero coupon Treasury instruments of equivalent maturity and portfolio risk.

While the calculation of $ECPV$ is important, as our equation indicates, a more inclusive representation of the exposure of a swap position involves some additional calculations. For example, as our model indicates, it is incorrect to assume, as is done in many writings on this topic,[23] that the expected replacement cost and the exposure of a swap is zero right after it is originated since the fees and other costs associated with the replacement of a swap, *ERFC,* are always positive and nonzero. While these costs may be a small

---

[23] See, for example, Dale F. Cooper and Jan R. Watson, "How to Access Credit Risks in Swaps," *The Banker* 137, no. 4 (February 1987), pp. 28–31; Mark Muffet, "Modeling Credit Exposure on Swaps," in *Conference on Bank Structures and Competition* (Chicago: Federal Reserve Bank of Chicago, 1987), pp. 473–96.

percentage of the notional amount of a large swap, they are likely to be a more significant proportion of the present value of net cash flows associated with all swaps, but especially so for the smaller swaps.

The estimation of the two probabilities in our model, P_{cd} and P_{lrc}, can be based on market yields and informed judgments that reflect the credit standing of the counterparties, local legal history of swap agreements, and the international credit standing of the countries involved. As interest rate swap agreements mature, while the risks due to legal and regulatory uncertainties might decrease, there will always be some country risk in swaps involving counterparties in different countries. It should be noted here that an estimate of the probability of default because of the poor credit standing of a swap counterparty, P_{cd}, may be based on the yield spread on the counterparty's bonds or other debt instruments. However, this credit-based probability of default may not be independent and may be correlated with the assumptions regarding the future movement of interest rates used in the calculations of risk and of the replacement costs of swaps.

CONCLUSIONS

This chapter has examined the nature of default risk in swap agreements. It suggests that because of the evolving nature of the swap market and the mostly untested nature of swap agreements, procedures for the assessment of swap risks should account for the risks due to the considerable legal and regulatory uncertainties that still surround swaps. Swap risk assessment procedures must not ignore these risks and the fees and costs associated with the replacement of a swap.

This chapter presents an extended procedure to assess and calculate swap risks that accounts for these institutional risks and additional replacement costs and fees. The model for assessing swap risk presented here is a more comprehensive representation of the exposure of a swap position, compared to other currently prevalent definitions of swap default risk. For example, this model for swap risk indicates that it is incorrect to assume that the expected replacement cost and the exposure of a swap is zero immediately after it is originated. Such swap exposure is not zero since the fees and other costs associated with the replacement of a swap are positive and nonzero from Day 1.

BIBLIOGRAPHY

Antl, Boris, ed. *Swap Finance*. London: Euromoney Publications Limited, 1986.

Arak, Marcelle; Arturo Estrella; Laurie S. Goodman; and Andrew Silver. "Interest Rate Swaps: An Alternative Explanation." *Financial Management* 17, no. 2 (Summer 1988), pp. 12–18.

Arak, Marcelle; Laurie S. Goodman; and Arthur Rones. (1986), "Credit Lines for New Instruments: Swaps, over-the-Counter Options, Forwards, and Floor-Ceiling Agreements." In *Conference on Bank Structure and Competition*. Chicago: Federal Reserve Bank of Chicago, 1986, pp. 437–56.

Bank for International Settlements. *Recent Innovations in International Banking*. Basel, Switzerland: Author, 1986.

Belton, Terrence M. "Credit Risk in Interest Rate Swaps." Working paper, Board of Governors of the Federal Reserve Banks, April, 1987.

Beidleman, Carl R. *Financial Swaps*. Homewood, Ill.: Dow Jones-Irwin, 1985.

Bicksler, James, and Andrew H. Chen. "An Economic Analysis of Interest Rate Swaps." *Journal of Finance* 41, no. 3 (July 1986), pp. 645–55.

Bierman, Harold, Jr. "Accounting for Interest Rate Swaps." *Journal of Accounting, Auditing, and Finance* 2 (Fall 1987), pp. 396–408.

Calavier, Michelle. "Swap's Judgment Day." *United States Banker*, July 1987, pp. 16–20.

Cooper, Dale F., and Ian R. Watson. "How to Assess Credit Risks in Swaps." *The Banker* 137, no. 4 (February 1987), pp. 28–31.

Cooper, Ron. "Still Plenty Room to Grow." *Euromoney*, October 1988, pp. 35–38.

Cunningham, Daniel P., and William P. Rogers, Jr. "The Status of Swap Agreements in Bankruptcy." Memorandum, Cravath, Swaine and Moore, 1988.

Dizard, John. "The Swap Market Shrugs Off Its First Defaults." *Corporate Finance*, May 1989, pp. 29–30.

Federal Reserve Board and the Bank of England. "Potential Exposure on Interest Rate and Exchange Rate Related Instruments." Staff paper, Federal Reserve System, 1987.

Felgran, Steven D. "Interest Rate Swaps: Use, Risk and Prices." *New England Economic Review,* November–December 1987, pp. 22–32.

Folks, R. William, and Raj Aggarwal. *International Dimensions of Financial Management.* Boston: PWS-Kent Publishers, 1988.

Henderson, Schuyler K., and Armel C. Cates. "Termination Provisions of Swap Agreements under U.S. and English Insolvency Laws." In *Swap Finance,* vol. 2, ed. B. Antl. London: Euromoney Publications Limited, 1986.

International Swap Dealers Association. *Code of Standard Wording, Assumptions, and Provisions for Swaps.* New York: Author, 1985.

Jackson, Dominique. "Swaps Keep in Step with Regulators." *Financial Times,* 10 August 1988, p. 22.

"A Little Local Difficulty." *The Economist,* March 18, 1989, p. 84.

Muffet, Mark. "Modeling Credit Exposure on Swaps." In *Conference on Bank Structure and Competition.* Chicago: Federal Reserve Bank of Chicago, 1987, pp. 473–96.

Morris, John. "A Swap over the Phone Is Binding." *Euromoney,* April 1987, p. 27.

Paul, Colin. "Legal Risk Involved in the Swaps Market." *Financial Times,* March 15, 1990, p. 12.

Peck, Rodney R. "Collateralisation of Swap Transactions." In *Swap Finance,* vol. 2, ed. B. Antl. London: Euromoney Publications Limited, 1986.

Sen, Bidyut. "The Pricing of Swaps." In *Swap Finance,* vol. 2, ed. B. Antl. London: Euromoney Publications Limited, 1986.

Smith, Clifford W., Jr.; Charles W. Smithson; and D. Sykes Wilford. *Managing Financial Risk.* New York: Harper and Row, 1990.

Turnbull, Stuart M. "Swaps: A Zero Sum Game?" *Financial Management* 16, no. 1 (Spring 1987), pp. 15–21.

Wall, Larry D., and John J. Pringle. "Alternative Explanations of Interest Rate Swaps: A Theoretical and Empirical Analysis." *Financial Management* 18, no. 2 (Summer 1989), pp. 59–73.

Weiner, Lisabeth, "Survey Shows Losses Are Low in Swap Market," *American Banker* 53, no. 2 (July 20, 1988), pp. 2, 23.

Whittaker, J. Greg. "Interest Rate Swaps: Risk and Regulation." *Economic Review,* Federal Reserve Bank of Kansas City (March 1987), pp. 3–13.

Wilson, Neil. "Portfolio of Trouble." *The Banker,* August 1989, pp. 9–13.

Wishon, Keith, and Lorin Chevalier. "Interest Rate Swaps—Your Rate or Mine?" *Journal of Accountancy,* September 1985, pp. 63–84.

CHAPTER 22

ACCOUNTING AND TAXATION FOR INTEREST RATE SWAPS

Frederick D. S. Choi
New York University
New York, New York

INTRODUCTION

Historically, contractual interest payments on debt instruments have been fixed over the life of the borrowing. Owing to the increased volatility of interest rates in recent years, debt instruments calling for variable interest payments have become a common feature of the financial scene.

The lower certainty of coupon cash payments associated with floating-rate obligations is generally viewed with mixed emotions. From a financing perspective, firms with fixed return streams tend to disfavor servicing variable-rate borrowings. Other things being equal, they normally prefer fixed-rate financing. Conversely, firms with variable earnings streams tend to favor floating-rate obligations.

The interest rate swap is a recent financial innovation designed to accommodate borrowers who may find it necessary to borrow on terms that conflict with their natural preferences.[1] It is basically an agreement between two parties to exchange interest payments

---

[1] Carl Beidleman, "Yield Enhancement Using Financial Swaps," in *The Handbook of International Investing*, ed. Carl Beidleman (Chicago: Probus Publishing Company, 1987), p. 599.

for a specific period of time on an agreed-upon notional value, and has, as its primary objective, the conversion of fixed-rate interest payments to floating-rate payments, or vice versa. The term notional value refers to a reference amount against which interest is calculated.

In this chapter, I examine some of the accounting and taxation issues associated with interest rate or coupon swaps. While such swaps can be effected in multiple currencies, the focus here is on swaps transacted in a single currency. Emphasis on a single currency framework in no way belittles the importance of the international dimension. On the contrary, international swaps arbitrage the ability of counterparties to access both domestic and overseas markets and exploit structural differences between domestic and international money rates and medium-term fixed rates. Accordingly, optimization of swap opportunities requires a global perspective.

Accounting measurement and taxation issues are first examined for corporate users of interest rate swaps. This is followed by an examination of accounting and taxation treatments for financial institutions. I conclude the chapter with a note on current trends in swap disclosure.

CORPORATE USERS

Interest rate swaps offer corporate financial managers a number of advantages in today's volatile financial markets. By enabling managers to change the nature of an existing asset or liability from fixed to floating, or vice versa, interest rate swaps enable companies to actively manage their interest rate exposure. They also allow managers to

1. Lower their all-in cost of borrowing by enabling counterparties to take advantage of their access to specific markets, capitalize on their differential credit rating, or exploit market inefficiencies.
2. Avoid renegotiating existing loan covenants on less-advantageous terms.[2]

---

[2] Larry D. Wall and John Pringle, "Interest Rate Swaps: A Review of the Issues," *Economic Review*, November/December 1988, pp. 25–26.

3. Unbundle the funding decision from the rate decision.[3]
4. Access credit markets on a more timely basis by circumventing registration or burdensome disclosure requirements.[4]
5. Obtain an off-balance sheet alternative to refinancing to the extent the swaps are related to an existing debt.[5]
6. Access fixed-rate funds from an investor universe that is separate and distinct from public and private markets, thereby preserving them for future direct financing.[6]
7. Speculate on the future trend in interest rates.[7]

Since the inception of the interest rate swap in the early 1980s, the volume of swaps has mushroomed, and this trend shows no signs of abatement.[8] In contrast, accounting, taxation, and regulatory provisions have not kept pace with this rapid development. At present, formal pronouncements that specifically address the accounting treatment of interest rate swaps are at an early stage of development. Accordingly, companies in the United States, and internationally, have sought guidance from (*a*) existing policies for financial instruments with similar characteristics and (*b*) fundamental concepts underlying the preparation of conventional financial statements. In the United States, for example, Statement of Financial Accounting Standards No. 80 (SFAS 80), which establishes standards for futures contracts other than currency futures, provides guidance that may be extended to interest rate swaps by analogy. Fundamental accounting concepts that have also proved helpful in shaping accounting policy include going concern, accrual, conservatism, consistency, and the general notion that financial accounting should attempt to reflect the economic substance of a transaction.

---

[3] Julian Walmsley, "Interest Rate Swaps: The Hinge Between Money and Capital Markets," *The Banker*, April 1985, p. 37.

[4] Jan G. Loeys, "Interest Rate Swaps: A New Tool for Managing Risk," *Federal Reserve Bank of Philadelphia Business Review*, May/June 1985, pp. 17–25.

[5] Frederick C. Militello, "Swap Financing: A New Approach to International Transactions," *Financial Executive*, October 1984, p. 34.

[6] Anthony J. Gambino, "Cash Management, Interest Rate Swaps, Risk Management Addressed by CPA's in Industry," *Journal of Accountancy*, August 1985, p. 68.

[7] Discussion Paper on Interest Rate Swaps, Financial Accounting Standards Board, January 28, 1985, p. 10.

[8] Phyllis Feinberg, *Corporate Cashflow*, April 1989, pp. 8–12.

Nature of Swaps

Understanding the nature of a swap position and its relationship to the financial position and performance of the reporting entity is useful in deciding on an appropriate measurement and reporting posture. Keith Wishon and Lorin S. Chevalier identify several helpful swap categories.[9]

1. *Matched Swaps.* In a matched swap transaction, there is an underlying interest-bearing liability or asset with terms similar to those of the swap contract. This occurs, for instance, when two counterparties that have each borrowed similar sums swap cash flows in order to convert a variable-rate borrowing into a fixed-rate obligation, or vice versa (this is illustrated in Exhibit 2).
2. *Unmatched Swaps.* In the case of an unmatched swap, parties contracting to pay or receive a stream of future cash flows have no other liability or asset related to the swap transaction. These one-sided, or "naked," positions are motivated by the desire to (a) hedge an overall risk exposure, or (b) speculate on the future trend in interest rates. They may also be undertaken as a temporary measure until a matched hedge can be arranged.
3. *Hedged Swaps.* A hedged swap is similar to an unmatched swap in that the exchange agreement bears no relation to an underlying liability or asset. It differs in that the firm entering into the swap arrangement has taken some action to hedge the interest rate risk (i.e., the potential impact of interest rate changes on a firm's reported performance). This hedging action may involve the purchase of a futures contract or the purchase or sale of Treasury securities, for example.
4. *Offsetting Swaps.* In this case, an entity such as a bank or broker acts as an intermediary between two swap positions that offset one another. While the intermediary retains the

[9] "Interest Rate Swaps—Your Rate or Mine?" *Journal of Accountancy*, September 1985, p. 74.

credit risk (i.e., the potential for loss arising from the non-performance of a swap counterparty), it eliminates all of the interest rate risk by arranging the offsetting positions.

Major Accounting Issues

As corporate borrowers are usually reluctant to take on speculative positions, they tend to favor matched swaps. In accounting for corporate users of swap products, fluctuating interest rates give rise to several issues, namely:

1. To what extent should interest rate swaps be recognized on the balance sheet? If they are recognized, how should they be valued?
2. What is the nature of revenues and expenses that arise from swap transactions and how should they be recognized in the income statement?
3. What are the tax implications of swap cash flows for market transactors?

To illustrate existing corporate treatments for interest rate swaps, consider the following case example. Alpha Company, hereafter referred to as Alpha, enjoys a triple-A credit rating and is able to borrow fixed-rate funds at 10½ percent and floating-rate debt at the London Interbank Offer Rate (LIBOR), a market-based index, plus ½ percent. Its investment portfolio generates a return that is tied to another variable-rate index, and Alpha is interested in matching that variable return stream with a variable-rate funding source. Beta Company (Beta) is a lesser-quality credit. As investors tend to demand greater premiums from lower-rated companies in fixed- as opposed to floating-rate markets, it can borrow fixed at 12 percent and variable at LIBOR plus 1½ percent.[10]

---

[10] Most swaps between corporate users are effected through an intermediary that will typically extract a fee for bringing the counterparties together, guaranteeing each leg of the transaction and collecting from, and making payments to, each of the counterparties. As accounting for intermediaries is considered separately, I purposely omit them from the example.

EXHIBIT 1
Interest Rate Differentials for Alpha and Beta

	Floating Rate	Fixed Rate
Alpha Company	LIBOR + 1/2%	10 1/2%
Beta Company	LIBOR + 1 1/2%	12%
Interest differential	1%	1 1/2%

As can be seen in Exhibit 1, although Alpha has an absolute advantage over Beta in both types of financing, it has a greater comparative advantage in borrowing fixed-rate funds. Consistent with the trade theory of comparative advantage, Alpha and Beta agree to an interest rate swap whereby Alpha pays Beta LIBOR plus 1 1/2 percent on the notional principal, and Beta pays Alpha a fixed rate of 11 3/4 percent on the same principal amount. Each borrows, by way of a bond issue, $100,000,000 for five years; Alpha borrows at a fixed rate of 10 1/2 percent, and Beta at LIBOR plus 1 1/2 percent, with rollover (repricing) dates occuring annually. Although each company will continue to service its own debt to maturity, they agree to swap cash flow streams in such fashion that Alpha ends up servicing Beta's borrowing and Beta servicing Alpha's debt. This is illustrated in Exhibit 2.

The net result of this swap is that Beta has transformed its variable-rate debt obligation into a fixed-rate debt at 1/4 percent

EXHIBIT 2
Swapped Cash Flows

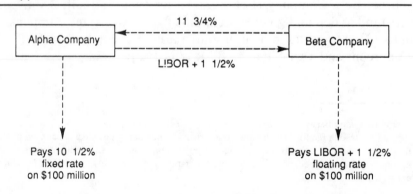

lower cost than if it had gone to the market directly. Alpha has also reduced its vulnerability to interest rate risk. Its payment of LIBOR plus 1½ percent to Beta is offset by fixed-rate receipts of 1¼ percent above its fixed-rate payment. This, in turn, leaves Alpha effectively paying LIBOR plus ¼ percent, which is ¼ percent lower than it would have achieved without the swap. Thus, the swap of cash flows has proven mutually beneficial in allowing both parties to the exchange agreement to raise funds at a lower cost than would otherwise be the case, while simultaneously hedging outstanding interest commitments.

In the foregoing swap arrangement, neither Alpha nor Beta exchange the notional principal of $100 million. While Alpha and Beta service each other's interest commitments, cash flows between the two are generally limited to any difference between the offsetting payment streams. Thus, Beta would remit a payment of $250,000 to Alpha, assuming that LIBOR remains unchanged at 10 percent and that interest payments are made at the end of each year.

Assume now that LIBOR rises to 10.5 percent at the start of the second year and remains at its new level through the next rollover date. In this case, Alpha Company becomes disadvantaged relative to Beta and would pay the latter an amount equal to the differential between the fixed versus floating swap cash flows, or $250,000 [= $100,000,000 × (.1175 − .12)]. If, instead, LIBOR had fallen from 10 to 9.5 percent, Beta would be disadvantaged relative to Alpha and would have to remit $750,000 to the latter [= $100,000,000 × (.1175 − .11)].

To recap, there is never an exchange of principal—neither at inception nor at maturity of the swap agreement. There are, however, periodic payments between the counterparties during the life of the swap, and the direction of these payments may reverse themselves depending on the future course of interest rates.

Accounting at Inception

Since there has been no exchange of principal at the inception of the swap agreement, accepted practice is to value the related debt obligation at its original transaction value. Differences of opinion, however, relate to the principal amount of the swap contract.

One viewpoint holds that swaps should be recorded on the balance sheet as an asset (receivable) and a liability (payable) in terms of the discounted present value of a swap contract's future payment streams.[11] In our case example, the swap agreement requires Beta Company to pay Alpha Company .25 percent on the notional amount of the matched obligation. Thus, at the inception of the swap agreement, Alpha has a receivable of $250,000. As the current interest rate may be considered an unbiased estimator of the future rate, Alpha's expectation is that this amount will continue for the next five years. Discounting this annuity at Alpha's effective cost of funds, 10.25 percent (= Alpha's fixed borrowing rate of 10.5 percent converted into a variable loan of LIBOR + .25 percent) yields a present value of $941,675. This amount would, in turn, be added to the carrying value of original debt and can be likened to a bond premium that would be recorded had a bond, carrying a coupon of 10.5 percent, been issued when the market rate of interest was 10.25 percent. Conversely, Beta would account for its periodic payment to Alpha as a bond discount. Accounting entries to record the original bond issue and the interest rate swap for Alpha and Beta are illustrated in Exhibit 3.

The foregoing accounting treatment is conceptually appealing as it takes into account a swap's future cash flows and the time value of money. Such practice, however, would not be consistent with established accounting practices for other forward agreements. Moreover, it would subject reported earnings to extreme volatility and, therefore, is not widely used. The more prevalent practice is to treat the swap principal as an off-balance sheet item. The major reasoning is that the amount to which the swap payments relate, $100,000,000 in our case example, is purely notional and will never be exchanged.[12]

---

[11] Joseph C. Rue, David E. Tosh, and William B. Francis, "Accounting for Interest Rate Swaps," *Management Accounting*, July 1988, pp. 43–49.

[12] John I. Tiner and Joe M. Conneely, *Accounting for Treasury Products* (Cambridge, England: Woodhead-Faulkner Limited, 1989), p. 49.

EXHIBIT 3
Swap Accounting at Inception: One Alternative

Alpha Company

Original bond issue:
1/1/1   Cash   100,000,000
            Bonds payable   100,000,000

Swap contract:
1/1/1   Swap (receivable)   941,675
            Bond payable[a]   941,675

Swap Accounting at Inception—Beta Co.

Original bond issue:
1/1/1   Cash   100,000,000
            Bonds payable   100,000,000

Swap contract:
1/1/1   Bonds payable   906,803
            Swap (payable)[b]   906,803

[a] $100,000,000 × .0025% = $250,000; $250,000 discounted for five years at 10.25% = $941,675.
[b] $100,000,000 × .0025% = $250,000; $250,000 discounted for five years at 11.75% = $906,803.

Accounting during the Swap Term

The ultimate gain or loss realized by a corporate swap user can be accurately assessed at maturity and will be represented by the net cash inflows realized at that time. The allocation of those gains or losses between accounting periods, as well as the nature of those gains or losses, has proved troublesome. Do the differential swap payments between counterparties during the swap term constitute gains or losses on independent financial transactions? Or do they constitute adjustments of a firm's funding costs? Should antici- pated swap cash flows be recognized? If so, how?

In a legal sense, one could argue that the cash settlements between the counterparties do not constitute interest flows; that is, they are not costs paid for the use of money. They are related to a separate transaction in which the rate decision has been separated from the funding decision. Accordingly, they could be viewed, and accounted for, as ordinary gains and losses generated from an operating transaction. This treatment, as we shall see, can have significant tax implications.

Alternatively, swap cash flows may be linked to the specific debt obligation whose face value provides a benchmark for future swap payments. This is appropriate if management's intention is to minimize its interest rate exposure on the obligation in question and structures the terms of the swap to mirror those of the obligation. In this sense, the swap may be considered an integral component of the funding decision. As principles of external reporting need not conform to tax law, at least in the United States, this treatment is the more common procedure adopted by corporate users. Accordingly, periodic payments under a swap agreement would be treated as adjustments of interest expense.

How, then, should anticipated swap cash flows be accounted for? In keeping with the cost principle, corporate issuers of debt seldom value these instruments at market. Thus, gains or losses inherent in a swap position would usually not be recognized. In industries where debt obligations are carried at market, however, marking swap contracts to market and recognition of such gains or losses as adjustments of funding costs would appear appropriate.[13]

To contrast these alternative treatments, let us return to our swap between Alpha Company and Beta Company. Based on our earlier assumption that LIBOR remains at 10 percent through the end of the first year, then rises to 10.5 percent at the start of Year 2, Alpha will receive $250,000 from Beta at year's end. Under the cost method described above, this payment effectively reduces Alpha's actual funding cost and is treated as a reduction of interest expense. Changes in the market value of the swap contract are ignored. For Beta, the $250,000 payment would be accounted for as an increase in its effective interest expense. This treatment is illustrated in Exhibit 4.

Under the mark-to-market approach, the swap contract, using present value of future cash flows as a surrogate of market value, would initially be accounted for as shown in Exhibit 3. The receipt of $250,000 by Alpha at the end of the first year essentially consists

---

[13] Wishon and Chevalier, "Interest Rate Swaps," pp. 76–77.

EXHIBIT 4
Accounting during Swap Term—Cost Method

Alpha Company

Swap receipt—first year:		
12/31/1 Cash	250,000	
Interest expense		250,000
Interest accrual—first year:		
12/31/1 Interest expense	10,500,000	
Cash		10,500,000
Swap payment—second year:		
12/31/2 Interest expense	250,000	
Cash		250,000
Interest accrual—second year:		
12/31/2 Interest expense	10,500,000	
Cash		10,500,000

Beta Company

Swap payment—first year:		
12/31/1 Interest expense	250,000	
Cash		250,000
Interest accrual—first year:		
12/31/1 Interest expense	11,500,000	
Cash		11,500,000
Swap receipt—second year:		
12/31/2 Cash	250,000	
Interest Expense		250,000
Interest accrual—second year:		
12/31/2 Interest expense	12,000,000	
Cash		12,000,000

of two components: (*a*) interest at 10.25 percent on the swap receivable and (*b*) a partial amortization of the swap receivable balance. Accrued interest on the receivable would be recorded as a reduction of interest expense of the period to reflect Alpha's effective interest cost. At that time, Alpha will also accrue its annual interest expense on its bond liability at the effective rate of 10.25 percent on the restated bond carrying value. Interest paid will be based on the contractual terms of the original bond agreement. Beta would record this transaction in converse fashion. Applicable accounting entries for the first year of the swap are displayed in Exhibit 5.

EXHIBIT 5
Accounting during First Year of Swap Term—Market Value Method

Alpha Company

Swap receipt—first year:

12/31/1	Cash	250,000	
	Interest expense[a]		96,522
	Swap (receivable)		153,478

Interest accrual—first year:

12/31/1	Interest expense[b]	10,346,522	
	Bonds payable	153,478	
	Cash		10,500,000

Beta Company

Swap payment—first year:

12/31/1	Interest expense[c]	106,549	
	Swap (payable)	143,451	
	Cash		250,000

Interest accrual—first year:

12/31/1	Interest expense[d]	11,643,450	
	Bonds payable		143,450
	Cash		11,500,000

[a] $941,675 × .1025 = $96,522.
[b] [($100,000,000 + $941,675) × .1025].
[c] ($906,803 × .1175.)
[d] [($100,000,000 − $906,803) × .1175].

At the beginning of the second year, interest rates have moved against Alpha. Accordingly, Alpha will now have to remit an interest differential of .25 percent to Beta. In the absence of information to the contrary, Alpha will adjust its records to reflect the revised cash flow expectation. As Alpha's bond issue can now be viewed as 10.5 percent debt issued at an effective rate of 10.75 percent, the carrying value of its bond would have to be adjusted as well. This adjustment will also affect its year-end accounting entries for the actual swap payment and interest expense accrual. Beta Company's adjustments and year-end accruals would, again, be made in converse fashion. The foregoing transactions analysis is illustrated in Exhibit 6. To assist the reader in working through the analysis, T-accounts summarizing the entries contained in Exhibits 5 and 6 are provided in the Appendix to this chapter.

EXHIBIT 6
Accounting during Second Year of Swap Term—Market Value Method

Alpha Company

Adjusting entry to reflect rate change—start of second year:

1/1/2	Bonds payable	1,567,967	
	Swap (receivable)[a]		1,567,967

Swap payment—second year:

12/31/2	Interest expense[b]	83,825	
	Swap (payable)	166,175	
	Cash		250,000

Interest accrual—second year:

12/31/2	Interest expense[c]	10,666,171	
	Cash		10,500,000
	Bonds payable		166,171

Beta Company

Adjusting entry to reflect rate change—start of second year:

1/1/2	Swap (payable)[d]	1,526,705	
	Bonds payable		1,526,705

Receipt of swap payment—second year:

12/31/2	Cash	250,000	
	Interest expense[e]		89,694
	Swap payable		160,306

Interest accrual—second year:

12/31/2	Interest expense[f]	11,839,694	
	Bonds payable	160,306	
	Cash		12,000,000

[a] ($941,675 − $153,478 + $779,770) where $779,770 is the present value of $250,000 at 10.75% for four years.
[b] [($941,675 − $153,478 − $1,567,967) × .1075]
[c] [($100,941,675 − $153,478 − $1,567,967) × .1075]
[d] ($906,803 − $143,451 + $763,352) where $763,352 is the present value of $250,000 at 11.75% for four years.
[e] ($763,352 × .1175)
[f] [($99,093,197 + 143,450 + 1,526,705) × .1175]

For a further discussion of the merits of market-based accounting for swaps, see Chapter 23.

Accounting for Swap Terminations
Some swap contracts allow parties to terminate the agreement prior to settlement for a fee. The fee will normally reflect the interest differentials between the fixed rate embodied in the swap

and fixed rates available in the market from the termination date to the original swap settlement date.[14] In our case example, assume that Alpha Company decides to terminate its agreement with Beta at the end of the first year. At that time, fixed rate funds for companies of comparable credit worthiness are available for 12.25 percent. Alpha would have to pay Beta approximately $1,510,713, the difference between the 12.25 percent and 11.75 percent specified in the swap agreement multiplied by the notional value of the swap and discounted for four years at the market rate.

While the calculation of this fee is straightforward, its accounting disposition is less so. Thus, should the fee be treated as a gain or loss and taken immediately to income? Or should it be deferred and amortized over the remaining life of the underlying swap instrument? Those who view the swap termination as analogous to the extinguishment of a debt obligation prior to maturity would argue that the $1,510,713 should be recognized in current income. The U.S. Financial Accounting Standards Board (FASB) has taken an opposing posture. Reasoning that most interest rate swaps are undertaken to hedge the interest rate risk on a related commitment, FASB considers the accounting provisions that are in effect for terminations of futures contracts to be applicable.

SFAS 80 generally requires that a gain or loss on a futures contract be recognized in the period during which there is a change in the market value of that contract unless it qualifies as a hedge of certain price or interest rate risk exposures. In this case the deferred gain or loss is treated either as an adjustment of the carrying value of the hedged item or deferred until the hedged item is subsequently sold or disposed of. Further, an adjustment of the carrying value of a hedged financial instrument should be amortized over the expected remaining life of the instrument.[15]

By analogy, the gain or loss on the early termination of a swap that hedges future interest payments should be deferred and recognized as interest is accrued. This treatment is especially appropriate where a company in the position of Beta Company immediately

---

[14] Tiner and Conneely, *Accounting for Treasury Products*, p. 58.
[15] Financial Accounting Standards Board, "Accounting for Futures Contracts," *Statement of Financial Accounting Standards No. 80* (Stamford, Conn.: Author, August 1984).

enters into a swap with another counterparty and uses the fee received from Alpha to offset its higher fixed payment to the new counterparty so that, in actuality, it is no better off then before the swap termination.

Corporate Taxation of Swaps

Business entities that are counterparties to a swap transaction face a number of issues regarding the tax aspects of interest rate swaps. These relate to (*a*) the amounts and timing of swap gains or losses, (*b*) the appropriate tax treatment of such gains or losses (ordinary versus capital gains treatment), and (*c*) the manner in which such gains or losses affect the double taxation of corporate income.[16] An international survey of tax provisions relating to interest rate swaps reveals efforts that are at a nascent stage of development.[17] As an international overview of such tax provisions is beyond the scope of this chapter, what follows is a brief overview of the U.S. scene as an illustration of this highly complex and unsettled subject.

In contrast to conventional accounting treatments discussed thusfar, swap cash flows are not viewed as interest expense or income for U.S. tax purposes. Although an interest rate swap is normally viewed in connection with the underlying debt obligation, the swap and the related debt instrument are regarded as separate transactions, as are the cash flows stemming from each. Accordingly, interest rate differentials that are received or paid by a swap user are viewed either as an ordinary gain or loss, or an ordinary business expense deduction.[18] There is a possibility, however, that swap payments may be reflected as adjustments to interest expense or income provided certain conditions are met; for instance,

---

[16] See Martin F. Belmore, "The Tax Treatment of Swaps in the United States," in *Inside the Swap Market*, 3rd ed. (London: IFR Publishing Ltd., 1989), pp. 187–203. For a parallel discussion of U.K. treatment of swap cash flows, see Eric Tomsett, "The Taxation of Swaps in the United Kingdom," in the same volume, pp. 181–85.

[17] Robert J. E. Henry, "International Taxation," in *Swap Financing Techniques*, ed. Boris Antl (London: Euromoney Publications Limited, 1983), pp. 73–97.

[18] Ibid., p. 74.

swap payments are made on a net, as opposed to a gross, basis and are related to interest expense on a financial obligation incurred, or interest income on a financial asset held, by the taxpayer. The manner in which swap payments are treated for tax purposes can have a significant effect on a U.S. corporation's foreign tax credit limit.

By the way of background, the United States adopts a worldwide principle of taxation and, thus, taxes income arising both within and outside its national boundaries. A direct consequence of this principle is that the foreign earnings of a U.S. multinational company are subject to the full tax levies of at least two countries. To prevent this from occuring, U.S. companies can elect to treat foreign taxes paid as a credit against the parent's U.S. tax liability. Generally, foreign taxes paid are creditable to the extent they do not exceed the foreign tax credit limitation. Foreign source gains increase the limitation and allow U.S. corporate taxpayers to claim additional credits for foreign taxes paid. Losses attributed to foreign sources reduce it.

Accordingly, swap payments that are treated as adjustments to non-U.S. source interest income increase a U.S. corporation's foreign tax credit limitation. Swap payments treated as adjustments to income expense, as opposed to noninterest treatment, also alter a firm's foreign tax credit limitation to the extent it is apportioned between U.S. and non-U.S. source items of income. For example, the allocation of interest rules under the U.S. Internal Revenue Code may increase the interest expense allocated and apportioned to foreign-source income if such payments were seen as interest, thus reducing the taxpayer's foreign tax credit limitation. While swap payments recognized as ordinary gains and losses also affect a U.S. taxpayer's foreign tax credit limitation depending on whether the gain from the swap is treated as U.S. or non-U.S. source, it is more difficult to attribute these to foreign sources. Any gain treated as U.S. source would have no impact on the foreign tax credit limitation.[19]

---

[19] Belmore, "The Tax Treatment of Swaps," pp. 153–54.

FINANCIAL INSTITUTIONS

Swap accounting for financial institutions (i.e., banks) is not as clear-cut as for industrial corporations. Like a nonfinancial entity, a bank can act as a principal in using swaps to hedge interest rate risk generated by its own balance sheet position and, in exceptional cases, to earn a trading profit by maintaining an unhedged position in a swap. In these instances, accounting issues confronting banks are not unlike those facing nonfinancial corporations. In addition, however, a bank can assume the role of an intermediary between two swap counterparties. Thus, whereas corporations typically engage in matched transactions, financial intermediaries can engage in unmatched and offsetting swaps as well.

Alpha Company and Beta Company, in our earlier example, may have utilized the services of Gamma Bank to arrange their coupon swap. In addition to delegating the administrative burden of the swap to Gamma Bank, Alpha and Beta may each be reluctant to assume the risk of default by the other. Hence, the use of a reputable financial intermediary. Accordingly, the swap arrangement might be structured as illustrated in Exhibit 7.

Gamma Bank's services may comprise locating and bringing swap counterparties like Alpha and Beta together, guaranteeing each leg of a swap transaction (i.e., assuming the credit risk that Alpha or Beta may default), acting as a collection and paying agent for swap flows between counterparties, and assuming interest rate

EXHIBIT 7
Swap Using Intermediary

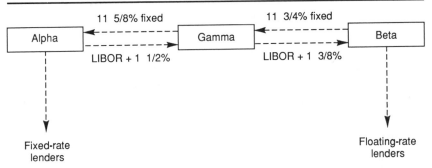

risk by warehousing a swap until a counterparty can be located.[20] The primary objective of the intermediary in these instances is to generate fee income. How to account for this income has proved controversial.

Accounting At Inception

As an intermediary, in the foregoing offsetting swap transaction, Gamma Bank has not guaranteed the underlying debt obligations of either Alpha or Beta; hence, the notional amounts would not have an impact on Gamma's balance sheet. If Gamma is acting purely as a broker between the counterparties, recognition of the swap contracts would not be appropriate. If Gamma positions itself as a principal between Alpha and Beta, accounting treatments discussed in connection with nonfinancial corporations would hold. In practice, since the swap transaction constitutes a contingent asset and liability from Gamma Bank's perspective, off-balance sheet treatment by way of footnote disclosure is gaining acceptance.

When Gamma Bank acts as a broker with no legal or economic interest in the swap transaction beyond its initial matching services, any fees received would simply be recognized as fee income when the services are performed. When Gamma acts as a principal between two counterparties, the issue becomes more complicated.

In Exhibit 7, Gamma Bank, in arranging an offsetting matched swap, earns a spread between what it receives from one counterparty and pays to the other. This differential is designed to compensate Gamma Bank for (a) arranging the swap, (b) administering the swap payments from and to counterparties, and (c) assuming credit risk that either Alpha or Beta may default. But how should Gamma separate out these three components and when should it recognize them in income?

In terms of the former, some feel that disaggregation of the spread into its relative components is an impossible task, or at best a very subjective process. Hence, no attempt is made to do so. In other cases, reasoned attempts consistently applied over time are

---

[20] Benjamin S. Neuhausen, "Accounting Guidelines for Swaps in the United States," in *Inside the Swap Market*, 3rd ed. (London: IFR Publishing Company, 1989), p. 176.

undertaken. Tiner and Conneely suggest one approach to doing so.[21]

In our example, Gamma Bank earns a spread of ¼ percent per annum on the swap arrangement. It thinks that interest rates could increase by 2 percent in a year and normally expects a margin of ⅜ percent for a standard commercial loan to comparable swap counterparties. Using the formula

$$P \times dI \times n \times M$$

where P = notional amount,
      dI = expected annual change in interest rates,
      n = number of years in the swap agreement, and
      M = margin between funding and loan rate applicable to the counterparty risk, for a standard commercial loan transaction.

Gamma Bank would break out its interest rate spread as follows:

Total swap income =
      $100,000,000 × ¼ percent × 5 years = $250,000

Credit risk assessment (annual) =
      $100,000,000 × 2 percent × 5 years × ⅜ percent = $37,500

The total swap income less the income for credit risk less the direct costs of servicing the swap transaction, would yield the arrangement fee.

Assuming that allocation procedures such as the foregoing are feasible, there is still the question of when the various fee components should be recognized. Practice is reportedly varied on this score.[22] Some banks do not recognize any income at the inception of the swap, preferring instead to recognize all income over the swap term. Some recognize, as arrangement fees, the direct costs of arranging the swap while recognizing the balance of its swap income over the life of the agreement. Still others estimate the

---

[21] Tiner and Conneely, *Accounting for Treasury Products*, p. 73.
[22] Eugene E. Comiskey, Charles W. Mulford, and Deborah H. Turner, "Banking Accounting and Reporting Practices for Interest Rate Swaps," *Bank Accounting & Finance*, Winter 1987–88, pp. 3–14.

portion of their fees that relate to credit risk assumption and ongoing servicing costs and recognize these annually while recognizing the balance as arrangement fee income at inception.

The latter practice is not in accord with recent FASB guidelines. SFAS No. 91 requires that banks defer loan origination fees (origination fees less origination costs) and amortize them over the loan term as yield adjustments. As swap origination fees are felt to be analogous to loan origination fees, parallel treatment is required.[23] Yet, are swap fees similar to loan origination fees? Is deferral of swap arrangement fees consistent with the matching principle, especially when much of the work in arranging a swap occurs up front? Once a swap is arranged, the major risk faced by the intermediary is the risk that a counterparty will default. Does allocation of all income over the life of the swap achieve a proper matching of risk and return? Current recognition of arrangement fees as fee income, with deferral and amortization of fees for ongoing servicing costs treated as fee income and assumption of credit risks as other operating income, appears more in accord with the substance of the underlying transaction.''

Accounting during the Swap Term

During the term of the swap, the financial intermediary, Gamma Bank in our example, will accrue both a swap receivable and a swap payable to Alpha Company and Beta Company, respectively. Since the right of offset applies here, the receivable and payable from Alpha would be netted as would the payable and receivable from Beta. Only the net amount due from, or due to, each counterparty would be disclosed in Gamma Bank's balance sheet. Fee income over the life of the offsetting swap would be recognized as described in the previous section.

If Gamma Bank acts as a principal and arranges a swap with another counterparty to hedge its own balance sheet exposure, the

---

[23] Financial Accounting Standards Board, "Accounting for Nonrefundable Fees and Costs Associated With Originating or Acquiring Loans and Initial Costs of Leases," *Statement of Financial Accounting Standards No. 91* (Stamford, Conn.: Author, December 1986).

accounting procedures would resemble those we illustrated with respect to Alpha Company and Beta Company in Exhibit 2. If Gamma Bank were using the swap to convert a fixed-rate obligation to a variable-rate debt to hedge a variable rate asset, any interest differential that it enjoyed would be accounted for as an adjustment to its interest expense. Moreover, any swap receivable from and payable to Gamma's counterparty would be recorded on a net basis in Gamma's balance sheet.

Perhaps the most difficult area of swap accounting for financial institutions relates to unmatched swaps. An unmatched swap might arise when a financial institution, such as Gamma Bank, enters a swap with Alpha company before locating a counterparty. Until it does so, Gamma Bank would be exposed to interest rate risk unless it were able to hedge this risk in some other fashion, for example, arrange an internal hedge with another banking affiliate. In this case, the swap position would be considered a speculation, and some form of market value accounting would be called for. One alternative would be to value the swap in accordance with the lower of cost or market rule. The problem in this regard involves determining when an impairment has occurred and whether such impairment is permanent. This is likely to be extremely difficult during periods of volatile interest rates. Assuming this treatment is followed, losses, in keeping with the principle of conservatism, would be recognized in current income; gains would be deferred. When a counterparty is eventually secured, income recognition procedures identified for matched swaps, enumerated above, would apply.

An alternative is to carry unmatched swaps at market until a counterparty is found. The unmatched swap would be marked to market at stipulated repricing intervals, and associated gains or losses recognized in current income. The question is how to obtain market prices that can be used to revalue a swap. Are secondary markets developed enough to offer reliable benchmarks? If not, would discounted cash flow analyses prove to be a reliable surrogate? If the latter can be answered in the affirmative, what discount rate should be used? Should it reflect an internally generated hurdle rate or a market-determined rate?

As secondary markets for swap instruments continue to evolve, the feasibility of using market benchmarks is improving. In the meantime, use of estimated market values based on the discounted present value of the favorable or unfavorable interest spreads using a bank's marginal cost of funds appears to be gaining acceptance.

Accounting for Swap Terminations

Accounting for a terminated swap in the case of a bank that is acting as a principal in hedging its interest rate exposure is similar to that of a nonbanking corporation. But such is not the case when a bank is a principal and serves as an intermediary between two counterparties. Consider again the swap scenario, depicted in Exhibit 7, where Gamma Bank arranges a swap between Alpha Company and Beta Company. Should Beta default, Gamma bank will have to recognize a loss on any receivable from Beta that proves uncollectible. It will also find itself with an unhedged position with respect to Alpha. Gamma Bank would have to mark its unhedged position with Alpha to market and recognize any loss incurred in maintaining an open position with Alpha in the current period.

If Beta were to voluntarily terminate its end of the swap by paying Gamma Bank a termination fee, the swap with Alpha would again be marked to market until a counterparty were found. If Gamma Bank intended to locate a new counterparty for Alpha, deferral of the termination fee would be called for. If not, current income would be affected.

Income Tax Treatment

The tax treatment of interest rate swaps for financial institutions is no more definitive than it is for nonfinancial entities. However, recent developments suggest that this financial innovation is undergoing substantial review, and new administrative guidelines are in the offing.

Until recently, up-front fees received by a financial intermediary in connection with an interest rate swap were treated as taxable income in the period in which received. This required deferred-tax accounting for institutions that amortized such fees over the life of the swap agreement. In February 1989, however, the U.S. Internal

Revenue Service (IRS) released Notice 89-21, which permits financial intermediaries to amortize such fees in a reasonable manner over the swap term. Still, the IRS leaves unanswered the question of what constitutes a reasonable method. Several amortization methods may be used: (*a*) straight line, (*b*) contingent payment, and (*c*) effective yield. For small institutions whose volume of swap transactions is not large, straight line amortization is probably sufficient. For institutions whose volume of swap activity is significant, the effective yield methodology illustrated in Exhibits 5 and 6 appears warranted.

Swap payments paid or received by the financial intermediary over the term of the swap agreement do not constitute interest income or expense. This, the reader may recall, stems from the fact that the swap agreement does not itself constitute an indebtedness between the financial intermediary and either of the counterparties. Accordingly, the swap payments are treated, for tax purposes, as normal business receipts and payments and reflected in current taxable income as such.

At the present time no regulations discuss whether a gain or loss will be recognized in the event a swap is terminated, voluntarily or otherwise, One should look to the substance of the event to formulate an appropriate tax posture. Assume one of the counterparties to an offsetting swap voluntarily terminates its side of the agreement and pays the intermediary a termination fee. How should this fee be treated? If the intermediary is in a position to immediately find a replacement counterparty, one could argue that the termination fee is no different than an up-front fee, which is the cost of arranging a replacement. In this sense, amortization of the fee to taxable income over the remaining swap term is defensible. On the other hand, if the search for a replacement counterparty subjects the intermediary to significant market risk, recognition of the termination fee as taxable income of the current period seems appropriate.[24]

---

[24] What constitutes significant market risk would probably depend on who the new counterparty is; e.g., a new counterparty versus the original counterparty that terminated the swap in the first instance.

RELATED DEVELOPMENTS

A major purpose of financial statements is to provide statement readers with information regarding the performance and risk dimensions of the reporting entity. Owing to the off-balance sheet nature of interest rate swaps, there is concern that those who rely on published financial statements currently receive insufficient information about the risks associated with these instruments, and consequently make suboptimal investment, credit, and regulatory decisions.[25]

New Capital Adequacy Guidelines

In the case of financial institutions, concern arises when one of the participants in a swap defaults. Under a swap agreement a bank agrees to make interest payments on behalf of the defaulted payer (credit risk). One danger is that the bank will not have the funds to continue making the payments (liquidity risk). Another is that interest rates may have changed so dramatically since the swap was initiated that the cost to the financial institution of finding a new counterparty to replace the defaulted company's obligation would be significant (interest rate risk).

As an example of this concern, banking regulators worry that banks may be undercapitalized, given the risky nature of their assets and obligations. Accordingly, bank regulatory authorities around the world are considering or proposing new regulations that would require increased capital levels at banks to reflect the risks of swaps in which banks function as intermediaries. Based on a framework adopted in July 1988 by the Basle Committee on Banking Regulations and Supervisory practices, which includes supervisory authorities from 12 major industrial countries, the U.S. Federal Reserve Board issued, in January 1989, new capital adequacy guidelines for state member banks and bank holding companies.[26]

---

[25] Financial Accounting Standards Board, Description of FASB Project on Financial Instruments and Off-Balance Sheet Financing, June 1986.

[26] "Final Guidelines Issued On Risk-Based Capital Requirement," *Federal Reserve Bulletin*, March 1989, pp. 147–48.

The guidelines establish a framework that sensitizes regulatory capital requirements to differences in risk profiles among banking organizations by taking off-balance sheet exposures explicitly into account in assessing capital adequacy. By 1992, banking organizations will be required to have capital equivalent to 8 percent of assets, weighted by their degree of riskiness. Risk weights assigned to off-balance sheet items are primarily based on credit risk. In the case of interest rate contracts, the risk-adjusted amounts (credit-equivalent amounts) are based on the following formula:

$$CE = RV + (NV \times ECF)$$

where CE = credit equivalent amount,
RV = replacement value,
NV = notional value, and
ECF = exposure conversion factor.

The first independent variable represents the cost to the bank of finding a replacement for a defaulted obligation; the second estimates the cost to the bank if interest rates have changed since the swap's inception. Specifically, the total replacement cost of contracts (RV) is obtained by summing their positive mark-to-market values. This current exposure is added to a measure of future potential increases in credit exposure. The latter is calculated by multiplying the total notional value of contracts (NV) by an exposure conversion factor (ECF) equal to 0.5 percent for contracts with maturities of more than a year (0 percent for one year or less).

To illustrate, assume that Gamma Bank is involved with a three-year single-currency fixed-to-floating interest rate swap with a notional principal of $10,000,000. The current replacement cost is assumed to be $200,000. The credit equivalent amount of this interest rate contract would be

$250,000 (= $200,000 + $10,000,000 × .005 percent).

Financial Disclosure Initiatives

To afford general-purpose financial statement readers the opportunity to better assess the risks associated with financial innovations, such as interest rate swaps, more and more accounting standard setters are considering initiatives calling for additional disclosure.

At the moment no formal pronouncement has been issued at the international level.[27] The Secretariat of the Organization for Economic Cooperation and Development (OECD), however, has stated that

> to improve the quality of financial statements, as recommended in the *OECD Guidelines for Multinational Enterprises*, it is essential that particulars of off-balance sheet transactions be disclosed in annual (or interim) reports of enterprises. Information should cover the accounting methods used (with particular reference to the treatment of such transactions in the income statement, whether for hedging or trading purposes), the amounts of the different types of commitment and information on the risks incurred, on an overall basis and for all financial instruments.[28]

At the national level, the United States has taken the lead in calling for enhanced disclosure. On July 21, 1989, the FASB issued a revised exposure draft entitled, "Disclosure of Information About Financial Instruments with Off-Balance Sheet Risk and Financial Instruments with Concentrations of Credit Risk." The proposed statement calls for the following information:

1. The face, contract, or notional principal amount and the amount recognized in the statement of financial position.
2. The nature and terms of the financial instruments and a discussion of the credit, market, and liquidity risk and related accounting policies.
3. The loss the entity would incur if any counterparty to the financial instrument failed to perform.
4. The entity's policy for requiring collateral or other security on financial instruments it accepts and a description of collateral on instruments presently held.
5. Disclosure of information about significant concentrations of credit risk in individual counterparties or groups of counterparties engaged in similar activities in the same region.

---

[27] Federation des Experts-Comptables Europeens, "Accounting and Financial Reporting for New Financial Instruments in Europe—Current Situation and Future Perspectives," in *New Financial Instruments: Disclosure and Accounting* (Paris: OECD, 1988), pp. 190–203.

[28] OECD Secretariat, "Disclosure and Accounting Treatment of New Financial Instruments," in *New Financial Instruments: Disclosure and Accounting* (Paris: OECD, 1988), p. 43.

If adopted as a Statement on Financial Accounting Standards, disclosure prescriptions contained in the exposure draft will be effective for fiscal years ending after December 15, 1989. Information with regard to Items 4 and 5 above will be effective for fiscal years ending after June 15, 1990.

Some observers of the international financial reporting scene feel that the FASB is asking too much.[29] Along similar lines, it is also felt that enterprises outside the United States are unlikely to be as forthcoming owing to (a) significant differences among countries regarding the amount, nature, and analysis of information required, and (b) the absence abroad of similarly extensive disclosure requirements for traditional financial instruments.[30]

While efforts such as the FASB's may seem overly ambitious, the trend toward more and better disclosure of interest rate products, such as coupon swaps, will continue. Banks and nonfinancial institutions, in competing for access to lower cost funds, will disclose what the market demands as long as doing so does not entail costs that exceed the perceived benefits. Until more definitive disclosure requirements are in place, one should look to practice for guidance. Evidence suggests that reporting entities are beginning to respond to user needs. A good example with regard to swap disclosure is the annual accounts of J. P. Morgan. Footnote 1 of their 1988 annual report, excerpted in Exhibit 8, sets forth Morgan's accounting policy for swap cash flows; footnote 18 provides information regarding swap risk.

CONCLUSION

Accounting treatment, taxation, and disclosure of interest rate swaps are still in a state of evolution. As swap products are finding increased acceptance around the world, the issues examined in this chapter are international in scope.

---

[29] See Malcolm Walley, "Interest Rate and Currency Swaps," in *New Financial Instruments: Disclosure and Accounting* (Paris: OECD, 1988), p. 98.

[30] Federation des Experts-Comptables Europeens, "Accounting and Financial Reporting," p. 196.

EXHIBIT 8

Example of Swap Disclosure in J. P. Morgan Annual Report for 1988
(Footnotes 1 and 18)

1. Interest rate swaps and currency swaps [*excerpts*]
   Income or expense associated with interest rate swaps and currency swaps, including all yield-related payments, is generally recognized over the life of the agreements. For swap transactions in which J. P. Morgan acts as a broker, arrangement fees are recognized currently in income.

* * * * *

18. Financial instruments
    J. P. Morgan uses various financial instruments for its own account in conducting trading activities and in managing its balance sheet risks. These instruments, which are not included in the financial statements, are reported in terms of nominal amounts, which do not necessarily reflect the underlying economic risks. The measurement of the risks associated with these instruments is meaningful only when all related and offsetting transactions are identified. A summary of obligations under certain of these financial instruments at December 31 follows:

In millions	1988	1987
Securities, interest rate futures and options, and precious metal contracts:		
Commitments to purchase	$26,381	$11,211
Commitments to sell	38,601	15,421
Future rate agreements and interest rate caps and floors:		
Future rate agreements sold and interest rate caps written	17,083	8,931
Future rate agreements purchased and interest rate floors written	11,377	3,085
Interest rate swaps:		
Less than one year	13,291	6,144
More than one year	60,405	52,408
Commitments to purchase foreign currencies and U.S. dollars:		
Spot, less than ten days	21,493	21,756
Forwards less than one year	82,043	65,593
Forwards one year and longer	6,365	6,324
Options	11,829	8,454
Currency swaps:		
Less than one year	6,034	5,121
More than one year	46,847	38,673

With regard to interest rate swap contracts, the amount at risk approximated $1.3 billion and $1.4 billion at December 31, 1988 and 1987, respectively. These amounts have been calculated by estimating the cost, on a present value basis, of replacing at current market rates all those outstanding contracts as to which J. P. Morgan would incur a loss in replacing the contract. The amount at risk, derived in this way, will increase or decrease during the life of the swaps as a function of maturity and market interest rates.

Owing to the different circumstances surrounding the use of coupon swaps, both within and between countries, it is unlikely that a single accounting treatment will communicate the economic substance of specific swap arrangements equally well. Accordingly, financial disclosures that provide statement readers with sufficient information to formulate reasonable assessments of the performance and risk dimensions associated with these, and related, financial innovations are likely to prove more helpful than measurement rules that mask the economic intent behind a given accounting treatment. Financial disclosure initiatives, such as those contained in the recent FASB exposure draft, are already under way. Both preparers and users of financial statements who have an interest in the outcome should take an active role in the process by which such standards are formulated.

APPENDIX: T-ACCOUNT ANALYSIS IN RELATION TO EXHIBITS 3, 5, and 6

Alpha Company

Bonds Payable

		1/1/1	100,000,000	Original bond issue (3)
		1/1/1	941,675	Discounted swap receipts (3)
12/31/1	153,478			Interest accrual (5)
1/1/2	1,567,967			Adjusting entry (6)
		12/31/2	166,171	Interest accrual (6)

Swap (Receivable)

1/1/1	941,675			Discounted swap receipts (3)
		12/31/1	153,478	Swap receipt (5)
		1/1/2	1,567,967	Adjusting entry (6)
12/31/2	166,175			Swap payment (6)

Interest Expense

		12/31/1	96,522	Swap receipt (5)
12/31/1	10,346,522			Interest accrual (5)
12/31/2	83,825			Swap payment (6)
12/31/2	10,666,171			Interest accrual (6)

Beta Company

Bonds Payable

		1/1/1	100,000,000	Original bond issue (3)
1/1/1	906,803			Discounted swap payments (3)
		12/31/1	143,450	Interest accrual (5)
		1/1/2	1,526,705	Adjusting entry (6)
12/31/2	160,306			Interest accrual (6)

Swap (Payable)

		1/1/1	906,803	Discounted swap payments (3)
12/31/1	143,451			Swap payment (5)
1/1/2	1,526,705			Adjusting entry (6)
		12/31/2	160,306	Swap receipt (6)

Interest Expense

12/31/1	106,549			Swap payment (5)
12/31/1	11,643,450			Interest accrual (5)
		12/31/2	89,694	Swap receipt (6)
12/31/2	11,839,694			Interest accrual (6)

CHAPTER 23

MARK TO MARKET VERSUS ACCRUAL ACCOUNTING FOR INTEREST RATE SWAPS

Keat Lee
ANZ
Melbourne, Australia
Ian Mordue
ANZ McCaughan
Melbourne, Australia

INTRODUCTION

Of all the financial instruments, swaps presents one of the most interesting challenges from the accounting perspective. Most of the issues in accounting for swaps are manifested in one form or other in accounting for other financial instruments on or off balance sheet. Therefore, a consistent framework and approach to accounting for swaps could be the precursor to a consistent framework and approach to the accounting for financial instruments in general.

This chapter seeks to identify some of the key issues in the accounting for swaps. In particular, it will address the logic of the mark-to-market method and draw attention to some of the pitfalls.

CHOICE OF METHODS

The two most generally acceptable methods of accounting for swaps are the accrual method and the mark-to-market method.

The *accrual method* essentially accrues the swap interest flows in the same manner as one would accrue interest on loans and deposits. In this method, the interest flows are seen as income earned and expense incurred over time. It doesn't matter if the swap interests are exchanged at the same periodic time intervals (e.g., half yearly fixed versus half yearly floating) or at different time intervals (e.g., one-year fixed versus quarterly floating); the interest flows are accrued at each reporting period for the period between last payment date and the reporting date.

The *mark-to-market method* takes into account changes in value of a particular instrument resulting from events such as changes in interest rates, exchange rates, credit risk of counterparties, etc. This method recognizes the dynamic nature of financial markets and places two portfolios on an even keel for comparative purposes. It removes the artificial distinction between realized and unrealized gains/losses. It is also less susceptible to manipulation, particularly where there is a highly liquid market and prices could be obtained objectively. The dollar values of assets and liabilities at two points in time (balance sheet dates) are comparable. The profits/losses resulting from the mark-to-market method are also more comparable than alternative methods.

A conservative version of the mark-to-market method is the lower of cost or market value. In this method, unrealized revaluation losses are recognized immediately while unrealized gains are not taken into account. This is for no other reason than applying the conservative accounting conventions in the historical context. This method can produce an apparently different profit result for two equally well performing entities merely through the timing of trades. Furthermore, in today's complex trading environment, where a portfolio is typically hedged by other instruments or combined in a single portfolio to take advantage of arbitrage opportunities, the lower of cost or market could produce significant distortionary results.

Moving further from these more established and acceptable methods, one could find variants such as up-front recognition of locked in profit or amortization of locked-in profits over time. These methods are less acceptable, despite their apparent simplicity, and generally do not have much theoretical basis.

The typical choice for accounting for swaps is therefore between the accrual method and the mark-to-market method. In choosing between the accrual and mark-to-market method, the purpose and effect of the swap transaction becomes important.

Applying symmetrical rules, swaps taken up to hedge an asset or liability (i.e., transform a floating asset or liability to fixed, or vice versa) should be treated in the same manner as the underlying instrument/exposure.

Therefore, if the asset/liability being hedged is accounted for on an accrual basis, the swap should also be accounted for on an accrual basis. If the underlying asset/liability being hedged is marked to market, then the swap should also be marked to market.

Where the swaps portfolio is managed as an independent trading portfolio, the mark-to-market method is generally regarded as superior to the accrual method for reasons described above. This is especially desirable for internal management information and increasingly adopted for external reporting purposes as well.

While the mark-to-market method means that profit and loss on swaps are essentially brought in up front, it also captures losses on open positions resulting from rate changes as and when they arise, which may not be captured by an accrual system. Furthermore, for major swap participants the risk weighting of swaps for capital adequacy purposes requires regular swaps valuation information.

MARKING SWAPS TO MARKET

On a mark-to-market basis, the profit and loss from swaps trading during a particular period comprises the following:

- Swaps interest flows (inflows less outflows).
- Accrued interest (closing less opening).
- Unrealized gains/losses from swaps book and funding costs/ benefits generated from any uneven cash flows.

To these one should add/deduct gains/losses from other synthetics (e.g., futures, FRAs, forward exchange contracts) hedging the swaps book and funding costs/benefits generated from any uneven cash flows.

Of the above items, the revaluation exercise probably presents the most interesting challenge.

Conceptually the revaluation of swaps is no different from the revaluation of other instruments. The objective of the revaluation is to establish the market value for the instrument, that is, the value for which the instrument could be liquidated. This is typically represented by the present value of the rights to, minus the obligations for, future cash flows.

Where there is no uncertainty about future cash flows (especially when the counterparties are both of equal blue chip standing), the theoretical market value of each swap is the net present value of the difference in cash flows between the contract rate and the current market rate, discounted using the swap rate for the remaining term. The swaps rates typically used are the midrate of the appropriate term.

Other factors may influence the value of the swap in question, including change in credit standing of the counterparty, the liquidity of the market, and the willingness of the counterparty to liquidate the swap or accept the obligation of a third party (as must happen if the rights to swap flows are assigned to a third party on sale of the swap or a parcel of swaps).

For medium- to long-term swaps the need to provide an allowance for further administrative and capital costs should also be considered if these are material, although one may argue that these are built into the swap spreads.

WHAT IS THE ESSENTIAL DIFFERENCE BETWEEN ACCRUAL AND MARK TO MARKET?

The main difference between the accrual method and mark-to-market method is essentially one of timing of recognition of economic events, as illustrated in Exhibit 1.

Accrual Method

The accounting profit that would be reported on the accrual method would be $200,000 per year, in this case in line with the cash flow.

EXHIBIT 1
Entity Has Two Fully Matched Five-Year Swaps with
Similarly Rated Counterparties

Swap 1

Notional principal amount	$100 million
Received fixed yearly in arrears	13.8% per annum
Receive floating yearly in arrears	LIBOR
Start date	31/12/1990
End date	31/12/1995

Swap 2

Notional principal amount	$100 million
Pay floating yearly in arrears	LIBOR
Receive fixed yearly in arrears	14.0% per annum
Start date	31/12/1990
End date	31/12/1995

Cash Flow ($000)

Year	Receive	Payment	Net
1991	$14,000	($13,800)	$ 200
1992	14,000	(13,800)	200
1993	14,000	(13,800)	200
1994	14,000	(13,800)	200
1995	14,000	(13,800)	200
			$1,000

Note: The floating legs of both swaps in this example cancel each other
out and are therefore not shown here.

What this is saying is that the net income from the swap is
earned progressively over the life of the swap despite the fact that
most of the effort relating to the swap is incurred up front.

Mark-to-Market Method

In applying the mark-to-market method, assuming the swaps midrates for the respective remaining term to maturity remain the
same throughout the life of the swaps, the profit and loss arising
from the above two swaps are as illustrated in Exhibit 2.

EXHIBIT 2

Mark-to-Market Method (Swap midrates constant over the term of the swap)

$000

Year	Term to Maturity	Swap Midrates (Percent)	Swap Revaluation		Swap Revaluation Net
			Swap 1	Swap 2	
1990	5 yr.	13.9%	$48,179	($47,491)	$688
1991	4 yr.	13.9	40,876	(40,292)	584
1992	3 yr.	13.9	32,557	(32,092)	465
1993	2 yr.	13.9	23,083	(22,753)	330
1994	1 yr.	13.9	12,291	(12,116)	175
1995	—	—	—	—	—

$000

Year	Swap Flows	Net Swap Revaluation		Profit
		Opening	Closing	
1990	—	—	$688	$ 688
1991	$200	($688)	584	96
1992	200	(584)	465	81
1993	200	(465)	330	65
1994	200	(330)	175	45
1995	200	(175)	—	25
Total profit				$1,000

Note: This ignores the reinvestment of the net swap flows, which is the same between the accruals and mark-to-market method.

Assuming swaps midrates changed, as they inevitably do, during the term of the swap, Exhibit 3 illustrates the profit and loss pattern of the two swaps through their five-year life.

Comparison of Methods

The patterns of profit for accrual and mark-to-market methods are illustrated in Exhibit 4.

In both cases, Exhibit 2 and Exhibit 3, the total profit/loss

EXHIBIT 3
Mark-to-Market Method
Swap midrates vary over the term of the swap

$000

Year	Term to Maturity	Swap Midrates (Percent)	Swap Revaluation Swap 1	Swap Revaluation Swap 2	Swap Revaluation Net
1990	5 yr.	13.9%	$48,179	($47,491)	$688
1991	4 yr.	11.0	43,434	(42,814)	620
1992	3 yr.	15.0	31,965	(31,509)	456
1993	2 yr.	18.0	21,919	(21,606)	313
1994	1 yr.	12.0	12,500	(12,321)	179
1995	—	—	—	—	—

$000

Year	Swap Flows	Net Swap Revaluation Opening	Net Swap Revaluation Closing	Profit
1990	—	—	$688	$ 688
1991	$200	($688)	620	132
1992	200	(620)	456	36
1993	200	(456)	313	57
1994	200	(313)	179	66
1995	200	(179)	—	21
Total profit				$1,000

from swaps on the mark-to-market basis over the term of the swap is $1.0 million, the same as with the accrual method.

The mark-to-market method essentially has the effect of recognizing the profit/losses up front. The rationale for marking to market is that, besides reflecting impact of fluctuations in interest rates, it also recognizes profit closer to where most of the economic efforts are made, that is, up front. Furthermore, this profit can be objectively assessed.

Supporters of the mark-to-market approach would argue that all the conditions necessary for recognition of income have been satisfied. Most swap trading activities would satisfy the income test suggested by R. T. Sprouse and M. Moonitz: "Revenues

EXHIBIT 4

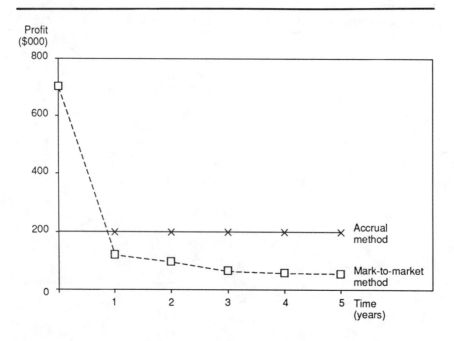

should be identified with the period during which the major economic activities necessary for the creation and disposition of goods and services have been accomplished, provided objective measurements of the results of these activities are available."[1]

IMPLICATIONS OF ADOPTING MARK-TO-MARKET METHOD

The timing of recognition of profit and loss arising from the adoption of mark-to-market method of accounting for swaps presents two potential problems.

First, where tax on swaps is paid on a mark-to-market basis, an organization stands the risk of paying too much tax and thereby turning a potentially profitable swap into a loss. Using the same illustration as before, assuming a tax rate of 50 percent and no lags

---

[1] "A Tentative Set of Broad Accounting Principles for Business Enterprises," Accounting Research Study No. 3, AICPA, New York, 1963, p. 47.

in timing of payment of tax, the tax paid on the two swaps on the mark-to-market basis compared to accrual basis are as shown in Exhibit 5. On net present value basis it is not difficult to see that the entity is worse off (by $115,000) by paying tax on a mark-to-market basis.

Second, where an entity has a policy of paying a certain proportion of profit as dividends, the mark-to-market method will result in relatively less capital than if the same dividend rate policy is applied on profit determined on an accrual basis.

Using the same example a 50 percent dividend rate will result in the relative capital positions at the end of the fifth year described in Exhibits 6 and 7 (assuming no tax, this example is equally valid if tax is paid on the same basis for both methods). In these exhibits, we have brought in interest or reinvestment of net swap flows because the cash flow impacts of the alternative methods are different and are critical to the comparative end positions.

In a dividends policy based on the accrual method, the retained earnings at the end of five years is higher than retained earnings based on the mark-to-market basis ($574,500 versus $481,600). It can be shown that in all cases except for a zero dividend policy, the entity will have less capital at the end if a fixed

EXHIBIT 5
Impact on Tax Liability (Mark-to-Market versus Accruals)

		$000		
Year	Accrual Profit	Tax @ 50 Percent	Mark-to Market-Profit	Tax @ at 50 Percent
1990	—	—	$ 688	($344)
1991	$ 200	($100)	96	(48)
1992	200	(100)	81	(41)
1993	200	(100)	65	(32)
1994	200	(100)	45	(23)
1995	200	(100)	25	(12)
	$1,000	($500)	$1,000	($500)
Present value (discount rate 13.9%)		($344)		($459)

EXHIBIT 6
Impact of Fixed Dividend Rate Policy
Applying the Accrual Method

Profit and Loss ($000)

Year	Accrual Profits	Interest on Cash Surplus	Total Profit	Dividends at 50 Percent	Cumulative Retained Earnings
1991	$200	—	$200.0	($100.0)	$100.0
1992	200	$13.9	213.9	(106.9)	206.9
1993	200	28.8	228.8	(114.4)	321.3
1994	200	44.7	244.7	(122.3)	443.7
1995	200	61.7	261.7	(130.8)	574.5

Cash Flow ($000)

Year	Net Swap Flows	Dividends (as above)	Net Cash Surplus	Interest on Cumulative Cash @ 13.9 Percent	Cumulative Cash
1991	$200	($100.0)	$100.0	—	$100.0
1992	200	(106.9)	93.1	$13.9	206.9
1993	200	(114.4)	85.6	28.8	321.3
1994	200	(122.3)	77.7	44.7	443.7
1995	200	(130.8)	69.2	61.7	574.5

dividend rate policy is applied to the mark-to-market method as opposed to the accrual method.

POSSIBLE SOLUTION

The tax and dividend problem highlighted above is basically due to the fact that the early recognition of profit has real cash flow (tax and dividend) implications. One possible solution is to impute a time value of money to the calculation of profit so that the two streams of profit recognized (i.e., accrual and mark to market) are equivalent in present value or future value terms.

In the above example, it means one would either recognize $200,000 per period as profit under the accrual method or $688,000 up front on making the deal (and no more subsequently) because

EXHIBIT 7
Impact of Fixed Dividend Rate Policy
Applying the Mark-to-Market Method

Profit and Loss ($000)

Year	Mark to Market Profits	Interest on Net Cash	Total Profit	Dividends at 50 Percent	Cumulative Retained Earnings
1990	$688.3	—	$688.3	($344.2)	$344.1
1991	95.6	47.8	$47.8	(23.9)	368.0
1992	81.2	(30.0)	51.2	(25.6)	393.6
1993	64.7	(9.9)	54.8	(27.4)	421.0
1994	45.8	12.7	58.5	(29.2)	450.3
1995	24.4	38.2	62.6	(31.3)	481.6

Cash Flow ($000)

Year	Net Swap Flows	Dividends at 50 Percent	Net Cash for Period	Interest on Cumulative Cash @ 13.9 Percent	Cumulative Cash Surplus (Deficit)
1990	—	($344.2)	($344.2)	—	($344.2)
1991	$200	(23.9)	176.1	($47.8)	(215.9)
1992	200	(25.6)	174.4	(30.0)	(71.5)
1993	200	(27.4)	172.6	(9.9)	91.2
1994	200	(28.9)	171.1	12.7	275.0
1995	200	(31.6)	168.4	38.2	481.6

$200,000 per period from 1990 to 1995 is indeed equivalent to $688,000 recognized at 1990.

Thus, in the same example the mark-to-market profits adjusted for the time value of money would be as shown in Exhibit 8.

The mechanics of the adjustment follows: Take the closing position for Year $199n$ and inflate the value by the one-year (Year $199n$) discount factor to impute the time value of the Year $199n$ closing to give the value for the time of Year $199 (n + 1)$ opening. For example, in Exhibit 8, 688, the closing mark-to-market amount for Year 1990, is inflated by 13.9 percent; $688,000 \times 1.139 = \$783,600$, and therefore the adjustment in 1991 is $783,600 - \$688,000 = \$95,600$, or $96,000 in Exhibit 8. In Year 1992, the

EXHIBIT 8
Mark-to-Market Profits Adjusted for Time Value of Money

			$000		
Year	Net Swap Flows	Opening	Net Swap Revaluation Adjustment	Closing	Profit
1990	—	—	—	$688	$688
1991	$200	($688)	($96)	584	—
1992	200	(584)	(81)	465	—
1993	200	(465)	(65)	330	—
1994	200	(330)	(46)	176	—
1995	200	(176)	(24)	—	—
					$688

adjustment is ($584,000 × 1.139) − $584,000 = $81,000, and so on.

The adjustment to opening revaluation each year has the effect of bringing two values, opening values and closing values, onto a comparable time value basis. It follows that within the year cash flows need to have a time value imputed to give the value for the time of the immediately succeeding year's opening. The reason is that within-the-year cash flows have been discounted when calculating the mark-to-market closing for the previous year.

Not only does this approach produce acceptable tax and dividend outcomes, it also makes financial statements produced using the modified mark-to-market method directly comparable with financial statements produced on an accrual basis. Indeed, the modified mark-to-market method satisfies the accounting dictum which requires published financial statements to give a true and fair view of the financial position and result of a company from time to time, whereas the conventional mark-to-market method generally practiced results in overreporting of profits.

The above modified mark-to-market method is not inconsistent with earlier published work by R. I. Chambers, which he termed Continuously Contemporary Accounting Systems (Co-

CoA).[2] In this system, all assets and liabilities are revalued to their current cash equivalents at each reporting date. All changes in value are taken through profit and loss. A capital maintenance adjustment is made against the resulting profit and loss to reflect the changes in general purchasing power of capital. Indeed, the modified mark-to-market method described above takes this concept even one step further to adjust for the full opportunity cost of capital.

The modified mark-to-market method is therefore recommended as the solution to problems associated with the conventional mark-to-market method.

---

[2] R. I. Chambers, *Price Variation and Inflation Accounting* (Sydney: McGraw Hill, 1980).

CHAPTER 24

INNOVATIONS, NEW DIMENSIONS, AND OUTLOOK FOR INTEREST RATE SWAPS

Carl R. Beidleman
Lehigh University
Bethlehem, Pennsylvania

INTRODUCTION

We have covered a great deal of ground in this volume since our initial discussion of the fundamental characteristics of cash flows in Chapter 1. We have trekked through the place of interest rate swaps in financial markets, the fundamental characteristics of basic swaps, the bells and whistles that have been added in the form of variations to plain vanilla swaps, and the development of the market for interest rate swaps, with data on its size and growth and the role of standardization in market development. This journey through swapland led us through numerous applications of swaps to some of the fundamentals of swap valuation and the conceptual relationships between interest rate swaps and alternative financial instruments that enable hedging of a swap portfolio, design of synthetic financial instruments, substitute or proxy approaches to solve numerous problems in financial management, or, simply to enable players to engineer cash flows that best suit their objectives. Final ground included items such as the credit exposure interest rate swaps entail, capital requirements imposed by regulators to help protect intermediaries against credit risk, default risk prospects, accounting methods and alternatives, and taxation of swapped cash flows. While termed *peripheral issues* in the sense that they are necessary to round out our full disclosure on interest rate swaps, these latter items are also central to the question of fully understanding the world of swaps, and they are essential to the decision whether or not to leave the role of being a swap spectator and to become actively engaged in the world of swaps.

As we covered this ground, there have been frequent references to the nature of the market for interest rate swaps and to improvements and refinements as these markets have developed. Little can be added in the way of subtleties to what has already been covered regarding market operation and efficiency, except to say that market developments have moved far more swiftly and completely than could ever have been envisaged even five years earlier. At that time, when I wrote the final chapter to the first edition of *Financial Swaps,* the market for swaps still relied on a type of arrangement format, where quoted prices took the form of indications rather than firm quotations, and counterparties were sought before a deal could be struck. There was little in the way of position taking or warehousing of swaps on the part of intermediaries. And swap documentation was nonuniform, adding to the difficulty of enlarging, reducing, or unwinding a swap position as conditions might warrant.

I predicted a movement from this sort of shadow market to a full-fledged market with active market makers taking positions on their own books, offering firm price quotations, cultivating extant applications and evolving new ones, and, of course, developing the standardized documentation and quotation mechanisms that were needed to improve the homogeneity of the product in its movement toward commodity status. Despite this vision, it must be confessed that I remain stunned and happily bewildered at the rapid growth and development of the interest rate swap market. Although I boldly spoke of a market size of $11 billion in 1984, the market has approached $1 trillion in 1989. This represents a compound growth rate of more than 200 percent per year. A market that more than tripled each year was hardly expected—and is hardly repeatable— but represents a staggering rate of increase that reflects the utility, versatility, and effectiveness of interest rate swaps and swap-like instruments and the creativity and ingenuity of swap providers, swap users, and their analysts. In the process, bid-ask spreads on plain vanilla interest rate swaps have fallen to a mere 10 basis points, which is further evidence of the improved efficiency of the market but which causes some observers to question its longer-run profitability.

As we made our way through swap country we have seen an evolution of instruments used to accommodate the need or desire to exchange cash flows of one configuration for cash flows of another. Although some of the more rudimentary instruments are still being used because of special features, the simplicity and advantages of interest rate swaps clearly make them one of the most advanced forms of long-date coupon cover to date. As instruments have become more polished and better understood, new applications for them have been found. This, in turn, has widened the usage of interest rate swaps and contributed to sizable improvements in market liquidity.

INNOVATIONS IN FINANCE

As in most other professions, improvements and new developments in finance have occurred in fits and starts, and the most significant advances are the result of attempts to find solutions to former impediments to the smooth flow of financing. The period since 1980 has been a golden age of financial inventiveness, as evidenced by the promulgation of new products and concepts including original issue discount bonds, zero coupon bonds, stripping of coupons from principal, defeasance, partly paid bonds, collateralized mortgage obligations (CMOs), interest only (IOs), principal only (POs), residuals, cards and cars (credit card– and automobile asset–backed securities), futures and options on almost anything, interest rate swaps, cross-currency swaps, commodity swaps, dual currency issues, and adjustable-rate preferred stocks.

Note that many of these innovative concepts have been in response to the problems imposed on financial managers by the high level and variability of both inflation and interest rates that have surfaced in recent years. The high and volatile rates of inflation across countries have caused wide fluctuations in interest rates, and, together, high and fluctuating inflation and interest rates have contributed to significant movements in exchange rates.

These modulations were facilitated by the movement from fixed to floating exchange rates in many of the developed countries in 1973 and, in the United States, at least, by the change in the orientation of the monetary authority from an emphasis on interest rates to monetary aggregates as targets of monetary policy in 1979.

In this final chapter we do not evaluate the merits of many of the more-or-less minor innovations in swap instruments, applications, or markets. We have already dealt with most of these. Instead, we focus on a number of significant possibilities that, if adopted, could have a massive impact on the market for interest rate swaps. The chapter ends with a summary of the importance of swap-like instruments to the contemporary financial mind-set, and vice versa, with a gentle reminder that if we are to enjoy the advantages of innovations in finance, we must be prepared to evaluate and deploy them wherever appropriate.

LOOKING FORWARD

Prospects for innovations in interest rate swaps should be examined from a number of dimensions. The primary issues of interest for the future include credit risk, types of swaps, innovations in the major applications ascribed to swaps, hedging, arbitrage and speculation, potential new roles for swaps, and improvements in the markets for swaps. In the following sections we treat each of these dimensions.

Credit Risk

Credit risk on interest rate swaps is rooted in the potential loss of the net payments of the differential interest flows to be made by the parties in the event one of them should fail to perform. This exposure is one-sided and declines with time. Its assessment has been ably discussed at earlier stages in this volume. At issue here is what changes may be seen in the future in order to better monitor and manage credit risk exposures.

Predecessors of swaps approached the problem of credit risk by requiring a *topping up* payment to be made when the present value of one set of cash flows differed from the present value of the counterset by more than some nominal amount, say 5 percent of par or principal. Similarly, modern futures contracts require a daily mark-to-market valuation, with an accompanying use or release of margin funds placed with the brokers by the respective counterparties. These procedures have been frowned upon by swappers because of their potentially onerous impact on cash flows, taxes, and accounting processes. Nevertheless, we have seen in Chapter 23 how a mark-to-market approach may be compared with alternative accounting procedures, and pressures to further ameliorate credit risk exposures may bring more attention to some form of mark-to-market book valuation for all outstanding interest rate swaps.

Inherent in the mark-to-market valuation method are margin or escrow requirements and their related cash flows. Using this method would, of course, remove one of the advantages financial swaps now enjoy over financial futures contracts. However, this approach would solve the major credit risk problems faced by swappers and swap intermediaries and eliminate the need to incorporate a provision for credit risk in swap spreads. Moreover, it could alleviate the requirement for capital that is now imposed by regulatory authorities on commercial banks, and, in the process, it could place commercial banks on an equal footing with investment or merchant banks with regard to capital requirements to support their swap portfolios. An alternative solution to this latter disparity is, of course, to impose capital requirements for swaps on the investment banks. These issues will receive considerable attention in the foreseeable future and may well result in the imposition and acceptance of some form of mark-to-market and margin requirements on financial swaps.

Variations to Interest Rate Swaps

The many variations to basic interest rate swaps that have been developed have been patiently covered in the foregoing material. While perhaps not exhaustive, our treatment has attempted to address variants such as forward swaps; prepaid swaps; amortizing swaps; extension swaps; step-up swaps; roller coaster swaps; options to add to or reduce an outstanding swap position; caps, floors, and collars on interest rates; off-market swaps, which require the making or receipt of a payment at inception; swaps using alternative floating-rate indices; and zero coupon swaps. This extensive menu leaves little to add but, given the ingenuity of swap dealers and users, it is not unlikely that we may see new additions to the basic swap menu. Possible new variants to basic swaps might be swaps embedded in new capital market issues; swap-futures contracts; discount swaps; swaps with an option on some equity or other commodity position; swaps whose floating-rate leg provides for cash flows determined by an equity index, an inflation index, or some commodity index; and earthquake or other act-of-God swaps. Other possibilities also exist. Their specification awaits the needs of users and the creativity of swappers and their market makers.

Innovative Applications

As indicated frequently in early chapters, the principal applications of interest rate swaps have been divided into strategies directed at hedging, arbitrage, or speculative objectives. As we look to the future it is convenient to focus on each of these major segments of swap usage.

Hedging
Interest rate swaps can be used to help manage interest rate risk. As they have achieved a type of commodity status with standardized terms and size, they have been used by an increasingly large number of finance managers for managing previously unprotected interest rate risk exposures. Hedging depends on the degree of the interest rate mismatch with regard to size and maturity. As interest rate swaps have been disaggregated by financial intermediaries, they have become available to hedge smaller and more unique exposures. It is likely that this process will continue to augment the growth of the swaps market and add to its liquidity.

The ongoing needs of financial institutions, institutional investors, and industrial firms to maintain the desired interest rate match can be expected to continue as finance managers become more aware of the damage that interest rate risk can cause, and as they recognize the positive role that interest rate swaps can play in managing that risk. While it is possible that interest rate mismatches, and their associated risk, could become less onerous if interest rate volatility were to decline markedly, the prospect of this occurring appears, at this writing, to be remote when one considers current approaches to monetary policy being employed throughout the world.

Hedging applications frequently arise because of other strategies that place a player in an exposed position. As such, interest rate swaps have been vital to the practice of financial engineering where intermediate cash flows are only incidental to the success of a financial strategy, provided that they can be altered at the final stage using a swap. The use of project finance concepts to fund a venture based on its internal cash flows often requires very sophisticated financial structures. These structures frequently set up undesired exposures that, in turn, rely on swaps to reconfigure the cash flows in order to meet investors' preferences. Swaps represent one of the building blocks that financial engineers can use to tailor a financial structure to meet a user's needs. Financial engineering has become an accepted practice but is still in its infancy. As it becomes more proven and develops new and exciting applications, its demand for interest rate swaps will proceed in lockstep.

Hedging applications for interest rate swaps will also follow from the far-reaching movement toward globalization of financial markets. Finance continues to move quickly into international areas where huge blocks of capital can be readily transferred from currency to currency. Competition is intensifying in both financial and nonfinancial industries where even smaller firms now face the need to move abroad and diversify. Improvements in transportation, communication, and computation have made these moves more feasible for many firms. The movement toward decreased regulations and controls has also assisted in this process. As a result, we no longer have purely domestic markets in most goods; to some extent nearly everything is now a commodity and is traded around the world. These changes have created niche opportunities for many small producers and suppliers to large firms and have enabled large firms to grow and compete in world markets. All of this will continue to have enormous implications for financial firms and for instruments such as swaps, which are relied upon to assist in managing the enormous flows of currency and debt service needed to accommodate the movement toward global integration.

The major significance of this for interest rate swaps is that we should expect to see a rapid development in the nondollar swaps markets that will nearly parallel the growth in the dollar market. As other currencies such as the D-mark or the yen become currencies of choice, their need for interest rate swaps for hedging purposes will mimic the dollar market. This movement will also produce corresponding demand for cross-currency swaps that are utilized to hedge exchange rate risk exposures. The extent of the growth in demand for swaps that can result from the now nearly ubiquitous movement toward global integration is difficult to imagine. It may be offset slightly by the (sluggish) trend in the European Community toward a single currency. On the other hand, looking farther out, this interruption in the growth in demand for swaps could be more than neutralized by the separation of the Soviet ruble into numerous national currencies, or in the admission of the East European currencies to the ranks of convertible currencies. Moreover, the impact of any significant amount of regular commerce with the Soviet block countries on the demand for financial swaps could be significant.

Arbitrage
Arbitrage applications of interest rate swaps are rooted primarily in the fact that inefficiencies in financial markets enable one player to enjoy some form of superior position or comparative advantage over other players in accessing one type of funds, say, short-term (floating-rate) versus another type, say, long-term funds. This primary example of the extraction of arbitrage gains due to market anomalies has been weakened since its inception in 1982, but it still offers benefits to swap market participants. Arbitrage tends to eliminate its own incentive; hence, it should be expected that arbitrage-motivated applications for swaps will wax and wane with time as new and different applications continue to appear, be exploited, and pass. They often depend on the presence of regulations or on differential regulations, tax rules, and accounting practices across countries. Arbitrage applications are also found in the differential treatment of swaps, futures, and securities by various regulatory authorities. Whereas certain securities or futures transactions may not be allowed in some jurisdictions, similar effects can be engineered through the use of swaps together with other

financial market instruments to accomplish a desired outcome or otherwise thwart the effect of a nuisance regulation. The extent to which arbitrage applications of interest rate swaps may develop will depend upon the degree of irritation caused by onerous regulations, the ingenuity of swappers and their market making representatives. Specifics are not easily predictable but the process that employs swaps to arbitrage market anomalies is well understood and will proceed in the future at a pace that approximates its past achievements.

Speculative Applications

Speculative uses of interest rate swaps depend primarily on a specific and firmly held view regarding the course of interest rates. If one believes that rates will fall, it is propitious to be a payer of floating-rates and a receiver of a fixed-rate on an interest rate swap. Conversely, if one believes that rates are about to bottom, a profit can be earned by being a payer of fixed and a receiver of floating interest payments. These opportunities have existed since the inception of swaps, but little has been documented on the activity of speculators or the speculative use of swaps. Perhaps the absence of data on speculative usage is understandable in that few such users would wish to disclose their speculative profits or be identified with their losses. Trading in swaps based on a shorter-term view of interest rates is a form of speculative use. Although it is believed to be practiced by many who are actively involved with swaps, little is known about the volume of its use or its overall profitability.

The absence of data on the speculative use of swaps may be due in part to the fact that swaps are off-balance sheet items and hence may not be reported to the public. These applications also generally rely on the taking of large positions. However, given the move toward large global interests, these limitations may become less obtrusive, and speculation using interest rate swaps may come of age during the lifetime of this book. It is not clear how this activity will be recorded or documented or whether it will be totally identified as speculative; it may simply take the form of failing to cover an exposure of a given book position when perceptions of rate movements suggest that gains could be realized by such a strategy.

New Roles for Swaps

The principal roles of interest rate swaps have been diligently addressed throughout this book. However, there is a conceptual role provided by swaps that may take on added significance in the coming years. Interest-rate swaps can be thought of as dual providers of service to users. An interest rate swap enables a counterparty to separate the credit risk inherent in a transaction from the interest rate risk associated with the deal. This splitting of risk may be important when considering investing funds for long periods of time. For example, a lender or investor may be content with the credit risk of a borrower but be unwilling to accept the interest rate risk of a long-term commitment. The combination of an interest rate swap with a grant of credit enables the lender to separate the interest rate risk from its exposure to the borrower. Hence, this lender effectively becomes a variable-rate lender to its client, with the full assumption of credit risk but not of interest rate risk. The other side of the swap might be a supplier of credit that has the ability to assume interest rate risk but with limited capacity to extend credit risk. In this situation, the provider of term funds (the receiver of fixed-rate payments) is insulated from the credit risk of the end user of credit by the introduction of the swap intermediary that bears the credit risk but not the interest rate risk of the transaction. As swap participants become more sophisticated regarding the management of different types of risk and better understand all the capabilities of an interest rate swap, these and other roles of swaps will find added application in the markets.

Market Efficiencies

While it may not seem possible given the present small bid-ask spreads on interest rate swaps, the markets will continue to experience marginal improvements in efficiency. There will also be increased specialization within the market, with some dealers catering to the higher volume applications in order to further reduce transaction costs. With the pressure of competitive forces, discount swaps may *not* be out of the picture. Specialization will also take other forms, including the handling of credit risk or interest rate risk, as appropriate, for the individual dealer. Others will specialize in the use of mathematics and extensive calculations necessary to utilizing financial engineering to its fullest or to laying off the risk inherent in a portfolio of swap instruments. These forces will be augmented by swap teams employed by users who sometimes become addicted to the search for swap opportunities. The free software and data service provided by some dealers and the ongoing offerings of seminars on financial engineering will facilitate these initiatives.

Swaps and financial futures markets may move closer together conceptually. But since a swap represents a stream of futures contracts and is freer from cash flow, accounting, and tax limitations, the separation of these markets remains assured in the near term. If mark-to-market valuation methods become a part of swap life, this distinction from futures will have been removed and, in the longer term, the markets may move closer together. Complete assimilation will not occur as long as the swap market retains its ability to tailor size, maturity, and appendages such as options, amortization, step-up provisions, and all of the other variations to basic swaps.

Commercial swaps represent an ingenious concept whose design was backed into through an attempt to simplify the awkwardness of back-to-back loans. Since the inception of commercial swaps in the late 1970s, their advantage has been proven repeatedly. Their future will be limited only by the creativity of market participants that employ them.

SUMMARY: CONTEMPORARY FINANCIAL MIND-SET

Considering ideas such as converting sizable amounts of floating-rate debt to fixed-rate debt at a propitious level of interest rates or hedging the risk of unknown interest rate outcomes requires a thorough knowledge of available instruments and an open willingness to use them. The same financial mind-set is necessary to implement interest rate swaps by potential players. Potential users must overcome the inertia of past resistance to financial innovation and acquire an understanding and confidence in what can be done with swaps and swap-like instruments.

People who have already used interest rate swaps agree that they are complex and require an initial investment in time and effort to develop the necessary proficiency and insight. However, after having developed a basic understanding and confidence in the underlying concept of swaps, initial users usually become repeat users. They take delight in their newly found ability to more effectively manage much of the interest rate risk in their balance sheet and/or income statement.

The potential to apply portfolio management concepts to liabilities places a responsibility on uninformed financial managers to acquire the skills necessary to deploy new financial concepts and tools. Despite the expenditure of time and effort required to obtain the needed skills, the advantages of improved control and decreased vulnerability to the ravages of interest rate risk have been the pleasant rewards to finance managers who have become proficient in deploying these contemporary financial tools. The flexibility provided by interest rate swaps as a means to hedge interest rate risk, exploit advantages inherent in market anomalies, or simply to make changes in a balance sheet in response to revised circumstances make them a very useful device easily accessible to informed financial managers. Their continued use and growth have been largely a function of their acceptance by managers of finance. I hope that this volume increases understanding of interest rate swaps and reduces the fear and apprehension formerly attached to swaps by financial managers, among others. If this can be accomplished, applications will continue to expand, liquidity will increase further, and financial management will be carried out more efficiently and expediently.

INDEX

Accounting and taxation
  accounting and reporting, risks due
    to, 439
  accounting at inception, 455–57,
    466–68
  accounting during swap term, 457–
    61, 468–70
  accounting issues, 453–57
  corporate users, swaps, 450–64
  financial disclosure, 473–76
  financial institutions, 465–71
  new capital adequacy guidelines,
    472–73
  non-U.S. dollar swaps, 223, 226–27
  swap categories, 452–53
  swaps' advantages to financial man-
    agers, 450–51
  terminations accounting, 461–63,
    470
Accruals accounting; *see* Mark-to-
  market vs. accruals accounting
Actual credit risk, 90
Adjustment flows, 241
Advantages, swaps, 102–4, 450–51
Aggarwal, Raj, 430, 432 n, 448
All-in cost (AIC), 235, 238, 247, 250
  nonpar swap, 255
Altering cash flows, existing liability,
  168–73
American swap option, 189
Amortizing swaps, 62, 127–28, 334
Amount at risk, 441–42
Analytical flows, 241
Antl, Boris, 447, 463 n

Arak, Marcelle, 138 n, 143, 413, 427,
  443 n, 447
Arbitrage
  application of, 88
  asset interest rate swap, 52–54
  call arbitrage structure, 198–204
  funding rates, 287
  innovative applications of, 499–500
  liability interest rate swap, 47–52
  locking in gain, 50
  and plain vanilla swaps, 87–89
  risk-controlled, thrift institutions,
    296–98
  sources of, 54–58
  and swaptions, 190, 192
  tax and regulatory, 134
Arrow, K. J., 143, 236 n
Asset based swaps, 176 .
  credits risk diversification, 183–84
  default risk on underlying security,
    184
  impact on primary market, 185–
    86
  impact on secondary and swap
    markets, 186
  liquidity, 185
  opportunities with, 182–83
  portfolio adjustments, 184
  rationale for, 182–85
  synthetic fixed-rate security crea-
    tion, 176–79
  synthetic floating-rate security crea-
    tion, 179–82
Asset hedge, 19

Asset interest rate swap arbitrage, 52–54

Asset management, retail market, non-U.S. dollar swaps, 217

Asset swap, 86

At-the-market swap, 72, 124

Banque Indosuez, 105

Basic bond and swap profiles, 193–95

Basic swap applications
  arbitrage, 87–89
  hedging, 81–84
  speculation, 81, 84–87

Basis risk, 77

Basis swap, 6, 62

Basle Agreement, 422, 423, 426–27

Basle Committee on Banking Regulations and Supervisory Practices, 472

Batlin, Carl A., 359

Bearer bonds, 39, 56

Beidleman, Carl R., 3, 98 n, 132 n, 143, 432 n, 447, 449 n, 492

Belmore, Martin F., 463 n

Belton, Terrence M., 414, 427, 447

Bennett, Dennis, 102 n, 106 n

Bicksler, James, 131 n, 143, 432 n, 447

Bierman, Harold, Jr., 439, 447

Bierwag, G., 82 n, 95

Bilateral credit risk, 90

Binomial options models, 211

Black-Scholes option model, 211

Bond futures hedging, 354–55

Bond/modified duration approach to hedging, 346–48

Book of swaps, 318

Bootstrapping, 273

Borrower's view, coupon risk, 8–10

Bretton Woods agreement, 29, 31–34

British capital markets, changes in stock and bond markets, 39–40

Brown, Jeffrey P., 114

Brown, Keith C., 61, 95

Calarier, Michelle, 431 n, 447

Callable bonds, 200–201

Callable debt, 63–64
  changing into
    floating-rate debt, 162–63
    noncallable debt, using callable swaps, 152–53

Call swaption, 189

Capital, defined, 422–23

Capital market applications
  callable debt creation, 163–64
  callable debt into floating-rate debt, 162–63
  callable debt into noncallable debt
    using callable swaps, 152–54
    using swaptions, 154–56
  cash flows alterations, existing liability, 168–73
  existing fixed-rate bond conversion into floating-rate instrument, 169–71
  fixing payment on floating-rate issue, 168
  floating-rate debt creation, 161–63
  floating-rate debt into synthetic fixed-rate debt, 151–52
  forward swaps, 166–67
  locking in attractive interest rates on existing high-coupon debt, 171–73
  locking in cost, future issuance, 166–68
  new issuance cost reduction, 148–66
  nonconventional debt
    FROGs into fixed-rate debt, 160–61
    inverse floaters into fixed-rate debt, 158–60
  nonconventional FROGs into floating-rate debt, 163
  putable debt creation, 164–66
  putable debt into floating-rate debt, 163
  putable debt into optionless debt, 156–58

Capital market applications—*Cont.*
  spread locks, 167–68
  synthetic floating, using vanilla
    swaps, 161–62
  synthetic optionless fixed-rate debt
    creation, 151–61
Capital market approach, plain vanilla
  swap, 72–76
Capital market transactions, swaptions and, 192–207
Cash flow module, and hedging, 334–
  35
Cash flows management
  cash flows characteristics, 3–4
  characteristics modification, 4–5
  coupon risk, 7–12
  financial characteristics, interest
    rate swaps, 12–13
  interest rate swap participants, 13–
    20
  and interest rate swaps, 5–6
  applications, 19–20
  liability management, 6–7
Cates, Armel C., 435 n, 448
Chambers, R. I., 490
Chen, Andrew H., 131 n, 143, 432 n,
  447
Chevalier, Lorin, 429 n, 448
Chicago Mercantile Exchange, 276,
  393
*Code of Standard Wording, Assump-
  tions and Provisions for Swaps*,
  112
COFI swaps, 120
Cohen, Deborah, 102 n, 106 n
Collateralized Mortgage Obligation
  (CMO), 44
Comisky, Eugene E., 467
Commercial banks
  regulation of, 422–27
  and swaps development, 107–9
Comparative advantages principle, 28
  29, 56–57, 131–33
Comprehensive view, swap risks,
  444–46
Conneely, Joe M., 456 n, 467 n

Contemporary financial mind-set, 502–3
Continental Bank, 105
Continuously Contemporary Account-
  ing Systems (CoA), 490–91
Contracts by currency, swaps, 220
Contractual flows, 241
Conventions and conundrums, inter-
  est rate swaps, 224–25
Conventions used in floating legs of
  swaps, 121
Convexity of bond, 351
Cooper, Dale F., 445 n, 447
Cooper, Ron, 431 n
Core capital, 422
Cornell, B., 329, 344
Corporate bond market, influence at
  longer maturities, 285–89
Corporate taxation, swaps, 363–64
Corporate tax planning, and off-mar-
  ket swaps, 166
Cost, after interest rate swap, 51
Counterparties, 197, 235, 254
Country risk, 339–40
Coupon effect, 124
Coupon risk
  borrower's view of, 8–10
  and interest rate risk, 7–8
  interest rate swaps function, 12
  investors' view of, 10–12
Coverage, Basle Agreement, 426–27
Crane, Robert, 418, 428
"Crazy" swaps, 334
Credit exposure and capital requirements
  Basle Agreement coverage, 426–27
  capital defined, 422–23
  commercial bank regulation, 422–27
  credit risk, 411–13
  empirical research, credit risk, 413–
    17
  exposure calculation, 423–26
  interest rate risk, 409–11
  management and directors' respon-
    sibilities, interest rate risk,
    421–22
  maturity matching credits, 419–21

Credit exposure and capital requirements—*Cont.*
  netting, swap payments, 426
  regulation, 417–27
  risk weighting, 423
  thrift regulation, 417–22
Credit risk, 411–13, 438, 495–96
  asymmetry of, 92–94
  diversification of, 92–93
  interest rate swaps, 20, 184
  plain vanilla swap, 89–94
Cross-currency interest rate swaps, 25
Cross-currency swaps, 362–69
  exposure, 361–72
  linkage with
    foreign currency interest rate
      swaps, 369–71
    U.S. dollar interest rate swaps,
      365–69
Cucchissi, Paul G., 188
Cunningham, Daniel P., 435, 447
Currencies, distinctions among, 223
Currency of cash flow, 4
Currency options, 43
Currency swaps, 25, 27, 318–20
Current exposure method, 423

Day-count mismatch, 244, 247
Day counts, 251
Dealer-oriented market structure, 65–
  66
Debreu, G., 143
Dedicated portfolio, 318
Default defined, 434–35
Default risk, underlying security, and
  asset-based swaps, 184
Default risk assessment
  accounting and reporting of swaps,
    risks due to, 439
  amount at risk, 441–42
  comprehensive view of risks, 444–
    46
  country or regulatory risk, 339–40
  default definition, 434–35
  default picture, 431

Default risk assessment—*Cont.*
  legal risks, 435–36
  market, legal, and regulatory as-
    pects of swaps, 434–40
  market structure, 437–38
  pricing risks, 441
  replacement cost of swaps calcula-
    tion, 442–44
  risks and market rate changes, 440–
    44
  risks in swap transactions, 432–33
Delta, and hedging, 356
Derivative products hedging, 348–56
Desensitizing cash flows to interest
  rate changes, 84
Determination source, 238
Detroit Edison, 105, 106
Differential credit risk premiums, 104
Differential swap, 254
  premiums and discounts, 252, 254
"Disclosure of Information about
  Financial Instruments with Off-
  Balance Sheet Risk and Financial
  Instruments with Concentration
  of Credit Risk" (FASB), 475–76
Discount, 254
Discount rate module, and hedging,
  335–37
Dizard, John, 436 n, 447
Duration, 82
Duration gap statistic, 85–86
Dynamic book, 67

Effective date, 235, 246, 251–52
Elmer, Peter, 418, 428
Empirical research, credit risk, 413–
  17
Estrella, Arturo, 433 n, 447
Eurobond market, 97–98
Euro-DM bonds, 39
Eurodollar (ED) futures, 276–77
Eurodollar FRN market, 288, 299
Eurodollar futures contract, 348–49
Eurodollar futures market, influence
  at shorter maturities, 283–85

Eurodollar strips, 390–93
extensions and refinements, 399–402
real world considerations, 398–99
strips versus swaps, 402–3
strip yield calculation, 393–97
Euromarkets, 38
European Currency Unit (ECU) bonds, 55–56
European swap option, 189
Evans, Ellen, 280
Even swaps, 252, 254
Event risk considerations, and asset-based swaps, 183
Exchange rate fluctuations, 1971–1989, 33
Executionary contracts, 76
Existing fixed-rate bond conversion to floating-rate instrument, 169–71
Expectations, and nontraditional yield curves, 382–85
Exposure calculation methods, 423–26
Extensions and refinements, strips, 399–402
Extension swaps, 127
Ex-warrant bonds, 183

Farrell, F., 83 n, 93, 95
"Fault" clauses, swap agreement, 435
Federal Home Loan Bank 11th District Cost of Funds Index, 100–101, 120
Federal Home Loan Bank Board (FHLBB), 106, 408, 419, 421
Federal Home Loan Bank of Atlanta variable advance rate, swaps index, 101
Federal National Mortgage Association (FNMA), 43
Federal Reserve AA Composite commercial paper rate, 281, 288
Federal Reserve Board, 7, 14, 34, 414, 472
Federal Savings and Loan Insurance Corporation (FSLIC), 436
Feinberg, Phyllis, 451 n

Felgran, Steven D., 410, 428, 437 n, 448
Financial Accounting Standards Board (FASB), on swap termination, 462
Financial deregulation, and growth of interest rate swaps, 37–41
Financial disclosure, 473–76
Financial innovation, 41–45
Financial market, and interest rate swaps
asset interest rate swap arbitrage, 52–54
Bretton Woods collapse, 31–34
financial deregulation, 37–41
financial globalization, 45–47
financial innovation, 41–45
floating-rate financing, 41–42
futures and options, 42–43
liability interest rate swap arbitrage, 47–52
money supply control, and monetary policy, 34–37
reasons for growth of swaps, 26–28
secularization, 43–45
source of arbitrage, 54–58
swap activity implications, financial markets, 58–60
swaps market development, 25–26
world economic environment, 1970s, 30–31
Financial markets globalization, 45–47
Financial strategy evaluation, 386–87
Finnerty, J., 83 n, 95
First coupon, 238
Fitzgerald, M. Desmond, 356 n
Fixed coupon, 238
Fixed-pay cash flows swapped to floating-pay cash flows, 117
Fixed-rate annuity, 332
Fixed-rate assets, 15
Fixed-rate bond markets, 286
Fixed-rate coupon, 235
Fixed-rate payers, 13–16
terminology regarding, 236
Fixed-rate payment, 235

Fixed-rate receivers, 18–19
Fixed-rate side, plain vanilla swap, 68, 69–71
Fixed-rate variation, 250–51
Fixing payment on floating-rate issue, 168
Flat, floating side of exchange, 67
Flexibility, swaps, 62
Floating index, 238
Floating index flat, 236
Floating-rate annuity, 332
Floating-rate buyers, 116–17
Floating-rate debt creation, 161–63
Floating-rate debt into synthetic fixed-rate debt, 151–52
Floating-rate financing, 41–42
Floating-rate generic standards, 248
Floating-rate indices, 190, 242–46
Floating-rate note position, 307
Floating-rate notes (FRN), 6, 39–40, 42, 44, 74–76, 82–83, 87–88, 160, 182, 217, 218, 254–55, 282, 330–32
Floating-rate payer, 16–18, 235, 288
  terminology regarding, 236
Floating-rate payment uncertainty, 240
Floating-rate receivers, 19–20
Floating-rate side, plain vanilla swap, 68, 69–71
Floating-rate variations, 242–50
Floating spread, 235
Fluctuations, six-month LIBOR rate, 1980–1989, 35
Folks, R. William, 432 n, 448
Fong, H. G., 337, 345
Foreign exchange risk, 26
Forward rate agreement (FRA), 276, 349–54
Forward swaps, 62, 125–27, 166–68
Francis, William B., 456 n
Frankfurt Interbank Offering Rate (FIBOR), 214, 215 n
FROGs, 160–61, 163
Frydl, E. J., 344
Functions, interest rate swaps, 12

Funding rates, arbitrage, 287
Fung, Kwun-wing, 415, 428
Futures and options, as response to market volatility, 42–43
Futures market approach, plain vanilla swaps, 76–81

Gambino, Anthony J., 451 n
Gamma, and hedging, 356
Generally accepted accounting standards (GAAP), 222
Generic equivalent cash flow approach (GECA), 252, 253
  valuation of, 241–42
Generic swaps, 240
  concentration on in early stages, 266
  terms, 238
Generic Treasury bill swap, 240
Germany
  swaps as proxy for short position, 219–20
  withholding tax repeal, 39
Globalization, financial markets, 45–47
Goodman, Laurie S., 138 n, 143, 147, 304, 413, 427, 443, 447
Government bond hedging, 354–55
Government National Mortgage Association (GNMA), 43, 44, 298
Government zeros, 335
Group of Ten, 422, 423
Growth of swaps, 28–29, 109, 281–82, 320–22

Hakansson, N., 143
Handjinicolaou, George, 25
Hedged swap, 452
Hedging
  asset hedge, 19
  bank's own funding, 219
  as basic swap application, 81–84
  benefits of swaps to thrifts, 421
  bond futures, 354–55

Hedging—*Cont.*
bond/modified duration approach
to, 346–48
cash flow exchanges and, 26–28
cash flow module and, 334–35
costs of, 301
delta, 356
derivative products, 348–56
discount rate module and, 335–37
Eurodollar futures contract, 348–49
fixed side of swap, 325–30
floating side of swap, 330–32
forward rate agreement, 349–54
gamma, 356
government bond and bond futures,
354–55
hedged instrument, 323–25
hedge ratios calculation, 395
hedging module, 339–42
innovative applications of, 497–99
interest rate cap, 354
interest rate swap, 352–54
portfolio approach to, 332–43
products for, 228–29
by proxy, 219–20, 222
risk, 356–57
strip hedge objectives, 395
and swaps' lack of variation margin
requirements, 103–4
and swaptions, 191–92
theta, 356
valuation module and, 338–39
vega, 356
Henderson, Schuyler K., 412, 425 n,
428, 448
Henry, Robert J. E., 463 n
High-coupon debt, locking in attractive interest rates on, 171–73
Hodges, S. D., 337, 338 n, 344
Hypothetical floating-rate note determination, 254–55

Iben, Benjamin, 266
Illiquidity, and non-U.S. dollar
swaps, 220–23

Immunization, interest rate risk, 82
Immunized portfolio, 318, 326–27
Implied interest rates, 380, 384, 385
Inception, accounting at, 455–57,
466–68
Income tax treatment, 470–71
Indexes, swaps, 100–101
Inflation
expectations of, 1980s, 35–36
worldwide, early 1970s, 32–33
Information broker, 63
Initial margin, 392
Innovations in finance, 494–95
Interest equivalents, 227
Interest payments of securities swaps,
239
Interest rate cap hedging, 354
Interest rate derivative products integration
bond/modified duration approach to
hedging, 346–48
Eurodollar futures contracts, 348–
49
government bond and bond futures,
354–55
hedging derivative products, 348–56
hedging risk, 356–57
interest rate cap, 354
interest rate swap, 352–54
Interest rate expectations, 378–79
and traditional yield curves, 382–85
Interest rate swap participants
natural fixed-rate, 13–19
natural floating-rate, 16–20
Interest rate swaps, 233 n, 266,
281
and exposure, 363–65
hedging and, 352–54
outstanding, 110
usage of, 360–61
variations on, 496–97
Intermediary functions, financial institution, 66–67
Internal Revenue Service, 116, 228
International money center banks, as
floating-rate payers, 17–18

International Swap Dealers Association (ISDA), 26, 62, 112, 282, 430, 434
Intrinsic value
swap, 74
swaption, 207–10
Inverse floaters into fixed-rate debt, 158–60
Investors, and interest rate swaps benefits, 36–37
Investor's view, coupon risk, 10–12
ITT, 99

Jackson, Dominique, 417, 428, 431 n, 448
Japanese banks, interest rate swap participation, 17
Japanese capital market, 40
Kalotay, A., 95
Kaufman, G., 85 n, 95
Kaufold, H., 82 n
Kawaller, Ira G., 390
Kimelman, Nancy J., 285 n
Krishman, Suresh E., 175

Lasseter, Victoria, 214
Lee, Keat, 479
Legal risks, 435–36
Levich, R., 344
Liabilities restructuring, swaps and, 282
Liability interest rate swap arbitrage, 47–52
Liability management, 6–7, 175, 375
retail market, non-U.S. dollar swaps, 216–17
Liability swap, 86
LIBOR (London Interbank Offering Rate), 5–6, 215 n
as floating-rate basis for swaps, 120, 266
Linkages, interest and cross-currency swaps

Linkages, interest and cross-currency swaps—*Cont.*
cross-country linkage, foreign currency interest rate swaps, 369–71
cross-currency linkage, U.S. dollar interest rate swaps, 365–69
cross-currency swap exposure, 365–72
cross-currency swaps usage, 362–63
interest rate swap exposure, 363–65
interest rate swaps usage, 360–61
Liquidity, and asset-based swaps, 185
Locking in arbitrage gain, 50
Locking in attractive interest rates on existing high-coupon debt, 171–73
Locking in cost, future issuance, 166–68
Loeys, Jan G., 451 n
Long-term fixed-rate debt, 130
Long-term floating-rate debt, 130

McCulloch, J. H., 344
Macfarlane, John, 233
Macirowski, T., 82 n, 96
McNulty, James E., 97, 101 n, 106 n, 407, 417 n, 428
Management and directors' responsibilities, interest rate risk, 421
Market, legal, and regulatory aspects, swaps, 434–40
Market completion, 134
Market efficiencies, 501–2
Market rate changes, and swap risks, 440–41
Market structure, and risk, 437–38
Market terminology, 234–37
Mark-to-market vs. accruals accounting
choice of methods, 479–81
comparison of methods, 484–86
differences between methods, 482–84

Mark-to-market vs. accruals accounting—*Cont.*
  implications, mark-to-market adoption, 486–88
  possible solution, 488–91
  profit and loss, mark-to-market basis, 481–82
Matched pair, 410
Matched swaps, 452
Matching principle modification, 374–75
Maturity, 238
Maturity date, 235
Maturity matching credit, 419–21
Militello, Frederick C., 451 n
Mismatches, 246–49
Modified duration, 304
Money supply control, and monetary policy, 34–37
Monroe, A., 95, 96
Moody's, 48
Mordue, Ian, 479
Morris, John, 436 n, 448
Mortgages, 15
Muffet, M., 414 n, 428, 445 n, 448
Multiparty transactions, 197–98
Multiple-period interest rate expectations, 379–82

Neal, Kathleen, 416, 428
Negotiated fixed rate, plain vanilla swap, 92
Netting, swap payments, 426
New capital adequacy guidelines, 472–73
Newhausen, Benjamin S., 466
New issuance cost reduction, 148–66
New roles for swaps, 501
Nonconventional debt
  FROGs into fixed-rate debt, 160–61
  inverse floaters into fixed-rate debt, 158–60
Nonconventional FROGs into floating-rate debt, 163
Non-LIBOR swaps, 120–22

Nonpar swaps
  all-in cost, nonpar swap determination, 255
  differential swaps, premiums and discounts, 252, 254
  even swaps, 252, 254
  hypothetical floating-rate note determination, 254–55
  secondary market or seasoned swaps pricing with GECA, 255–56
  variation of even and differential swaps with GECA, 254–56
Non-par-value swaps, 62, 255
Nontraditional yield curves, and interest rate expectations, 382–85
Non-U.S. dollar swaps
  accounting considerations, 223, 226–7
  asset management applications, retail market, 217–18
  currency distinctions, 223
  future of, 228–29
  liability management, retail market, 216–17
  overcoming illiquidity, 220–23
  usages of, 214–15
  users of, 215–20
  wholesale market, 28–30
Nonvanilla deals, 333
Notional principal, 417
  amount, 235
  by currency, swaps, 221

Off-balance sheet restructuring, 87–89
Off-market swaps, 62, 114–16
Offsetting swaps, 452–53
Offsetting transactions, 218–19
Off-the-run Treasury issues, 326
On-the-run securities, 237
Open bond positions, alternative to, 219
Original exposure method, 423, 424
Outstanding swaps, estimated volume of, 1988, 28
Over-the-counter swap market, 233

Parente, Gioia, 280, 285 n, 298 n, 300 n
Par value swap, 72
Pay-fixed party, 67
Pay-fixed swap, 73
Payment frequencies, 238, 250–51
Payment-frequency mismatch, 246–47
Payout diagrams, 193
Peck, Rodney R., 435 n, 448
Pitman, Joanna, 428
Plain vanilla swaps, 61–62
  and arbitrage, 87–89
  capital market approach, 72–76
  credit risk on, 89–94
  futures market approach, 76–81
  hedging, 81–84
  LIBOR swap, 111
  market pricing conventions, 67–72
  speculation, 81, 84–87
  and synthetic floating, 161–62
  trends in swap market structure, 63–67
Portfolio adjustments, 184
Portfolio approach, swaps management
  cash flows module, 334–35
  currency swaps, 318–20
  discount rate module, 335–37
  hedging, 330–32
  hedging instrument, 323–25
  hedging module, 339–42
  portfolio approach, swaps hedging, 332–43
  swaps and portfolio management, 343–44
  variation module, 338–39
Potential credit risk, 90, 92
Premium, 254
Premium or discount, 238
Prepaid swaps, 125
Price risk, 8
Price sensitivity of swap, 306–10
Pricing convention, swap market, 67–72
Pricing date, 238
Pricing risks, 441

Primary market impact, asset-based swaps, 185–86
Pringle, John J., 132 n, 133, 134, 143, 407, 429, 432 n, 448, 450 n
Project-finance swaps, 334
Putable debt, 163–66
  into optionless debt, 156–58
Put-call parity, swaptions, 211–12
Put swaption, 189

Rate exposure management, 134
Rate quotation conventions, swap market, 69
Rationale, asset swaps, 182–85
Realistic considerations, strips, 398–99
Receive-fixed party, 67
Regulation
  commercial banks, 422–27
  credit exposure and capital requirements, 417–27
  thrift institutions, 408, 417–22
Regulatory arbitrage, 134
Regulatory risk, 440
Reinvestment rate risk, 8
Replacement costs of swaps, 442–44
Replacement swap, 90–92
Reset frequency, 238
Reset-frequency mismatch, 249
Reuters floating rate, 242
Risk
  accounting and reporting, 439
  amount at, 441–42
  asymmetry of, 437
  bilateral credits, 90
  comprehensive view of swaps, 444–46
  country, 339–40
  coupon, 7–12
  credit, 20, 89–94, 184, 411–17, 438, 495–96
  default, 184, 434–46
  event, 183
  foreign exchange, 26
  hedging, 356–57

Risk—*Cont.*
  interest rate, 5–6, 82, 224–25, 409–
    11, 421
  legal, 435–36
  and market rate change, 440–41
  potential credit, 90, 92
  price, 8
  pricing, 441
  regulatory, 340
  reinvestment, 8
  weighting of, 423
Risk-based capital proposal, FHLBB,
    421–22
Risk-controlled arbitrage, thrift insti-
    tutions, 296–98
Risk-free rates and credit premiums
    combinations, 134–38
Risk weighting, 432
Rogers, William P., Jr., 112 n, 435 n,
    447
Rones, Andrew, 138 n, 143, 413, 427,
    443, 447
Ross, Daniel R., 233
Rue, Joseph C., 465 n
Ruff, Craig, 420, 428

Schaefer, S. M., 335, 337 n, 338 n,
    344, 345
Seasoned swap, 249 n
Secondary market impact, asset-based
    swaps, 186
Secondary market or seasoned swaps
    pricing with GECA, 255–56
Securitization, 43–45
Sen, Bidjut, 441 n, 448
Sensitizing cash flows to interest rate
    changes, 84
Settlement date, 235, 238
Short- and long-date interest rate
    swap strategies
  expectations and nontraditional
    yield curves, 382–85
  financial strategy evaluation, 386–
    87
  interest rate expectations, 378–79

Short- and long-date interest rate
    swap strategies—*Cont.*
  modified matching principle, 374–75
  multiple-period interest rate expec-
    tations, 379–82
  short-date strategy evaluation, 376–
    78
  and theory of term structure of
    interest rates, 376
Short- and long-term first fixed-rate
    period, 251
Short-date strategy evaluation, 376–
    78
Short or long first floating-rate period,
    249–50
Short-term debt, 130
Showers, Janet, 233
Silver, Andrew, 433 n
Simon, Katrina, 416, 428
S&L syndrome, 14–15
Smirlock, N., 82 n, 96
Smith, C., 81 n, 95, 96
Smith, C. W., 132, 134, 345, 428
Smith, C. W., Jr., 132 n, 134 n, 143
Smith, D., 88 n, 95, 96
Smith, Donald J., 61
Smithson, C. W., 81, 95, 96, 132, 134,
    143, 345, 428, 409 n, 414 n
Sources of arbitrage, 54–58
Speculation
  innovative uses of, 500
  and plain vanilla swaps, 81, 84–87
  and swaptions, 181
Spread, 238
Spread locks, 167–68
Spreads above or below floating-rate
    index, 242–46
Sprouse, R. T., 485
Standard and Poor's, 48
Standardization, swaps, 109–12
Statements of Financial Accounting
    Standards (SFAS), 226–27, 439,
    451, 468
Step-up swaps, 128–29
Steiber, Sharon L., 97
Strips, 335; *see also* Eurodollar strips

Student Loan Marketing Association
(Sallie Mae), 98–100, 111
Supplemental capital, 422
Swap, corporate, and U.S. Treasury
markets, relationships between,
294–96
Swap activity, implications for financial markets, 58–60
Swap amortization, 62, 127–38, 334
Swap analysis complexities, 239–40
Swap categories
asset-based, 176–86, 296–98
basis, 6, 62
callable, 152–54
COFI, 120
"crazy," 334
cross-currency, 25, 228, 361–69
currency, 25, 27, 318–20
deferential, 252, 254
even, 252, 254
extension, 127
forward, 62, 125–27, 166–68
generic, 234, 237–39, 240, 266
interest payments, 239
interest rate, 12, 19–20, 25–65, 110,
360–61, 374–85, 496–97
liability, 86
LIBOR, 111, 120–22
non-LIBOR, 120–22
nonpar, 235
non-U.S. dollar, 28–30, 214–27
off-market, 62, 114–16, 166
offsetting, 252–53
par value, 72
plain vanilla, 61–96, 111, 161–63,
187–89
prepaid, 125
seasoned, 249
securities, 239
step-up, 128–29
unmatched interest rate, 346
Swap duration, 304
price sensitivity of swap, 306–10
swap position, 305–6
over time, 310–13
Swap market, 63–67
day-count mismatch, 247

Swap market—*Cont.*
day counts, 251
effective date, 251–52
fixed-rate variations, 250–51
floating-rate uncertainty, 240
floating-rate variations, 242–50
generic swap, 234, 237–39
interest payments or securities
swapping, 239
market terminology, 234–37, 238
mismatches, 246–49
payment frequencies, 250–51
payment frequency mismatch, 246–
47
pricing conventions, 67–72
rate quotation conventions, 69
reset frequency mismatch, 249
short and long
first fixed-rate period, 251
floating-rate period, 249–50
spreads above or below floating-rate
index, 242–46
swap analysis complexities, 239–40
valuation methodology
generic swaps, 240
nongeneric swaps, 142
Swap market development, 97–99
advantages of swaps, 102–4
and agency costs, short- and long-
term debt, 133
commercial banks and investment
bankers and, 107–10
comparative advantage principle
and, 28, 29, 56–57, 131–33
indexes used, 100–101
market growth, 28–29, 109, 281–82,
320–21
risk-free rates and credit premium
combinations with swaps, 134–
37
and standardization, 109–12
swap preference conditions, 139–42
swap tailoring, 99–100
thrifts and, 106–7
U.S. corporations and, 104–6
Swap market impact, asset-based
swaps, 186

Swap maturities, 1987, 110
Swap option valuation, 207–12
Swap payment structure, 51
Swap position, and duration, 305–6
Swap preference, conditions for, 139–42
Swaps and swaptions for debt transformation, 150
Swap spread curve, shape of, 289–93
Swap spreads, forces behind
    asset-based interest rate swaps, 296–98
    corporate bond market, 285–89
    Eurodollar futures market, 283–85
    growth of swap market, 281–82
    hedging costs, 301
    interest rate swap, corporate, and U.S. Treasury markets relationships, 294–96
    risk-controlled arbitrage, thrift institutions, 296–98
    shape of swap spread curve, 289–93
    swap and other financial markets, 280–81
    synthetic Eurodollar fixed-rate investments creation, 300
    synthetic Eurodollar floating-rate investments creation, 298–300
Swap spreads widening, 1989, 183
Swap tailoring, 99–100
Swap term, accounting during, 457–61, 468–70
Swap terminations, accounting for, 461–63
Swaption-driven arbitrage transactions, 190
Swaptions applications
    arbitrage, 192
    basic bond and swap profiles, 193–95
    call arbitrage structure, 198–204
    in capital market transactions, 192–207
    hedger, 191–92
    intrinsic value, 207–10
    multiparty transactions, 197–98
    payout diagrams, 193

Swaptions applications—*Cont.*
    put call parity, 211–12
    speculator, 191
    swap option valuation, 207–12
    swaption profiles, 196–97
    synthetic put bond structure, 204–7
    time value and volatility, 210–11
Swap valuation, 268–69
    yield to maturity approach, 267–68, 269–72
    zero coupon approach, 267, 272–78
Synthetic Eurodollar fixed-rate investments creation, 300
Synthetic Eurodollar floating-rate investments creation, 298–300
Synthetic fixed-rate security creation, and asset-based swaps, 176–79
Synthetic floating, using vanilla swaps, 161–63
Synthetic floating-rate liability, 86
Synthetic floating-rate security creation, and asset-based swaps, 179–82
Synthetic noncall bond, 202
Synthetic optionless fixed-rate debt creation, 151–61
Synthetic put bond structure, 204–7
Synthetic securities, 116–20

Tax and regulatory arbitrage, 134
Taxation; *see* Accounting and taxation
Tax considerations, non-U.S. dollar swaps, 223, 227–28
Tax planning, off-market swaps, 166
TED spread, 285
Terminations, accounting for, 470
Term structure of interest rates, 376
Theta, and hedging, 356
Thrift Bulletin 13 (FHLBB), 421
Thrift institutions
    and development of swaps, 106–7
    and hedging risk, 26–27
    regulation of, 408, 417–22
Time value, swaptions, 210–11
Tiner, John I., 456 n, 462 n

Tomsett, Eric, 463 n
Tosh, David E., 456 n
Trade date, 235
Trends, swap market structure, 63–67
Tuffli, Reto M., 188, 346
Turnbull, Stuart M., 132 n, 143,
    432 n, 448

U.S. corporations, and swaps market,
    104–6
Uncertainty, floating-rate payments,
    240
Unilateral credit risk, 90
Unmatched interest rate swaps, 346
Unmatched swaps, 452
Use value, of swaps, 74

Valuation, even and differential swaps
    with GECA, 254–56
Valuation formulas, 268–69
Valuation methodology
    generic swaps, 240
    nongeneric swaps, 241
Variable-rate instruments, 15
Variation margin requirements,
    swaps' lack of, 103–4
Variation module, and hedging, 338–
    39
Variations
    even and differential swaps with
        GECA, 254–56
    fixed-rate, 250–51
    floating-rate, 242–50
    interest rate swaps, 496–97
Variations, basic swaps
    amortizing swaps and step-up
        swaps, 127–29
    extension, 127
    forward, 125–27
    non-LIBOR, 120–22
    off-market, 114–16
    prepaid, 125
    synthetic securities, 116–20
    zero coupon, 122–25

Vasicek, O. A., 337, 345
Volatility
    interest and exchange rates, 33–34
    market, 42–43
    swaptions, 211

Wakeman, Lee M., 81 n, 96, 132,
    134, 143, 297 n, 317, 345, 346,
    411 n, 427, 428
Wall, Larry D., 132 n, 133, 134, 143,
    407, 415, 428, 429, 432 n, 448,
    450 n
Walmsley, Julian, 70 n, 95, 96, 451
Warehouse approach, 333
Watson, Ian R., 445 n, 447
Weaver, Samuel C., 374
Wedding cake swap, 335 n
Weiner, Lisabeth, 431 n, 448
Whittaker, J. Gregg, 413, 429, 444
Wholesale market, and non-U.S.
    dollar swaps, 218–20
Wilson, Keith, 439 n
Wilson, Neil, 436 n, 448
Wishon, Keith, 448
Withholding tax, dollar-denominated
    bonds, 38–39
Withholding tax issues, 228
World Bank, 58
World Bank–IBM swaps, 1981, 25
World economic environment, 1970s,
    and growth of swaps, 30–31
Worldwide inflation, 1970s, 32–33

Yawitz, J., 82 n, 96
Yield-to-maturity approach, swap
    valuation, 267–68, 269–72
Zero coupon approach, swap valua-
    tion, 267, 272–78
Zero coupon curve, 272, 337
Zero coupon swaps, 122–25, 267–68
Zero economic value at origin, 74–75
Zero swaps, 334